THREE
on the
TOWER

The Lives and Works of
Ezra Pound, T. S. Eliot and
William Carlos Williams

THREE
on the
TOWER

The Lives and Works of Ezra Pound, T. S. Eliot and William Carlos Williams

by Louis Simpson

Our spirit, shut within this courtyard of sense-experience, is always saying to the intellect upon the tower: "Watchman, tell us of the night, if it aught of promise bear."

—WILLIAM JAMES

WILLIAM MORROW & COMPANY, INC., NEW YORK 1975

Library of Congress Cataloging in Publication Data

Simpson, Louis Aston Marantz (date)
  Three on the tower.

  Bibliography: p.
  Includes index.
  1. Pound, Ezra Loomis, 1885-1972. 2. Eliot, Thomas Stearns, 1888-1965. 3. Williams, William Carlos, 1883-1963. I. Title.
PS3531.082Z836   811'.5'209   74-26952
ISBN 0-688-02899-3

Book design by Helen Roberts

This book is dedicated to my mother.

Preface

In 1908 Isadora Duncan "in a short loosely hung Grecian dress, with bare feet and arms, danced a series of Greek dances from Gluck's *Iphigénie en Aulide,* reproducing the postures of Greek dancers as portrayed on ancient vases." [1] Isadora Duncan embodied the New Spirit. So did Ezra Pound with his red hair and cape. He saw himself as a troubadour poet, a Ronsard, another Villon. He left the United States, spent some months in Venice, then traveled to London.

His timing was perfect. In the following years London was a vital center of the arts—there was nothing in Philadelphia to compare with it. There was a Post-Impressionist exhibition. The Russian ballet arrived in London. There was Futurist art . . . shouting of poems while a drum was beaten. There was political turmoil in Ireland. There were suffragette outrages. There was *Blast.*

> OH BLAST FRANCE
> pig plagiarism
> BELLY
> SLIPPERS
> POODLE TEMPER
> BAD MUSIC
>
> BLESS ALL PORTS
> scooped out basins
> heavy insect dredgers
> monotonous cranes

> stations
>   lighthouses, blazing
>   through the frosty
>   starlight, cutting the
>   storm like a cake [2]

The period ended with the Great War, which produced sixteen million casualties. The human body, having been newly sensitized, was lacerated and flayed. Afterwards everyone had shell shock. It was to this postwar generation that *The Waste Land* spoke. "My nerves are bad to-night. Yes, bad. Stay with me." [3]

Ezra Pound, T. S. Eliot and William Carlos Williams made their reputations with short, intense, imagistic poems. There was, however, the question of how to continue—we live by the senses but at the same time we must have an aim that is not dependent on the senses. "Life itself" is incoherent, as a Great War plainly shows. "Our spirit," says William James, "shut within this courtyard of sense-experience, is always saying to the intellect upon the tower: 'Watchman, tell us of the night, if it aught of promise bear.' " [4]

We are still looking for ways to continue. Therefore I have written about Pound and Eliot and Williams, each of whom went on to create a significant body of work. I have discussed their ideas as though they were new—and indeed, as they are necessary I believe them to be new. The poetry, however, is what matters—ideas are only points of departure—therefore I have concentrated on the poetry. Not the poem just by itself but as part of an ongoing process of creation.

I have attempted to enter into the process. To do this I have had to understand each man's life—his connections with other people, his attitudes and beliefs. My rule has been to give these matters as much importance as he himself gave them. Williams wrote continually about his life, therefore I have talked about it in detail. Eliot hardly ever writes about his, but when he does it seems confessional. Pound, for all his volubility, gives little away; he writes about himself in the *Cantos,* but nothing personal, and this is the way I have dealt with him.

I had to write this book to clarify my ideas. There are talented poets in the United States, but we need to consider where we are going. Pound, Eliot and Williams seem to have touched all the bases—with one possible exception, surrealism, though a case can be made for Eliot's poems being surrealist, if we admit that surrealist writing may have logical connections. Each of these men was remarkably fertile in ideas; even their failures are interesting, because they demonstrate an idea.

I could not have written the book without the help of these people: my wife, Dorothy; my editor, Robert Levine, who gave encouragement and advice; Jean Robinson and Merridy Darrow, who worked on the manuscript; and my research assistant, Jean Carr.

I
Ezra Pound, or Art

1

1908

ON 21 October 1908, Ezra Pound wrote a letter from London to his friend William Carlos Williams in Rutherford, New Jersey. Pound had published his first book and Williams hadn't liked it —he thought it too bitter. Pound said, "Remember, of course, that some of the stuff is dramatic," and he explained that the thought in the poem wasn't to be taken as his own; it was the thought of the character named in the title. "I wish," he said, "you'd spot the bitter, personal notes and send 'em over to me for inspection." He thought that Williams must have been reading "in the wrong tone of voice." However, he added, Williams might be right, for Hilda agreed with his opinion.[1]

Hilda was Hilda Doolittle, daughter of the Professor of Astronomy at the University of Pennsylvania. Pound had been in love with her. He had been in love more than once: with Hilda Doolittle of Philadelphia and Mary Moore of Trenton. With a face he had seen in passing—the girl in Chestnut Street.[2] With pictures in galleries and visions of fair women evoked by words in the air.

In Venice it had been Ruth Heyman, a concert pianist. Her mother's family went back to the American Colonies, her father's to the Diaspora. She was older than Pound. He offered her the gift of his poetry, "even as Ronsard gave it./ Seeing before him, one sweet face grown old."[3]

He called a "press recitation" at the Liceo Benedetto Marcello.

One night he came to her room having shaved off one of his sideburns. He said that it was to "put down Vanity," and that he would shave the other as well. This he accomplished.

He offered to give up poetry in order to manage her concert tours, and in his role as impresario sent a notice to the Paris edition of the *New York Herald:*

> Katharine Ruth Heyman, whose American tournée is predicted as the event of the coming piano season there, may give certain concerts in Paris on her way West.
>
> Her playing in London before sailing is also to be announced.
>
> Venice   E. P.[4]

He was proud of the professional tone: the words "tournée" and "certain concerts" had the imperious air necessary in announcements of this kind.

Then, suddenly, Ruth Heyman left Venice, and the flame went out. *A Lume Spento.* Where love had been, a wisp of candle smoke. When he published his first book, at the press of A. Antonini, Cannaregio, 923, the title page bore the words:

> This Book was
>
>   LA FRAISNE
>   (The Ash Tree)
> dedicated
>
>   to such as love this same
>   beauty that I love, somewhat
>   after mine own fashion
>
> But sith one of them has gone out very
> quickly from amongst us it is given
>
>   A LUME SPENTO
>   (With Tapers Quenched) [5]

This was the book Williams had found too bitter. He had used the word "anarchy" and questioned Pound's air of a vagabond, another Villon. A writer had to be careful; he was being watched by "the eyes of a too ruthless public."

Pound answered that he didn't give a hoot for the public, ruthless or otherwise. "Damn their eyes. No art ever yet grew by looking into the eyes of the public."

He proceeded to list the kind of stuff the public expected of poets:

1. Spring is a pleasant season. The flowers etc. etc. sprout, bloom etc. etc.
2. Young man's fancy. Lightly, heavily, gaily, etc. etc.
3. Love, a delightsome tickling. Indefinable etc. etc.
4. Trees, hills, etc. are by a provident nature arranged diversely, in diverse places.
5. Winds, clouds, rains, etc. flop thru and over 'em.
6. Men love women. (More poetic in the singular, but the verb retains the same form.)
7. Men fight battles, etc. etc.
8. Men go on voyages.

He told Williams that he was aiming to paint the thing as he saw it. He was aiming at Beauty. He wanted to be free of didacticism and as original as possible. Utter originality was out of the question, but if you used another man's ideas you should at least be better than he was.

London was ahead of the States. The reason Williams hadn't appreciated *A Lume Spento* was that he hadn't been able to, he was out of touch. Pound was using "rules of Spanish, Anglo-Saxon and Greek metric" that were not common in the English of Milton or Miss Austen. "I doubt, however, if you are sufficiently au courant to know just what the poets and musicians *and* painters are doing with a good deal of convention that has masqueraded as law." [6]

This was typical of Pound—he was always telling people they did not know as much as he did. The habit made him enemies— they would not forgive his superior airs.

Williams was fond of Pound and would not be offended. At first, perhaps . . . but he would quickly get over it. "Pound," he wrote, "is a fine fellow; he is the essence of optimism and has a cast-iron faith that is something to admire. If he ever does get blue nobody knows it, so he is just the man for me. But not one person in a thousand likes him, and a great many people detest him and why? Because he is so damned full of conceits and affectation. He is really a brilliant talker and thinker but delights in making himself just exactly what he is not: a laughing boor. His friends must be all patience in order to find him out and even then you must not let him know it, for he will immediately put on some artificial mood and be really unbelievable. It is too bad, for he loves to be liked, yet there is some quality in him which makes him too proud to try to please people. I am sure his only fault is an exaggeration of a trait that in itself is good and in every way admirable. He is afraid of being taken in if he trusts his really tender heart to the mercies of a cruel crowd and so keeps it hidden and trusts no one." [7]

Williams wrote this, in a letter to his mother, when he was at the University of Pennsylvania. The subject, Pound, was to occupy him all his life.

Pound was enjoying London. There were opportunities for a writer—even one whose tastes ran to troubadour poets. Shortly after coming to London he heard of a vacancy at the Polytechnic in Regent Street. He applied and was appointed to deliver a series of lectures on "The Development of Literature in Southern Europe." So he now had an income of sorts, and would not have to sail back to America ignominiously in the steerage.

At first he had taken a room at Miss Withey's boardinghouse in Duchess Street, which he couldn't afford. It was an aristocratic neighborhood with carriages and grooms. Then he moved to cheaper quarters in Langham Street.[8] He had very little money. He became thoroughly familiar with eggs fried to the consistency of rubber, bacon with knots of gristle that could break a tooth, and many cups of tea. He learned how to wrap himself in layers of wool against an English winter. He now knew what it was like to live through an English Sunday.

A hundred years ago the poet Heine had stayed at Number 32, Craven Street in the Strand. On his return to Germany he uttered a cry on behalf of poets everywhere: "Don't send a poet to London."

But Pound was happy. In comparison with Indiana where he had been teaching, London was Heaven.

He was a great walker, finding shortcuts to the British Museum. There was much to look at: automobiles, red open-topped buses that had replaced horse-drawn vehicles, men wearing top hats and women wearing furs. He discovered the Vienna Café near the Museum, where you could order half portions. He explored the bookshops in Charing Cross Road, and he walked in Trafalgar Square with its "glint of straw blown from horses' feeds, the shine of bits of harness, the blaze of gold lettering along the house fronts." [9] There was the wonder of the Underground—trains running in cool, white, brilliantly lighted tunnels.[10]

But the most important thing was that he was surrounded by fellow artists, the kind of people he had yearned for in Indiana. "I am homesick," he had written, "after mine own kind." [11] And now he had come home.

In December 1908, he published his second collection of poems, a pamphlet titled *A Quizaine for This Yule*. Again it was a small edition of a hundred copies. As Christmas was approaching the pamphlet sold out, and the publisher, Elkin Mathews, printed a second edition. This was a small but heartening success.

In February 1909, Mathews introduced him to the Poets' Club that met at the United Arts Club in St. James's Street. The night they went, G. B. Shaw and Hilaire Belloc were present. Pound thought it a bore. By April, however, a group of young poets had split off from the Club and started to meet on their own. On April 22 he went to one of their meetings. It was there that he met T. E. Hulme, F. S. Flint and other people with new ideas about poetry.

Ideas were badly needed. Years later, looking back on the state of poetry in Britain between 1890 and the time he got there, Pound would say that it had been "a horrible conglomerate compost, not minted, most of it not even baked, all legato, a doughy mess of third-hand Keats, Wordsworth, heaven knows what, fourth-hand Elizabethan sonority, blunted, half-melted, lumpy." [12]

This was true. Writing in general is always a doughy mess. Sometimes this is improved by a few people to whom writing matters more than anything else. At the beginning of the century there were novelists such as Conrad and James who discussed the craft of fiction. In poetry, however, the situation was different— there seemed to be no intellectual curiosity. A. E. Housman polished his lyrics until they were perfect; Kipling wrote ballads that could be sung in music halls—another kind of anonymity. William Butler Yeats and Thomas Hardy were writing poetry, but the first was Irish and the second was remembered as the author of novels. There was no movement in poetry, no gathering of men and ideas.

There had been a cult of Beauty in the nineteenth century. Beauty was praised by Ruskin in his writings on art and architecture; by Pater, who spoke of the life of art as burning "with a hard, gem-like flame"; [13] by Swinburne and Rossetti in poems that were sensual, speaking of

> The heavy white limbs, and the cruel
> Red mouth like a venomous flower . . .[14]

The Pre-Raphaelites made paintings of beautiful women with long hair and heavy-lidded eyes, men equally beautiful in armor, and beautiful scenes with flowers, or rooms ornate with cloth and gems.

The cult of Beauty seemed inseparable from debauchery. Poets at the end of the nineteenth century in England wrote about whores as though they were madonnas and hinted at a sin "that dared not speak its name." Some of the poets were drunkards. And there were rumors of worse things happening in France.

The founding, in 1894, of *The Yellow Book,* an illustrated magazine publishing essays, fiction, and verse, seemed to mark the triumph of the cult. The contributors were called "decadent," yet there was a section of the public that avidly read their poems and stories or looked at their paintings. The poems of Ernest Dowson were more "modern" than the poems of Swinburne: Swinburne had sung rapturously of passion—Dowson seemed exhausted by it. The drawings of Aubrey Beardsley were scandalous and fascinating.

Some people seemed to be transforming their very lives into art. The most flamboyant was Oscar Wilde, whose wit on the stage proved entertaining to the public. It seemed that the most precious attitudes would not meet with disapproval if they were entertaining.

Then Wilde was arrested and charged with twenty-five counts relating to "acts of gross indecency." He was found guilty on all charges except one, and sentenced to two years' confinement with hard labor. Housman remarked, "Oh they're taking him to prison for the colour of his hair," but irony cannot stem a tide. Poets and artists and people of that kind had been taught a lesson. Beauty was suspect; little was heard about her at the opening of the new century.

But when Pound arrived in London things were beginning to change. "London," he wrote Bill Williams, "deah old Lundon is the place for poesy." [15]

2

Portrait of a Man
With a Blue Earring

IN *Return to Yesterday* Ford Madox Ford recalls Pound's appearance in the streets of London. He would see Pound coming toward him "with the step of a dancer, making passes with a cane at an imaginary opponent. He would wear trousers made of green billiard cloth, a pink coat, a blue shirt, a tie hand-painted by a Japanese friend, an immense sombrero, a flaming beard cut to a point, and a single, large blue earring." [1]

And William Carlos Williams says that Pound had "A beautifully heavy head of blond hair of which he was tremendously proud. It was really very beautiful hair, wavy. And he held his head high. I wasn't impressed, but I imagine the ladies were." [2] The hair is also described as being "crinkly, thick, reddish-gold hair brushed straight back from his forehead," and his beards and moustaches "came and went in rapid succession." [3]

It is said that an anonymous "Virgin's Prayer" was being circulated among the avant-garde:

> Ezra Pound
> And Augustus John
> Bless the bed
> That I lie on. [4]

At least two ladies were impressed: Mrs. Shakespear, "the most charming woman in London," and her daughter Dorothy. Pound visited them on a winter's day; he talked while Dorothy Shakespear sat on a low stool and listened.

Much was forgiven because he was an American. The English are inclined to forgive foreigners for their lapses of taste and manners—they haven't had the advantage of an English upbringing. And Americans were expected to be picturesque. London had seen Bret Harte, Joaquin Miller and Mark Twain. It wasn't likely to be upset by an American Ronsard. In fact, one or two of the English were grateful for Pound's informality. When Brigit Patmore met him at a party, she was struck by the fact that the "long, slim young man leaning back in a low chair, withdrawn into his clothes," actually smiled at her. "The very un-Englishness of this pleased me," she said.[5]

Pound was making a name for himself. Some people disliked his affectations, others were put off by his dogmatic opinions, but there were those who agreed with the *Evening Standard and St. James Gazette:* "Mr. Pound is a poet, though a fantastic one." [6]

This was on the occasion of his publishing a new collection of poems, in April 1909. The book, *Personae,* attracted unusual notice, considering that before this he had published only two pamphlets in editions of a hundred and two hundred copies. *Personae* received an important review by Edward Thomas writing in *The English Review.* Thomas praised Pound's "directness and simplicity." He said, ". . . he is true in his strength and weakness to himself, full of personality and with such power to express it that from the first to the last lines of most of his poems he holds us steadily in his own pure, grave, passionate world." [7]

The English Review numbered among its contributors famous writers such as Thomas Hardy, Joseph Conrad, Henry James, W. H. Hudson and H. G. Wells. This favorable notice in its pages made Pound a bit of a celebrity. He had the honor of being poked fun at in *Punch*—a paragraph announcing "the new Montana (U.S.A.) poet, Mr. Ezekiel Ton, who is the most remarkable thing in poetry since Robert Browning. . . . He has succeeded, where all others have failed, in evolving a blend of the unfettered West, the vocabulary of Wardour Street, and the sinister abandon of Borgiac Italy." [8]

The impression that Pound came from the "unfettered West" seems to have been current. In fact he came from Wyncote, ten miles north of Philadelphia. He was born in Hailey, Idaho, where his father worked in the Land Office, but when Ezra was eighteen months old the family moved back East. The climate of Hailey did not agree with Isabel Pound—Hailey is five thousand feet above sea level—and it was a rough town. Hailey had only one street, lined with saloons, and men still wore revolvers in those days.

They traveled in the Great Blizzard of '87, behind the first rotary snow plow. When Ezra coughed the inventor of the plow would give him some sugar steeped in kerosene.[9]

They lived in New York for a while, at a boardinghouse on East Forty-seventh Street run by the Westons, Isabel Pound's relatives. The Westons could trace their line back to the Colonies. They were related to the poet Henry Wadsworth Longfellow. Against that, Homer Pound could throw his own father into the scales: Thaddeus Pound, Lieutenant-Governor of Wisconsin and three times elected to Congress.

Then they moved to Philadelphia where Homer Pound was employed as an assayer at the Mint. Ezra liked to visit his father's place of business. He once saw men shoveling silver coins into counting machines, by the light of gas flares.[10] It left an unforgettable impression. The men at the Mint would tell stories about gold. There were cunning men who would cover a bar of lead with gold, making places where the bar was gold all the way through. That was one of their ways of swindling people.

One day Dorothy Shakespear and her mother took Ezra Pound to meet William Butler Yeats. Yeats lived in Woburn Place on a first floor. The room was dimly lighted and hung with Pre-Raphaelite pictures.

Yeats was "the greatest living poet" [11]—in fact, Pound had come to London because Yeats was there. That and the need to make a living . . . In Venice he had been living on potatoes and barley soup.

Once in a poem he had expressed his longing for "kin of the spirit."

> . . . that know and feel
> And have some breath for beauty and the arts.[12]

Now they were about him, listening to Yeats read from his poems. Yeats read in a chanting voice. He put down the book and spoke of his youth in Ireland, how in his walks he would talk to the peasants and they told him about the fairies. He spoke of traveling to Paris and meeting Mallarmé. Of the importance of dreams . . . A "symbolic child" dreamed that it saw a woman shoot an arrow into the sky.[13] He spoke of the nobility of the soul that poets must have and was lacking to the present age. There was a beautiful woman, known to him personally, who had spent a whole day playing with a hawk someone sent her from Donegal.[14]

On Sundays Pound would go and talk to Victor Plarr, who, like Yeats, had been in the Rhymers' Club back in the nineties. Plarr was the librarian of the Royal College of Surgeons, but all his joy lay in the past, talking about the doomed men of the *fin de siècle*. He had known Ernest Dowson, who spent all his money on women of the street, and Lionel Johnson, who drank himself to death. Literally . . . It was said that he died by falling off a stool in a pub.

Pound was attending the meetings of the Poets' Club. They talked about technique and discussed foreign verse forms, including the "free verse" of the French Symbolist poets. They wrote imitations of Japanese *tanka* and *haiku,* and read Provençal songs. At one of their meetings, at the Tour Eiffel restaurant in Percy Street, Pound read his poem "Sestina: Altaforte" so loudly and expressively that the management placed a screen around the table. This poem was published by Ford Madox Hueffer in the June issue of *The English Review,* of which he was the editor. It was Pound's first appearance in a British magazine.

T. E. Hulme was the Club's most brilliant member. He wanted to rid poetry of its Romantic trappings and replace this with real knowledge—which, as he was a religious man, meant the truths of religion. And by restoring wit in poetry he wished to restore a sense of its human connections. A poem titled "Autumn" that Hulme read to the Club exhibits his ideas, as do all his seemingly innocuous little poems.

> A touch of cold in the Autumn night—
> I walked abroad,
> And saw the ruddy moon lean over a hedge
> Like a red-faced farmer.[15]

The poem rejects a Romantic, would-be "cosmic" pose, in favor of life as it is observed. The infinite is brought down to earth. In another poem, titled "The Embankment," Hulme would say:

> Oh, God, make small
> The old star-eaten blanket of the sky,
> That I may fold it round me and in comfort lie.[16]

Again, the aim is to make thought "concrete" by writing in images, and to prevent vagueness, Romantic dissipation of the self.

Hulme's ideas were based on the doctrine of Original Sin. Jean Jacques Rousseau had tried to make man out to be innately good. This was Romanticism, and it hadn't worked: experience taught men that they were wretched. For they were born with Original Sin and, left to their own devices, would fall into error. They could only be saved by the truths of religion. Romanticism made for pride, wickedness, and bad writing. Romanticism was endlessly writing about oneself, trying to fill the universe with oneself. "Romanticism," said Hulme, "is spilt religion." [17]

Equally important as a source of ideas was Ford Madox Hueffer (who later changed his name to Ford Madox Ford). Hulme's anti-Romanticism and his insistence on writing in images, together with Hueffer's insistence on a conversational style, would be the main Imagist principles. But the time was not yet; Pound did not grasp the importance of these lessons; in his poems he still was imitating the archaic diction of the Provençal poets, the "medi-evalism" of Dante Gabriel Rossetti and William Morris, the languid tones of early Yeats. He was taken with the precious attitudes that had been current in the nineties. For the nineties were daring to return, and Beauty had been seen in the vicinity of the British Museum.

Pound's "Ballad of the Goodly Fere" was in the manner of the Pre-Raphaelites. It could almost have been painted, with a red-haired Christ and exact details of the armor worn by the soldiers. Pound wrote it when he was living in Langham Street. He had been to a café in Soho the night before, and had been angered by a "certain sort of cheap irreverence" that was new to him. He lay awake, and the next morning when he set out for the Museum he had the first four lines in his head. He wrote the rest of the poem at a sitting, "on the left side of the Reading Room, with scarcely any erasures." [18]

From Langham Street he moved to Islington in north London, a dismal region of gray-yellow brick houses. And from there he moved to Hammersmith. Finally, in September 1909, he dis-covered Church Walk.

This was in Kensington, off the High Street. He rented a room from Mrs. Langley at Number 10. It had a "cast-iron fireplace, one hob on each side of the bars, and a pair of good windows looking south." [19] Mrs. Langley was "a yeoman's daughter from the north." He couldn't praise her enough: the Langleys were "positively the best England can produce at ANY level." [20] There was only one drawback: he couldn't stand the persistent ringing of the bells of St. Mary Abbots, close by. Brigit Patmore recalled how "he would cross the room with that peculiarly light step of his and shut the windows as soon as they began." [21]

In October, Elkin Mathews published a new collection of Pound's poems, titled *Exultations*. But on this occasion Edward Thomas was not pleased. Pound, he wrote, was "so pestered with possible ways of saying a thing that at present we must be content to pronounce his condition still interesting—perhaps promising—certainly distressing." [22] In private, writing to Gordon Bottomley, he expressed revulsion and took back his earlier praise of Pound's work: "Oh I do humble myself over Ezra Pound. He is not and cannot be very good. Certainly he is not what I mesmerized myself—out of pure love of praising the new poetry!—into saying he was and I am very much ashamed and only hope I shall never meet the man. . . ." [23] Thomas was to go through a further change six months later: he thought that he might have overreacted: "It was very treacherous & my severity was due to self-contempt as much as dislike of his work." [24] For Pound, literary life was not going to be plain sailing. It was possible to bring someone you did not know to the verge of hysterics simply by publishing a book.

Between *Personae* in 1909 and *Ripostes* three years later, Pound's reputation went into a decline. "Nearly to a man the reviewers of *Ripostes* were dissatisfied with the change in Pound's verse." [25] The increasing "realism" of Pound's writing hardly accounts for the dissatisfaction—there had been plenty of cynical poetry in England, and people had merely been amused. The trouble was that he was beginning to criticize editors, journalists, publishers, and standards of taste.

> This *papier-mâché*, which you see, my friends,
> Saith 'twas the worthiest of editors.
> Its mind was made up in "the seventies" . . .[26]

Indeed! Who did he think he was?

Wyndham Lewis tells a story that shows how unpopular Pound was becoming. Lewis was in the habit of lunching at the Vienna Café, near the British Museum, with "an entertaining group of people who were mostly drawn from the official ranks" of the

Museum. They were mostly middle-aged scholars, though there was a poet named Streatfield who had been a friend of Samuel Butler's and whose "high crowning laugh partook of the orgasm."

One day it was announced that an American poet named Ezra Pound would be joining them for lunch. Several of those present had already seen him, and "it was reported that S. had pronounced him a Jew. S. had an excellent nose for Jews, it was claimed: he had a gift that enabled him to detect a Jew under almost any disguise—something like water-divining, a peculiar and uncanny gift. And S. had affirmed (and coming in at that moment S. confirmed it, with a dainty sideways nod—as he hung up his overcoat—of his large pink countenance, decorated with a powerful white moustache) that this 'young American poet' was undoubtedly a crypto-semite, of the diaspora of Wisconsin."

It is a pity Proust was not there. The hand that created Baron Charlus would have delighted in the anti-Semites at the Vienna Café.

When Pound came in, Lewis tells us, he was mildly surprised to see "an unmistakably 'nordic blond,' with fierce blue eyes and a reddishly hirsute jaw, thrust out with a thoroughly Aryan determination." Then he paid no further attention to Pound. But he heard his voice, "the staccato of the States," and sensed that "there was little enthusiasm." Most of the party thought that Pound was indeed a Jew, disguised in a ten-gallon hat. Lewis heard them saying so afterwards, that Pound was a "red Jew . . . a subtle blend, but a pukka Kosher." When Pound left, says Lewis, he whirled off, "bitterness in his heart, if I know my Ezra." This, according to Lewis, was Pound's "first taste of the English." Pound "had no luck with the English, then or at a later date, and was always in this country the perfect fish out of water—hardly a Jewish trait!" With this closing remark, which reveals his own opinion of Jews, Lewis ends his story.[27]

The picture Lewis gives of Pound's relationships with English people up to this time—Lewis places the incident in or about 1910 —seems manifestly false. Pound had English friends and we know from his activity that he was not the fish out of water Lewis describes. In fact, the description is more suitable to Lewis himself, who was always picking a quarrel. But it may be true of Pound after 1910. His dislike of British officials, publishers, and patrons of the arts could have been intensified by incidents such as the one Lewis describes. Meeting a few Englishmen like "S." who "with a dainty sideways nod" confirmed his being a Jew would have made Pound shun the type.

The incident may be important for another reason. Suppose Pound heard that he had been taken for a "red Jew." Stories like this do get around—Wyndham Lewis, for one, would have been glad to carry it. Pound's reaction would have been to make it clear that he was not a Jew—to make it as clear as possible. Pound had only the normal amount of prejudice that came with a Christian upbringing. The later Pound, however, is a notorious anti-Semite. The episode at the Vienna Café, when he himself was taken for a Jew, and one or two other incidents of the kind, may have set him moving in the direction of anti-Semitism.

In 1910 Pound's Polytechnic lectures were published as *The Spirit of Romance*. Then he returned to the States for a visit. He saw his parents in Philadelphia, then he explored New York. He called on Yeats's father and met John Quinn, lawyer and patron of the arts. Hilda Doolittle came to New York and together they went over to New Jersey to see Bill Williams.

While in America Pound worked on translations of Cavalcanti and began to take an interest in the elegies of Propertius. He published his first American book, *Provença*, with Small, Maynard and Company of Boston. This included the best of the poems in *Personae* and *Exultations,* together with new poems that would be published in England with the title *Canzoni.*

He spent Thanksgiving Day with Williams in Rutherford.

On 22 February 1911 he sailed for Europe. He would not return to the States for twenty-eight years.

On his return to London he stayed only a day or two, then crossed to Paris. He traveled in Italy and north to Giessen in Germany where Hueffer was living in order to obtain a divorce. Pound arrived bearing a copy of *Canzoni* and read it to Hueffer. Hueffer's reaction was startling—he rolled on the floor. In this way he gave Pound to understand that his style was hopelessly out of date. "That roll," Pound said afterwards, "saved me at least two years." [28]

Hueffer believed that "poetry like everything else, to be valid and valuable, must reflect the circumstances and psychology of its own day." [29] His criticism gave Pound the push he needed into modernism; he cast archaisms overboard and developed a more direct, conversational style.

Pound returned to London. In October Hilda Doolittle came on a visit. Another important event was his meeting A. R. Orage, editor of *The New Age*. Between 30 November 1911 and 22 February 1912 Orage published a series of articles by Pound titled "I Gather the Limbs of Osiris." The first installment was Pound's translation of "The Seafarer" from the Anglo-Saxon. These articles amounted to a statement of Pound's aesthetics. He showed that he had ideas—he was not just another dilettante with a cape and cane.

As Pound became more serious his ideas aroused ridicule. The hostile reviews of *Ripostes,* he said, cost him many of his readers. "The public doesn't like to be surprised and the new poems had been surprising, even a little shocking." [30]

The reviewers claimed to be making their judgments on behalf of the public. But, in fact, the reviewers were acting on their own behalf. They had to protect themselves. Anything that was off the beaten track, that they couldn't understand, that might offend some powerful person, represented a threat to them. If they gave it their approval they were risking their jobs. Therefore, the reviewers were timid and at times repressive in their judgments.

Pound began to think of "editors, critics, the press generally, and in the end the whole of society" as "locked into a deadening stiffness, a resistance to anything that was genuinely new." [31] He became a critic of the literary establishment and the economic system that supported it. Up to this time he had indeed been a bohemian, thumbing his nose at society and at the same time hoping that it would reward him, making an exception in his case because of his extraordinary talent. Art would solve everything and make him famous. Now, however, he discovered that he must play according to the rules or be excluded. But he was not willing to be another dull poet like Abercrombie, another writer of "belles lettres" like Quiller-Couch. He would have to do battle. There was no alternative—he would have to gather his ideas and set about being a poet in earnest.

3

Gathering the Limbs of Osiris

POETRY, Pound says, began with someone's having a "very vivid and undeniable adventure" and being called a liar, whereupon he saw that no one would understand if he said that he "turned into a tree," so he made a myth instead—"a work of art that is—an impersonal and objective story woven out of his own emotion, as the nearest equation that he was capable of putting into words." [1] And he says, "Poetry is a sort of inspired mathematics, which gives us equations, not for abstract figures, triangles, squares, and the like, but for the human emotions." [2]

He was learning to make these equations. One way of telling a story "impersonally and objectively" is, strangely enough, for the author to tell it as though he were one of the people actually in the story. He creates a character and speaks through it—this is what is meant by a "persona"—as though he were an actor in a play speaking to the audience. The reader isn't called upon to believe, only to listen. The reader gets to know the character, and as the character believes certain things and acts as though they were true, the reader comes to believe them too. This kind of dramatic writing is sleight of hand, substituting one thing for another; our attention is diverted from the narrative to the person telling it, and as he is before us and we can hear him speaking, our belief in his reality leads us to believe the story he tells. At times, also, there is dramatic irony—the reader seems to know more than the character, who is involved and cannot see all around him. This

18

gives the reader a sense of his own superiority and makes him more
willing to believe the tale.

In Pound's poems, as in the poems of Robert Browning, the
persona may use a tone of "impassioned expostulation":

> Bah! I have sung women in three cities,
> But it is all the same . . .
> > "Cino" [3]

> Damn it all! all this our South stinks peace.
> > "Sestina: Altaforte" [4]

This is a way of getting the reader into the poem, of making an
argument out of nothing, beginning with a stage, a character, and
some visible agitation. If the speaker is agitated we want to know
why and what will happen next. A calm, unperturbed character
has nothing to reveal. Drama is agitation, and the best dramatic
writers are those who know how to start a quarrel.

Thus, in "Cino" the speaker begins by declaring that he is fed
up with women.[5] In "La Fraisne" an old man tells us that he has
run away from the world into the woods, that he has found a
bride "That was a dog-wood tree some syne," and that men say he
is mad.[6] His memory is failing, his thoughts trail off in dots—the
most important dots in English poetry, says Richard Ellmann,[7] for
they are an innovation, an early attempt to show fragmentation of
thought, what Pound in *Mauberley* will call "a consciousness dis-
junct" and other writers will call "the stream of consciousness."

> Once there was a woman . . .
> . . . but I forget . . . she was . . .
> . . . I hope she will not come again.[8]

Dramatic writing enables the poet to pretend—he can say things
that, if he were speaking in his own person, would be obviously
untrue. Pound uses the dramatic monologue for this purpose, but
he also uses it when he is speaking his mind. To express his inmost
thoughts he may use another writer's style or the style of another
period. Thus, the "Envoi (1919)" in *Hugh Selwyn Mauberley* is
written in archaic diction reminiscent of English poetry in the
sixteenth century. Yet the thought is perfectly sincere—this is
certainly not said in mockery: ". . . change hath broken down/
All things save Beauty alone." [9] The passage against vanity in
Canto LXXXI is in the style of a past age: "What thou lov'st well
is thy true heritage . . ." [10] Readers agree that this is Pound speak-

ing for himself, and here too he is speaking in a style taken from tradition. Some men, when they wish to speak their mind, step forward in person. With Pound the process can be exactly the opposite—in order to speak his mind he uses another man's voice or even a quotation.

Pound's use of the dramatic monologue was learned from Browning. There are readers who do not understand why he imitates and borrows and quotes so much. It is because to Pound traditions are alive:

> To have gathered from the air a live tradition
> or from a fine old eye the unconquered flame
> This is not vanity.[11]

"A return to origins invigorates because it is a return to nature and reason." [12] Pound is like the medieval craftsman who cares above all that a thing be well made, and will borrow his tools to make it, and does not care whose name it bears.

In some early poems Pound imitates the troubadours. He is a poet wandering the roads, thinking of women.

> Eyes, dreams, lips, and the night goes.
> Being upon the road once more,
> They are not.[13]

His allusions may be obscure, in the manner of "trobar clus." And his language is sprinkled with archaisms to give the impression of a bygone age. It is odd to find one of the leaders of modern poetry starting out with obsolete words—"destrier" for "horse"—but though the language is archaic, the spirit is experimental. He writes with an ear for the musical phrase, not the ticktock of iambic feet. Pound is going far afield at a time when poets in England are content to plod in the old worn ruts of meter and to write about love and nature in the same old ways.

In an essay about the twelfth-century troubadour Arnaut Daniel, Pound shows what he thinks lyric poetry should be. Daniel was an innovator—he made new rhymes. He rediscovered style, "a manner of writing in which each word should bear some burden, should make some special contribution to the effect of the whole." Daniel made a unity of words, rhythm and music. Moreover, he was accurate in his observations of nature.[14]

Pound uses established meters and line lengths, but he may strike off into something completely unconventional. The first

three lines of the following passage are fairly regular, with ana-
pestic feet.

> Aye, I am wistful for my kin of the spirit
> And have none about me save in the shadows
> When come *they*, surging of power, "DAEMON,"
> "Quasi KALOUN." S.T. says Beauty is most that, a
> "calling to the soul." [15]

The fourth line leaps into the future—it would not be surprising
to find it in the *Cantos*. Pound has broken off writing "poesy" and
given his thought direct. The fourth line brings into the poem
the sound of a man's thinking; the rhythm has changed from a
regular beat to accord with "the inner form of the line." [16] When
Pound has learned to write this kind of verse consistently it will
carry the weight of thought in the *Cantos*.

Donald Davie finds Pound's characteristic rhythm in a "breaking
of the line near mid-point." Davie is speaking of Pound's "Sestina:
Altaforte," the poem he read so loudly in the restaurant.

> The verse-lines are true units, rhythmically and in meaning; and
> yet each of them is broken near the center much more forcibly
> than by a caesura in traditional accentual-syllabic meters. The
> break in "I have no life/save when the swords clash" depends
> upon a rising beat before the break, crammed against the em-
> phatically falling rhythm of the trochee "save when." But this
> is not true of other lines where the break apart is just as pro-
> nounced. In any case, this breaking of the line near mid-point
> (which Pound at this stage cannot maintain through a whole
> poem) was to be the hall mark of his writing in verse.[17]

In the winter of 1911–12 Pound published a series of articles
in A. R. Orage's magazine, *The New Age,* along with translations
from Anglo-Saxon, Provençal and Tuscan poetry. The articles,
titled "I Gather the Limbs of Osiris," show his ideas about poetry
in general. He describes meter in English as being made out of
Latin, French and Anglo-Saxon systems—measuring by quantity,
number of syllables, number of stressed syllables, or alliteration.
There are several systems of rhyming and "the Spanish system of
assonance." "It is probable," he says, "that all these systems concern us," and he ends his explanation of meter with a prophecy:
"It is not beyond the pales of possibility that English verse of the
future will be a sort of orchestration taking account of all these
systems." [18]

"Orchestration" is a fair description of what Pound's mature style will be, shifting from one meter to another as the mood takes him, and already in the early poems there are indications of free verse. He is breaking the pentameter—"To break the pentameter, that was the first heave" [19]—by using various feet and line lengths. In "I Gather the Limbs of Osiris" he hints at rhythms that cannot be measured. There is "the inner form of the line." Perception of this is instinctive: "Some people 'see colour' and some 'line.' " He doesn't want to start a "babel" of "post-impressionists in rhythm," people searching their hearts for the right sound; nevertheless, while some people can hear quantity and others can hear stress, there are fewer who can feel rhythm by "the inner form of the line." This inner form is all-important; it is their sense of it that gives Milton and Yeats mastery of rhythm in verse. [20]

Pound's early poems point toward more ambitious work, but they are also important in themselves. One of the poems that appeared in his first book, *A Lume Spento,* now stands at the head of *Personae,* the volume of his collected shorter poems. " 'The Tree,' " says Hugh Witemeyer, "describes the kind of metamorphic experience (displacement from the poet's self into another mode of experience) out of which many poems in the volume *Personae* grow." [21] As we have seen, Pound thought that poetry originated in some kind of metamorphosis, a "very vivid and undeniable adventure" in which a man "turned into a tree." [22]

The range of form and style is large, from ballad to free verse. The "Ballad of the Goodly Fere," published in 1909, hit the taste of the public. Jesus is described as a lover of the outdoors and boon companion.

> Aye lover he was of brawny men,
> O' ships and the open sea. [23]

As Pound remarked, if he had been content to write this kind of poem over and over again he might have been a popular writer. [24]

At the other extreme is "The Return," written three years later. Yeats called it "The most beautiful poem that has been written in the free form, one of the few in which I find real organic rhythm." [25] The poem seems to be about pagan gods who have become weak and troubled. It is written in cadences, unrhymed.

> See, they return; ah, see the tentative
> Movements, and the slow feet. . . . [26]

According to R. Taupin "The Return" is an imitation of the rhythm of a poem by Henri de Régnier, "Les Médailles d'Argille." K. L. Goodwin suggests that it gave Aldington and H.D. a model for their own "Greek" style.[27] "The Return" is a sophisticated, thoroughly "modern" performance, in every way superior to the "Ballad of the Goodly Fere."

"The Seafarer" (1911) shows Pound's method of translating which, when he is so inclined, produces not so much a translation as a new poem in the spirit of the original.[28] In translating "The Seafarer" he aims to reproduce the "feel" of the original by reproducing Anglo-Saxon sounds, whether or not they correspond literally to the meaning of the original. This way of translating offended scholars who believed that translation must be literal to be accurate. Pound provoked their wrath by stating in print that his version of "The Seafarer" was "as nearly literal" as any translation could be. Obviously it is not. Where the Anglo-Saxon has *wrecan* ("to make, compose") Pound has "reckon." Where the Anglo-Saxon has *sumeres weard* ("guardian of summer") he has "summerward." And so on. Moreover, there are unfortunately some mistakes, as when Pound misreads *purh* ("through") as *pruh* ("coffin") and translates it as "tomb." [29] Nevertheless, his translation conveys the important meanings of the Anglo-Saxon, and— which the literal way of translating failed to do—Pound has translated into poetic English, finding new equivalents for old emotions. This was his contribution as a translator—he showed that to translate accurately you must do more than find words that have the same meaning as words in another language. Literal translation sounds like no language at all. The aim of translation is to find words that bring over the sense and spirit of the original so that they are understood. Therefore the translator must aim at making an "equation" rather than a literal translation.

One of the best known of the early poems is "Portrait d'une Femme." [30] As verse it is conventional iambic pentameter—the concept is what is memorable. Pound may have been reading Laforgue, especially "Légende" where Laforgue speaks of: "A woman you see on empty days,/ Seated at her table, in a room that smells of winter." [31] We know that when T. S. Eliot came to describe neurotic, civilized woman he remembered Laforgue. In any case, whether the concept is borrowed or not, Pound has seized on it for the twentieth century. This is one of the earliest portrayals in English of the modern woman who embodies "civilization and its discontents." Her head is filled with "Ideas, old gossip, odd-ments of all things." She has no character, it seems, yet she holds a fascination—those who visit her "take strange gain away." Per-haps having no character is the prerequisite for being a per-sonality—"Nothing," Pound says, "that's quite your own./ Yet this is you." [32]

What the lady evidently lacks is a direction, a reason for liv-ing at all. In Eliot's description of her, in *The Waste Land*, she will be hysterical, a web of nerves. Finally she is a vampire.

> A woman drew her long black hair out tight
> And fiddled whisper music on those strings
> And bats with baby faces in the violet light
> Whistled and beat their wings.[33]

This modern view of culture is rooted in the past. We are again looking at *La Gioconda* with Pater: "She is older than the rocks among which she sits; like the vampire, she has been dead many times, and learned the secrets of the grave. . . ." [34] But where Pater saw beauty, Eliot sees despair.

The reader of the poems in *Ripostes* (1912) may wonder what it was that made reviewers hostile and, according to Pound, lost him some of his English readers. The poems aren't shocking. Yet they show a sincerity, a seriousness about the act of writing, that is opposed to the smooth, commercial stream. Pound spoke of "One average mind—with one thought less, each year." [35] To attack the average, to "speak of perfection" is, as Pound says elsewhere, to get yourself disliked.[36]

Perfection was what he was after, to convey "an exact impres-sion of exactly what one means in such a way as to exhilarate." Not that poetry was to be void of mystery, but artists "discrimi-nate . . . between one kind of indefinability and another." He said, "Technique is the only gauge and test of a man's lasting sincerity." [37]

All his life he held to this. He believed that art was supreme and that it might be taught. For this reason other men accepted him as their teacher, and men of strong, original talent—Yeats, Eliot, Joyce—were willing to listen to his instructions. But insist-ing on technique and striving for excellence is likely to make average people uneasy, and they are the ones who run the world.

4

Il Miglior Fabbro

"England is as dead as Mutton."
> Pound to Harriet Monroe, November 1913

" 'Harriet' is a bloody fool."
> Pound to Amy Lowell, November 1913 [1]

IN August 1912 Harriet Monroe wrote to Pound from Chicago asking him to contribute to a new magazine she was starting called *Poetry*. He accepted and so set in motion one of his careers, that of impresario, chivvying Harriet or anyone who was in a position to publish good writing. "My idea of our policy is this: We support American poets—preferably the young ones who have a serious determination to produce master-work. We import only such work as is better than that produced at home. The best foreign stuff, the stuff well above mediocrity, or the experiments that seem serious, and seriously and sanely directed toward the broadening and development of the Art of Poetry." [2]

He contributed his own poems to *Poetry* and tried to educate Harriet: "Poetry must be *as well written as prose*." [3] She dug in her heels. She thought that he preferred foreign poetry to the native product, while he on his side tried to cure her of provincialism. When he sent her T. S. Eliot's "The Love Song of J. Alfred Prufrock"—"the best poem I have yet had or seen from an American" [4]—she raised objections and delayed printing for eight months. Finally he broke off his formal connections with *Poetry*, but he continued to send Harriet letters of advice.

He had dealings with Amy Lowell, who, having heard of the

Imagists, arrived in England with the hope of becoming an important figure in the movement. Amy Lowell was the perennial rich American woman who takes up art and tells everyone what it is. Usually she is content to command a salon. But not Amy—she wanted to be a leader of the new poetry. Pound, on the other hand, wanted her to publish a magazine and make him the editor. He thought she had the money—a natural conclusion, since she appeared in London with her own car and chauffeur and was staying at the Berkeley Hotel.

But Amy wanted to be courted for her poetry, not her cash, and when she realized that Pound was making fun of her—at an "Imagist Dinner" she gave, someone mentioned her poem "In a Garden" and the line "Not the water, but you in your whiteness, bathing," and someone else pointed out that she was stout, whereupon Pound brought in a tub, big enough for her to sit in, and suggested that she start a new school, *Les Nagistes* (The Bathers) [5] —well, Amy got the point. She withdrew to America, taking poems by five Imagists with her, and published her own anthologies. In letters she remarked sadly that Ezra was in a decline, nobody wanted to have anything to do with him any more. [6]

Pound was willing to deal with people such as Harriet and Amy because he wanted to see good writers published. In December 1913 he wrote a letter to James Joyce, asking him to send something for *The Egoist,* or for *Poetry* or *The Smart Set,* for which he was able to solicit contributions though not accept them. [7] He arranged to publish a poem by Joyce—"I Hear an Army." When he had read *Dubliners* and the first chapter of *A Portrait of the Artist as a Young Man,* he became an admirer and defender of Joyce's work. He reviewed *Dubliners* in *The Egoist* (July 15, 1914) [8] and found a literary agent who would handle *The Portrait.*

At the same time, he discovered T. S. Eliot, who was studying philosophy at Oxford, and began to promote Eliot's work.

There were others, such as Robert Frost, whose work he promoted until they showed that they had different aims. Thirty years later when Pound was in a desperate situation they came to his defense. They remembered his devotion to writing and all he had done for others at no profit to himself, indeed at times when he himself was barely able to make a living.

How did he live in those years? By writing—mainly reviews and

articles. It was damned hard work. In the winter of 1913–1914
W. B. Yeats wanted a secretary, and Pound agreed to be it. He
had admired Yeats for years, imitating his poetry at times—"La
Fraisne," Pound says, was written in a mood similar to that of
"Mr. Yeats in his 'Celtic Twilight.' " [9] Recently, influenced by
Hulme's dislike of the Romantic, and Ford Madox Ford's (Huef-
fer's) insistence on informality, Pound had become wary of Yeats.
Yeats hearkened back to Symbolism and the Romantic. Writing in
Poetry, January 1913, Pound explained that Ford and Yeats were
opposed—Ford was objective, Yeats subjective. Yeats was "the only
poet worthy of serious study" but his way was "very dangerous."
Nevertheless, Pound thought that Yeats could still be taught
something—he was willing to be "modern"—and he persuaded
Yeats to submit some poems to *Poetry*. He could not resist re-
writing the poems slightly as they passed through his hands, to
Yeats's indignation.[10]

Yeats on his side found Pound's poetry perplexing—the free
verse was "devil's metres." He wrote to Harriet Monroe that
Pound was "certainly a creative personality of some sort, though
it is too soon yet to say of what sort . . . His experiments are
perhaps errors, I am not certain; but I would always sooner give
the laurel to vigorous errors than to any orthodoxy not inspired." [11]

For three winters, 1913–1916, Pound went with Yeats to Sussex
as his secretary. There is an affectionate account of this in the
Cantos. Pound recalls the voice of "Uncle William downstairs
composing":

> that had made a great Peeeeacock
>   in the proide ov his oiye
>   had made a great peeeeeeecock in the . . . [12]

He recalls that Yeats would not eat ham for dinner because
peasants ate ham for dinner. He read Wordsworth aloud to Yeats
"for the sake of his conscience," but Yeats preferred "Ennemosor
on Witches," and they read Doughty's *The Dawn in Britain*.[13]

In April 1914, Pound was married to Dorothy Shakespear, the
good listener, daughter of "the most charming woman in London." Their life together was a confusion of journalism, writing
poetry, translating, editing, being interested in new painting,
sculpture, and music. Pound made his own furniture and played

tennis. Looking at this period of Pound's life when he was becoming disillusioned with the state of poetry in England it is clear that he must also have been happy.

What was Imagism? In histories of literature, a movement that started about 1909 with Hulme's group of poets who met in restaurants and that came to an end in 1917 when Amy Lowell published the third of her anthologies of Imagist poets. The flourishing time when ideas were generated was shorter, 1912 to 1913, when Pound was in charge. The Imagist movement produced a handful of small poems that are still fresh and sparkling, but nothing grand.

Imagism, however, is more important than the history of a movement. The influence of Imagist principles has been large. In accordance with these principles Pound, Eliot and Williams did much of their work, and this influenced hundreds of other poets. The principles have also taken effect in prose—the stories of Ernest Hemingway, for example, were written in a manner of which the Imagists approved, and Hemingway has been imitated everywhere. There are novelists in France and Russia who, though they may not be conscious of it, owe their styles to Imagism. The little seed of the Imagist movement made a great tree with twigs and leaves spreading over the world.

Imagism did not begin with the movement, and the more we pursue its beginnings the more they recede. Pound himself seems to have thought that Imagism began in the nineties. In *Hugh Selwyn Mauberley* he dwells considerably on the nineties—Mauberley, who lives through the Imagist period in London, keeps harking back to the nineties. The librarian "Verog," who is actually Victor Plarr, reminisces about Dowson and other worthies of the *fin de siècle*. Following the cult of Beauty and "art for art's sake," hoping to make one small, perfect thing in enamel or bronze, this is Mauberley's métier, as it was for artists of the nineties. There were poems written at that time—Oscar Wilde's "Impressions," William Sharp's "Transcripts"—which, had they been written in free verse, would seem Imagist.

Speaking of *Mauberley* reminds us that there were writers before the *fin de siècle* who "spoke of perfection." Flaubert, of course, and Gautier. . . . Flaubert is Mauberley's "true Penelope," and in the course of the poem there are phrases taken from Gautier's book, the title of which being translated is *Enamels and*

Cameos. The Imagists, too, work on hard surfaces to make them shine brilliantly.

When we think of the Imagist style we are reminded of English translations of Greek lyrics. There is the same clarity and emphasis on sense perception. Some of Pound's and Aldington's and most of H. D.'s poems are written in a lucid "Greek" manner. They assume that Greek feelings were as clear as the sky and running water. Pound says that Imagism stands for "hard light and clear edges," for "a certain clarity and intensity." Whether this is true of the Greeks is not the point—it is the Imagist view of the Greeks, as it was the view Keats had of the Greeks. To think like a Greek is to be clear. Also, it means to think through the senses. Keats put it extremely: "O for a life of Sensations rather than of Thoughts!", and spoke of testing poetry on the pulse, of loading every rift with ore.

The history of ideas frequently contradicts itself. Imagism, as Hulme conceives it, is opposed to Romanticism, yet on this point Imagist thinking has definite resemblances to the thinking of Keats.

Keats might have seen the contradiction as part of a drama. The ideas writers have, literary movements, the lives of writers, are drama—it is a mistake, and hopelessly confusing, to expect them to lead to truth. If we wish to arrive at truth we must study something else. As the lady said to Rousseau, "Give up ladies and study mathematics."

It was a Greek, Aristotle, who said that nothing can be known by the mind unless it has first been perceived by the senses. The Imagist poets are always evoking sense perceptions. Indeed, Imagist poetry was sometimes called "physical poetry"—John Crowe Ransom used this term for it. Hulme insisted so strongly on the physical properties of Imagism that many people believe that Imagism was just a description of objects and actions. Some Imagist poets themselves seem to have believed it—their poems are stiff as brocade, small as a fragment of glass. Hulme said that poetry was "a compromise for a language of intuition which would hand over sensations bodily. It always endeavours to arrest you, and to make you continuously see a physical thing, to prevent you gliding through an abstract process . . . Images in verse are not mere decoration, but the very essence of an intuitive language." [14]

There it is—"images." And Pound said that he organized the Imagist movement "on the Hulme basis." [15] The impression that

Hulme was the main theorist may, after all, be right. There is no doubt that the study Hulme's group made of Japanese poems, *haiku* and *tanka,* had a great deal to do with the conception of Imagist poetry.[16]

This reminds us that Imagism may have had a source in Japanese art, which became a vogue at the end of the nineteenth century. The painter Whistler, by his use of objects Japanese, did much to stimulate the vogue. Imagism owes something to Whistler.

And to painting . . . Pound says so, speaking of his famous little Imagist poem, "In a Station of the Metro."

> The apparition of these faces in the crowd;
> Petals on a wet, black bough.

He says that the experience "should have gone into paint." The faces he saw in the Metro became "an equation . . . not in speech, but in little splotches of color." He is careful to say, however, that it is not Impressionist painting, because "The state of mind of the impressionist tends to become cinematographical . . . the cinematograph does away with the need of a lot of impressionist art." [17]

Perhaps the true founder was Henry James. Pound met James in London in 1912, and met him again—"The massive head, the slow uplift of the hand, *gli occhi onesti e tardi,* the long sentences piling themselves up in elaborate phrase after phrase, the lightning incision, the pauses, the slightly shaking admonitory gesture with its 'wu-a-wait a little, wait a little, something will come' . . ." [18]

Hugh Kenner speaks of James's "refusals and eschewals, his way of only half-naming things or presenting them by way of analogy." Indirection . . . this is surely a principle of Imagism. He says that "James's great sensibility brought in a generation. But for that sensibility *Prufrock* is unthinkable, *Mauberley* is unthinkable." He speaks of James as "The mind unviolated by an idea," holding converse with particulars, "mute particulars, mute mental particulars, the act of perception and the act of articulation inextricably one." [19] Bravo! We are inclined to give the palm to Henry James as the true founder of Imagism.

There was another master novelist who said something that has a bearing on this point. Conrad says that "A work of art should carry its justification in every line." (Pound will call this "intensity" and "concentration.") Conrad says that "All art . . . appeals primarily to the senses" in order to "reach the secret spring of responsive emotions." "My task which I am trying to achieve is, by the power of the written word to make you hear, to make you feel—it is, before all, to make you see." [20] Doesn't this say it all, and were the Imagists different?

Conrad collaborated with Ford, and a few years later Ford rolled on the floor in front of Pound and showed him the way to a modern style. Conrad and Ford insisted on "presentation." This is at the heart of Imagism—present, don't explain.

There are other claimants—Henri Bergson, for example. In April 1911 Hulme attended a conference at Bologna in the course of which Henri Bergson lectured on "the image." He spoke of "a receding and vanishing image" that stood halfway between concrete intuition and complex abstraction. The image, said Bergson, haunted the philosopher; it seemed to come closer to his meaning than the conceptual expressions into which intuition was translated. When Hulme came back to London that winter he gave some lectures on Bergson at the home of Mrs. Franz Liebich. Pound attended. Fresh from his translating of the poems of Guido Cavalcanti, Pound, by his account, explained to Hulme "the difference between Guido's precise interpretive metaphor, and the Petrarchan fustian and ornament, pointing out that Guido thought in accurate terms; that the phrases correspond to definite sensations undergone. . . ." As Pound tells it, Hulme fell silent. Then he remarked, "That is very interesting . . . That is more interesting than anything I ever read in a book." [21]

So, is it possible after all that Pound invented Imagism?

Or was it Remy de Gourmont? According to Gourmont, language originated in words that were like sense perceptions, these degenerated into words that were ideas, and these became words that were just vague sentiments. "An idea is only a sense-perception that has faded." [22]

The truth is, no one invented Imagism, or everyone did. When an invention is needed and the time is right for it, people come upon it independently. Who invented radio? Ideas that were seized on by Pound and directed as the Imagist movement were discovered elsewhere by others and given other names. Pound, however, put the ideas to work. His way of taking an idea that had been neglected or not understood—at least, not in English— stating it clearly, and showing how it can be applied, practically amounted to saying it for the first time. Pound was, like Thomas

Alva Edison, a genius at practical mechanics. It is hard to draw a line between this and invention.

In the spring or early summer of 1912, Pound says, H. D., Richard Aldington and he agreed upon three principles:

1. Direct treatment of the "thing" whether subjective or objective.
2. To use absolutely no word that does not contribute to the presentation.
3. As regarding rhythm: to compose in the sequence of the musical phrase, not in sequence of a metronome.

He says, "An 'Image' is that which presents an intellectual and emotional complex in an instant of time. I use the term 'complex' rather in the technical sense employed by the newer psychologists, such as Hart, though we might not agree absolutely in our application.

"It is the presentation of such a 'complex' instantaneously which gives that sense of sudden liberation; that sense of freedom from time limits and space limits; that sense of sudden growth, which we experience in the presence of the greatest works of art.

"It is better to present one Image in a lifetime than to produce voluminous works." [23]

We see that in Pound's view Imagism is a great deal more than "physical poetry." It is, indeed, rather mysterious. In another place he points out that the Imagist poet depends on the creative, not upon the "mimetic or representational" part of his work. "The author must use his *image* because he sees it or feels it; *not* because he thinks he can use it to back up some creed or some system of ethics or economics." [24] (An interesting remark, in view of Pound's later didactic development in the *Cantos.*)

These sentences and other sayings by the Imagists—notably the preface to Amy Lowell's anthology, *Some Imagist Poets,* published in 1915—do not amount to a definition. Imagist poems were clear, Imagist theory was not. There was, Pound said, a certain "doctrine of the image," but it would only start useless controversy to let the public have it. [25] (Bergson's idea, probably, was what he had in mind.)

But though the theory is not clear, when we read Imagist poems we see exactly what they were up to—the best of the Imagists, that is, for they were soon imitated by a swarm of free-verse writers,

many of whom had no talent at all. These Imagists drc
and Eliot back to reading Gautier and writing tight
stanzas.

The good Imagist poems are moments of perception arrived at
through the senses. There must be a triggering device; this is
something seen, heard, touched, smelled, or tasted.

> Green arsenic smeared on an egg-white cloth,
> Crushed strawberries! Come, let us feast our eyes.[26]

These lines evoke the senses of sight, touch ("smeared . . .
crushed") and taste. It is possible also to imagine that we are
smelling crushed strawberries, and the sound of the syllables involves the fifth sense. But this is elementary—the triggering device
is there, but not much of an explosion. Writing has to be more
than this, more than a sensory experience—it has to show us something we have not seen, heard, touched, smelled, or tasted. Poets
have always known this . . . Milton in "Lycidas" saw life at odds
with art, and Keats explored the problem at some length. If poetry
is an illusion of life, why not just choose life—lying on the grass,
making love, drinking wine? Keats thought that creating illusions
of life would lead you naturally to create illusions that were more
enjoyable than life, and this would lead you to dispense with life
altogether, "to cease upon the midnight with no pain." In short,
to die. Whereupon you would be just earth, unable to sense anything at all. Therefore, instead of regarding art as an illusion,
Keats determined by an effort of will to use art as a means of getting through to reality, which was not found in life but somewhere
else.

It is not through its philosophy, however, that a movement in
art is best understood. The way is through a study of its technique. To understand Imagism we need to see what an image is
and how it works. This is the way Samuel Johnson went about
understanding metaphysical poetry—he studied the conceit. Let
us therefore look at the image which, as we look at it, will not be
very different from the metaphysical conceit. In the image—we are
speaking of the Imagists' use of the term, for there have been
other uses—in the image of 1912, two things are put together.
Pound says, "The 'one image poem' is a form of super-position,
that is to say, it is one idea set on top of another."[27] The mind
moves from one to the other. Or it may be two actions that are
juxtaposed, or a thing and an action. Or there could be several

things and actions. Indeed, it is possible to conceive of an image that would continue for a long time, with many connections between things and actions and complex movements of the mind between them all. It is possible to think of an entire Canto or a whole book as one complex image.

For the moment let us stay with the idea of a simple image consisting of two parts juxtaposed. In Pound's little poem "In a Station of the Metro" there are faces and there is a black wet bough. The mind moves from one to the other, connecting them, comparing, finding resemblances and differences. The number of resemblances and differences it finds is up to the mind, naturally.

The image consists of the parts *and* the movement. It isn't static, nor is it composed of just any objects placed side by side. They have to be significant objects, and they have to be put together so that something happens. This is the key, this is why it isn't enough just to collect objects. You have to select, and in order to select you must have something in mind. You have to be—this is the catch—a poet. *"Mais, d'abord il faut être un poète."* [28]

On this obstacle Amy stumbled, and many others with her. You had to be the kind of person Henry James described, "on whom nothing is wasted." You had to have had—Pound's phrase—"a delightful psychic experience."

(It strikes us there may be something lacking in a kind of poetry that takes its origin from a "delightful experience." Terror, perhaps. Wordsworth said "beauty *and* terror." The Imagists, if the above description of their works is complete, seem to have provided for beauty but not for terror. This will be one of the criticisms of Pound's *Cantos*. But it is not a valid criticism of Eliot's poems. So, it is not a lack in the theory—there can be terrifying images enough if the poet's temperament runs that way.)

Juxtaposition of different things may serve to double an effect or undercut it, to create effects of irony, humor, or pathos. In the following poem, "Fan-Piece, for Her Imperial Lord," Pound juxtaposes two things.

> O fan of white silk,
> > clear as frost on the grass-blade,
> You also are laid aside.[29]

A woman is speaking of the man who has deserted her. Earl Miner comments: "We must not overlook the importance of the super-

posed image to this theme. The resemblance of the silk of the fan
to the frost on the grass is not one only of color. The point is that
the clear frost melts quickly in the morning sun, that beautiful
fans are used by imperial princes for only a short time, and that
even a woman's beauty will serve as an attraction for only a
season." [30]

In the *Cantos* juxtaposition will be used to show metamorphosis, the changing of one thing into another, the breaking of solid
surfaces that allows a permanent idea or god to emerge. ("A god
is an eternal state of mind.") [31] The supernatural often makes its
appearance through metamorphosis—a man turning into a tree,
one financial system turning into another. Pound's image, composed of parts in an active relationship, allows the supernatural
to be seen. The image is an opening, "a 'magic moment' or moment of metamorphosis, bust thru from quotidien into 'divine
or permanent world.' Gods, etc." [32] The eyes of a sea beast become the eyes of a girl, and these are the eyes of Helen, "destroyer
of men and cities." [33]

Images, then, aren't ornaments, hung on an idea to adorn it.
They are the poem itself. "The image," Pound says, "is itself the
speech." [34] This may be a way to distinguish images from metaphors and similes in their traditional English use. Metaphors and
similes are often used for adornment, to illustrate an idea that is
explicitly stated. The poet makes a statement about love, say, or
old age, then finds a metaphor to illustrate it.

> That time of year thou mayst in me behold
> When yellow leaves, or none, or few, do hang . . .

There is a time lag, therefore a separation, between thought and
experience. The more elaborate the comparison, as in Milton's
epic similes, the harder it is to "feel" the thought. An imagist
poem, on the other hand, concentrates on giving you the experience—handing over sensations bodily, as Hulme said. Imagist
writing aims to make you feel, rather than to tell you what feeling is like. This is done by using many images. Also there is concentration, achieved by cutting out the creaky hinges of simile
and metaphor, the "like's."

"Go in fear of abstractions," Pound said.[35] The Imagists were
against any kind of abstraction or vagueness in the use of language. The Symbolists had been abstract. "The symbolist's *symbols* have a fixed value, like numbers in arithmetic, like 1, 2, and

7. The imagiste's images have a variable significance, like the signs *a*, *b*, and *x* in algebra." Symbolism was usually associated with mushy technique.[36] Symbolism was a throwback to Romanticism, Hulme's "spilt religion," drifting off as a gas. Imagism, on the other hand, was the new kind of classicism that made you feel more alive. "The natural object is always the *adequate* symbol." [37]

Pound made working rules for the Imagist. For rhythm: "Don't chop your stuff into separate *iambs*. Don't make each line stop dead at the end, and then begin every next line with a heave." He adjured the poet to "behave as a musician." [38] He said, "I believe in an 'absolute rhythm,' a rhythm, that is, in poetry which corresponds exactly to the emotion or shade of emotion to be expressed." [39]

For rhyme: "A rhyme must have in it some slight element of surprise if it is to give pleasure." [40]

For language: "Use no superfluous word, no adjective which does not reveal something." [41]

Such was the theory. The movement went as follows. In October 1912, H. D. brought Pound a number of poems which he forwarded to Harriet Monroe. Pound says that in fact he started the movement in order to publicize H. D.'s work. The poems were published in the January 1913 issue of *Poetry*. They were "Hermes of the Ways," "Orchard"—originally titled "Priapus," but Harriet was having none of it—and "Epigram."

Richard Aldington and F. S. Flint also published Imagist poems.

The March 1913 issue of *Poetry* carried a brief essay, "Imagisme," under Flint's name. The "three principles" given above, "Direct treatment of the 'thing,'" et cetera, are taken from this essay. Though it bears Flint's name, it seems that Pound wrote it. In conversation with Patricia Hutchins in the fifties Flint said that Imagism had been a young people's joke, "not at all that serious." He described how Pound arrived one day with an "interview with himself" already written, and wanted him to sign it. Flint declined to do so. He revised the "interview" after Pound had left, and sent it to him. Pound made further improvements.[42]

The same issue of *Poetry* carried Pound's "A Few Don'ts by an Imagiste."

In January 1914 *The Egoist*, edited by Pound and Aldington, started publishing Imagist poems contributed by Flint, Aldington,

Pound, H. D., Amy Lowell, John Gould Fletcher, Wil
Williams, D. H. Lawrence and others.

In spring 1914 Pound published an anthology, Des
that included work by eleven poets. Besides those nan
there were Skipworth Cannell, Allen Upward, John ......os,
James Joyce and Ford Madox Hueffer. With this Pound ended
his role as impresario and Amy Lowell took over. Imagism was
discussed in the newspapers; there were parodies, sudden conver-
sions, etc. Imagist poems appeared in the United States in *Poetry*
and *The Little Review* edited by Margaret Anderson and Jane
Heap. In London, Imagist poets continued to publish in *The
Egoist*. On 1 May 1915 *The Egoist* published a "Special Imagist
Number" that included a "History of Imagism" by Flint.

In 1915, 1916 and 1917 Amy Lowell published her anthologies
in Boston. The poets included Aldington, Flint, H. D., Amy herself, John Gould Fletcher and Lawrence. After 1917 "Imagism
was no longer a movement; it had become a tool, which each poet
could adapt to his own use." [43]

By the time his Imagist anthology appeared Pound no longer
thought of himself as an Imagist. He was in another movement.
Not really a movement . . . just a "gang." It didn't even have
a name until he gave it one—Vorticism.

It began with a quarrel. Wyndham Lewis and a number of
fellow artists broke with Roger Fry and his Omega atelier over a
commission that Lewis claimed Fry had appropriated from
Spencer Gore and himself. The "rebel" artists—Lewis, Edward
Wadsworth, Frederick Etchells, Cuthbert Hamilton, and C. R.
W. Nevinson—established a Cubist Art Centre in Great Ormond
Street. Financial backing was provided by Kate Lechmere, whom
Lewis met in Paris. Pound joined the Centre mainly as propa-
gandist; he contributed a wall sign that announced: "End of the
Christian Era." [44]

Lewis' quarrel with Fry gave the group a feeling of solidarity.
There was also a need to make themselves heard above the up-
roar of Futurism. The Futurists were taking over everything; any
kind of art that had an unusual color, shape or sound was being
labeled Futurist.

The inventor of Futurism was an Italian, F. T. Marinetti,
painter, poet, and maker of manifestoes. Marinetti thought of
the word "futurist" and its opposite, "passéist." Having done this

he had done the main thing. A "Manifesto of Futurism" appeared in *Le Figaro,* 20 February 1909. In the years that followed there would be Futurist pronouncements on painting, sculpture, architecture, cinema, clothing, war, women, drama, music, politics, and music halls.[45]

William C. Wees has pointed out the resemblance between Marinetti's ideas and those of Marshall McLuhan fifty years later. Marinetti "hoped to open people's eyes and ears to the industrial urban mass culture that even in 1910 drew western man inside the boundaries of a 'global village.' " There was a new "world-consciousness," thanks to wireless and newspapers. Marinetti said, "The inhabitants of a mountain village can, every day, in a newspaper, follow with suspense the movements of the Chinese rebels, the English and American Suffragettes, Dr. Carrel and the heroic sledges of the Arctic explorers." With this new world-feeling men did not want to know about the past—they wanted to know what was happening now.[46]

In painting, the Futurists developed a technique known as Simultaneity. There might be multiple stages of an action or several things happening at once. They pointed out that a running horse does not have four legs but twenty. The best-known painting in the genre is Balla's "Dynamism of a Dog on a Leash." Futurist paintings involved the spectator by means of "force-lines," angles, curves and swirls "intended to represent the energies and forces of life extended into the composition of the work." [47]

In poetry Marinetti's "wireless imagination" produced "words at liberty" *(parole in libertà),* a "crude, telegraphic report of events and sensations." The Futurist poets did away with syntax, punctuation, and meter. They replaced these old conventions with simple onomatopeia, mathematical and musical notations, and other "non-verbal effects." "Words at liberty" created impressions and sound effects. Finally, this kind of writing evolved into pictorial poetry—today it would be called concrete poetry—such as Apollinaire wrote in *Calligrammes.*[48]

Marinetti came to England in April 1910. In March 1912 he came again, bringing with him Boccioni, Carrà and Russolo. This was the occasion of the first international exhibition of Futurist works. The catalogue of the exhibition presented Marinetti's "First Futurist Manifesto" and other statements. In 1913 the Futurists came again. In September of that year Harold Monro devoted a large part of *Poetry and Drama* to discussing Futurism.

There were also translations of poetry by Marinetti, Buzzi, and Palazzeschi.

> We race
> We rise
> We must sing a new song of our speed
> We must chant a new hymn of ascent.
> Soon we shall make ourselves lungs of the sponge
> of the spaces and wings of the plumes of the clouds.
> O mankind of yesterday
> you may bury a spear in your bosom! [49]

The Futurists loved machinery: automobiles, airplanes, dreadnoughts. They glorified war and held women in contempt. They were going to destroy museums, libraries, academies of every kind, and fight against "moralism, feminism, every opportunistic or utilitarian cowardice."

"Let's go! Mythology and the Mystic Ideal are defeated at last. . . . We must shake the gates of life, test the bolts and hinges." [50]

The public loved it. Futurist exhibitions and performances were crowded.

Pound, Sturge Moore, and Richard Aldington, who tells the story, brought Marinetti to see Yeats in Woburn Place. Marinetti spoke no English, and Yeats would not speak Italian, for "he would not talk a language of which he was not a master." So Pound and his friends acted as interpreters. Yeats read some of his own poems, "which Marinetti would have thought disgustingly *passéistes* if he had understood them." Then Yeats through Sturge Moore asked Marinetti politely to read something. "Whereupon Marinetti sprang up and in a stentorian Milanese voice began bawling:

> *Automobile,*
> *Ivre d'espace*
> *Qui piétine d'angoisse, etc."*

Yeats had to ask him to stop because the neighbors were banging on the floor, the ceiling, and the walls.[51]

English avant-garde artists were in danger of being strangled by the octopus doing its steps in public under the direction of Signor Marinetti. They had played along with the Futurists, agreeing with their revolutionary frame of mind. But they did not agree with Futurist styles of painting—representation of flux and "empathetic" appeal, drawing the spectator into the picture. They thought Marinetti's infatuation with the automobile ridiculous. The English artists were tired of being called Futurists—they had ideas of their own.

In Berlin in the winter of 1912–13, T. E. Hulme heard Wilhelm Worringer lecturing on art. Worringer divided art into two kinds, "empathetic" and "abstract." Empathetic art was "organic . . . permeated by the viewer's 'activity' and 'inner life,' his empathy with the work of art." Abstract art on the other hand was "inorganic" and "life-denying." It repelled the viewer's attempt to merge his feelings with the work of art.[52]

On 22 January Hulme gave a lecture at Kensington Town Hall on "Modern Art and Its Philosophy." Hulme's argument, as he admitted, was "practically an abstract of Worringer's views." And it owed nothing to the prancing Italian. Hulme substituted the word "geometric" for "abstract"; instead of "empathetic" he said "vital." Geometric art was angular and lifeless; it presented the human body in "stiffness and cubical shapes." It reflected a sense of man's separation from nature, and its finest expressions were in Byzantine, Indian and Egyptian art. In contrast, vital art was soft and naturalistic, and the pleasure it gave was empathy. It reflected a pleasant relationship between man and his environment. Vital art had reached its fulfillment in the Renaissance, and Western art had been under its influence ever since.[53]

Hulme's point was an attack on vital art and the Renaissance. It was "the business of every honest man at the present moment to clean the world of these sloppy dregs of the Renaissance." Hurrah for geometry and down with chiaroscuro!

So Hulme abandoned what he had learned from Bergson—*élan vital,* intuition, flux and all that rot. He was now demanding art that would be like the machine, rigid and exact. An art of hard surfaces. Also, he rejected Post-Impressionism. Only a few years ago the Post-Impressionists had had their exhibition that stood the town on end. They too had rejected the Renaissance, in favor of primitive art. But Hulme shifted the "base of attack" from Africa, Polynesia and Egypt to twentieth-century England. The antidote to Giotto was not Gauguin. Hulme wanted nothing of Gauguin maids, banyan trees, and palm-leaf drapery. The legs of the Eiffel Tower were more like it. The concepts of the graceful and beautiful, Hulme said, were to be replaced by the "austere, mechanical, clear cut and bare." He was interested in art that had a structure like that of a machine.[54]

The Cubist Centre was forced to close—Lewis was a poor manager—but the group continued to be active, rallying behind Hulme's ideas. Later on, Lewis would have a falling-out with Hulme, resenting his admiration of the sculptor Jacob Epstein, but for a while they were collaborators. The sculptor Gaudier-Brzeska also was associated with the group. A definite "group-style" was beginning to emerge. "By 1914 much of Lewis' own work had taken on the mechanical qualities Hulme praised; so had Bomberg's, Wadsworth's, Roberts', Gaudier-Brzeska's and several others, including Epstein's. His 'Rock-Drill' (first exhibited in March 1915) perfectly fulfilled Hulme's criteria." [55]

The effects they were aiming at were described by members of the group in similar terms. Gaudier said, "sharpness and rigidity"; Lewis said, "rigid reflections of stone and steel"; and Pound said, "hard light, clear edges." Instead of multiple images and blurred, merging forms such as the Futurists produced, the Vorticists' "machine aesthetic" produced "static, rigidly geometrical, and nearly or completely abstract designs." [56]

They set about making it clear to the public that they were not Futurists. They stated that while Marinetti's message had been necessary, it was also Italian and "southern." England, after all, had led the world in the creation of machinery—Englishmen had invented modern life; therefore they should have more to say on the subject than anyone else.[57]

The Englishman C. R. W. Nevinson had gone over to Marinetti. On 12 June 1914, Nevinson and Marinetti were scheduled to perform at the Doré, together with the Futurist painters Russolo and Piatti, "Inventors and Contractors of Noise-Tuners." This was an opportunity for the English artists to show that they were not Futurists. They sent letters to the newspapers repudiating Marinetti and Futurism. Then they turned up at the performance. Marinetti recited his "Battle of Adrianople" with "machine-gun noises, whinnies and yells, at the top of one of the most powerful sets of lungs in Europe, accompanied by Nevinson on the bass drum." [58] The Lewis contingent, led by Lewis himself, T. E. Hulme, and Gaudier-Brzeska, heckled vigorously. Other Vorticists present were Epstein, Etchells, Wadsworth, and a cousin of Wadsworth "who was very muscular and forcible." [59]

It was Pound who thought of the symbol of the Vortex—depicted in *Blast* as an inverted cone, whirling and drawing everything into itself, yet at rest. The origin seems to be a passage he wrote in "I Gather the Limbs of Osiris." Much of his thought was generated in this series of articles written for Orage and published in 1911–12. Under the heading "Technique" Pound said, "Let us imagine that words are like great hollow cones of steel of different dullness and acuteness." The word-cones were charged with a force like electricity, "or rather, radiating a force from their apexes—some radiating, some sucking in." When three or four words were in exact juxtaposition the energy of one word would be multiplied by the energy of another. "The peculiar energy which fills the cones is the power of tradition, of centuries of race consciousness, of agreement, of association; and the control of it is the 'Technique of Content,' which nothing short of genius understands." [60]

This, it seems, was what Vorticism meant to Pound as a poet. He was not very successful, however, as a member of the group. When the first issue of *Blast,* the Vorticist magazine, came out on 2 July 1914, Pound's contribution was disappointing. The Vorticists went beyond Hulme in invoking the energies of a "primitive, barbaric will that could produce a 'bareness and hardness' satisfying to a primitive 'Art-instinct' and appropriate to a modern world of machine forms." [61] But all that Pound could come up with was insults in verse—the feelings behind them rather soft than otherwise. There was nothing in the poems Pound published in *Blast* that suggested the new forms of machinery. A schoolboy thumbing his nose would have done as well.

> You slut-bellied obstructionist,
> You sworn foe to free speech and good letters.[62]

He was aiming at Juvenalian satire, and in a letter to Joyce he spoke of "ithyphallic satiric verse," [63] but it came out as remarks about "gagged reviewers" and "those who pat the big-bellies for profit."

Wyndham Lewis' writing came closer to bringing over into words the principles that were clearly visible in sculpture or paint.

> Our Vortex is fed up with your dispersals, reasonable
>   chicken men.
> Our Vortex is proud of its polished sides.
> Our Vortex will not hear of anything but its disastrous
>   polished dance.[64]

The most original pages of *Blast,* however, were not verse or prose, but lists of people and things that were blasted and people and things that were blessed.

The "Manifesto" of July 1914, BLASTED: the English climate, French (Gallic) gush and bourgeois fussiness, the English aesthete, English humor, sport, and the "years 1837 to 1900" (Victorianism). It blasted:

SENTIMENTAL HYGIENICS
ROUSSEAUISMS (Wild Nature Cranks)
FRATERNIZING WITH MONKEYS
DIABOLICS—raptures and roses of the
erotic bookshelves

Blasted were the British Academy and the Bishop of London. A. C. Benson the popular novelist. Otto Weininger, who had written a book of popular psychology titled *Sex and Character*. Marie Corelli. And Rabindranath Tagore.

Blasted was Ella Wheeler Wilcox, poet, and Sir Edward Elgar, O. M., who wrote the coronation march for George V.

Blasted were do-gooders such as Norman Angell, author of *The Great Illusion*, and Sidney Webb, the Fabian Socialist.

Blasted was "Rev. Pennyfeather (Bells)," because Reverend Prebenday Sommerset Edward Pennefeather, Vicar of Kensington, was held by Pound to be personally responsible for the ringing of the bells of St. Mary Abbots Church. On the coronation of George V the bells were rung for three and one-half hours. Pound wrote years later: ". . . vigorous anti-clerical phase ensued." [65]

BLESSED were: England for its ships, sailors, ports, industrialization. And English humor, because this was a "great barbarous weapon."

Blessed were: "Cold, magnanimous, delicate, gauche, fanciful, stupid, ENGLISHMEN."

Hairdressers were blessed. So was "French vitality."

Blessed were Suffragettes, Ulsterites, the Pope and the Salvation Army. Boxers and music-hall entertainers. Aviators.

The founder of Lyons Corner Houses, "where the man in the street could have his cup of tea in clean, convenient, modern surroundings," was blessed.

So were Chaliapin, Lydia Yavorska (an actress and producer), Granville Barker, R. B. Cunningham Graham, Frank Harris, and James Joyce. Finally, the Vorticists blessed people who had been good to them: the avant-garde, one or two critics, and Madame

August Strindberg, proprietor of the Cave of the Golden Calf, who had let them eat on tick. Also, Lord Howard de Walden, president of the Contemporary Arts Society that had purchased Lewis' "Laughing Woman" in 1913, and Kate Lechmere, who had financed the Centre, and a solicitor named Rayner, and Leveridge, the printer of *Blast*.

It hurts to tear oneself away from the Vorticists. This seeems to be their fate . . . something else came along, the war, and that was that. For a short time in the spring of 1914, however, Vorticism was "all the rage." [66] At gatherings all over London the subject was sure to come up. The Vorticists, said R. A. Scott-James, "engaged in propagandism with the combined earnestness and lightheartedness of sportsmen." [67]

Vorticism, said another observer, "was the affirmation of the revolt against humanism." [68]

But the war was a revolution against humanity, and the smaller Vortex was swallowed up in the greater.

The Futurists welcomed the onset of war with joyful cries; they rushed to meet it. It was noisier than the Battle of Adrianople. The cannon, the mortars, the machine guns! Marinetti and his troupe of moustache-waxing entertainers were no longer heard from.

The Vorticists also went to war. But this was not what they had had in mind. They did not share the Italian silliness about loud noises and rushing along. In a short time Vorticism had petered out—"Wyndham Lewis and Roberts did not adhere to strict Vorticist principles in their war paintings; and naval camouflage hardly promised to sustain a flourishing art movement." [69]

Gaudier-Brzeska, perhaps the most talented of them all, was killed in a charge at Neuville St. Vaast, on 5 June 1915.

Pound gave Vorticism . . . the Vortex. Poetry has often owed something to painting; in France during these years the poet Apollinaire developed a concept of Simultaneity in lines of verse. One thing would occur alongside another, with no chronological order.

> Three gas lamps lighted
> The boss has T.B.
> When you've finished we'll play backgammon
> A conductor who has a sore throat [70]

French painters pointed out that the poets had learned Simultaneity from them, not the other way round.

But on this occasion it was a poet who taught the painters. Pound's Vortex explained at a glance what the artists were trying to achieve. Pound said, "All experience rushes into the vortex . . . [It] is every kind of whirlwind of force and emotion. Vortex. That is the right word, if I did find it myself." Lewis said that there was "a great silent place" where all the energy was concentrated. "And there at the point of concentration is the Vorticist." [71]

What did Pound get out of Vorticism? He said that it had awakened his sense of form, made him "more conscious of the appearance of the sky where it juts down between houses, of the bright pattern of sunlight which the bath water throws up on the ceiling, of the great 'V's' of light that dart through the chinks over curtain rings." All these, he said, were "new chords, new keys of design." [72] He summed up his new sense of form in the phrase, "planes in relation," and in his book on Gaudier-Brzeska explained what was meant by this.

> The pine-tree in mist upon the far hill looks like a fragment of Japanese armour.
> The beauty of this pine-tree in the mist is not caused by its resemblance to the plates of the armour.
> The armour, if it be beautiful at all, is not beautiful *because* of its resemblance to the pine in the mist.
> In either case the beauty, in so far as it is beauty of form, is the result of "planes in relation."
> The tree and the armour are beautiful because their diverse planes overlie in a certain manner.[73]

William C. Wees concludes his discussion of Pound's part in the Vorticist movement with the remark that "This vivid sense of abstract visual form helped Pound cross over from Imagism to Vorticism, declaring, as he made the crossing, that a poem is Imagist in so far as it 'falls in with the new pictures and the new sculpture.'" [74]

But why did Pound feel that he must cross over from Imagism to Vorticism?

Imagism was emotion caught in a moment of time. This had produced masterpieces such as the small, perfect poems of H. D. But suppose the poet wished to make something larger. Suppose he wanted to write about history. Clearly the Imagist principles, tending as they did to brevity and perfection, would no longer serve.

What was needed was a new concept of the image as a funnel through which history, ideas, everything could come roaring.

Pound saw the Vortex as a "radiant node or cluster . . . from which, and through which, and into which, ideas are constantly rushing." [75]

Vorticism, however, was not Impressionism—Futurism had been merely "accelerated Impressionism." [76] The Vorticist was to be thought of as "directing a certain fluid force against circumstance, as *conceiving* instead of merely reflecting and observing." [77]

The Vortex was a form. Imagism in the hands of Amy Lowell— the "hippopoetess" H. D. called her—had become shapeless and nonvisual. But the Vortex was a "radiant node or cluster." The Vorticist poet could write about everything, and it would be poetry. A stillness.

There were two kinds of images: "subjective" images that rose in the mind, and "objective" images. "Emotion seizing upon some external scene or action carries it intact to the mind; and that vortex purges it of all save the essential or dominant or dramatic qualities, and it emerges like the external original." [78] Pound was preparing to write about the "external original," that is, the world. "The poet's specific job is to observe the situation, come to a well-defined idea of what's right and what's wrong with it and what can be done to rectify the wrong, and then to put the ideas into action." [79]

In 1913 Pound met an American woman, Mary Fenollosa, whose husband Ernest, deceased, had studied Japanese and Chinese literature in Tokyo. She turned over to Pound the translations and notes her husband had made, giving him a free hand to edit and publish the material. There were sixteen notebooks of rough translations of Chinese poetry and Noh dramas, and an essay by Ernest Fenollosa on "The Chinese Written Character as a Medium for Poetry."

This started Pound making his own translations of Chinese and Japanese poetry into English. Fenollosa's essay and notes confirmed Pound in his belief that writing depended on images. From Fenollosa he gathered that the Chinese written character was a picture—the character for "horse" looked like a horse. Chinese writing consisted of visual components that were brought together and that acted upon one another to form the picture of an idea, an "ideogram."

People who know Chinese say that Fenollosa and Pound were

mistaken. Fenollosa was interested in the small number of Chinese characters that depict something or unite depictions, but these amount to only about a tenth part of the written language. Most Chinese characters specify a sound and tell the reader which of its homonymous meanings to select. Fenollosa did not want to believe this—the concept of characters as pictures was too attractive—so he decided that the pictorial clues to most of the characters had been lost.[80]

As he read Fenollosa's notes on the Chinese ideogram, Pound conceived of making ideograms in English. Words in English did not depict things but it might be possible for writing to present images from which, as from a picture, the reader would gather an idea. The advantage would be that the idea rose out of the language, that is, out of nature, history, the consciousness of the race. It would not be imposed.

Pound kept this in mind when he came to write the *Cantos*. The theory seems to have worked in that it enabled him to write. The theories poets have usually serve this purpose, unless theory gets in the way of writing and spoils it entirely. Yeats had his gyres and Pound had a belief in scientific, objective writing.

But he knew that the theory was inadequate. It is the poet who selects the images. Nature does not select them, nor does history, nor the consciousness of the race. It is not possible to write any more than it is to live without being "subjective." The personality of the poet is of the utmost importance. Personality is a fact; personality is part of the "objective" universe. In this sense, then, everything is "objective." Or nothing is. Thought begins to go around in circles when we divide thinking into "subjective" and "objective" parts.

Pound tried to reconcile the idea of the poet as observer and the idea of the poet as Vorticist who puts ideas into action. The contradiction is resolved if we think of the poet as the kind of sculptor who carves with the grain of the material, finding as well as making the form he desires. His art is a collaboration between his will and the material—as Wordsworth said, eye and ear both create and perceive.[81] The poet is a sculptor—not one who models in clay, imposing his own "subjective" idea entirely. "Poet as sculptor" is Donald Davie's view of Pound's art, and it is a good one.[82] In any case, if there is still a contradiction between Pound's idea of the poet as observer and the poet as creator, the perplexity is not his alone; it is endemic to man, who feels that he can act yet knows that his life is circumscribed. Pound's perplexity reflects the human condition—he is after all a poet, not a philosopher.

Though the theories poets have may be illogical, in practice their theories make poems and therefore, curiously, they become true. Wordsworth's claim that poetry is to be found in the language used by men is illogical, for the poet must have an *a priori* idea of what poetry is, if he is to find it. Yet the theory enabled Wordsworth to realize a pastoral world inhabited by characters who are full of wisdom. Similarly, Pound's concept of the ideogram enabled him to write portions of the *Cantos* as a series of observations from which the reader may draw his own conclusions.

Cathay marks another, equally important step in Pound's development. Making his versions of the Chinese showed him a new way to write lines of verse. Instead of repeating a pattern of feet, the Chinese poet repeats a grammatical structure, usually subject, verb, object. In Pound's versions the line is frequently a complete sentence; this is followed by a line that has the same order of syntax. This device, known as parallelism, has been used before in English poetry—the Psalms of David, the poems of Christopher Smart and Walt Whitman depend on it. Pound uses parallelism, however, in a way that may be original: parallel to an abstract statement runs a statement that is concrete, so that the reader "conspires"—Donald Davie's word—to give the abstraction equal weight.

> Flying snow bewilders the barbarian heaven.
> Lice swarm like ants over our accoutrements.
> Mind and spirit drive on the feathery banners.
> Hard fight gets no reward.[83]

We consent to the opinion in the fourth line because the line has the same grammatical construction as the lines coming before that presented indisputable facts.

Repeating a syntactical pattern rather than repeating feet—this is the writing by the "sequence of the musical phrase, not in sequence of a metronome" that Pound had been recommending for some time.[84] Donald Davie explains that in traditional English verse, "the finest art was employed in running over the verse line so as to build up larger units of movements such as the strophe, the Miltonic verse paragraph . . . the sustained dramatic speech." Therefore the line was submerged in larger, more intricate rhythmical units. But when, as in Pound's translations, the line is considered as the unit, there emerges "the possibility of 'breaking' the line, of disrupting it from within, by throwing weight upon smaller units within the line." [85]

In the following line there are four units of rhythm: "Horses, his horses even, are tired. They were strong." [86] The pauses are made for reasons of grammar—they are not made to accommodate feet, a certain number of feet within the line, running on to make a paragraph of verse. The rhythm of the sentence is the rhythm of the line, and verse comes close to speech.

Cathay, like "The Seafarer" and *Homage to Sextus Propertius,* goes beyond translation in its freedom, the freshness of its imagery and language, and the suppleness of the line. These versions of Chinese and Japanese poetry read as though they were original poems by Pound. One poem in particular, "The River Merchant's Wife: A Letter," after a poem by Li Po, has frequently been reprinted in anthology selections of Pound's work. "The River Merchant's Wife" is famous for the persona—Pound has achieved mastery in the form of the dramatic monologue he has practiced from the beginning; he is now able to speak in a voice that seems perfectly detached from himself. The voice does not speak directly to the reader; it seems to be overheard; so we are led to believe in it, and as the voice is trained in the habit of modesty—it speaks not of its own sorrow but of the sorrowful noise the monkeys are making—we are induced to provide the emotion ourselves.[87]

The imagery in *Cathay* is predominantly visual—we are looking at a tapestry with green grass and willows, water, a drifting boat, a blue cloud. Or at a desolate landscape through which a tired army is moving. In one poem at least, imagery goes beyond the visual to reveal the mystery that, for Pound, lurks behind the veil of things. This is, in "Separation on the River Kiang," the image of "The long Kiang, reaching heaven." [88] In an Imagist poem, Pound says, "one is trying to record the precise instant when a thing outward and objective transforms itself, or darts into a thing inward and subjective," [89] and he says that "the natural object is always the adequate symbol." [90] The sail drawing away on the river makes us feel the smallness of man and the immensity of grief.

When *Cathay* was published Britain had been at war with the Central Powers for eight months. Pound sent some of the poems to Gaudier-Brzeska, who was in the trenches. Gaudier-Brzeska read "Lament of the Frontier Guard."

Who has brought the flaming imperial anger?
Who has brought the army with drums and with kettle-drums?
Barbarous kings.
A gracious spring, turned to blood-ravenous autumn . . .[91]

Gaudier-Brzeska could look out on a muddy landscape over which lines of barbed wire were strung, and hear the rolling of artillery. He said in a letter to Pound, "The poems depict our situation in a wonderful way."

Gaudier-Brzeska died in that war. So did T. E. Hulme.

These fought in any case,
and some believing,
            pro domo, in any case.[92]

5

Into the Vortex

Much conversation is as good as having a home.

Homage to Sextus Propertius

BIOGRAPHY has to be an equation—it cannot be a literal translation. The object is to know what a man did, felt and thought. A mere collection of facts won't accomplish this purpose. In fact, there are times when ideas are far more important than facts. When, for example, William Blake says that he has been talking to the Prophet Isaiah, this is clearly more important to Blake than it would have been to meet a member of the Royal Academy in the flesh.

Now Pound had a meeting with Walt Whitman and, as he usually did, adopted the mannerisms of his new friend. It was the missionary voice in Whitman that appealed to Pound and he imitated it in "Commission."

> Go, my songs, to the lonely and the unsatisfied,
> Go also to the nerve-wracked, go to the enslaved-
>   by-convention . . .[1]

In another mood he would recall Gourmont and speak of eroticism as an intellectual principle. He adopted Gourmont's pose of a man who spoke his mind frankly—"a writer's one pleasure."[2] He wrote for people who had the brains to understand and thumbed his nose at the others.

But if he wished to tell an anecdote neither Whitman nor

Gourmont could serve his turn, and he remembered Gautier. Then the words "delicate" and "white" appeared in the poem.

> This lady in the white bath-robe which she calls a peignoir,
> Is, for the time being, the mistress of my friend,
> And the delicate white feet of her little white dog
> Are not more delicate than she is . . .[3]

The mask is that of a man of the world with refined tastes who views life with equanimity. He is a superior person. This is the attitude Pound assumes when he writes the sketches of "contemporary manners" that appear in *Lustra* (1916)—he chooses his words with a precision that borders on distaste, picking up a subject with tongs in order to show it to the reader.

> The little Millwins attend the Russian Ballet.
> The mauve and greenish souls of the little Millwins . . .[4]
>
> . . . .
>
> The small dogs look at the big dogs . . .
> They consider the elderly mind
> And observe its inexplicable correlations.[5]

At times he is so disdainful that he prefers to view life through the medium of literature or translation.

Translation provided the mask that enabled him to write his first long poem. In 1917 he began composing versions of the *Elegies* of Sextus Propertius, a Roman poet of the first century A.D., contemporary with Virgil and Horace. Pound took passages from the second and third books of the *Elegies,* sometimes translating closely and sometimes leaving out lines or adding to Propertius's words. He pieced together, to form new wholes, passages that in the original were separated. His aim was to "bring a dead man to life, to present a living figure." [6] Perhaps the best word for the result is "imitations." To say that Pound's versions are translations raises expectations that must be disappointed, for there is not an exact correspondence of meanings—in places, unfortunately there is downright mistranslation. Pound's errors fixed the attention of critics upon his understanding of Latin so that they failed or were unwilling to see where departures from the original were intended, and they missed the point of the whole. Pound has set about creating a fictional Propertius; his Propertius is more humorous than the original and "he is unpatriotic where Propertius was quite the reverse." [7]

In March 1919 four sections of "Propertius" came out in *Poetry*. This drew upon Pound's head the contempt of W. G. Hale, Professor of Latin at the University of Chicago. In a letter to *Poetry* he said that Pound had made Propertius seem flippant, which he wasn't. Then he pointed out several errors of translation. "Mr. Pound mistakes the verb *canes,* 'thou shalt sing,' for the noun *canes* (in the nominative plural masculine) and translates by 'dogs.' Looking around then for something to tack this to, he fixes upon *nocturnae* (genitive singular feminine) and gives us 'night dogs'!" Hale was positively offended by Pound's rendering of a passage in Propertius that meant "my lady" or "young ladies." Pound had rendered this as "the devirginated young ladies." This, in Hale's opinion, was decadence. He concluded that if Pound were professor of Latin "there would be nothing left for him but suicide." He advised him to "lay aside the mask of erudition . . . if he must deal with Latin, I suggest that he paraphrase some accurate translation, and then employ some respectable student of the language to save him from blunders. . . ." [8]

There have been other people over the years who have found Pound's "mask of erudition" intolerable. They refuse to concede his claim that he is bringing dead men to life, and prefer their authors in a literal translation.

Others, however, who read Pound with sympathy feel that *Homage to Sextus Propertius* is a masterpiece. Pound's Propertius is a wry poet in an age of imperial warmongering. His Muse is "no more than a girl"—that is, he is a poet of love, especially the loose loves and adulteries that were current in Augustan Rome. His poems are made to be read by a girl while she is waiting for her lover. Propertius's own love affair with Cynthia is treated with superb cynicism. One morning he goes to see her unannounced.

> And Cynthia was alone in her bed.
> I was stupefied. [9]

There is a good deal of eroticism in this writing. Cynthia sends a message telling him to come

> *At* once!!
> "Bright tips reach up from twin towers,
> "Anienan spring water falls into flat-spread pools." [10]

Conscious that great deeds are afoot and that other poets are making a reputation by hymning them, Propertius attempts something in the heroic vein:

> Up, up my soul, from your lowly cantilation,
>   put on a timely vigour. . . .[11]

But Apollo calls him an idiot and says, "Who has ordered a book about heroes?" [12] So Propertius renounces Calliope, the Epic Muse, and continues to write "something to read in normal circumstances," [13] consoling himself with the thought that he will be read by "the devirginated young ladies." His poems will travel, and

> I shall have, doubtless, a boom after my funeral,
> Seeing that long standing increases all things
>   regardless of quality.[14]

As with some poems in *Lustra,* "Propertius" is written in "translatorese," a pompous, circumlocutory style borrowed from the Loeb classics. Pound uses English words that sound like Latin—to give the effect of Latin he may even use Latin:

> A Trojan and adulterous person came to Menelaus
>   under the rites of hospitium. . . .[15]

The pomposity is frequently undercut, however, by using plain twentieth-century words:

> And besides, Lynceus,
>   you were drunk.[16]

If translating by ear leads Pound astray at times so that he misunderstands Latin, it also makes for lucky hits. Thus

> O me felicem! O nox mihi candida . . .

is rendered into the happiness of a child or savage:

> Me happy, night, night full of brightness . . .[17]

At times as we read *Propertius* we feel another presence, the ample waistcoated form of Henry James. It is he who conducts the language, discriminating among shades of meaning in order to arrive finally at the exact shade that truth requires.

For example, Propertius has a friend, Lynceus, who has always been glad to do him a service, carrying messages to Cynthia and reporting her demeanor. Now Propertius discovers that Lynceus has seduced her, or more likely has been seduced. This is how Propertius expresses his resentment.

> . . . in one bed, in one bed alone, my dear Lynceus
>   I deprecate your attendance.[18]

The delicacy with which Propertius suggests that the event has been the result of a praiseworthy wish on Lynceus's part to serve him, thereby offering Lynceus a reasonable excuse if he wishes to take it, transforms a sordid matter entirely—it is no longer sordid. The sentence has increased our awareness of how the meaning of a thing may be changed by the manner of saying it. Life is transformed into style, and we are no longer at the mercy of accidents— the infidelity of a mistress, the treachery of a friend.

In this instance, however, the disparity between life and style is a little too large, and there is parody. Pound wishes affectionately to point out what is "phantasmagoric" about James's concept of style as reality. There is in James no plain speaking such as is found in Remy de Gourmont. "The gods had not visited James, and the Muse, whom he so frequently mentions, appeared doubtless in corsage, the narrow waist, the sleeves puffed at the shoulders, a la mode 1890–2." The scenes and characters of James are like paper flowers sealed inside glass paperweights. James is concerned with "mental temperatures." Gourmont on the other hand "is interested in hardly anything save emotions," and these depend on sex. "You could . . . have said to Gourmont anything that came into your head. . . . Gourmont prepared our era." [19]

When T. S. Eliot edited a selection of Pound's poems he excluded *Homage to Sextus Propertius* because, he said, readers who did not know the original could not appreciate Pound's version. This is nonsense and Eliot must have known it—there is no need to read Latin in order to understand Pound's poem in English. It is more likely that Eliot excluded the poem because it might be shocking and offensive. The talk about sex and, more important, the satire of imperialism might have offended important people. Pound was satirizing the warmakers and poets such as Henry Newbolt who urged their countrymen to battle.

> He thrills to Ilian arms,
>   He shakes the Trojan weapons of Aeneas . . . [20]

Eliot preferred to play it safe and not, as Pound's editor, be thought to be agreeing with his views. It has to be said of Eliot that he courted the good opinion of society. This was never true of Pound.

If we think of what was passing for poetry in England at this time, Pound's achievement in *Propertius* is all the more remarkable. These were the years when the Georgian Poets became popular. Recent attempts to resuscitate them have failed to make them out to be more than writers of pretty lyrics and descriptive poems lacking in ideas. Two or three had unusual talent—Walter De La Mare, Siegfried Sassoon, and D. H. Lawrence, who was associated with the Georgians in the beginning. But most were content to prattle about nature in rhyme. One much-quoted Georgian poem was directed to a fat woman the poet had seen from a train; he was sorrowful because she was wearing gloves and so was not in contact with nature. It did not seem to occur to the poet that he himself, sitting in the train, was even more insulated. Or that some people cannot help being fat. Thoughts such as these did not bother the Georgian Poets—they just wrote. It was poetry by amateurs for an audience of amateurs, and it suited the British public down to the ground. The Georgians were the fellows to read, not the lah-di-dah stuff concocted by aesthetes in Bloomsbury. To read a poem by J. C. Squire was to know that here was a man you could have a pint with; you might, in a pinch, send him in to bat.

This was the condition of poetry in England when Pound published *Homage to Sextus Propertius*. As time goes by, the zest with which he wrote becomes more apparent, while nature, as described by the Georgian Poets, seems to have faded.

Pound liked to make an "exhibit," citing a passage that would give the "feel" of a writer's talent. And Pound's life is best viewed in this way; a slide of his activity over a few months as poet, journalist and critic will do as well as a description of everything he did.

In September 1919 Pound and his wife returned to London from a trip to the Continent. They had been to the South of France and the Pyrenees.

He obtained the post of drama critic on *The Outlook*. It was the kind of well-paid job he had always wanted.

The Ovid Press published forty copies of the fourth Canto, and *The Little Review* was publishing Fenollosa's essay, "The Chinese Character as a Medium for Poetry."

Pound received the "Cyclops" episode of Joyce's *Ulysses* and told John Quinn that it was perhaps the best thing Joyce had done; the parody of styles was as good as Rabelais. "Our James is a grrreat man." [21]

In a series of articles, "The Regional," being published in *The New Age*, he discussed the problems of the artist in the modern world, with examples from history, contemporary England, and his own experiences in Provence. He attacked provincialism and expounded Major C. H. Douglas's ideas about overproduction.

For Pound had discovered Douglas's theory of Social Credit, which he was to expound all his life and explain in the *Cantos,* boring some readers to tears while others say that without the financial theory the *Cantos* would be mere dilettantism.

Major Douglas's Social Credit theory was based on three criteria: Real Wealth, the power to produce goods; Real Credit, the trust in that power of production; Financial Credit, the estimate of that power in the form of money. While Real Credit is determined by the trust of the whole community in their economy, Financial Credit is determined by a few bankers. The bankers, by charging interest on loans, take back more than they give, and thus disrupt the balance between Real and Financial Credit. Without regard for production the bankers flood the economy with loans to collect interest; when the economy is saturated the bankers provoke wars to create new debts. The endless succession of wars is a result of this cycle. The solution: take Financial Credit out of the hands of the bankers and put it in the hands of the government.[22]

This was the creed Pound now adopted. He wrote articles about Social Credit and urged it in letters to friends, acquaintances and strangers. Monetary reform was the secret he had been waiting for all his life; the son of the assayer Homer Pound had always been fascinated with money and suspected there was a conspiracy. One of his earliest published poems, "Cino," hints at a secret known to the rich which he, Cino, could reveal if he had a mind to. And where would the rich be then?

> And all I knew were out, My Lord, you
> Were Lack-land Cino, e'en as I am,
> O Sinistro.[23]

In October the Egoist Press published Pound's *Quia Pauper Amavi,* a collection of poems including *Homage to Sextus Propertius* and Cantos I, II, and III. These versions of the *Cantos* he later revised considerably. By December he had written Cantos V, VI and VII and drafts of Cantos XIV and XV.

Early in 1920 *Quia Pauper Amavi* was reviewed favorably by Eliot in *The Athenaeum* and by Ford in *Piccadilly,* but savaged by Robert Nichols in *The Observer.* Nichols accused Pound of obscurity, of writing "poor prose cut into lengths," and vulgarity.[24]

He said, "Mr. Pound is not, never has been, and, almost I might hazard, never will be a poet. He is too hard, too clever . . ." Robert Nichols was one of the Georgian Poets whom Pound had ridiculed for their ignorance.

At the end of May 1920 Pound and his wife went to Italy. They traveled to Venice, then to Sirmione for Dorothy's health. She had been ill and the doctors thought the air in Sirmione would do her good. While they were still in Sirmione, Pound's *Hugh Selwyn Mauberley* was published in London at the Ovid Press in an edition of two hundred copies. In the same month, June, Pound's friend Elkin Mathews published *Umbra,* a collection of Pound's early poems including translations from Cavalcanti and Daniel, and also including original poems by T. E. Hulme.

Some people think that *Hugh Selwyn Mauberley* is Pound's best poem. In the opinion of F. R. Leavis, Pound's standing as a poet rests on *Mauberley,* for his early poems are interesting only as examples of the development of technique, and the *Cantos* appear to be "little more than a game," Pound's allusions having no value to anyone else.[25] Other critics have agreed that *Mauberley* is a masterpiece and have gone to some trouble to explain it. But the explanations are too ingenious to be convincing. The parts of *Mauberley* are brilliant, but out of focus when we look at the work as a whole.

It has been said that when he wrote *Mauberley* Pound wished to separate himself from the aesthete he had been, the poet who dreamed of beauty and who would have been happy living in the nineties. Pound was now preparing to embark on a career as epic poet. He was about to describe the Inferno ruled by Usury. In order to launch forth he must first exorcise "Mauberley," the aesthete in himself. This was his intention and some critics say that he succeeded. Hugh Kenner says, "That poem ended his 'aesthetic' period; the 'sensitive' man who did not know what was going on he peeled off like a shed skin and called Hugh Selwyn Mauberley."[26] This may have been Pound's intention, but whether he succeeded is another matter.

Hugh Selwyn Mauberley is in two parts. The first begins with an epitaph, "E. P. Ode . . . ," in which Pound describes his own career as it might have been described by someone who was not sympathetic. "E. P." was "out of key with his time." Then Pound's own voice takes over, commenting on London and the age, the cheapening of values by commerce. The second part deals with an aesthete named Mauberley. He is, it seems, an engraver, a maker of small, static images. But it seems he is a writer too, for we are told that he has been excluded "from the world of letters." Mauberley has no artistic drive and no sexual drive either. He lives for the moment, reminiscing, unable to see any larger social meaning—"Mildness, amid the neo-Nietzschean chatter." Finally he travels to the Pacific and dies in a hedonist's paradise, listening to "the phantasmal sea-surge."

This is how *Hugh Selwyn Mauberley* reads, and how most people come back to reading it after they have read the critics. The trouble begins when we try to get beneath the surface or to make sense out of it as a whole—that is, as a continuous work with a consistent point of view. In the first place, who is "E. P."? Common sense tells us that it must be Ezra Pound, but common sense isn't enough in this instance; in fact, the readings given by some critics depend on E. P.'s not being Pound. And Pound himself made a remark that supports this. Speaking of the commentators on *Hugh Selwyn Mauberley* he said, "The worst muddle they make is failing to see that Mauberley buries E. P. in the first poem; gets rid of all his troublesome energies." [27] From which we must conclude that Pound was either as muddled as his commentators or trying to make the confusion worse, for there is nothing to support this view. Mauberley and E. P. do not even meet. If Pound thought he was using Jamesian narrative techniques when he wrote *Mauberley*—from remarks he made it seems that he had some such idea—it is fortunate that he did not go in for novel-writing.

In the second part, titled "Mauberley," there are lines applying to Mauberley which could be applied to E. P.

> His true Penelope
> Was Flaubert . . .[28]

For three years Mauberley is "diabolus in the scale," and we have been told that E. P. struggled for three years. They have both been excluded from "the world of letters." So we must think that Mauberley and E. P. are the same person. But Mauberley is an engraver, a maker of medallions, while there is no reason to think that E. P. was anything but a writer. E. P. "strove . . . to maintain 'the sublime,' " while Mauberley is timid and ineffectual, "lacking the skill/To forge Achaia." So Mauberley and E. P. are not the same person, after all.

If we try to find a consistent point of view *Hugh Selwyn Mauberley* doesn't make sense. And whatever Pound's intentions may have been, Parts One and Two do not hang together. There are two distinct sequences: the first about life in London before the war, with some reminiscences of the nineties; the second about a character named Mauberley who resembles Pound in that they are both aesthetes. But there is no other resemblance. As Espey suggests, they could have frequented the same artistic circles, but it is unlikely that they would have had much to say to each other.[29] Pound is quite superior to the mild, ineffectual Mauberley.

"Exactly," says the critic, "Mauberley is Pound's lesser self. He buried his aestheticism with Mauberley." But there is no similarity between the kind of aestheticism practiced by Pound, with a ring in its ear, and the shy behavior of the medallionist. Pound may have set out to portray himself as Mauberley. But something happened—he got carried away—he created a fictional character, as he had with Propertius. Mauberley turned out to be quite different from himself. So writing about Mauberley hadn't changed anything.

Pound was already writing the *Cantos,* putting ideas into action and aiming to build a new civilization. No doubt in writing *Mauberley* he intended to say goodbye to London and his own "aesthetic period." But taking up a cause or writing a poem will not rid a man of his affections. Pound's instinct for self-preservation as an artist was stronger than his will to change. The lover of Beauty "in the old sense" would remain, though to be sure at times it is hard to find him under the torrent of propaganda. Pound is still an aesthete in the *Cantos,* and *The Pisan Cantos* are the work of a man who, after all, puts the love of beauty before Social Credit.

Some critics, however, do not admit this. William Cookson, who believes that Pound's aestheticism was buried in *Mauberley,* also believes that what counts in Pound's poetry is his ideas about history and money—"even," says Cookson, "if they were proved to be mistaken." [30]

To think that ideas about aesthetics are less important than ideas about money is to adopt the philistine view. Pound himself once expressed this view, just as at the end of his life he said that the *Cantos* were a botch, but we need not accept the opinions of an author about his own work when they are contradicted by the work itself. Pound was interested in monetary reform as a means to an end, which was the creation of beauty.

Hugh Selwyn Mauberley, then, is a sequence of loosely related poems followed by a series of poems dealing with a character

named Mauberley. Espey has shown how much Pound drew on
when he was composing these poems, what he learned from Gautier and Flaubert, what from Henry James. Donald Davie has
given as a likely source the *Imaginary Letters* Pound wrote for
The Little Review in 1918. The supposed author of the letters is
an aesthete named Walter Villerant. He is devoted to art, he is
evidently an American expatriate, he quotes Gourmont's "Con-
sérvatrice des Traditions Milésiennes," a line that turns up in
Mauberley.[31]

There are other possible sources. For example, it is possible that
when he created Mauberley Pound drew on the life of the poet
Rupert Brooke. Pound had already written a poem about Brooke,
alluding to an experience he had in Tahiti. The poem, "Our
Contemporaries," came out in BLAST in July 1915, after Brooke's
death while on active service in the Dardanelles. Brooke was a war
hero and Pound was criticized for showing bad taste. There wasn't
in fact much to complain about—"Our Contemporaries" goes as
follows:

> When the Taihaitian princess
> Heard that he had decided,
> She rushed out into the sunlight and
> Swarmed up a cocoanut palm tree.
>
> But he returned to this island
> And wrote ninety Petrarchan sonnets.[32]

In *Personae* the poem has a footnote in French which, being translated, reads as follows. "This is about a young poet who followed
the Gauguin cult to Tahiti itself (and who is still with us). As he
was very handsome, when the tawny princess heard that he was
willing to grant her his favors she showed her happiness in the
manner we have described. Unfortunately his poems are concerned only with his own subjective feelings, in the Victorian style
of the 'Georgian Anthology.' "

The poem offended Brooke's idolators. Pound, writing to Harriet Monroe, said that he had made an error in publishing it but
had meant no harm. He had nothing against Brooke, who "got
perhaps a certain vivid poetry in life and then went off to associate
with literary hen-coops like Lascelles Abercrombie in his writings
. . . If he went to Tahiti for his emotional excitements instead of
contracting diseases in Soho, for God's sake let him have the credit
for it." [33]

He also said, "Other young men have gone, and will go to

Tahiti." [34] "Going to Tahiti" meant hedonism, drifting off in subjective moods. It is true that Brooke died not in Tahiti but the Dardanelles, but this seemed just as far away from London. Brooke's patriotic fervor may have struck Pound as merely subjective, an attempt to escape reality. Everyone remembers Brooke's poem:

> If I should die, think only this of me:
> That there's some corner of a foreign field
> That is forever England.[35]

But Mauberley's epitaph could also be applied to Brooke:

> Here drifted
> An hedonist.[36]

There are differences between Brooke and Mauberley, of course, but they had one important thing in common—they were both "concerned only with their own subjective feelings." This was, in fact, the most important thing about them. So Pound, with Brooke in mind, wrote out the fate of a purely subjective man and called it Mauberley. At the same time he was able to say what he really thought about Rupert Brooke without again drawing upon himself the wrath of the public.

Most of *Hugh Selwyn Mauberley* is written in quatrains. In reaction against the shapeless free verse of the "Amygists" Pound and Eliot decided to write rhymed quatrains in the manner of Gautier. Eliot wrote "The Hippopotamus," "Whispers of Immortality" and other poems, and Pound wrote the *Mauberley* poems. They are concentrated, so much so that readers cannot make out all the meanings. It is not always clear, for example, whether Pound means what he says or is being ironic. It is not possible to know, in the "Envoi," to whom these words refer: "Hadst thou but song/ As thou hast subjects known. . . ." Is the poet speaking to his book, or is the book speaking to the woman who "sang me once that song of Lawes"? [37] Pound's readers become so accustomed to being puzzled that they find meanings where none are meant. One critic reads the line, "Dowson found harlots cheaper than hotels" to mean "Dowson thinks extensive whoring will cost him less than a bourgeois existence in hotels." [38] The plain sense, of course, is that Dowson found it less costly to stay with a whore for the night than to pay for a hotel room.

There is however, a noticeable difference in style between the

astringent quatrains of Part One and the quatrains dealing with
Mauberley's fate in Part Two.

> Drifted . . . drifted precipitate,
> Asking time to be rid of . . .
> Of his bewilderment [39]

In Part One, Pound deplores the commercialization of art and
he sneers at democracy:

> All men, in law, are equals.
> Free of Pisistratus,
> We choose a knave or an eunuch
> To rule over us.[40]

He feels superior to his subject and removed from it; "objective,"
witty quatrains are a suitable form for this commentary. There
follow two impassioned condemnations of war, written in free
verse. We see that Pound has hit on usury—thanks to his meeting
with Major Douglas—as the theme he will use from now on. The
quatrains resume, casting backward in time to the Pre-Raphaelite
period and the nineties, presumably to explain how the present
age came into being. There are four portraits of contemporaries:
Arnold Bennett, Ford Madox Ford, and two women with preten-
sions to culture. There is an "Envoi (1919)" with the conclusion,

> . . . change hath broken down
> All things save Beauty alone.[41]

This conclusion does not support the theory that when Pound
wrote *Mauberley* he was ridding himself of aestheticism.

In Part Two the commentary changes into something quite different. Imagination comes into the poem; Pound begins imagining
what it is like to be Mauberley; the language takes on the hesita-
tion, the sliding, the very sound of Mauberley's existence.

> Lifting the faint susurrus
> Of his subjective hosannah.[42]

He shares Mauberley's "subjectivism." This is better than commentary, it is creation.

6

His True Penelope

The beauty is not the madness.
Canto CXVI

P OUND left England in December 1920. The most pressing
reason was money—he was being shut out of the market. Orage,
writing about Pound in *The New Age,* said, "Much of the Press
has deliberately closed by cabal to him; his books have for some
time been ignored or written down, and he himself has been compelled to live on much less than would support a navvy." [1] Eliot
said the same: "The fact is that there is now no organ of any
importance in which he can express himself, and he is becoming
forgotten. It is not enough for him simply to publish a volume
of verse once a year—or no matter how often—for it will simply
not be reviewed and will be killed by silence." [2]

Pound believed there was a conspiracy—the word had gone
round to shut him out because he was threatening the usurious
capitalist system on which publishers depended. He relates the
crucial incident in *How to Read.* He thought of making a twelve-
volume anthology "in which each poem was chosen not merely
because it was a nice poem or a poem Aunt Hepsy liked, but because it contained an invention, a definite contribution to the
art of verbal expression." He took the outline to an agent with
an explanatory letter, and the agent took them to a publishing
house, without first reading the letter. Two days later Pound
received a message from the agent asking him to come and see
him at once. Pound found the agent "awed, as if one had killed
a cat in the sacristy. Did I know what I had said in my letter? I

did. Yes, but about Palgrave? I did. I had said: 'It is time we had
something to replace that doddard Palgrave.' 'But don't you know,'
came the awestruck tones, 'that the whole fortune of X . . . &
Co. is founded on Palgrave's Golden Treasury?' " Since that day,
Pound tells us, no book of his has received a British imprimatur
until the appearance of Eliot's "castrated edition" of his poems.[3]

There is another point he might have mentioned. Francis
Turner Palgrave's grandfather was Meyer Cohen, a Jewish stock-
broker. This may very well have contributed to Pound's belief in
a conspiracy of financiers, publishers and rich Jews who aimed
at maintaining the status quo.

But there is no need to discover a conspiracy in order to explain Pound's lack of success. How many people want to read
translations of Cavalcanti? Or explanations of Chinese poetry?
And some editors may have had personal reasons. Pound was too
brash—his stuff was unsalable, yet he put on such airs!

For the next twenty years, at the height of his powers as a
creative artist, Pound would be out of the public eye. He had
asked for it with his contempt for popularity—"No art ever yet
grew by looking into the eyes of the public." [4] London, he said,
was full of pimps and vermin who had smothered discussion of
KNOWN FACTS about literature and done their best to prevent the distribution of C. H. Douglas's ideas. They were responsible for competitive armament and treason.[5] Nevertheless,
Pound's isolation when it came was chilling. It accounts for some
dull stretches in the *Cantos*—he was talking to himself. To some
extent it accounts for his polemics—he had to create the audience
that was denied him, to change the world so that people would
read his poetry. And it made him ignorant of what was happening in the world, so that he backed Mussolini.

The Pounds moved to Paris and settled in a ground-floor apartment on rue Notre Dame des Champs, in Montparnasse. They
had brought over their books, paintings and sculpture, and Pound,
who had a knack with carpentry, made the furniture.

He was working on an opera, *Le Testament,* about the life of
Villon. He met fellow writers and artists—Cocteau and Picabia
struck him as exceptionally intelligent. He read the parts of
Joyce's *Ulysses* and forwarded them to *The Little Review* in New
York, until the Society for the Prevention of Vice prosecuted the
editors and they were enjoined to stop publishing Joyce's work.
Thereupon the publisher who was going to publish it as a book

pulled out. But Sylvia Beach, who ran the Shakespeare and Company bookshop in Paris, undertook to publish it.

There were visitors from America—Alfred Kreymborg, editor of *Broom*, and a young poet, E. E. Cummings, who had published some remarkable poems in *The Dial*.

He did a job of editing Eliot, helping him put his new long poem in shape. In the summer of 1921 Eliot became ill with, he said, "an emotional derangement which has been a lifelong affliction. Nothing wrong with my mind." [6] He went to Margate to convalesce, and from there to Lausanne. On his way back to London he came to see Pound, bringing with him the manuscript of a poem he had written while convalescing. Pound suggested changes. He struck out the first fifty-four lines, a description of some "gents" having a night on the town, so that the poem began with the line, "April is the cruellest month, breeding . . ." He made other suggestions, some of which Eliot accepted. When Eliot went back to London he continued to correspond with Pound about revisions of *The Waste Land*. It was finished at the end of the year. Pound told Eliot that he had written "the longest poem in the English langwidge." "Complimenti, you bitch. I am wracked by the seven jealousies, and cogitating an excuse for always exuding my deformative secretions in my own stuff, and never getting an outline." [7]

The stuff of which he spoke was the *Cantos*.

He had been planning the *Cantos* since 1904, he told the interviewer. He was an old man when he said this, and memory faltered, but it was true that he had always had some large work in mind. When he wandered on the roads of Provence he was gathering the sound:

> Sound slender, quasi tinnula,
> Ligur' aoide: Si no'us vei, Domna don plus mi cal,
> Negus vezer mon bel pensar no val.[8]

From Burgos he gathered an image:

> My Cid rode up to Burgos,
> Up to the studded gate between two towers . . .[9]

And from Venice:

> I sat on the Dogana's steps,
> For the gondolas cost too much, that year,
> And there were not "those girls", there was one face . . .[10]

He had knowledge to begin with that no one else had, "six centuries that hadn't been packaged. It was a question of dealing with material that wasn't in the *Divina Commedia*. Hugo did a *Légende des Siècles* that wasn't an evaluative affair but just bits of history strung together. The problem was to build up a circle of reference—taking the modern mind to be the medieval mind with wash after wash of classical culture poured over it since the renaissance. That was the psyche, if you like. One has to deal with one's own subject." [11]

So it was to be history evaluated. As for method, "I don't know about method. The *what* is so much more important than how." [12] This, from the poet who had always insisted on technique! It is plain that poets aren't philosophers—they contradict themselves all over the place. The remark, it seems, was defensive—people were always talking about his technique while his ideas were not taken seriously.

Method was essential. He had hit on the method of getting to know a period by seeing it through the eyes of one of the leading statesmen, a Bismarck or Gladstone. "Having become really conversant with the activities of either of these men, would not almost any document of the period fall, if we read it, into some sort of orderly arrangement? Would we not grasp its relation to the main stream of events?" [13]

Besides history there was myth. He saw himself as an Odysseus voyaging toward his homeland. Or like Ovid he observed the metamorphoses, the changing of one thing into another, at which moment the god, or permanent idea, becomes visible.

He wrote about his life, things he had seen or heard. This was to run through the epic, one of the threads that bound it. But it wasn't to be subjective, not "the growth of a poet's mind." It was the mind looking out on the world, across the sea-wet rail. It might look into Circe's ingle or a place where men were manufacturing arms and planning to foment a war—in either case it would be more interesting than the poet's mind. The poem was a voyage of exploration, *periplum,* and the mind wasn't the subject—the subject was the world.

Therefore the *Cantos* would deal with facts. It was the ideogramic method—"presenting one fact and then another until at some point one gets off the dead and desensitized surface of the reader's mind, onto a part that will register." [14]

The Romantics expressed their emotions, and Symbolist poets dreamed. An age of science demanded the poet of facts.

In 1924 Pound moved to Italy. He said, "France has no writer of first magnitude." [15] This was an exit line rather than an explanation.

We have it from William Carlos Williams that Dorothy Pound didn't like Paris. When he was there the Pounds happened to be there too, on a return visit. His first glimpse of Dorothy was significant: "The erectness of the British walk, the shoes, but especially the design of the hat she had on, could never have originated in the French capital." She conceded nothing of her Englishness to the French. She disliked them intensely, she told him, and also the Paris winter, "neither fish nor flesh." [16]

Maybe Pound felt that he could not shine in Paris. Gertrude Stein's remark about him is famous: she said he was a village explainer—excellent if you were a village—if not, not.

Perhaps he felt that he needed more space for his domestic arrangements. He was having an affair with the violinist Olga Rudge—more like a second marriage. In July 1924 Pound was in Italy with Olga Rudge, at Bressanone. There she gave birth to a female child. They named her Maria. In Paris two months later, Dorothy Pound gave birth to a male child. They named him Omar.[17]

Pound and Olga Rudge gave Maria to be raised by foster parents at Gais in the Tyrol. Omar Pound was raised by his grandmother, Olivia Shakespear, in England.

Pound, his wife, and Olga Rudge lived in Rapallo, on the Mediterranean seventeen miles south of Genoa. The Pounds lived in one house, Olga Rudge in another. Fortunately, how they all got along is not germane to the understanding of Pound's art. He does not write about his wife or his mistress. If this had been William Carlos Williams the case would have been different, but Pound was a man of ideas first, life later.

Pound seems to have handled his separate households *en grand seigneur*—in the spirit of Remy de Gourmont's *The Natural Philosophy of Love,* which he undertook to translate. "Nothing," says Gourmont, "so favours marriage, and consequently, social stability, as the *de facto* indulgence in temporary polygamy. The Romans well understood this, and legalized concubinage. One cannot here deal with a question so remote from natural questions. To condense an answer into the briefest possible space, one would say that man, and principally civilized man, is vowed to the couple, but only endures it on condition that he may leave and return to it at will. This solution seems to conciliate his contradictory tastes, and is more elegant than the one offered by divorce, which is always the same thing over again; it is in conformity not only with human, but also with animal tendencies. It is favourable to the species, in assuring the suitable upbringing of children, and also the complete satisfaction of a need which in a state of civilization, is inseparable either from aesthetic or sentimental pleasure." [18]

Maria—who when she grew up and married was Mary de Rachewiltz—wrote a book about her early years. It is worth reading for the glimpses it provides of Pound as a family man. From time to time her father, whom she called "Babbo," and her mother, whom she called "Mamile," would come to see her. Sometimes they took her away with them for a few days.

Babbo took her to see *Snow White,* and they sat through it twice. Once, after an Astaire-Rogers movie, on the way home Babbo tapped and leapt. He encouraged her to do likewise "and 'get nimble.' " This was in Venice. When they got back to the flat on the Canal Grande where they were staying, there was a noise from Babbo's room. He had thrown off his coat and jacket— "he leapt and tap-danced more freely." Mamile had quite a bit of difficulty persuading him to stop, so as not to disturb the other guests. "Babbo was mortified and sorry; it was hard for him to keep still before having fully danced out the rhythm he had absorbed." [19]

At school she was desolated when Babbo wrote her a scolding letter for having ordered an expensive Latin-German missal and charged it to him. He gave her rules of conduct: she was to understand clearly and to make herself understood. "Education is worth nothing unless one has these two habits." [20]

When she was older she read Babbo's writings and translated some *Cantos* into Italian. "They don't say that," she told him (*"Non si dice"*), and "Time they did," he said.[21]

During the war she admired Babbo's loyalty to the Fascist cause: "Idealism and heroism were by no means all on the side of the partisans. Babbo was infected by a desperate fighting spirit and faith." [22] She could not understand what he had done to make people angry. Babbo was listening to a distant drum and trying to save the world. ". . . as for the purity of the race—what's wrong in wanting to preserve that, as long as the issue isn't disturbed and blown up artificially?" [23]

Pound's parents came to Rapallo and decided to stay. The Yeatses came and stayed. Other old friends turned up—Aldington and Fordie.

Pound was busy writing *Cantos* and articles and keeping up with his correspondence. For example: the Alumni Secretary of the University of Pennsylvania had written requesting a contribution for the graduate school of arts.

A hell of a lot the University had done for this alumnus when he came back from Crawfordsville licking his wounds! It had been his first job—at Wabash College as an instructor. One day a delegation of students, "about-to-flunks," called on the president of the college to complain about Pound's swearing and smoking. It was said that he was the "Latin Quarter" type. Then one night he was discovered having supper in his apartment with a girl from a traveling show. She was stranded and hungry, and it hadn't been convenient to carry her dinner across the hall, but try explaining that to the provincial Presbyterian mentality! [24]

So he had been fired. He had hoped that the University of Pennsylvania, seeing that they had given him a degree, would be willing to give him a job. But they weren't having any. If they had given him work he would probably still be in Philadelphia. Instead, he had gone into exile.

This letter required an answer:

"All the U. of P. or your god damn college or any other god damn American college does or will do for a man of letters is to ask him to go away without breaking the silence." [25]

Louis Zukofsky wanted to come to Europe. Pound weighed the pros and cons, and wrote Williams. "Dear Willyum the Wumpus: How badly does Zuk want to git to Yourope? And how badly OUGHT he?"

"I have allus held," he assured Williams—Bill was known to be touchy on this subject—"that sometime somehow *god damn* etc. something ought to git started ON THE BLOODY SPOT (especially as ole Europe ain't what she wuz).

"However, if it merely means killing off yet another generation . . ."

By which he meant, wouldn't it be an act of mercy to save Zukofsky from the usual fate of the artist in America?

Did Zukofsky have any resources (fiscal)? Would it weaken his fiber to be helped? Was it right to add yet another to an unpaid profession "in which even the old stagers are havin hell's own helluva to pay for their beer and sandwiches?" And once he came over, could he stand repatriation? [26]

Zukofsky did make the journey. Pound paid for his ticket and Zukofsky arrived in Rapallo. This coincided with a visit of the English poet, Basil Bunting. Bunting had what is called the artistic temperament—his meals had to be served.[27]

It was like Pound to pay for Zukofsky and put up with Bunting. Improvident for himself, he was mindful of the needs of others—if they had talent. Rapallo was like a Renaissance village, with Pound as patron of the arts, within his slender means. Writing in *This Quarter,* Hemingway said: "So far, we have Pound the major poet devoting, say, one-fifth of his time to poetry. With the rest of his time he tries to advance the fortunes, both material and artistic, of his friends. He defends them when they are attacked, he gets them into magazines and out of jail. He loans them money. He sells their pictures. He arranges concerts for them. . . . He advances them hospital expenses and dissuades them from suicide. And in the end a few refrain from knifing him at the first opportunity." [28]

The Pounds lived in a flat on the fifth floor of the Albergo Rapallo. From the terrace, while Pound worked, he looked south over the sea. On the twenty-third of March the swallows would fly directly over on their way to two streams in the vicinity. There they rested before flying north again.[29]

There were days when he longed for a visitor and the sound of English. What was the Possum doing? And Bill Williams back in Jersey?

To be interested in many things is as good as having a home. He was studying Frobenius. The German anthropologist had given him the word *paideuma.* It meant the whole energy of a race, from their ideas down to the things they knew in their bones. Patterns of energy.[30] It was the Vortex—it validated the *Cantos!* Frobenius had discovered evidence of a civilization extending from Africa into Europe. Some of the evidence was in folktales, confirming Pound's own use of Ovid.

There are two kinds of Ovidian metamorphosis in the *Cantos*. One kind involves transmission of knowledge—an idea, image, archetypical figure or "god" passing through various languages and situations. The other kind is more basic, a change of form— man into hawk, woman into swallow.

> and the wind out of Rhodez
> Caught in the full of her sleeve.
> . . . the swallows crying.[31]

"To a primitive mind the guarantee of the supernatural nature of a subject is its capacity to alter form dramatically." [32]

Gods—"A god is an eternal state of mind" [33]—aren't set apart from the world, they are in it, whether it be nature or a work of art. "The natural object is always the adequate symbol." [34] At the moment of metamorphosis the god-idea is revealed. Some god-ideas reveal themselves repeatedly. The love goddess reveals herself as Helen of Troy, Eleanor of Aquitaine, and other beautiful women. She is signaled by her eyes:

> eyes of Picasso
> Under black fur-hood [35]

Ordinary human females may embody the goddess, especially when they are making love. The goddess is frequently destructive, "destroyer of men and cities." [36] She causes confusion, "basis of renewals." [37] Counterpointing the theme of fatal beauty is the theme of fidelity, in Cunizza, Marguerite of Chateau Rousillon, and other women.

The myths and fables in the *Cantos* point to archetypical human situations. "It is a basic principle of *The Cantos* that all related characters can merge or meet, into one another." [38] Myths reveal what is constant about human behavior, especially the kind that raises a moral problem.

A man has to see through things and find what makes them tick. Pound peered through the fog of history and saw usury. "Money and sex and tomorrow" [39] were the interests men had in common. He had been thinking about money for years before he came in contact with the good Major and Social Credit. He had always known there was a conspiracy to keep money out of the hands of people like himself. In his first book he said that he could expose the conspiracy if he had a mind to and bring down the rulers:

> But you "My Lord," God's pity!
> And all I knew were out, My Lord, you
> Were Lack-land Cino, e'en as I am,
> O Sinistro.[40]

Usury was the prime cause of human misery—"Here is the core of evil." [41] Not until he came to the end of his life would he see that usury was not a cause but a symptom.

> re USURY
> I was out of focus, taking a symptom for a cause.
> The cause is AVARICE.

> Venice, 4th July, 1972 [42]

The opposite of usury would be government based on a banking system that kept money in circulation—didn't let a few people pile it up and then lend money at exorbitant rates of interest. For instance, there was the Monte dei Paschi in Siena. Founded in 1624 by Ferdinand II of Tuscany, this bank had credit backed by the Sienese public lands, and it was still going strong. There had been similar instances in China. History went through cycles, the same principles took effect everywhere, civilizations rising or falling.

"You allude too much," Basil Bunting told him, "and present too little." [43]

> Hast 'ou seen the rose in the steel dust
>   (or swansdown ever?) [44]

Kenner comments: "One quoted phrase annexes Jonson's stanza to bring this lady, barely seen, into being at the end of the first Pisan Canto." [45]

In fact the quoted phrase annexes nothing. Even if the reader does happen to know the passage Pound has in mind, the allusion doesn't work as poetry—Jonson's poem is remote and in no measure recreated by Pound's referring to it. If the reader doesn't know the passage he has to look it up, by which time he is far from poetry. There are stretches in the *Cantos* that consist of little more than references. They must have been easy to string together—they are impossible to read with pleasure and therefore they teach us nothing. The so-called Chinese cantos are especially arid for this reason. Pound got them out of a book. Anywhere we open them there is this kind of dead reference:

> Came Ming slowly, a thousand, an hundred thousand
> the pirate Kouetchin came to him
>   At court, eunuchs and grafters [46]

Moreover, Pound's facts are incomplete and sometimes they are unreliable. Dekker points out that Pound's version of Sigismondo Malatesta's life omits whatever Pound considers irrelevant, and that his portrait of Sir Basil Zaharoff is a caricature. A poet must select, of course, but then what becomes of the claim that he is writing history?

The frequency of Pound's allusions, the dead stretches, the unreliability of his "facts," are a serious obstacle. Pound's admirers, however, do not admit this. In their eyes everything that he did was good. Faced with adverse criticism, their method is to assert the exact contrary. Thus Cookson asserts, "The main elements in Pound's poetry and prose are neither obscure nor literary." [47] Kenner says, "The words that can be looked up in a dictionary and the fields of reference that can be checked in the encyclopaedia are not the content of the poem." [48] With no apparent humor Emery says, "The reader who can bring order out of the apparent confusion of the Pisan cantos will find no significant difficulties in the *Rock-Drill* if he has available copies of Couvreur's *Chou King*, Philistratus's *Life of Apollonius,* and T. H. Benton's *Thirty Years' View.*" [49]

Readers may think that, to have attracted such admirers, Pound must be a poet to avoid. This would not make the admirers unhappy. They want Pound all to themselves; inhabiting the *Cantos* they have a sense of participation and intimacy with the author that they do not wish disturbed. "In this sense," Dekker says, "Pound's work is not a poem, it is a conspiracy."

Once Eliot asked in print, "What does Mr. Pound believe?" Pound replied, "I believe the *Ta Hio.*" [50] This was the *Great Learning* of Confucius which he translated. Confucian ideas are at the center of the *Cantos* and spelled out in Canto XIII.

> If a man have not order within him
> He can not spread order about him . . .
>   . . . . .
> And if the prince have not order within him
> He can not put order in his dominions.[51]

Confucius put family relationships first—if a man committed

murder his father should hide him. Confucians were opposed to the mysticism of the Buddhists and other religious sects. Their Paradise was of this world. "The men of old wanting to clarify and diffuse throughout the empire that light which came from looking straight into the heart and then acting, first set up good government in their own states." [52]

Under a good government everyone would have a sense of living and working creatively. The work might be only a small thing such as making a fishing lure, but it would have "the light of the doer, as it were/ a form cleaving to it." [53] In the earthly paradise artists would be free to do as they liked. This was how Sigismondo Malatesta had contracted with the artisans who built the Tempio at Rimini.

> And for this I mean to make due provision
> So that he can work as he likes
> Or waste his time as he likes . . .[54]

Democracy, however, did not support the artist. Democracy crushed the individual and the perception of beauty.[55]

The remedy, then, was to have not democracy but its opposite, a strong ruler who would govern according to Confucian principles and support the arts. Pound found what he was looking for in Benito Mussolini. In December 1933 he collaborated with F. Ferruccio Cerio to make a film scenario on the history of Fascism. This was rewarded with an invitation to come to Rome and meet Mussolini. The meeting took place on 30 January. Pound brought with him—or perhaps he sent in advance—a copy of *A Draft of XXX Cantos.*

Mussolini said that the work was *"divertente"*—entertaining. To Pound this was a sign of Mussolini's superior intelligence and showed that the *Cantos* were suitable for men of action. When Pound said he was trying to put his ideas in order, Mussolini asked, "Why do you wish to put your ideas in order?" This was another sign of superior intelligence. He had caught the point of the *Cantos* before the aesthetes got there.[56] From that day on Pound referred to Mussolini as "the Boss." He hung on a wall the letter that had invited him to come to Rome for an interview, and he kept a scrapbook of Mussolini's activities.

In Pound's opinion the American people were "too hog lazy and too unfathomably ignorant to use the mechanism they [had] inherited to better economic and intellectual advantage." [57] From the vantage of Rapallo he proceeded to inform them, writing letters to U.S. Senators and Congressmen pointing out the error of their ways. He saw no need for a revolution in government—what he wanted was social and intellectual revolution.[58]

When Italy invaded Abyssinia he said the Italians weren't fighting battles, they were making roads.[59]

In 1939 Pound returned to the United States for a brief visit. He stayed in Washington for a fortnight, discussing monetary reform and politics with Senators, Congressmen and government officials. From his own account, in a conversation with Senator Borah he offered to serve in some official capacity, but Borah said, "[I] am sure I don't know what a man like you would find to *do* here." [60]

During this visit to the States Pound was awarded an honorary degree of Doctor of Letters by his alma mater, Hamilton College. The citation stated that he had led "a full life of significance in the arts." On this occasion he engaged in a heated public quarrel with H. V. Kaltenborn—Pound praising Mussolini.

Then he returned to Italy. He expressed the opinion that American education was full of "syphilis" and her intellectual life full of "dryrot." [61] Roosevelt was an evil man surrounded by sinister advisers; if there was a war he would bring America in.

In January 1941 he started making broadcasts on Rome Radio's American hour.

According to Mary de Rachewiltz, Pound tried to leave for the States after Pearl Harbor, but was told there was no place for him on the last clipper out—the seats were reserved for diplomats and the press. If he and his family wanted to leave it would have to be by boat.[62] But this was dangerous. There was some talk of his going to Portugal. Pound corroborates this part of the story —but, he says, he would have been cooped up in Lisbon for the duration. Besides, his parents were living in Rapallo and they were too old to travel.[63]

So he stayed in Italy. And when Italy and the United States were at war he resumed his broadcasts. This is the explanation he gave:

Interviewer: . . . were you conscious of breaking the American law?

Pound: No. I was completely surprised. You see I had that promise. I was given the freedom of the micro-

	phone twice a week. "He will not be asked to say anything contrary to his conscience or contrary to his duty as an American citizen." I thought that covered it.
Interviewer:	Doesn't the law of treason talk about "giving aid and comfort to the enemy," and isn't the enemy the country with whom we are at war?
Pound:	I thought I was fighting for a Constitutional point. I mean to say, I may have been completely nuts, but I certainly *felt* that it wasn't committing treason.

In the interview Pound went on to say that he had been work-ing for years to prevent war. He wasn't telling the American troops to revolt. He said again that he had thought he was deal-ing with an "internal" question of constitutional government. "And if any man, any individual man, can say he has had a bad deal from me because of race, creed, or colour, let him come out and state it with particulars. The *Guide to Kulchur* was dedicated to Basil Bunting and Louis Zukofsky, a Quaker and a Jew." [64]

Whether or not Pound committed treason, to most Americans he stood condemned for his racist outpourings. It has been said in his defense that when he used the word "kike" he meant "usurer." "International Jewry," Mary de Rachewiltz explains, was the true enemy, "whether the bankers and cannon merchants were Jews or Gentiles." [65] But if Jews were not the "enemy," why speak of Jews? Most people consider Pound to have been an anti-Semite. Passages such as these from his writings incline them to think so:

> Wellington was a jew's pimp.[66]
> . . . .
> Democracies electing their sewage
> till there is no clear thought about holiness
> a dung flow from 1913
> and, in this, their kikery functioned, Marx, Freud.[67]
> . . . .
> the yidd is a stimulant, and the goyim are cattle in
> gt/ proportion and go to saleable slaughter [68]

Broadcasting from Rome, Pound told Americans that for the United States "to be making war on Italy" was "just plain non-sense." Mussolini and Hitler were their true leaders: "You follow

Mussolini and Hitler in every constructive act of your govern-ment." He said, "You are not going to win this war."

> Well, you have been fed on lies, for 20 years you have been fed
> on lies, and I don't say maybe. And Mr. Squirmy and Mr. Slimy
> are still feeding it to you right over the BBC radio, and every
> one of the Jew radios of Schenectady, New York and Boston . . .[69]

But the war was not won by Hitler and Mussolini, and at the beginning of May 1945, the American Army was in Rapallo. Two partisans knocked on Pound's door—"Two common ex-Fascist convicts," says Mary de Rachewiltz indignantly. They said, *"Seguici, traditore,"* and Pound followed, slipping a volume of Confucius into his pocket. As he stopped to leave the key with the woman who lived on the ground floor, he made a noose with his hands around his neck.[70]

The partisans turned him over to the army. Olga Rudge came looking for him . . . an American Army major went to Pound's house and took away his typewriter. Three weeks later he was removed to the Disciplinary Training Center near Pisa—"in an open jeep," says Mary de Rachewiltz, "handcuffed to a Negro accused of rape and murder." [71] When he got to the DTC he was put in a cage.

Pound suffered indignity and discomfort, and his admirers have written about this with feeling. Yet, to read their descrip-tions of history is to enter a strange world. Hugh Kenner describes the hardships Pound suffered in the DTC at Pisa, but the reader will look to Kenner in vain for an equally graphic description of life under Fascism or in a German concentration camp. He describes the war fought by the Allies in Italy as "bombing their way up the Peninsula." He describes America in these words: "The bicycle chain swings in a suburban street. An eye is gouged out. Crowds walk past death indifferently. And the New World's century is under way." [72]

But we should not let the irascibility of Pound's apologists be added to his own so that he seems a kind of monster.

He was brought to Washington and indicted on a charge of treason. He was examined by four psychiatrists who reported that he was "suffering from a paranoid state." They said that he was "insane and mentally unfit for trial" and in need of care in a mental hospital. On 21 December 1945, the court ordered that Pound be sent to St. Elizabeth's Hospital for treatment and examination. Accordingly he was sent to St. Elizabeth's and there confined.

It takes nerve to be a poet, especially if that is all you are. Williams was an obstetrician, Eliot an editor at Faber, Stevens a vice-president of the Hartford Insurance Company, but Pound was just a poet. It takes nerve, and he had it, but there were times when he thought of "mighty poets in their misery dead," and of poets who were not so mighty but whose fates were just as sad.

> Johnson (Lionel) died
> By falling from a high stool in a pub.[73]

He remembered the view of the philistine: "The 'Nineties' tried your game/ And died, there's nothing in it." [74]

How clever of Mr. Nixon to see that E. P. was in the nineties game! Some critics say that Pound worked his way out of it, burying the aesthete Mauberley, but for a moment Pound saw to the heart of the matter. He was able to see the truth when he pretended to be someone else, and as Mr. Nixon he saw that E. P. was an aesthete of the kind that had flourished in the nineties. *Au fond* he was a lover of Beauty and Art.

But Beauty wasn't enough. You couldn't sit around waiting for Inspiration—in between times it could drive you to drink. A man needed to use his brains all the time—he needed an epic idea.

There was life—comedy and tragedy—but he wasn't strong on life. He envied the old man in Dorset—generations had gone into his making, centuries of living close to the soil, wash upon wash of culture producing finally a language with knots in it, prose with a grain, poems rooted strongly yet with queer, unexpected branchings. In order to write about life you had to have grown like Hardy for generations in one place.

E. P. wasn't able to write about people, their feelings. He wasn't strong on feelings. What did they add up to anyway? Family life, the religion of the Jews, with God the Father ordering people about . . . The Jews basked in the intravaginal warmth of the family, lending money at exorbitant rates, and the goyim went to the slaughter. So much for feelings and so-called humanitarianism. There was too much misplaced pity in the world, spoiling what was good.

> Compleynt, compleynt I hearde upon a day,
> Artemis singing, Artemis, Artemis

> Agaynst Pity lifted her wail:
> Pity causeth the forests to fail,
> Pity slayeth my nymphs,
> Pity spareth so many an evil thing.[75]

In an age of usurers and arms manufacturers poetry had to be based on something more tangible than feelings—it had to be based on "a sufficient phalanx of particulars." [76]

Some attempt to put one's ideas in order is unavoidable, and most people are satisfied to work out a loose system of beliefs that enables them to function. Some of the beliefs may be contradictory, but the looseness accommodates it—by exercising what Keats called "negative capability" they manage to function. "Negative capability," Keats said, is the ability to be "in uncertainties, mysteries, doubts, without any irritable reaching after fact and reason." [77]

Pound was reaching after fact and reason and becoming increasingly irritable. And this is what some critics congratulate him on—that he got past poetry and took up economics! As time went by his idea of what was permissible in the way of a system narrowed down. It was Social Credit or nothing.

> . . . the lot of 'em. Yeats, Possum and Wyndham
> had no ground beneath 'em.
> Orage had.[78]

He put his ideas about economics into his epic. It would begin in "the Dark Forest," cross the Purgatory of human error, and end in the light.[79] At the same time it would be the justification of his life—the poem was a *periplum*, a voyage into the unknown, coincident with his life. He "hoped to become, while writing the poem in public, the poet capable of ending the *Cantos*." [80]

These were his intentions. But in fact there was too much to do and confusion set in. Not planned confusion, "the basis of renewals." . . . He was attempting nothing less than a history of the world. This made for sketchiness in the execution—the insufficiency of the Cantos about Hell, for example. There were too many allusions, for he couldn't cover everything and hoped that an allusion would be enough. But for some readers, reading the *Cantos* is like listening to a man play a piano with every other key missing.

Yet "out of all this beauty something must come"—an aesthete's faith if ever there was one.[81] This is said "Under white clouds, cielo di Pisa," a quarter century after Pound is supposed to have taken leave of his aesthetic self. He remembers "the sky's glass leaded with elm boughs," [82] and says it again with a slight change: "Twilit sky leaded with elm boughs." [83] He is still an Imagist, and the poets of the nineties are with him on this voyage.

His intention had been to get rid of E. P. who

> Observed the elegance of Circe's hair
> Rather than the mottoes on sun-dials.[84]

If Ezra Pound had had his way E. P. would have passed from men's memory and a Vorticist would have taken his place, an epic poet who expressed the *paideuma*, tribal characteristics. But what the *Cantos* do express is the love of art. This is the true Penelope to whom E. P. is returning.

> Broken our strength, yea as crushed reeds we fall,
> And yet the art, the art goes on.[85]

In the December 1930 issue of *Front* Pound stated his "Credo." There is nothing here about economics—there is much about beauty in terms that would have appealed to Swinburne and Dowson. Pound said, "I would replace the statue of Venus on the cliffs at Terracina. I would erect a temple to Artemis in Park Lane. I believe that a light from Eleusis persisted through the middle ages and set beauty in the song of Provence and of Italy." [86]

On the deepest level of his mind, where art was concerned, Pound was the opposite of the anti-Semite and the Fascist. Technique is love—to make a thing well is to give the best of oneself to mankind. Pound believed that men could work together to build "the city of Dioce, whose terraces are the colour of stars." [87] At the exit of his Inferno he placed the builders of cities:

> the new sky,
>   the light as after a sun-set,
>   and by their fountains, the heroes . . .[88]

At the end of the war when he was in the prison cage at Pisa with trouble enough to drive thought out of the head of an ordinary man, Pound turned in reverie to a time when men worked together and there could be "honesty of mind/ without overwhelming talent." He added sadly, "I have perhaps seen a waning of that tradition." [89] Tradition, passing on wisdom and skill from one man to another, one country to another, one generation to another—this is what Pound loved, and the love of this is what he teaches.

> Thus the light rains, thus pours, e lo soleills plovil
> The liquid and rushing crystal
>   beneath the knees of the gods.[90]

7

Cloud's Processional

TWEEDLEDUM says that style isn't as important as content. Tweedledee on the other hand says that what you say doesn't matter but only how well you say it. On 20 February 1949 the Fellows of the Library of Congress voted with Tweedledee for style and awarded the first Bollingen Prize for poetry to Ezra Pound. The prize was one thousand dollars, for the best book of "American verse" published during the year. It was awarded for *The Pisan Cantos.*

Pound was under an indictment by the government of the United States for "knowingly, intentionally, wilfully, unlawfully, feloniously, traitorously and treasonably" adhering to the enemies of the United States and giving "aid and comfort" to these "enemies." There seemed to be a great difference between the opinion of Pound held by American intellectuals and that held by the government.

The poet Robert Hillyer wrote articles in *The Saturday Review of Literature* attacking Pound and the jury that had given him the prize. People took sides, some congratulating Hillyer on the stand he was taking, others defending the jury. The jurors were well-known "modern" poets—Eliot and Auden among them —so that the controversy went beyond the question of Pound's guilt and the prize, it became a quarrel between those who were for "modern poetry"—Pound, Eliot and their followers—and those who were for some other kind of poetry that would speak to and for the American people. The proponents of this other kind of poetry named Robert Frost as an example.

One night the members of the Poetry Society of America gathered at the Waldorf Astoria to dine and reassure one another. Speaking from the platform Robert Hillyer compared Pound's *Cantos* to the scribblings of a lunatic. He also criticized Archibald MacLeish. MacLeish, too, it seemed, was part of the conspiracy Hillyer was exposing. Then John Ciardi took the microphone away from Hillyer and said that he was a friend of MacLeish and was ashamed to have sat at the same table with Robert Hillyer. W. H. Auden, who was also at the speakers' table, began to cough in his handkerchief. He slipped away behind a screen—one moment he was there, the next he wasn't. The members of the Poetry Society were thunderstruck, their pistachio ice cream melting on their plates. They were accustomed to complaining about modern poetry, and they thought Pound was tucked away safely in a mental hospital. Who would have thought the old man to have had so much blood in him?

The cause of the controversy was in St. Elizabeth's Hospital in the District of Columbia, within arm's reach of the government he had offended. Doctors had decided that he wasn't competent to stand trial. "In our opinion, with advancing years his personality, for many years abnormal, has undergone further distortion to the extent that he is now suffering from a paranoid state which renders him mentally unfit to advise properly with counsel or to participate intelligently and reasonably in his own defense." [1] The indictment remained on the books and Pound was kept in an insane asylum. It was agreed that he wasn't really crazy but if he behaved himself the government would pretend that he was.

Pound's wife came to visit him every day. He had a supply of books and magazines. And he had many visitors. Whenever Eliot was in the States he would make a special journey to St. Elizabeth's. There were other poets and critics who came to pay their respects to the Old Man Mad About Letters. Delighted to have their company Pound bustled about, making tea. Sometimes he would lecture them on economics. At other times, disconcertingly, he would be silent and stare them in the eye.

There were also disciples such as John Kasper, who came to see him and then went forth to preach hatred against Negroes and Jews. For a man who claimed that he was not a racist Pound was remarkably unfortunate. He was more unfortunate than the man in Molière's play, for he kept getting into the same galley.

When Kasper began making a name for himself as a rabble-rouser
the newspapers revealed that he was Pound's disciple. A businessman and poet named Harry Meacham went to see Pound. He
reminded Pound that his friends were trying to persuade the government to release him, and asked him to state publicly that he
did not approve of Kasper. "Well," Pound said, "at least he's a
man of action and don't sit around looking at his navel." [2]

Thirteen years after the partisans knocked on his door and
said, "Come along, traitor," Pound was set free. He sailed back
to Italy, and the first thing he did on arriving was to give the
Fascist salute and tell the reporters that America was a lunatic
asylum.

There is a passage denouncing Vanity in *The Pisan Cantos.*

> How mean thy hates
> Fostered in falsity,
> Pull down thy vanity . . .[3]

The passage is dear to anthologists, for it is a quotable whole in
an unquotably long poem. It is especially valued as evidence of
Pound's change of heart—he has stopped railing and is reconciled
to the world. On consideration, however, this is not what happened. The line, "The total dirt that was Roosevelt," appears in
Canto LXXXVII, a long time after Pisa.[4]

It is not even clear that Pound includes himself in his denuncia-
tion of vanity. The passage says, "Pull down thy vanity," it does
not say, "I am pulling down mine."

Pound on Vanity had been, as usual, a dramatic impersonation, a monologue in the style of a period. Pound did not change
his opinions when he wrote about vanity, any more than he had
renounced a part of himself when he created the character Bertrand de Born, "stirrer up of strife," or Mauberley the aesthete
and follower of the cult of Beauty. The role of humility, if we
assume that Pound does include himself among those to whom
the Canto is addressed, was just another of his *personae.* He himself was not to be reconstructed, either by doctors or the state.
His discontents were "unremovably/ Coupled to nature." [5]

For a time the barbarians had been stronger. They had placed
him in a cage, six feet by six and a half. Through wire mesh with
metal strips welded over the wire he looked out on other cages
containing murderers, rapists, deserters from the Army of the
United States. The Disciplinary Training Center was surrounded

with barbed wire that slanted out at the top, supported on what looked like gibbets. It was possible that he would be hanged or at least die of pneumonia. Dust blew into the cage and he was wet when it rained. He slept on concrete, wrapped in two blankets. His cage was lit by the glare of a reflector. In the hours before dawn the cold mist made his teeth chatter and his limbs to shake. During the day he was not allowed out for exercise though other prisoners were. He paced to and fro in the cage, striking with an imaginary tennis racket, shadowboxing. Then they gave him more blankets and a pup tent to keep out the rain.

He began to have bouts of panic. He suffered from amnesia. The top of his head felt empty. So they moved him from the cage to a tent in the dispensary.

For a time he was held in one place. Then he saw that there were creatures for whom this time was all, this place the whole world. At dawn he observed the ants.

> And now the ants seem to stagger
> as the dawn sun has trapped their shadows [6]

One of the qualities he had admired in Arnaut Daniel was his exact observation of nature. Yeats on the other hand saw everything as a symbol—gazing at Notre Dame he saw it enclosed in a larger significance. For one man who could look at nature and report what he saw, there were a hundred who were purblind, saw trees as men walking. But

> When the mind swings by a grass-blade
> an ant's forefoot shall save you [7]

Now a wasp had built her cell on the roof of his tent. As he watched a new wasp emerged, the color of grass, climbed down to the earth, "to carry our news/ to them that dwell under earth." [8] The newborn wasp would sing in the bower of Kore and have speech with Tiresias.

It had taken the mother wasp half a day to make her cell out of mud. It had been a devil of a time before Ezra Pound hit on the right way to make his first Canto. He found it in Andreas Divus's translation of Homer, picked up in a bookstall on the Seine. Divus had translated Greek into Latin. As the Greek sounded to Divus, primitive and heroic, so would Anglo-Saxon, the sound of "The Seafarer," be to twentieth-century readers who

spoke English. He began the first, Homeric Canto with the sound
of Anglo-Saxon.

> Circe's this craft, the trim-coifed goddess.[9]

He had gone with Odysseus under the earth and poured the
libation of blood. The dead rose and their spirits drank of the
blood—they spoke to him and through him. The *Cantos* were a history of ghosts, with many crowding round him—the helmeted ghost
of Sigismondo Malatesta, the white ghost of Helen, the ghost
of John Adams. They spoke together, a confusion of tongues. In
the midst of their conversing one would vanish and another take
his place.

Last of all came Mussolini, his eyes staring, his mouth hanging
open. His naked feet were covered with blood.

> the twice crucified
> where in history will you find it? [10]

Roosevelt had made war on Mussolini. Pound had done his best
to prevent it. He had tried to tell people in America about usury,
warn them against Roosevelt and the Jews. They had chosen to
ignore his warnings. Well, it was no longer his responsibility—
they would have to suffer the consequences.

He wrote at night the bits of poetry he composed during the
day. They let him use the typewriter in the dispensary. They let
him keep his copy of Confucius and his dictionary of Chinese.
He also had a Bible—Jehovah was okay with the officials. He had
The Pocket Book of Verse—this last found in the john.

He was getting back the sound of American, listening to the
guards. " 'If you had a f . . . . n' brain you'd be dangerous.' " [11]
Not having lived Stateside as they called it so many years he had
lost touch with demotic American. Someone said that when he
tried to write American it sounded like *Our American Cousin*,
the play Lincoln saw the night he was shot. As Hem used to say,
they said many things.

He had been out of touch. But he wouldn't, to save his life,
have spent it like Bill Williams in a town in New Jersey. There
was a defect there. Doting on the plain and ugly. Puritanism.
Williams was like one of the spirits in Dante that walked with
eyes fixed on the ground, by preference. Nor would he have
wanted to stay in London like Eliot, getting timider and timider.

The Possum had taken to religion—he was some sort of deacon in his church. There was a defect there. Of courage. A lack of joy. No, even if he hanged for it he preferred the view from his tent, the morning sun rising, the shadows of the ants, like centaurs, having disappeared.

A group of prisoners was being run over to the obstacle course. In the distance he could see the *"torre qui pende,"* the leaning—no, hanging—tower. He could see a patch of white, the *battistero.* And above Pisa the clouds. They were as fine as any in the Peninsula.

The tower was of white Carrara marble. Beauty formed out of chaos, the female. "By prong have I entered these hills." [12]

He was being compelled to think about his life. There was nothing else to do, no access to a library. His life was in the past. Well, the muses were daughters of memory, and what he had seen and heard was indisputable fact. When he spoke about what he himself had witnessed no one could question his authority. When he wrote about the past, even his ideas took on a feeling of reality—for they were part of his life. In themselves neither valid nor invalid, ideas became believable when they were treated as part of the story of his life—when, so to speak, they became fiction. Then everything seemed to fit—the shadow of the guard, the shouting of the drill instructor, the sow on the other side of the barbed wire with her farrow, "matronly as any duchess at Claridge's." [13] The black man, Walls, had lent him a razor to shave with. It seemed perfectly natural. There was a man named Clower he remembered he might owe money to. That too seemed natural and went into the poem.

In former days when he wrote about present matters he would harangue the reader. But now there was nothing more to be gained. As Chaucer said, "who wrestles for the world will get a fall." So now he just wrote about life—London, for example, the gulls on the Serpentine, the sunken garden. He wrote about people he had known before the war. Before which war? The war before which everything. He recalled "Uncle William/ labouring a sonnet of Ronsard." [14] And there were lesser men and women. He had a hundred ghosts.

When he was old he lived with Olga Rudge—in winter at her small house on Calle Querini in Venice, in summer at her house at Sant' Ambrogio in the hills above Rapallo. "Down below lived Dorothy." [15]

He was famous—some thought him a great poet and in any case he was a monument. As the years passed he became more and more silent; visitors might be confronted with a man who sat the whole time saying nothing. "He was just out of it," said one who had been through the experience.[16]

When Eliot died Pound traveled to England to attend the memorial service in Westminster Abbey.

Every year he visited the music festival at Spoleto, the most famous person there. He was invited back to the States to be honored and gazed at. His peculiar views didn't seem to matter to young men who had learned about poetry in the university. They were taught that the poem was a thing complete in itself, existing apart from history. The poet's intentions didn't matter —to think they did would be the "intentional fallacy."

To the young American who came to interview him and who asked about his "devotion to technique" he replied that "the *what*" was much more important than how.[17] The interviewer listened to this without turning a hair. It seemed that these days Ezra Pound could say anything and it would go into print without anyone's turning a hair. The world had changed—people took for granted attitudes that, when he was young, had to be fought for. When he was a young man poetry had been dying of sentimentality. So he had insisted on "objectivity." Now poetry seemed to be dying of objectivity. Poetry had always been dying of something as far back as he could remember.

Looking at the clouds he saw his life receding. "In the 'search for oneself,' in the search for 'sincere self-expression,' one gropes, one finds some seeming verity. One says 'I am' this, that, or the other, and with the words scarcely uttered one ceases to be that thing." [18]

There was a man walking on a road lined with poplars. There was a man in a London street, wearing a broad hat and a cape— he looked bohemian, a "Latin Quarter" type. There was a man in a restaurant reading a poem in a loud voice to a table full of people. The manager came up with the waiter, carrying a screen —they placed it around the table to hide the poetry readers from the other people in the restaurant. There was a man sitting in a cage near Pisa, his red hair covered with dust.

He had been a vagabond all his life. He had not been willing to stay in one place, settle for one style.

> One dull man, dulling and uxorious,
> One average mind—with one thought less, each year.[19]

He hadn't been willing to be dull, but had kept slipping from one role into another, "casting off, as it were, complete masks of the self in each poem." [20]

He watched his many selves take shape and fade. Seeing them fade was his life.

> Nothing that's quite your own.
> Yet this is you.[21]

II

T. S. Eliot,
or Religion

8

The Author of Prufrock

IN 1669 an Englishman named Andrew Eliot, a leatherworker by trade, came to Massachusetts from the village of East Coker in Somerset. His name is in the register of the First Church at Beverly. He was a witness at the Salem witch trials, but afterwards he recanted, and it is said that for the rest of his life he regretted having taken part. Andrew Eliot's descendants were prominent in New England history. They were Presbyterians, then they were converted to Unitarianism.

In 1834, William Greenleaf Eliot, having graduated from the Harvard Divinity School, went out to St. Louis, Missouri, where he founded the first Unitarian chapel and, in 1857, founded Washington University. He was a writer on "ethical and philosophical questions, and set the standard of conduct for his descendants, any deviation from which would be sinful. They had a sense of public service described by the poet T. S. Eliot as "an uncomfortable and very inconvenient obligation to serve upon committees." [1] Robert Sencourt, in his memoir of Eliot's life, says that William Greenleaf's descendants "admired him as a hero, they worshipped him as a saint, and they loved him for the fine old gentleman he was." At the same time we are told that he "towered over his family as over his congregation," and that his daughter-in-law, Charlotte Eliot, "lived in his shadow." [2] This is the familiar picture of a Victorian patriarch, righteous, awe-inspiring and, it is to be hoped, benevolent. Of the fourteen children born to William Greenleaf Eliot's wife, five survived. The second son, Henry Ware Eliot, graduated from Washington University, of which his father was president, but instead of going into the ministry he went into business as a wholesale grocer. When this failed he became a partner in the Hydraulic Press Brick Company. He rose to be president, collected paintings, was active in the St. Louis Philharmonic and Choral Societies, and served on the governing board of the University. Henry Ware Eliot married Charlotte Chauncey Sterns. She too came of a Boston family that had been among the early settlers. Charlotte Eliot wrote a life of her father-in-law, William Greenleaf Eliot. She also wrote a poem—rather, a series of short verses with prose in between—to which she gave the title, *Savonarola, A Dramatic Poem.*

The poet T. S. Eliot was their seventh child. He was born on 26 September 1888, and christened Thomas Stearns Eliot.

He seems to have been a delicate child. We are told by Sencourt that as a child Eliot suffered from hernia "and so was rather coddled." Also, there was an Irish nurse "who frequently talked to the child about God." She took Tom with her to her church, which was Catholic. In this way, says Sencourt, Eliot was exposed to the Catholicism that he would come to prefer to the "prim moralizing Unitarianism which he had learned at home as the religion of a model grandfather." [3] T. S. Matthews in his biography of Eliot says that the nurse, Annie Dunne, was "the first exciting woman in Tom Eliot's life," and that the child saw the difference between the "liturgical order and richness of the Mass" and the "bloodless prolixities of Unitarian prayer meetings." [4] This may have been true, but a man has many experiences in the course of his life and what matters is his thinking, that is, the way the mind works through the data presented to it and the way it arrives at a conclusion. This process, however, can only be suggested and may hold no attraction for the general public. An Irish nurse is more appealing.

Eliot's father was a Unitarian, a teetotaler, a nonsmoker, and a model citizen. We are told, however, that he was "stone deaf, middle-aged, and remote." To entertain the children he would draw faces on their boiled eggs. He also drew cats, and he made a point of calling nasturtiums "nestertians" in the hope that one of them would correct him. He was a good chess player and his handwriting was untidy. He seems to have been an Edward Learish character whose love of cats and untidy handwriting, at least, were inherited by the poet.[5]

Eliot's mother, Charlotte, was forty-five when he was born (his father was forty-seven). Matthews tells us that she was "one of those admirable women who have strict standards of conduct and no intimate friends, and who are admired, disliked, and feared by all who know them." [6] Matthews tells us that her handwriting was "uncompromisingly ugly." He has an ever harsher judgment: Eliot's mother "did not like children. She never said so; she bore seven and did her maternal duty by them, but none of them needed to be told how she felt." She kept a watch over the children's reading and there were certain "vulgar" books, *Tom Sawyer* and *Huckleberry Finn* among them, that Tom was forbidden to read.[7]

Next to the Eliot house was a girls' school called Mary Institute —this too had been founded by his grandfather—which Eliot's sisters attended. A high brick wall separated the schoolyard from the Eliots' back garden. The wall had a door in it and there was a key to the door. If he stood in the back garden he could hear the voices of the children playing in the schoolyard. At the end of the day when they had gone he would enter the schoolyard and sometimes venture into the building.[8]

The Mississippi, the "strong brown god—sullen, untamed and intractable," [9] the scent of ailanthus in the spring, and voices of children who, when he arrives on the scene, have vanished, are in the poems Eliot wrote many years later. So is the sea, for Henry Ware Eliot built a house at Gloucester, Massachusetts, and the family spent summer vacations there. Eliot would recall "peering through sea-water in a rock-pool, and finding a sea-anemone for the first time." [10]

He began early as a writer. He wrote a life of George Washington in ten lines, and before he was ten founded, edited, and distributed to members of his family a periodical titled *Fireside*. He liked "martial and sanguinary" poetry such as "Horatius," "The Burial of Sir John Moore," "Bannockburn," Tennyson's "Revenge," and the border ballads. Then for three years he lost his liking for poetry altogether; the only pleasure he derived from Shakespeare was "the pleasure of being recommended for reading him." At the age of fourteen, however, he saw an extract from Fitzgerald's *Omar Khayyam* and had the overwhelming sensation of entering a new world of feeling. "It was like a sudden conversion; the world appeared anew, painted with bright, delicious and painful colours. Thereupon I took the usual adolescent course with Byron, Shelley, Keats, Rossetti, Swinburne." This period persisted until he was nineteen or twenty.[11]

But only a part of an author's imagery comes from his reading. It comes, says Eliot, "from the whole of his sensitive life since early childhood."

> Why, for all of us, out of all that we have heard, seen, felt, in a lifetime, do certain images recur, charged with emotion, rather than others? The song of one bird, the leap of one fish, at a particular place and time, the scent of one flower, an old woman on a German mountain path, six ruffians seen through an open window playing cards at night at a small French railway junction where there was a water-mill; such memories may have symbolic value, but of what we cannot tell, for they come to represent the depths of feeling into which we cannot peer.[12]

He was sent to school at Smith Academy in St. Louis. The hernia prevented his participating fully in games, so he studied and read for pleasure. He was taught Greek and Latin, the history of Greece and Rome, English and American history, elementary mathematics, French and German. "Also English! I am happy to remember that in those days English composition was still called *Rhetoric*." [13] After his discovery of *Omar Khayyam* he wrote some gloomy quatrains. At sixteen he published a few pieces of verse and prose in the *Smith Academy Record*. "A Fable for Feasters" is in the graveyard humor of *The Ingoldsby Legends,* telling of monks and a ghost. In "A Lyric" he was imitating Ben Jonson:

> The flowers I gave thee when the dew
>   Was trembling on the vine,
> Were withered ere the wild bee flew
>   To suck the eglantine.[14]

This was better poetry, his mother told him, than any she had written herself. Eliot comments, "I knew what her verse meant to her. We did not discuss the matter further." [15] He also composed a valedictory poem and read it on Graduation Day.

From Smith he went to Milton Academy in Massachusetts, where he received further grounding in basic subjects, including Greek and Latin.

In 1906 Eliot entered Harvard College. At this time the president was Charles William Eliot, a distant cousin of Eliot's grandfather, William Greenleaf Eliot. President Eliot was a Unitarian and a man for the new century, liberal and progressive in his views. He did not hold with the anthropomorphic view of religion, with references to a Holy Ghost or a Mother of God. He was against morbidly dwelling on sin. The religion of the future would seek to prevent disease and would lead to universal goodwill. It was "benevolent materialism." [16] The teachings of Jesus would be brought in line with education, social service, research in medicine and, as Gatsby might have said, "needed inventions."

In his reading in modern languages and literature Eliot came across Flaubert's portrait of the chemist Homais, whose ideas about religion were similar to President Eliot's: "My God is the God of Socrates, of Franklin, Voltaire and Beranger! . . . I cannot worship an old fogey of a God who walks round his garden with a stick in his hand, lodges his friends in the bellies of whales . . ." He was reading French poets; he had discovered Baudelaire, who had a better style than President Eliot and who loathed materialism. Moreover, in his browsings at the Union he had picked up a copy of Arthur Symons' *The Symbolist Movement in French Literature.*

Conrad Aiken, who was at Harvard with Eliot, remembers him as an undergraduate: "a singularly attractive, tall, and rather dapper young man, with a somewhat Lamian smile." [17] Eliot was painfully shy but tried to overcome this by going to dances and parties. He felt very much out of place. He had been born in the South—St. Louis being practically the South in its atmosphere and way of life. He himself had what he called a "nigger drawl" (people in St. Louis said "nigger" and spoke contemptuously of Jews and other strangers). But he wasn't really a Southerner, for his family came from the North and looked down on all Southerners. So he was never really anything anywhere. He thought he was more of a Frenchman than an American, and more of an Englishman than an American. Yet, the United States of America up to a hundred years ago had been "a family extension." [18]

During these years he continued to spend his summer vacations at Gloucester. Samuel Eliot Morison, the historian who was Eliot's cousin, says that "Tom was not only steeped in the lore of Cape Ann; he became familiar with the encompassing ocean." Eliot would sail with a friend named Harold Peters out beyond the rocks known as the Dry Salvages. When there was fog they would listen for the "groaner," the whistling buoy east of Thacher Island, and the "wailing warning" of the diaphone on the island.

They grew familiar with "The sea howl/ And the sea yelp," "The distant rote in the granite teeth." [19]

He was beginning to write poetry, and contributed poems to the *Harvard Advocate* of which he was an associate editor. They were what might be expected of an adolescent who had been reading Romantic and Victorian poets. The writing shows a sense of rhythm and sound. But there is something more, a quality described years later by a character in one of Eliot's plays:

> a sudden intuition, in certain minds,
> May tend to express itself at once in a picture.[20]

The ability to render thought in images is evident in lines Eliot wrote when he was still an undergraduate.

> The peacocks walk, stately and slow,
> And they look at us with the eyes
> Of men whom we knew long ago.[21]

Suddenly his manner changes—it is no longer Tennyson and Swinburne, it is Jules Laforgue. "Laforgue," says Eliot, "was the first to teach me how to speak, to teach me the possibilities of my own idiom of speech." [22] As Sencourt says, it was as though Eliot had met Laforgue in person; he submitted not only to Laforgue's way of writing but his way of life.[23] When he sat down to write it was as though he were the reincarnation of Laforgue. He now wrote as a man of the world, speaking with irony. In one poem he describes Romeo and Juliet

> in the usual debate
> Of love, beneath a bored but courteous moon . . .[24]

Romeo is stabbed by a servant and thus spared the longueurs of life, the disenchantment. The narrator remarks that "Blood looks effective on the moonlit ground," and that this is "The perfect climax all true lovers seek!"

It is curious how authors find their affinities. The writer a writer needs may not be a grand figure: to the contrary, he may only strike a certain note. Laforgue is no great figure in the literature of France, but to Eliot he was all-important.

When he writes in the manner of Laforgue he expresses his boredom and sometimes he gives vent to spleen—a vague, nervous irritability. If irritability is too strong a word, let us say a gnawing sense of the ridiculous. With spleen he regards a "satisfied procession/ Of definite Sunday faces" on their way to church.[25] Everything about ordinary life—teatime, children and cats in the alley—increases his dejection. He visualizes the arrival of the procession, Life, with hat and gloves in hand, impatient at being kept waiting "On the doorstep of the Absolute." The poem "Spleen" marks an advance: Eliot is beginning to deal with people and ideas rather than flowers, peacocks, and marionettes.

Between Laforgue's life and Eliot's there are resemblances; this is not surprising, for Eliot imitated Laforgue. They were both expatriates: Laforgue was born in Uruguay in 1860 but moved to France at an early age. Laforgue dressed like an Englishman and carried an umbrella. He kept his personal life out of his work and very little is known about him. One further fact should be mentioned: Laforgue was married in London at St. Barnabas's Church. Shortly before Eliot married for the second time he discovered that he was to be married in the same church as Laforgue. This is one of the coincidences in a man's life that prove nothing yet demand to be noticed. Coincidences such as this drive men to art, where facts have some significance.

Eliot turned to Laforgue and the French Symbolists because, he says, there was no poet in England or America who could be of use to a beginner in 1908.[26] The poetry being written at this time was watered-down Romanticism. It was necessary to go to another language or another age for models. The Symbolists taught that poetry "must transmute life into a new incarnation of thought and rhythm."[27] So did the Jacobean dramatists, instinctively. In both the appeal was to mind through sense perception. "In both, too, the interest was dramatic, in contrast to the reflective and descriptive modes of the eighteenth and nineteenth centuries, and to that of the subjective lyric."[28] In dramatic poetry there was a distance between the author and the subject, therefore the poet was able to view life all around, himself included. He was not carried away by his own emotions.

Eliot says that he does not know of any other writer who formed his style by studying Laforgue and the Jacobean dramatists. It was an original place to start. "He has actually trained himself *and* modernized himself *on his own*," Pound would say after meeting Eliot.[29]

He had been reading Dante, who remained for him a supreme poet. He read Donne and the Metaphysicals. He had come across odd authors such as John Davidson whose "Thirty Bob a Week" with its colloquial speech and imagery taken from mean streets indicated what might be done in the way of realism.

After receiving the BA he continued at Harvard as a graduate student working toward the Master's. He enrolled in a course taught by Irving Babbitt: "Literary Criticism in France with Special Reference to the Nineteenth Century." This was more than a course in French literature, it was confirmation for Eliot of attitudes he already held. Babbitt disliked the liberal mind; he was against the free-elective system at Harvard and in life. "The function of the college . . . should be to insist on the idea of quality." Babbitt wanted a sense of authority and claimed to have found it in the classics, the "unbroken chain of literary and intellectual tradition which extends from the ancient to the modern world." The classics appealed to man's higher reason and imagination and enabled him to participate in "the universal life." The classical spirit was marked by restraint, discipline, proportion and law.

Babbitt called his position humanism. The humanist believed that "the man of today, if he does not, like the man of the past, take on the yoke of a definite doctrine and discipline, must at least do inner obeisance to something higher than his ordinary self, whether he calls this something God, or, like the man of the Far East, calls it his higher self, or simply the Law."

Babbitt thought that most of the harm in the world was caused by people who trusted to their feelings. "In the name of feeling Rousseau headed the most powerful insurrection the world has ever seen against every kind of authority." Romanticism was the father of lies and Rousseau was its prophet. Romanticism meant lack of discipline, individualism, stress on sensation, primitivism and the glorification of spontaneity. Romanticism was the cause of the excesses of modern life—humanism the corrective.[30]

Much of Eliot's later writing, especially his attack on Romantic attitudes, is consistent with the teachings of Babbitt. He continued to respect Babbitt after he himself had decided that humanism was too vague, that he needed the dogma of the church.

Conrad Aiken speaks of a lady in Boston whom Eliot visited: "The oh so precious, the oh so exquisite, the Jamesian lady of ladies, the enchantress of the Beacon Hill drawing room . . . afterwards to be essentialized and ridiculed (and his own pose with it) in the Tsetse's '*Portrait d'une Femme.*' "[31] Eliot seems to have found a situation in real life that could be dealt with in the style of Laforgue: a woman demanding greater intimacy and a man who is unwilling or unable to give it. He squirms under her reproaches; he feels that he is craven and ridiculous; but he keeps returning nevertheless. The Circe of the drawing room takes her place in Eliot's poetry with the punctiliously dressed, balding middle-aged man.

In 1910 he wrote the "Portrait of a Lady." He also wrote two "Preludes" and the first part of "The Love Song of J. Alfred Prufrock."

After receiving the MA he decided to pursue his studies in France, at the University of Paris. He was there in the autumn of 1910, attending lectures by Henri Bergson. He was "at odds with Bergson's optimism from the outset," but Bergson's idea of instinctive consciousness, breaking down orderly thought into a stream of disconnected impressions, may have contributed to the seemingly free flow of thought in Eliot's "Rhapsody on a Windy Night" and other poems.[32]

He was tutored by the novelist Alain-Fournier, whose enthusiasm for Dostoievsky led him to read that author—another possible cause of the breaking down of orderly thought. He met the critic Jacques Rivière, who later became the editor of *Nouvelle Revue Française.* He came to know Charles Maurras, the leader of *Action Française,* a movement dedicated to nationalism, the Catholic church, and anti-Semitism. He read novels by Charles Louis Philippe. *Bubu de Montparnasse,* an account of the lives of prostitutes and pimps, made a strong impression; it was not like anything he had known in Cambridge or St. Louis. From this novel he borrowed the scene for his own third "Prelude," a woman's getting out of bed in a dirty room. Another novel by Philippe, *Marie Donadieu,* supplied Eliot with more ideas about low life and more phrases for poems.[33]

He made a friend, Jean Verdenal. This is the man to whom his first book is dedicated:

> For Jean Verdenal, 1889–1915
> mort aux Dardanelles

There follows a passage of four lines from Dante's *Purgatorio.* Dante is being guided through purgatory by Virgil. They meet the spirit of the Roman poet Statius, who stoops and tries to clasp Virgil's feet in homage. Virgil stops him with the reminder that they are both only shadows. Statius replies, and these are the lines Eliot uses, "Now you can understand the quantity and warmth of the love I have for you, so that I forget how unreal we are and treat shadows as though they were solid." [34]

In an essay that at Eliot's insistence had to be withdrawn from circulation, the critic John Peter has proposed that the relationship between Eliot and Jean Verdenal was more than friendship, it was a "close romantic attachment." [35] There is no way to discover whether this is true or not. Eliot reacted to the mention of this critic's name with "acute sensitivity." [36] If, as Swift imagines in *Gulliver's Travels,* there is a place in another life where critics meet authors, it would be edifying to be present when Thomas Stearns Eliot meets John Peter.

During this year Eliot wrote the third and fourth "Preludes" and "Rhapsody on a Windy Night." It is possible that "La Figlia Che Piange" also belongs to this period. Then, in the summer of 1919, he traveled in Northern Italy and in Germany as far as Munich. There he finished "The Love Song of J. Alfred Prufrock."

Writing is not always a pleasure, it may be a burden and obsession. The poet "has something germinating in him for which he must find words; but he cannot know what words he wants until he has found the words. . . . He is oppressed by a burden which he must bring to birth in order to obtain relief . . . he is going to all that trouble, not in order to communicate with anyone, but to gain relief from acute discomfort." [37]

The poet's mind is "a receptacle for seizing and storing up numberless feelings, phrases, images, which remain there until all the particles which can unite to form a new compound are present together." [38] The coming together of particles cannot be willed, there must be a "passive attending upon the event." When the event occurs, however, the poet consciously finds the right words in which to make his communication. This requires "frightful toil," mainly the labor of self-criticism. [39]

The impulse to create is not the same as merely feeling. Eliot agrees with Flaubert's idea of the impersonality of art: the artist is a man who feels, but he knows how to separate himself from his feelings and use what he needs in order to create a work that will mean something to other people. "The more perfect the artist the more completely separate in him will be the man who suffers and the mind which creates; the more perfectly will the mind digest and transmute the passions which are its material." [40]

In a sense one cannot be an artist until one has ceased, oneself, to live. "One is prepared for art when one has ceased to be interested in one's own emotions and experiences except as material . . . Personal emotion, personal experience is extended and completed in something impersonal—not in the sense of something divorced from personal experience and passion. No good poetry is the latter . . . Not our feelings, but the pattern we make of our feelings is the centre of value." [41]

Such are Eliot's views of the process of artistic creation. He had not yet set them down in words, but when he did the process he described was that which had led to the creation of *Prufrock and Other Observations,* and to the creation of all his poems, with the possible exception of *Four Quartets,* which seems the result of having decided to write rather than having been driven to it by an obsession.

In Munich he sat at a table looking at chestnut trees and finishing "Prufrock." The citizens walked by with an air of bourgeois respectability. There were children in sailor suits—German dreadnoughts were being built as rapidly as possible in order to match the British navy—and officers in resplendent uniform escorting blonde women, future mothers of the race. Here were strength, vigor and the consciousness of a national destiny. In the midst sat a tall young American with a Roman nose and placid eyes—a face somewhat lacking in color, rather gray in fact—composing a poem that expressed disenchantment.

It may have begun as a rhythm. In poetry sometimes, and in some poets a great deal of the time, there is a feeling of rhythm before there is anything else—before the precise words, sounds, images, or ideas. "I know," says Eliot, "that a poem, or a passage in a poem, may tend to realize itself first as a particular rhythm before it reaches expression in words, and that this rhythm may bring to birth the idea and the image; and I do not believe that this is an experience peculiar to myself." [42]

He speaks of the poet as a person with "auditory imagination . . . the feeling for syllable and rhythm, penetrating far below the conscious levels of thought and feeling, invigorating every word; sinking to the most primitive and forgotten, returning to the origin and bringing something back, seeking the beginning and the end." [43]

"Prufrock" has a pleasant rhythm, lines of varying length with an iambic beat—it is not free verse by any means—and there are plenty of rhymes to tie the lines together, even for people who like poetry to be the way it used to be, regular and predictable. "Prufrock" moves with a semblance of freedom, but it is freedom within familiar patterns of rhyme and meter. What is the poem about? It is not far from being the work Flaubert said he wished to compose, that would be about nothing at all, sustained only by its style. As Prufrock describes the uselessness of doing any-thing, his inability to communicate his meaning to anyone, as he visualizes what the evening would be like if he went, without ac-tually going, Prufrock—like Pyrrhus in the play, "like a neutral to his will and matter"—does nothing. Then, lest we should think that his indecisiveness has heroic proportions, he rids us of this hope too. "No! I am not Prince Hamlet, nor was meant to be." [44]

The poem is practically a demonstration of the "modernist" theory that style is everything, subject unimportant. "It is never what a poem *says* that matters, but what it *is*." This remark by I. A. Richards is quoted by Eliot in *The Use of Poetry and the Use of Criticism;* [45] the New Criticism that prevailed in academic circles from the nineteen-thirties until only yesterday was founded on this belief. Art does not depend on the world, nor does it seek to change it. Poetry is about itself, the experience we have when we are reading the poem. The poem is about what it will be—the poem has a vision of itself in accordance with which it starts and proceeds, arranging matters in detail—rhythm, the choice and order of words, images and ideas—in order to arrive at the result foreseen. What Eliot says of his life in *Four Quartets* is true of the life of the poem: "The end is where we start from." [46]

The poem, however, takes its material from the world, for we think best in images. "Prufrock" begins with an image of the evening "spread out against the sky/ Like a patient etherised upon a table." [47] This observation is now as famous, in the United States at any rate, as the remark made by Keats's urn. To the first readers it must have been startling. It was not the kind of thing they were accustomed to finding in poems. You could see the operating table and you could almost see the slops. Things didn't get any better as you went through dingy streets looking into cheap hotels and restaurants. This was followed by a remark about women in a room talking about Michelangelo. Then there was a fog, and mumbo jumbo, highbrow talk about preparing a face "to meet the faces that you meet." It was confusing and to some readers it was pretentious; Eliot was obviously pulling the public's leg, like the fellow in France who painted people with two noses.

If they had been readers of French poetry they would not have been surprised. They would have met with references to hospitals and street scenes in the poetry of Baudelaire. In Laforgue they would have found the tone of self-deprecation, the hesitations and withdrawals, the pondering over motives, Prufrock's inability to speak out, his feeling—it almost amounts to a faith—that life is a dead end.

Prufrock says, "I am Lazarus, come from the dead." [48] Hugh Kenner remarks: "Eliot's unvarying dramatic method is to set loose, in a drawing room full of masks, some Lazarus." [49] What Lazarus knows is death. How Eliot came at an early age by the knowledge of the fear of death is anyone's guess, but he had this knowledge and it gave him authority. The knowledge of fear, and his capacity for transferring it by means of an image to the reader's senses, enabled him to move immediately to the front of living poets.

The other thing Prufrock knows is that we cannot tell each other exactly what we mean. Each of us is enclosed by his experience of the world. At best we see only bits of other people, the mere externals, and the words that consciousness prepares may be the least revealing aspect of ourselves. We see a pair of arms "braceleted and white and bare/ (But in the lamplight downed with light brown hair!)." [50] The arms are not attached to a person. Someone asks us a question, and we try to think of an answer—but in order to know what the question meant we would have to be the person who asked it, and any answer we gave would be misunderstood. When we walk through a street we see men as shirt sleeves smoking pipes. The word surrealism has not yet been invented, but there is an air of surrealism in this poetry: the deserted street winds into the emptiness of a dream; the man truncated by the window is like a man by Magritte standing in a reverie. Magritte likes to put a lion in a room, and so does Eliot: the evening enters and stretches out like a cat beside Prufrock.

If we wish to explain what is meant by "modern poetry" we have to reckon with the idea of intensity. Ever since Poe declared that poetry must be short and intense, that in effect there could be no such thing as a long poem, a certain kind of poet—we must be on guard against trying to include everyone in these generalities—has been putting a premium on intensity. The aim is to excite or astonish the reader. Ezra Pound elevates this intention into a rule: "Incompetence will show in the use of too many words." The object is "to charge language with meaning to the utmost possible degree . . ." This is done by "throwing the object (fixed or moving) on to the visual imagination," and "inducing emotional correlations by the sound and rhythm of the speech." [51] It is well that he mentions rhythm and sound, for this description of intensity would lead the reader to think that it is to be arrived at by means of visual images alone. But there may be images that evoke rhythms or sounds.

"Prufrock" is especially rich in visual images. Prufrock's behavior is concentrated by the bald spot in the middle of his hair, his tie-pin, his possible trouser cuffs. His life, as everyone knows, is measured out with coffee spoons. His cogitating is pinned to the wall like a moth or butterfly. His profoundest self is hidden beneath the sill of consciousness; it is seen from the side of the boat as

> a pair of ragged claws
> Scuttling across the floors of silent seas.[52]

Eliot carried this crab a long way from Gloucester where he saw it, to deposit it in just the right place. But was this the right place? Was his decision to put the crab in right or wrong?

He was to say later,

> I pray that I may forget
> These matters that with myself I too much discuss
> Too much explain.[53]

This is read as a statement about Eliot's struggle to believe, and it is so by the context. We are inclined to think that the most important thing in a poet's life is what he believes, or else we look for an Irish nurse. The poet is likely to do so himself. But the most important thing may be his wanting to set things right, to put them exactly where they belong in order to finish a poem.

9

"The horror! the horror!"

IN September 1911 Eliot returned to Harvard with a malacca cane and a Gauguin "Crucifixion" which he hung up in his room.[1] He registered for courses leading to the PhD in philosophy. He was appointed a teaching assistant, he participated in the seminars of Josiah Royce, and in time he became president of the Philosophy Club. Moreover, he undertook Oriental studies. "Two years," he says, "spent in the study of Sanskrit under Charles Lanman, and a year in the mazes of Patanjali's metaphysics under the guidance of James Woods" left him "in a state of enlightened mystification." [2]

He took boxing lessons, Conrad Aiken recalls, from "an ex-pugilist with some such monicker as Steve O'Donnell," [3] and for three years he wrote no poetry.

In the summer of 1913 Eliot bought a copy of F. H. Bradley's *Appearance and Reality*. He had probably read Bradley before this; in any case, he now began reading Bradley with a view to writing a dissertation on his ideas. Thus Eliot yielded to the third influence on his life and thought. First Laforgue, then Babbitt, then Bradley. But it would be an error to think that reading Bradley brought Eliot anything really new; he found in Bradley the confirmation of ideas he already had. Perhaps not so much his ideas as his intuitions. Though Eliot wrote no poetry in these years, he was reinforcing his feelings as a poet.

Bradley is not easy to understand, and it is not reassuring to be told by critics that his ideas cannot be paraphrased.[4] It appears that reading Bradley demonstrates what Bradley argues: the total enclosing reality of immediate experience. As with Flaubert or Henry James, Bradley's style is his meaning.

Eliot knew that every man was imprisoned in the world of his own experience. He had written poetry on this theme. In Bradley he found a reasoned explanation of what he had discovered through temperament and intuition.[5] Bradley argued that the mind could not be separated from what the mind perceived. Bradley does not speak of a subjective self, but of moments of experience—composed of subject and object together—which he calls "finite centers." External sensations are as private to the mind as its own thoughts and feelings. "In either case my experience falls within my own circle, a circle closed on the outside; and, with all its elements alike, every sphere is opaque to the others which surround it . . . In brief, regarded as an existence which appears in a soul, the whole world for each is peculiar and private to that soul." [6]

This passage by Bradley, which appears as a footnote to *The Waste Land,* states a theme that appears repeatedly in Eliot's verse. We have seen it in "Prufrock." It is implied by the woman's complaint in *The Waste Land:* "I never know what you are thinking." [7] It is chanted by Sweeney:

> I gotta use words when I talk to you
> But if you understand or if you dont
> That's nothing to me and nothing to you [8]

Eliot is still discussing it in *Four Quartets:*

> Trying to learn to use words, and every attempt
> Is a wholly new start, and a different kind of failure [9]

The inability of the mind to detach itself from what it perceives —the immersion of the self in experience, so that the self may be said not to exist at all, instead there is a continuum—this view of life continued to haunt Eliot. In psychoanalytic terms, there is no ego boundary. The mind is continually being bombarded by sensations and unable to withdraw. In fact, there is no mind, no thinking, only an illusion of mind and thought. The self is lost in the immensities of infinite space that terrified Pascal. No form of belief is possible, for in order to believe one must believe in something separate from oneself. But there is nothing separate from oneself.

"In feeling the subject and object are one," Eliot states in his thesis on Bradley. As long as he could feel no separation between his mind and his sensations he would be the poet of despair the world thought he was. (Eliot denies that in *The Waste Land* he expressed his own disillusionment.[10] He wishes to seem impersonal. But there is nothing impersonal about his poetry; to the contrary, we are conscious of his drawing on personal experience. The statements that artists make about their intentions are not to be taken as final; as Eliot says, a poet when he is a critic argues for positions he needs for his immediate work, and he is likely to change his opinions.)

As long as Eliot agreed with Bradley that each mind is imprisoned by experience, like Prufrock he would not be able to have a clear idea about anything. "The particular has no language." [11] He would not be able to take hold of life, for if there is no "I" that feels itself separated from a "You," there is no affective life. In theological terms, for a man to know himself he must have a feeling of separation from God, a sense of sin. In order to have any kind of happiness, man must feel that he has fallen from absolute happiness. But if there is no feeling of separation, if there is only one indistinguishable mass of existence, the perceiving mind being one with its sensations, in the world and of the world, there is only a purgatory of sensations.

The mind in Eliot's poems was a sensitized surface that reacted convulsively to sensations.

> His soul stretched tight across the skies
> That fade behind a city block,
> Or trampled by insistent feet . . .[12]

It was this almost painful sensitivity, expressing itself in images, that caught and fixed the reader's attention.

When Bertrand Russell visited Harvard, Eliot attended some of his seminars. Russell did not notice Eliot until he made an unexpected remark: they had been discussing Heraclitus, and Eliot said that Heraclitus reminded him of Villon. The comparison of the philosopher of fire and the poet who wrote of passion stayed in Russell's mind and led to their later friendship. In exchange, Eliot would portray Russell as "Mr. Apollinax."

> In the palace of Mrs. Phlaccus, at Professor Channing-Cheetah's
> He laughed like an irresponsible foetus.[13]

(Eliot has a gift for making up names: "Professor Channing-Cheetah" seems just right for an old Boston family with some Hispanic aberration. Like most of Eliot's inventions in this line, it is unforgettable.)

In 1914 Eliot was awarded a Frederick Sheldon traveling fellowship. He was to go to Marburg in Germany and attend lectures by Rudolf Eucken.

He had been in Marburg only a fortnight when war broke out. He proceeded to London—instead of studying at Marburg he would study at Oxford. In the meantime he found lodgings near Russell Square.

On September 22 Eliot met Pound. He had read Pound's *Personae* and *Exultations* when he was an undergraduate. The poems did not excite him at the time—nor, for that matter, was he excited by the poems of Yeats—he was "too much engrossed in working out the implications of Laforgue." But he did consider Pound's to be "the only interesting poems by a contemporary." [14]

Pound immediately recognized Eliot's talent and did everything he could to push him forward. At the same time he enlarged Eliot's mind. "Mr. Eliot was lifted out of his lunar alleyways and fin de siècle nocturnes, into a massive region of verbal creation in contact with that astonishing didactic intelligence, that is all. 'Gerontion' (1920) is a close relative of Prufrock, certain matters filtered through an aged mask in both cases, but 'Gerontion' technically is 'school of Ezra.' " [15] This is the estimate of Wyndham Lewis, who was on the spot. Grover Smith says that "Eliot has seldom imitated Pound." [16] This may be true, but in his use of history in "Gerontion" and elsewhere, in his use of myth, in the increased range of his ideas, Eliot owes much to the example of Pound's wide-ranging, uninhibited, less coherent mind.

There are signs of Pound's manner in the poems Eliot wrote after their meeting: "Morning at the Window," "Aunt Helen," "Cousin Nancy," and "Mr. Apollinax." "The poems," says Grover Smith, "contain an element missing from those of the Laforguian period—a kind of levity like Pound's own in such poems as 'The Bath Tub' and 'Phyllidula.' And the device of bathos, exemplified also in the opening lines of 'Prufrock,' is typical of Pound's work in *Lustra*." [17] In Eliot's "The Death of Saint Narcissus" the protagonist imagines a series of metamorphoses, one of these being metamorphosis into a tree, reminiscent of Pound's poem "The Tree" in *A Lume Spento*. "Saint Narcissus" was submitted by Eliot to *Poetry* in 1915, then withdrawn. It was the germ of more important work: the opening line, "Come under the shadow of this gray rock," [18] slightly altered, would find its way into *The Waste Land*. The words, "He could not live men's ways, but became a dancer before God," [19] pointed the direction of his life and thought.

Eliot was admitted to Merton College, at Oxford, in the middle of October. This was F. H. Bradley's college, and Eliot's supervisor, Harold Joachim, was a Bradleyan.

At Merton he met E. R. Dodds, who introduced him to a poetry-reading group, the Coterie. At one of their meetings he read "The Love Song of J. Alfred Prufrock," and the members are said to have been impressed. He met Aldous Huxley and I. W. Earp, who later became art critic on the *New Statesman*. Neither then nor later would Eliot have any difficulty meeting people. He was, says Wyndham Lewis, "A sleek, tall, attractive transatlantic apparition—with a sort of Gioconda smile." He was "a Prufrock to whom the mermaids would decidedly have sung, one would have said, at the tops of their voices—a Prufrock who had no need to 'wear the bottom of his trousers rolled' just yet; a Prufrock who would 'dare' all right 'to eat a peach'—provided he was quite sure that he possessed the correct European table-technique for that ticklish operation. For this was a very attractive Prufrock indeed, with an alert and dancing eye—*moqueur* to the marrow, bashfully ironic, blushfully *tacquineur*. But still a Prufrock!" [20]

In the spring of 1915 Eliot was meeting a young woman named Vivien Haigh-Wood. Sacheverell Sitwell says that they first met on the river, that "she was playing a phonograph in a punt alongside his." [21] They saw each other at parties, they went out together, then suddenly they were married. The ceremony was performed by a registrar in Hampstead. Neither the family of the bride nor the groom's family were informed in advance.

Vivien Haigh-Wood was a small, dark, quick-witted girl who liked dancing. She was attractive to men and had had at least one serious affair when Eliot met her.

Why were they married in secret? No one has revealed the answer. To be married in secret, to be confirmed in the Church in secret—such was Eliot's preference, and he can hardly be blamed for it, but when he became a public figure his habit of secrecy led to rumor and speculation. It was said that Vivien Haigh-Wood was a schoolmistress whom he had seduced and felt obliged to marry. She was not, in fact, a schoolmistress, and with her *thé-dansant* temperament it seems doubtful that she would have felt that a man had to marry her just because they had a little bit of harmless fun.

What is certain is that her nerves were bad. They are the most famously bad nerves in literature. She had migraine headaches and internal ailments that the doctors diagnosed as "intestinal catarrh." She had to take drugs for her ailments, but if her brother Maurice is to be believed, she was not addicted, and he seems to have been a truthful man.[22] On the other hand, the stories about her being promiscuous seem to be true. But this is rushing matters. For the time being Vivien is a bride, Eliot is a groom, and they are looking for a way by which he can earn their bread and butter.

In July Eliot traveled to America to see his family. Vivien, pleading fear of submarines, did not accompany him. He spent three weeks in East Gloucester, explaining to his parents why he had married an Englishwoman without asking their advice, why he was not planning to finish his degree at Harvard and become a professor, and why he was thinking of living in England rather than America. He may not have had a clear idea of his intentions when he arrived, but he had when he left. He understood that he could not bring himself to be what his parents wanted him to be. They managed, however, to arrive at a compromise: he would finish his dissertation on Bradley, and his father would continue his small allowance. They parted with hard feelings on both sides; he was proving a terrible disappointment.

Then he returned to England. He never again saw his father.

In September he took a schoolteaching job in the town of High Wycombe for a stipend of £140 and one meal a day. He taught French, mathematics, history, geography, drawing and swimming. Then he got a better job at Highgate Junior School, better because it was in London, in Hampstead, and he was paid £160 plus dinner and tea. So he followed in the steps of Samuel Johnson, to whom he has been compared, driving schoolboys to their tasks. John Betjeman, who was one of the boys, remembers Eliot as "a tall, quiet usher . . . whom we called 'The American Master.' "[23] Betjeman presented a manuscript of his own poems to the master, who returned them without comment.

It was fatiguing work. Wyndham Lewis describes Eliot at about this time, arriving at a dinner engagement, haggard and apparently at his last gasp. He would take his place at the table. Then, having given his face "a dry wash" with his hands, he would draw on some reserve of energy and be "as lively as ever he could be or any one need be." [24]

At this point Bertrand Russell, whom we last saw holding forth at Professor Channing-Cheetah's, returns in the flesh. He undertook to befriend his former pupil and his pupil's rather pretty wife. "In Bertrand Russell," says Kojecky, "the Eliots had both a landlord and a friend. On occasion he arranged a convalescent holiday for Vivien . . ." [25] Indeed he did—he even went so far as to accompany her himself, leaving her husband at home, and got thanked for it in the bargain.

After dining with the Eliots and meeting Vivien for the first time, Russell wrote a letter about them.

> I expected her to be terrible, from his mysteriousness; but she was not so bad. She is light, a little vulgar, adventurous, full of life—an artist I think he said, but I should have thought her an actress. He is exquisite and listless; she says she married him to stimulate him, but finds she can't do it. Obviously he married in order to be stimulated. I think she will soon be tired of him. He is ashamed of his marriage, and very grateful if one is kind to her.[26]

Russell was kind. He made over to Eliot £3,000 worth of debenture stock as a gift. (Eliot later returned the certificates).[27] He invited the Eliots to come and live with him in his small flat, and they accepted. Then he took Vivien with him to Torquay. Russell explains it in these words: "Mrs. Eliot was ill and needed a holiday. Eliot, at first, could not leave London, so I went first with her to Torquay, and Eliot replaced me after a few days." [28]

"Replaced me" is a good phrase. It seems more than likely that Russell seduced Vivien, or vice versa. Her husband, however, seems not to have been aware of it. He was wonderfully naive, or else he was wonderfully complacent. We find him writing to Russell:

> Dear Bertie, This is wonderfully kind of you; really the last straw, so to speak, of generosity. I am very sorry you have to come back, and Vivienne says you have been an angel to her . . . I am sure you have done everything possible, and handled her in the very best way; better than I. I often wonder how things would have turned out but for you. I believe we shall owe her life to you, even.[29]

Later on, Russell analyzed the Eliots' marriage and Vivien's character. He said that he had been fond of them both and had tried to help them in their troubles until he discovered that "their troubles were what they enjoyed." He noted Vivien Eliot's impulses to be cruel to her husband, "not with simple but with Dostoievskian cruelty." And he said, "She is a person who lives on a knife edge, and will end as a criminal or a saint—I don't know which yet. She has a perfect capacity for both." [30]

She was to end as neither. She ended as a nuisance and a burden. But during the early years of their marriage she had spells of vivacity and she taught her husband to fox-trot. But she saw nothing wrong with going dancing with someone else—for instance, three Canadian flyers who picked her up.

We are told that Eliot treated her with tenderness: once when they were in a chemist's shop, to buy some aspirin, she undertook to demonstrate a ballet step. "She held on to the counter with one hand, rose on her toes and held out the other hand which Tom took in his right hand, watching Vivienne's feet with ardent interest while he supported her with real tenderness . . . most husbands would have said, 'Not here, for Heaven's sake!' " [31]

As Richard Ellmann has said, 1914–15 was the pivotal year for Eliot: he decided to give up philosophy for poetry, to marry, and to stay in England.[32]

Having moved from Oxford, the academic atmosphere proving uncongenial, and settled in London, he saw much of Pound, who was then organizing the Imagist movement. He met Pound's associates: F. S. Flint, Richard Aldington and his wife H. D., Ford Madox Hueffer, Violet Hunt, Wyndham Lewis, and the sculptor Gaudier-Brzeska. At this time Pound had a way of dividing the world into sheep and goats, saying of someone who was not an Imagist or Vorticist, "Il n'est pas dong le mouvmong." Eliot wanted very much to be "dong le mouvmong."

He was not, however, an Imagist in the narrow sense of the word—a maker of bric-a-brac. Hugh Kenner says that Eliot's "Preludes" are not Imagist poems for in Imagism the natural object was always the adequate symbol, while in "Preludes" the natural object "implies an ache, a yearning after significance." [33] In other words, Eliot was not an Imagist but a Symbolist. Marion Montgomery seems to agree when he says that in Eliot's poetry there is "a flight from particular things in which Hulme expected the poet to find beauty. There is an uneasiness in Eliot's personae as they find themselves in the presence of 'the thousand sordid images' of which their souls are constituted." [34] Grover Smith limits Eliot's actual involvement in the Imagist movement to the summer of 1915, when he submitted "The Death of Saint Narcissus" to *Poetry* in Chicago. He speaks of Eliot's "brief flirtation" with Imagism.[35]

While it is true that Eliot's images are symbolist in their power to suggest a further meaning, it is an exaggeration to deny the influence of the Imagist movement upon his work. More and more we are coming to see that Imagism, though it may have been short-lived as a movement, continued to influence writers after the movement ceased. Imagism was replaced by theories more complicated than the idea that "the natural object is always the adequate symbol," nevertheless, the emphasis given to this principle continued to be felt. There are passages in Pound and Eliot's later writing that owe a great deal to Hulme and Ford, their insistence upon "objective" images and the sound of living speech. Unfortunately, Pound and Eliot were capable of forgetting Imagist principles altogether and writing in a language that would have made Ford roll on the floor.

Eliot began publishing his poems in 1915. "Prufrock" appeared in *Poetry* in June. Pound had a hard time persuading Harriet Monroe to take it: she preferred Vachel Lindsay, whose "The Chinese Nightingale" that year received *Poetry*'s first prize— "Prufrock" came second. In July, Eliot published "Rhapsody on a Windy Night" in *Blast*, Wyndham Lewis's Vorticist magazine. In September, Pound placed the "Portrait of a Lady" in Alfred Kreymborg's *Others*. In October, three more poems by Eliot appeared in *Poetry,* and five came out in Pound's *Catholic Anthology.*

He was beginning to get a name; in the meantime he had to make a living. He augmented his schoolmaster's salary by giving lectures in French and English literature, first for the Oxford University Extramural Department, then for London University and the London County Council. He prepared and delivered some sixty-five lectures. The twelve-page descriptive syllabus of the course in "Modern French Literature" that Eliot gave at Oxford is preserved at Harvard in the Houghton Library. It shows the heavy influence of Babbitt and predicts Eliot's attitudes during the next decade. The emphasis is not on imaginative literature but on political, religious and philosophical works in prose.

"Nineteenth century tendencies" are traced back to Rousseau, Babbitt's *bête noire*. Rousseau struggled against authority in religion and aristocracy and privilege in government. He exalted personal feelings over the typical; he stressed feeling rather than thought. Rousseau was for humanitarianism—belief in the fundamental goodness of human nature. He deprecated form in art and glorified spontaneity. He was egotistical and insincere.[36]

"Romanticism," Eliot said, "stands for *excess* in any direction. It splits up into two directions: escape from the world of fact, and devotion to brute fact. The two great currents of the nineteenth century—vague emotionality and the apotheosis of science (realism) alike spring from Rousseau." [37]

Sometimes during these lectures Eliot would read Hulme's poem, "The Embankment," in which a "fallen gentleman"—a former Romantic—forswears the sound of fiddles and the ecstasy he used to seek.[38] Now he sees that "warmth's the very stuff of poetry." He wishes to wrap the sky around him like a blanket and be comfortable. In Classicism there is comfort, in Romanticism, pneumonia—a point of view contrary to the popular view of these matters.

On evenings when he was not lecturing, and on weekends, Eliot did literary work—he wrote book reviews. At first, as he had been trained as a philosopher, he confined himself to reviewing books about philosophy, religion or ethics. For the *International Journal of Ethics* and the *New Statesman* he reviewed books with titles such as *Theism and Humanism, Social Adaptation, The Ultimate Belief,* and *Philosophy and War.* Between 1916 and 1918 he contributed some twenty reviews.

By April 1916 he had finished the thesis on Bradley. It was sent to Harvard and Josiah Royce pronounced it very good. But the boat on which Eliot had booked passage to the States did not sail, so he did not appear for his *viva voce* examination and was not awarded the degree. His parents were disappointed—Charlotte Eliot wrote to Bertrand Russell that she had "absolute faith in his Philosophy but not in the vers libres."

In 1917 he gave up schoolteaching and relied on what he could earn by reviewing. It was a desperate move; he must have hated teaching. Then he obtained a position in the Foreign and Colonial Department of Lloyd's Bank in Queen Henrietta Street. This is one of the dramatic surprises in Eliot's managing of his career; just when we think we are able to understand him, he eludes our

grasp and assumes a new role. From Grub Street to banking . . .
and banking in earnest, no nonsense about it. He took his duties
seriously, so that his literary friends, who were mystified, would
twit him with it. Virginia Woolf suggested that he might rise to
be branch manager. Eliot did not deny it, he merely smiled.

In June, through the efforts of Pound and John Quinn, he was
appointed assistant editor of *The Egoist,* succeeding Richard
Aldington. *The Egoist* was "an individualist review" edited by
Harriet Shaw Weaver. The title was conceived by Dora Marsden:
the egoist was the moral opposite of the slave; the egoist was "the
free man or woman, unamenable to pressures directing him towards what he ought to be, but fully alive to what he is, and
ready to take responsibility for what he does and thinks." The
image of the egoist appealed to Harriet Weaver. Whitman's *Leaves
of Grass*—"I celebrate myself, I sing myself"—was one of her
favorite books.[39] This seems unlikely company for the author
of the lectures against Rousseau, but Eliot may have felt that he
would be able to hold the job without being understood for the
anti-individualist that he was. On the literary side *The Egoist*
had already been brought by Aldington into the Imagist camp.

It was through Pound that Eliot obtained his position on *The
Egoist,* and through Pound that he came to know John Quinn,
who became, on a small scale, Eliot's patron. Either Pound or John
Quinn contributed £5 and later another £7 toward Eliot's salary
on *The Egoist.* John Quinn arranged the American publication
of Eliot's 1920 *Poems* and, in 1921, *The Sacred Wood.* In 1922 he
arranged the publication of *The Waste Land* on terms advantageous for the author.

Eliot has acknowledged Pound's efforts on his behalf and praised
him as an impresario, a friend to struggling writers. Pound's efforts
on behalf of Eliot were untiring. In 1916 he took him to the first
performance of Yeats's play, *At the Hawk's Well,* in Lady Cunard's
drawing room in Cavendish Square. The time was to come when
Eliot would be considered welcome in these drawing rooms while
Pound himself was excluded.

Eliot gained more from Pound than an entry into literary circles. He gained from Pound's ideas: his recommendation of the
poems of Arnaut Daniel and the criticism of Remy de Gourmont,
his advice to read Gautier. Eliot gained from the example of
Pound's diligence. Years later he said that Pound's great contribution to the work of other poets had been "his insistence upon the

immensity of *conscious* labour to be performed by the poet." [40]

Pound understood the differences between Eliot and himself. It was his ability to see differences that made him helpful—he did not attempt to shape others in his image. When Eliot brought Pound some pages of headstrong criticism in which he laid about him right and left, Pound said, "That's not your style at all. You let *me* throw the bricks through the front window. You go in at the back door and take out the swag." [41] And this was, in fact, what came to pass. Pound insulted people, and when he started harping on Social Credit he was regarded as a crank, so that finally editors did not want to see his work. Eliot, on the other hand, expressed his ideas in reasonable prose; if there was anything revolutionary about the content it was disguised by the suavity of the saying. Eliot offended no one who was important to his career, and in time came to be regarded as the most influential of critics.

Hugh Kenner says that in his essays for the London *Times* Eliot was parodying the style of the usual reviewers, that it was parody when he wrote: "The existing monuments form an ideal order among themselves, which is modified by the introduction of the new (the really new) work of art among them." [42] This, says Kenner, is a "charmingly comic sentence." But Kenner's view is too ingenious—writers are never as Machiavellian as in the provinces they are supposed to be. Eliot at times wrote pompously because he was capable of being pompous, especially when holding forth on matters such as tradition.

His work at Lloyd's was exhausting. In 1917 Vivien Eliot told Pound that her husband had not done any work on poetry for weeks; he came home from the bank exhausted and fell asleep until bedtime. When the war came to an end he was made responsible for unraveling debts and claims of the bank in connection with the peace treaties. He worked in a room underground, the heels of pedestrians tapping on the glass skylight overhead. He may have felt that he was learning something about history. "History has many cunning passages, contrived corridors . . ." [43] In any case, he had a head for figures, and banking was less harmful to the muse than being, God save the mark, a professor. When I. A. Richards offered to put his name up for a lecturer at Cambridge, he declined the gambit.

The war unhinged everybody. Europe has never recovered from the four years' bloodletting on the Western Front. This still remains the Great War; a generation grew to middle age under its

shadow. If they themselves had not seen lines of men rising out
of trenches and walking forward into shellfire, machine-gun bullets
and barbed wire, they had heard about it from their brothers,
certain photographs were indelibly printed on their consciousness.
With the war came a loss of confidence in government, God, and
culture. It became perfectly acceptable to say that you did not
give a damn about culture, since it had led to all that.

Eliot was one of "the men of 1914," though he came no closer
to the trenches than Torquay. He was well suited, by his constitu-
tion, to express the general sense of malaise and disillusionment.
Another generation might have found his messages unacceptable,
but at this time the prophet of doom and the audience were in
accord. Eliot was a doubting man. He was like Henry Adams in
his own description of that worthy: "Wherever this man stepped,
the ground did not simply give way, it flew into particles." [44] There
is another observation so unexpected that it has the air of having
been drawn from the writer's experience and hastily applied: what
kept Adams "intelligent and uneducated" was "an incapacity for
sensuous experience." Eliot adds: "It is possible that men ripen
best through experiences which are at once sensuous and intellectual." [45]

Something was certainly missing in the sensuous quality of
Eliot's marriage. Vivien's haste to commit adultery may have
wounded him in his self-esteem. It has been suggested that he was
"psychically impotent." In any case, the marriage was a misfortune.
Richard Ellmann says, "In the Grail legends which underlie *The
Waste Land*, the Fisher King suffers a Dolorous Stroke that maims
him sexually. In Eliot's case the Dolorous Stroke had been marriage." [46]

Marriage, however, was not the cause of Eliot's troubles. His
sad views existed in embryo long before he met Vivien. She had
not formed his heart. With another woman he might have had
a happier view of marriage. The author of unwisdom in *The
Cocktail Party*, who says of life, "The best of a bad job is all any
of us make of it," [47] might have been replaced by a less severe
critic—as when Eliot married for the second time he was. But the
dissatisfactions, the nervous intensity, the anguish, were constitutional, and they were the source of the kind of poetry he wrote.
He chose Vivien because she was necessary to his grief.

There is an air of mystery about Eliot. Though he is the most
"personal" of poets—the images in his poems are like the content

of dreams—he prefers to speak in an assumed voice. His life, also, was concealed by a variety of roles. He was the bank clerk, punctiliously garbed with bowler and umbrella; the pontificating critic; the editor at Faber. He disappeared behind the door of his church. The cause of these evasions appears to have been psychological—he speaks of "an aboulie and emotional derangement which has been a lifelong affliction. Nothing wrong with my mind. . . ." [48] "Aboulie" means "morbid absence of will." The world came rushing in and he could not meet it head on.

His "aboulie," however, was favorable to the production of art. "Absence of will" put him in a receptive frame of mind so that he could receive impressions. Art, like sex, is a field in which the battle is not always to the strong: it is the one whose "nerves are exposed" who is the strong man of the arts. He must also, of course, have the ability to select what he needs and shape it into a work of art. Mere receptivity is not enough.

It has been said, even by friendly critics, that Eliot is not a universal poet. One commentator says that "he lacks a ready power of empathy, of self-projection into the points of view of others." [49] But he had plenty of empathy for certain types—a Prufrock, a Madame de Tornquist "in the dark room/ Shifting the candles." [50] And though people like to think of art as all-embracing, and point to a Tolstoy as evidence that it can be, art that represents an unusual condition may have a powerful effect.

Avant-garde art always seems "narrow," and it is often called "morbid." The paintings of the Post-Impressionists, for example, that now seem idyllic, were at first called "pathological." The paintings of Manet, Van Gogh, Matisse, Bonnard, Vuillard, Signac, Vlaminck, Derain and Rouault struck one spectator as "the works of idleness and impotent stupidity, a pornographic show." [51] A critic declared, "The emotions of these painters (one of whom, Van Gogh, was a lunatic) are of no interest except to the student of pathology and the specialist in abnormality." [52] It may be that any extension of imagination, as it has first to destroy the old order, strikes people as "morbid." In time, however, they may see that it is the symptom of a larger health. At any rate, the public does not seem to mind a certain amount of morbidity. Once they have got past the barriers set up by the guardians of the old, they flock to the new. Time after time, the artist who is true to his own view of experience turns out to be speaking for others.

Eliot's "aboulie" was not peculiar to him. "In the absence of a spontaneous, natural, creative relationship with the world which is free from anxiety, the 'inner self' thus develops an overall sense of inner impoverishment, which is expressed in complaints of the emptiness, deadness, coldness, dryness, impotence, desolation, worthlessness, of the inner life." [53] This description of schizophrenia by R. D. Laing is like a description of the people in *The Waste Land*. Eliot understood the sickness of Western civilization at the time of the Great War, and of certain aspects of that civilization at all times.

His diagnosis was not that of the doctors—he perceived it as a spiritual sickness. Michael Goldman has said, "We might do well to consider whether Eliot's vision does not suggest . . . that schizophrenia is a spiritual as well as a mental disorder." What to the medical practitioner was a matter of "nerves" or "insanity" Eliot saw as a matter of evil.[54] Dante had said, "In His will is our peace"—to Eliot, "morbid absence of will" was unwillingness to be with God. The feeling of "an aboulie" was like damnation. "The schizoid individual," says Laing, "exists under the black sun, the evil eye, of his own scrutiny. The glare of his awareness kills his spontaneity, his freshness; it destroys all joy." [55] It was this condition that Eliot perceived as a spiritual crisis and expressed in images that haunted a generation.

He said that he disliked the word "generation." He was supposed to have expressed the "disillusionment of a generation," but this was nonsense. He might have expressed for some people "their own illusion of being disillusioned," but that did not form part of his intention.[56] The disclaimer, like Eliot's insistence on "impersonality," has little to do with the effect his poetry has on readers. Still, there is a point: Eliot's poems usually describe a spiritual crisis; but the author, to borrow a phrase from F. Scott Fitzgerald, did not become identified with the objects of his horror or compassion.[57] The writing was overcoming the horror.

Many writers have described a psychological or spiritual struggle, but Eliot describes it with peculiar intensity. For Eliot a feeling of despair was symptomatic of the struggle for salvation. Men live more intensely when they come to grips with their deep feelings —even with despair—these are the "intimations of immortality" they have longed for. The cause may not be pleasurable, but it makes for gladness in the writing. It is the emotion with which

Eliot perceived the desolate condition of the world around him that makes his descriptions unforgettable. Eliot's poems have an emotional intensity unmatched in English when they describe states of fear and anxiety. For equivalents we must go to the French of Baudelaire, the Italian of Dante.

In his long essay on Dante, Eliot says that "poetry not only must be found *through* suffering but can find its materials only *in* suffering." [58] During these years, with the assistance of his wife, he was gathering the materials. We are told that Vivien was given to making derogatory remarks; she would find a bad motive for everything people said or did, her husband not excepted. There were those who found her charming. As a hostess, says Mrs. Patmore, who was married to Richard Aldington, Vivien was "endearing, quiet, attentive to her guests without fuss and a very intelligent listener." [59] But this state did not last. When she was in one of her moods it was exhausting to talk to her: she would meet the simplest remark with a nervous intensity: "Why did you say that? What do you mean?"

> 'What are you thinking of? What thinking? What?
> 'I never know what you are thinking. Think.' [60]

In January 1919 Eliot's father died, still believing that his son had turned out badly. This, too, gave Eliot grief for his writing.

> On a winter evening round behind the gashouse
> Musing upon the king my brother's wreck
> And on the king my father's death before him . . .[61]

No one who met the affable, if somewhat fatigued, young man who appeared on weekends would have suspected the depth and complexity of his mental processes. Eliot attended tea parties at the Sitwells' in Bayswater. He accepted weekend invitations to Garsington, Lady Ottoline Morrell's house near Oxford. No description of the period would, as they say, be complete without a mention of Lady Ottoline Morrell. Aldous Huxley's *Crome Yellow* is a comic, Peacockian *roman à clef* of life at Garsington, with Bertrand Russell, who had been Lady Ottoline's lover, wandering through the scenes, together with other "personages" who were once well known. Lady Ottoline inspires a few satiric lines by Pound in *Mauberley,* and D. H. Lawrence, too, writes about her in *Women in Love,* as "Hermione Roddice." Invariably those she patronized repaid her with the coin that is tendered in such cases: ridicule. It seems she had taste enough to attract writers and artists to her country house, but not enough intelligence to appreciate them. But perhaps it is never possible to appreciate such people as they think they deserve.

On weekends forty or fifty undergraduates, including Aldous Huxley, would come over from Oxford and Lady Ottoline's weekend guests would encounter the horde at a party that went on all day. Virginia Woolf presided over the literary conversations. E. M. Forster was there, "a quiet little chap," said Wyndham Lewis, "of whom no one could be jealous, so he hit it off with the 'bloomsburyites,'" and was appointed male opposite number to Virginia Woolf." [62]

There is a photograph of Virginia Woolf with Eliot and Vivien.[63] Virginia Woolf is standing between them; she looks gaunt and leathery; she has manifestly appropriated Eliot, who gazes with a smile into the camera. To Virginia's left, separated by a definite gap, stands Vivien, toes together, head slightly lowered, eyes very dark in the shadow of her hat. She looks like a sulky child with two grown-ups. It is only fair to say that in another photograph taken at Garsington, of Vivien by herself sitting on a bench, holding an open parasol and looking off to the right, she has a cute figure and piquant face, like a soubrette.[64]

Having met with the approval of Virginia, Eliot began to frequent those houses in Bloomsbury over which she ruled with an iron hand, and Bloomsbury was the center of avant-garde, literary London. Then, with the publication of *Prufrock and Other Observations,* Eliot made his mark. Only five hundred copies were printed by the Egoist Press, but the number was not important, what mattered was the quality of the audience. At a weekend at Garsington, Clive Bell handed out copies and Katherine Mansfield read "Prufrock" aloud. Clive Bell was the husband of Virginia Woolf's sister, Vanessa. The intelligent American with his charm and keen sense of humor, so unexpected in an American, had arrived.

10
Mug's Game

"Poetry is not a career, but a mug's game."
T. S. Eliot

ELIOT posts a warning: "I believe that the critical writings of poets . . . owe a great deal of their interest to the fact that the poet, at the back of his mind, if not as his ostensible purpose, is always trying to defend the kind of poetry he is writing, or to formulate the kind that he wants to write." [1] In this view, Eliot's literary criticism was the by-product of his "private poetry-workshop." [2] Nevertheless, his sentences were memorized and codified. In the course of an essay on Ben Jonson, or Dante, or the style of the sermons of Lancelot Andrewes, Eliot would make remarks on the nature of art, and these were joined by his readers to make a philosophy. Eliot disclaimed the intention of being a scholar or the leader of a school of criticism,[3] but he did not disclaim the results. To see the famous critic denying any intention of being taken so seriously leaves an impression not of modesty but pride. What might he not have done if he had made the effort!

Eliot began writing literary criticism for *The Egoist,* which he helped to edit, *The Athenaeum,* of which Middleton Murry was editor, and the *Times.* He met Murry at Garsington; Murry wanted him to come and work with him on *The Athenaeum,* but Eliot preferred the security of the bank. He was introduced by Aldington to Bruce Richmond, editor of *The Times Literary Supplement.* "After about six months of cautious work," says Aldington, "I finally talked Richmond into agreeing to have lunch with Eliot." Eliot turned up in strange guise—a beard that he had grown while on a trip to Switzerland, and a Derby hat. In spite of this, Eliot and Richmond hit it off. "In five minutes he had completely captivated Richmond, as he can captivate any intelligent person." [4]

So it was that Eliot's unfailing charm prepared a way for his career. His first contribution, an essay on Ben Jonson, appeared in the *Times* on November 13, 1919. In the following essays that he wrote for the *Times* he concentrated on Elizabethan and Jacobean drama.

It is worth looking at the essay on Ben Jonson. It begins: "The reputation of Jonson has been of the most deadly kind that can be compelled upon the memory of a great poet." [5] The sentence might have been written by the other Johnson, Samuel. "Compelled upon" has an archaic ring and therefore the sound of authority. Eliot proceeds: "To be universally accepted; to be damned by the praise that quenches all desire to read the book; to be afflicted by the imputation of the virtues which excite the least pleasure; and to be read only by historians and antiquaries— this is the most perfect conspiracy of approval." The sentences are dramatic. In reading Eliot's criticism of men who have been dead these hundreds of years, one feels that one is witnessing a drama the ending of which is still uncertain. This accounts for the popularity of his writing and answers the puzzlement of those who have not been able to account for Eliot's reputation as a critic on such slight grounds. His criticism, like his poetry, is extraordinarily interesting because it is dramatic. Moreover, as with a drama where we do not take what the characters say as expressing the mind of the dramatist, in Eliot's criticism we are to understand that he is speaking for the living body of his creative work, in that time and place, not as a philosopher.

Eliot began as a critic with a Symbolist bias, arguing that the work of art must be criticized apart from moral considerations. He blamed Matthew Arnold for having succumbed to the "almost irresistible temptation . . . to put literature into the corner until he cleaned up the whole country first." [6] Upon this attitude was built the New Criticism, which concentrated attention upon the text, its structure, style, and meaning, independent of the author's intention or the circumstances surrounding its creation. "When we are considering poetry we must consider it primarily as poetry and not another thing." [7] By the time, however, that this way of reading was fairly established among centers of learning, Eliot had moved to a position that amounted to a reversal. In 1928, in the preface he wrote for the new edition of *The Sacred Wood,* he reminded the reader that "a poem, in some sense, has its own life . . . its parts form something quite different from a body of neatly ordered biographical data . . . the feeling, or emotion, or vision, resulting from the poem is something different from the feeling or emotion or vision in the mind of the poet." But he added, "On the other hand, poetry as certainly has something to do with morals, and with religion, and even with politics perhaps, though we cannot say what." [8] In the same year, in an essay on Julien Benda's *The Treason of the Intellectuals,* Eliot said, "You cannot lay down any hard and fast rule of what interests the *clerc,* the intellectual, should or should not have. All you can have is a standard of intellect, reason, and critical ability which is applicable to the whole of a writer's work." [9] The work draws upon the writer's attitudes toward politics or religion or culture; criticism therefore must deal with these matters. The reversal coincides with Eliot's conversion to Anglo-Catholicism and his proselytizing—a change that lost him readers who did not share his views.

A selection of the essays, made with the care that goes into selecting poems for a book, was published on 4 November 1920. *The Sacred Wood* established Eliot as a critic; it is still the best introduction to his critical thinking, and for sheer readability he never surpassed it. *The Sacred Wood* has a quality lacking in Eliot's later criticism: high spirits. He is having fun, making provocative remarks, giving the reader something more, or something less, than he bargained for.

"Poetry is a superior amusement." [10]

"When one creative mind is better than another, the reason often is that the better is the more critical." [11]

The sayings have not grown weak with time—today they are just as provoking. Now that romantic attitudes are again fashionable, many poets would feel compelled to disagree. Poetry is not an amusement, it is in dead earnest, and to be able to think as a critic is not to be a poet at all. Such are the current shibboleths.

"Some one said: 'The dead writers are remote from us because we *know* so much more than they did.' Precisely, and they are that which we know." [12]

There is Eliot's notorious saying . . . "Poetry is not a turning loose of emotion, but an escape from emotion; it is not the expression of personality, but an escape from personality. But, of course, only those who have personality and emotions know what it means to want to escape from these things." [13]

On this and other remarks was founded the legend of Eliot's "impersonality." But, as some readers have pointed out, there is nothing "impersonal" about his writing.

Only at times in *The Sacred Wood* do we come across the pompous, pontificating voice that will be common in Eliot's later writing. "Mr. More has, it seems to me, in this sentence just failed to put his finger on the right seriousness of great literary art; the seriousness which we find in Villon's *Testament* and which is conspicuously absent from *In Memoriam;* or the seriousness which controls *Amos Barton* and not *The Mill on the Floss.*" [14] The snobbishness of this would be hard to beat. It must have been intimidating when it first appeared in the *Times,* whose average readers were not given to reading *Amos Barton* or to scholarship of any kind. Looked at now, however, the remark is ridiculous and the author is a prig—a prig who created others, complete with umbrellas, rising out of these essays in a cloud and descending on universities everywhere. They are still with us, writing their uninspired prose. When Eliot speaks of being "serious" a remark such as the one said to have been made about Alfred De Vigny seems to be called for: *"Ces Vigny m'emmerdent avec leur dignité."*

The best known of Eliot's *sententiae* occurs in the essay on "Hamlet and His Problems." This is the description of the "objective correlative." Mario Praz says that the phrase was first mentioned by Washington Allston in 1850, in *Lectures on Art.*[15] A closer source is Pound's description, in 1918, of the origin of myth. It seems that it was Pound who stated the idea, but Eliot who brought it to the attention of the public and was given the credit. According to Pound, a man would have some "very vivid and undeniable adventure"—for instance, he "turned into a tree." But when he told someone about it he was called a liar. So he made a myth instead, "a work of art that is—an impersonal or objective story made out of his own emotion . . ." [16]

Eliot says, "The only way of expressing emotion in the form of art is by finding an 'objective correlative'; in other words a set of objects, a situation, a chain of events which shall be the formula of that particular emotion; such that when the external facts, which must terminate in sensory experience, are given, the emotion is immediately evoked." [17] In other words, the artist embodies his feelings in his work so that when the work is understood, so are his feelings. Is there anything original about this idea? Doesn't "work of art," or the word "fiction," or "poem," imply that a thing has been made? And for what purpose was it made but to convey the maker's feelings? Is Eliot, with a deal of pomp and circumstance, merely saying what everyone knows? Merely adding a bit of jargon to the pedant's store? Eliot has been accused more than once of using pretentious language in order to say little or nothing. Aldous Huxley called Eliot's criticism "a great operation that is never performed; powerful lights are brought into focus, anaesthetists and assistants are posted, the instruments are prepared. Finally the surgeon arrives and opens his bag—but closes it again and goes off." [18]

There is a way of saying something, however, that is as good as saying it for the first time. The description of the "objective correlative" was one of the places where Eliot moved poetry in his time, and prose too, in a new direction. It was a reminder of the need to embody thought in dramatic action or speech, or in a narrative, or in images. At the same time it was an admonishment against using art as "self-expression." The intention was to restore to art some of the communal properties it had had in the age of Shakespeare, or in Dante's Italy. As we have seen, Pound preceded Eliot in this road, but Pound's voice was not heard while Eliot's in *The Egoist, The Athenaeum, The Times Literary Supplement,* and later *The Criterion,* influenced a widening circle.

Eliot disclaims his influence: "I fail to see any critical movement which can be said to derive from myself, though I hope that as an editor I gave the New Criticism, or some of it, encouragement and an exercise ground in *The Criterion.*" [19] But in fact his influence was overwhelming. Robert M. Adams speaks of his generation's having accepted Eliot "wholesale . . . not only 'Prufrock' and *The Sacred Wood,* but an attitude toward the entire European past, a modification of its 'pastness,' and a spirit of inquiry that seemed to us life-giving." [20] Edmund Wilson, a man of Eliot's generation and one who was not impressed by the mere appearance of authority, says that "Eliot's opinions, so cool and even casual in appearance, yet sped with the force of so intense a seriousness and weighted with so wide a learning, have struck oftener and sunk deeper in the minds of the postwar generation of both England and the United States than those of any other critic." [21]

What was it they found so appealing? The attitude toward the past that Robert Adams speaks of, and the "life-giving" spirit of inquiry . . . these were surely a large part of Eliot's attraction as a critic. The qualities are exhibited, for example, in his essay on "Tradition and the Individual Talent." As Pound before him, Eliot gives readers the feeling of an ongoing life of art to which they may contribute. It is a more comforting view than the Romantic, which gives the impression that art is born anew with each man and dies with him, so that art has a quality of desperation. Readers don't mind being told that "Tradition . . . cannot be inherited, and if you want it you must obtain it by great labour." [22] Youth has never minded being called to great tasks (it's the small ones they object to). At the same time Eliot's readers may take comfort in the thought that everything does not depend on "genius," the gift so dear to the Romantics. "Talent" is just as good—in fact, it is better, for talent is something you can work with. Genius you either have or you haven't; genius is unreliable to say the least; at any rate it is unclubbable.

Besides, he wrote so well. In the twentieth century, now that we have seen the result of the style of a Churchill, or the lack of style of a Nixon, we can hardly deny that style is a practical force. Eliot's style was the voice of common sense, pointing to the obvious. There were idiosyncracies, too, that lent the writing charm—the way Eliot used the pronoun "we," for example, implying that the reader was among the happy few. Outside in the dark were multitudes who did not understand, wailing and gnashing their teeth.

This idea may be nonsense: "The more perfect the artist, the more completely separate in him will be the man who suffers and the mind which creates." [23] Yet it is well written: it has clarity and a nice balance of phrases, one against the other. When a sentence sounds right, so does the idea.

As I have said, this is dramatic writing. It is suspenseful to see, in the famous paragraph about the two gases, the platinum, and the acid, what is going to happen next. "The mind of the poet is the shred of platinum." [24] Who would have thought it! As the lady says in Proust's novel, "There has been nothing like it since the table-turning."

Note that during this passage the reader has the illusion of assisting at an experiment, and believes that he has been gifted with powers of analysis. As Eliot told him, "A critic must have a very highly developed sense of fact," [25] and "Comparison and analysis . . . are the chief tools of the critic." [26]

The reader knew he was the sort of person Eliot had in mind when he wrote, "There is no method except to be very intelligent." [27]

It is a common error to think that Romanticism searches for new forms of art while classicism clings to the old. The opposite is more likely to be true, for in his need for self-expression the Romantic writer does not wish to study technique, especially the technique of a time or culture other than his own. This was the case in 1920: Romantics clung to the style of Tennyson; classicists such as Pound and Eliot sought for new forms and language in the poetry of the troubadours, in French, Italian and Chinese poetry.

The attitudes in Eliot's poetry are the same as those expressed through his criticism. But as the poetry seems experimental in form, some critics have said that it is contradictory to the spirit of Eliot's criticism: the poetry, they say, is Romantic, the criticism traditional. They point to the "personal" feelings in the poetry as opposed to the "impersonality" recommended by Eliot in his essays.[28] This point of view is based on a misconception of the nature of classical art. From *Oedipus Rex* to the present, classical art has dealt with "personal" situations. It is not the subject of a work of art that determines whether it is "classic" or "Romantic," but the treatment of the subject. Eliot's poetry is full of personal feelings; the treatment, however, is not at all Romantic.

He is perfectly acidulous in the poems written from 1917 to 1919. He has been repelled by "Amygism," the spate of inchoate, post-Imagist free verse. Ezra Pound in reaction wrote rhymed quatrains in the manner of Gautier; the result was *Mauberley*. At Pound's instigation Eliot did the same and the result was "The Hippopotamus," the Sweeney poems, and "Whispers of Immortality." Eliot's critics have different views of the value of this writing. Grover Smith, who is usually calm as he goes about explaining the references in Eliot's poems and the meaning of his symbols, becomes positively offended with the poems of this period. They are "nothing for Eliot to be proud of . . . the skeleton in his poetic cupboard." [29] (It is difficult to think of them as a skeleton in a cupboard, however, for they have frequently been reprinted.) Smith says that the poems are precious, "an exhibition of functional plagiarism, a triumph of mystification." On the other hand, Elizabeth Drew says that Eliot's poetry "has taken on an enriched vigour and expansion." [30]

Besides lines from Gautier there are traces of Corbière (*Mélange Adultère de Tout*) and Rimbaud, and "Whispers of Immortality" owes as much to Eliot's reading of Marvell and Donne as it does to Gautier. But there is no end to listing the influences upon Eliot. He wrote with consciousness of a tradition—he would have said that it was the only way to write. Sometimes his poetry is inspired by a wish to update or correct literature of the past, and some of his best poetry, *The Waste Land* for example, is as much a criticism of literature as it is of life.[31] Accordingly he would imitate, borrow, and, to use his own word, steal from other poets. "Immature poets imitate; mature poets steal; bad poets deface what they take, and good poets make it into something better, or at least something different." [32] (This, like other sayings by Eliot, is an echo of Pound. In a letter to William Carlos Williams in 1908 Pound said, "It is only good manners if you repeat a few other men to at least do it better or more briefly. Utter originality is of course out of the question.") [33]

When Eliot began to publish there were critics who thought that when they showed that he had taken a line from another poet they had triumphed over him. (When the poems became famous they were not so sure, but still they were annoyed.) These critics did not share Eliot's and Pound's view that traditionally literature is a communal art. In fact, they were not acquainted with the idea, and if they had been they would have rejected it. Critics who were offended by Eliot's use of quotations were confirmed Romantics: in their view it was every man for himself. They put a very high price upon individualism. They were the property owners and capitalists of literature.

Eliot's "Whispers of Immortality" contains whispers by no fewer than three poets: Gautier, Webster and Donne, with perhaps D. H. Lawrence making a fourth.[34] The poem by Gautier, "Carmen," from which Eliot borrows two lines, pays homage to sensuality. This is an approximate translation of the ending of Gautier's poem:

> In her attractive ugliness
> There's salt, the fresh astringency
> Of Venus in her nakedness
> Leaping out of the bitter sea.

But Eliot treats sensuality with ridicule:

> Uncorseted, her friendly bust
> Gives promise of pneumatic bliss.[35]

and with disgust:

> The sleek Brazilian jaguar
> Does not in its arboreal gloom
> Distil so rank a feline smell
> As Grishkin in a drawing-room.[36]

These are among the lines readers cite when they wish to prove that Eliot is disgusted with sex. There are other places: "In *Lune de Miel*," says Rossell Hope Robbins, "there is no response to the decent joy and freshness of young married love; all that the disgusted Eliot can see are sweaty legs covered with flea-bites." [37] It is true that readers will look in vain for the decent joys of sexual intercourse in Eliot's writings, and now that something about his first marriage has been revealed people are attributing his disgust with sex to the frustrations of his private life. The argument from circumstance is stronger if we turn to the 1920 edition of Eliot's poems, *Ara Vos Prec,* and read the "Ode" he later suppressed.

> When the bridegroom smoothed his hair
> There was blood upon the bed.[38]

But Eliot's marriage was not the fundamental reason for his writing about sex the way he did. Another man might have found another woman. Eliot brought his disaffection with him; it was necessary to the development of his poetry. He had a feeling of emptiness and desolation, he was cut off from other people. At the same time he was moving toward the kind of religion best suited to his temperament. There are other, wider kinds—Eliot's religion, however, was the kind in which sexual intercourse is a bar to salvation.

"Whispers of Immortality" shows the close connection between Eliot's poetry and the ideas expressed in his criticism.

> Donne, I suppose, was such another
> Who found no substitute for sense . . .[39]

This anticipates by three years his essay, "The Metaphysical Poets," where he speaks of the "mechanism of sensibility" in the poets of the seventeenth century, which could "devour any kind of experience." [40]

> To seize and clutch and penetrate;
> Expert beyond experience.[41]

In the essay he says, "A thought to Donne was an experience; it modified his sensibility." He argues that the thinking of the seventeenth-century poet was one with his sense perceptions. At a later time, the age of Milton and Dryden, a "dissociation of sensibility" set in, a split between thought and sense perception. Consequently the language of poetry became vague and meaningless. (In terms of the craft, poets no longer wrote in images and their language lost its bite.) These observations lead Eliot to describe the poetic temperament; the mind he is describing is his own. "When a poet's mind is perfectly equipped for its work, it is constantly amalgamating disparate experience; the ordinary man's experience is chaotic, irregular, fragmentary. The latter falls in love, or reads Spinoza, and these two experiences have nothing to do with each other; or with the noise of the typewriter or the smell of cooking; in the mind of the poet these experiences are always forming new wholes." [42] The poet's mind is an associating sensibility in which thought and sensory experience are immediately related.

In the Sweeney poems Eliot projects a character as unlike himself as possible. He told Nevill Coghill that he thought of Sweeney as "a man who in younger days was perhaps a professional pugilist, mildly successful; who then grew older and retired to keep a pub." [43] Eliot does not throw himself into the character as Pound might have done—he looks at Sweeney from outside—but there is some envy mixed with his descriptions of Sweeney's hairy body, the low dives he frequents, his vulgarity. The fascination Eliot brought to his reading of novels about French prostitutes is exhibited in his poems about Sweeney in a tavern and a brothel.[44]

Eliot's anti-Semitism emerges in "Burbank with a Baedeker: Bleistein with a Cigar."

> The rats are underneath the piles.
> The Jew is underneath the lot.[45]

"The question whether 'Burbank with a Baedeker' was anti-Semitic," says Grover Smith, "is obviously not a pressing one." [46]

Not pressing for Grover Smith, but conceivably pressing for Jews: one Jew in whose house Eliot was staying as a guest happened to read this poem—she then asked him to leave.[47] In later years Eliot denied that he was an anti-Semite and seemed not to understand why people thought him one. "It is a terrible slander on a man," he told William Turner Levy. "And they do not know, as you and I do, that in the eyes of the Church, to be anti-Semitic is a sin." [48] Nevertheless, it is not uncommon among Christians. Those who fail to see anti-Semitism in Eliot's writings—as with Pound, some of Eliot's admirers are wonderfully unobservant on this point—must themselves live where anti-Semitism is so much a part of the normal order of things as to be taken for granted. There are enough anti-Semitic remarks in Eliot to place him among those who in the nineteen-twenties and -thirties encouraged anti-Semitism and made it possible for Jew baiters to thrive.

Pound was outspoken, Eliot more discreet. In "The Hippopotamus" he poked fund at the lukewarm faith of the Established Church; in "A Cooking Egg" he satirized Sir Alfred Mond, the founder of Imperial Chemical Industries, and in *"Le Directeur"* he mocked "the conservative director of the *Spectator*." But these were safe targets. Eliot's satire was intended to amuse, not change society. The poems of the 1917 to 1919 period, like Lytton Strachey's debunking portraits of "eminent Victorians," assured the reader of his own superiority. One might have predicted that the author would be a writer of clever satiric verse, more intelligent than most but no more important. One would have been wrong.

11

Margate Sands

HE had a long poem in mind.[1] But he had to set his lands in order . . . clearing up debts between Lloyd's Bank and the Germans. He had to put *The Sacred Wood* together and see it through the press. He had to find a less noisy place to live. He could not get any work done or ever rest.[2] And when the Eliots did move to Clarence Gate Gardens it was too expensive. In the spring of 1921 he complained to John Quinn of the lack of *"continuous time,"* not getting more than a few hours together for himself, which broke the concentration required for turning out a poem of any length.[3]

He had, however, managed to produce a number of lines. And there were pieces he had written at one time and another that might be fitted in. For instance:

> Full fathom five your Bleistein lies
> Under the flatfish and the squids.
> Graves' Disease in a dead jew's eyes!
>   When the crabs have eat the lids.
>   Lower than the wharf rats dive
>   Though he suffer a sea-change
>   Still expensive rich and strange
>
> That is lace that was his nose
>   See upon his back he lies
> (Bones peep through the ragged toes) . . .[4]

But he reconsidered and put Bleistein to one side. The tone was wrong—too many people, as it was, thought of him as a wit or satirist.[5] But the tone he had in mind was deeper than satire.

> . . . I will show you something different from either
> Your shadow at morning striding behind you
> Or your shadow at evening riding to meet you;
> I will show you fear in a handful of dust.[6]

Still, the theme of drowning was important . . . in some way associated with his father.

> Full fathom five thy father lies;
> Of his bones are coral made . . .[7]

Henry Ware Eliot had loved the sea. He owed his father a memorial. So he kept the lines about Bleistein at the back of the manuscript.

He pushed pieces around. Sometimes there was the glimpse of a scene. Sometimes it was as though he were in a room where people were speaking. If he could only make out the words . . . Things kept coming back. What the charwoman had told Vivien, about a conversation with her friend . . . "You ought to be ashamed, I said, to look so antique." [8]

He was in the Starnbergersee at Marburg with the Lithuanian girl. She had fair hair coiled in braids above her forehead. She said she was "echt deutsch," a real German, and laughed, showing white teeth.

He was reading a book titled *My Life,* by Countess Marie Larisch, when a line leaped out of it:

> And when we were children, staying at the arch-duke's,
> My cousin's . . .[9]

Sometimes a vista would open and he felt the long movement of the poem, like a swell at sea. It came from a long way off, bringing toward him the odors of an unknown life, rank and exotic. Then the movement ceased. There was not a breath of air. Only the blank sheet of paper. When he looked at anything he had written it was just scribbling . . . a heap of fragments.

In August of 1920 Vivien thought he needed a holiday, so he went off with Wyndham Lewis. Their destination was Quiberon Bay, but on the way they stopped in Paris to see James Joyce. Eliot and Joyce had never met.

Pound had given Eliot a parcel wrapped in brown paper to

deliver to Joyce. Eliot discharged himself formally of the commission. When the parcel was opened it revealed a pair of old
brown shoes and some clothes that Pound, out of the kindness of
his heart, had collected for the indigent Irish novelist. The scene
ended with Joyce's telling his son that he would not be home for
dinner, and handing him the shoes. They exchanged words—like
"a couple of neapolitan touts," says Wyndham Lewis—and the
son rushed off "with the shoes beneath his arm, his face crimson
and his eyes blazing with a truly southern ferocity."

Joyce was proud; he set out to remove the impression made by
Pound's gift of an old pair of shoes. The whole time Eliot and
Lewis were in Paris, he insisted on paying for their meals and
drinks. He treated Eliot with cool politeness; he seemed not to be
aware that he was a poet. Eliot thought him arrogant. "I should be
better pleased," he said grimly, "if he were less polite." [10]

Nevertheless, Eliot read *Ulysses* in manuscript. In November
1923, reviewing *Ulysses* in *The Dial*, he said that Joyce had discovered in "the continuous parallel between contemporaneity and
antiquity" a way of shaping the "futility and anarchy" of modern
life. "Instead of narrative method, we may now use the mythical
method. It is, I seriously believe, a step forward making the
modern world possible for art." [11]

There were other influences. Conrad Aiken says that "in the
winter of 1921–22" he would meet Eliot for lunch twice a week,
and Eliot always had with him a pocket edition of Dante.[12]
(Aiken's dating is wrong—it must have been in summer, for that
winter Eliot was not in London.) Dante's *Commedia* was very
much on Eliot's mind as he prepared his own. There are echoes of
Dante in *The Waste Land,* as in other of Eliot's works: "I had not
thought death had undone so many." [13] He was also conscious of
Baudelaire as he wrote. Baudelaire knew about "morbid absence
of will"—he had called it Ennui. "You! hypocrite lecteur!—mon
semblable—mon frère!" [14] Baudelaire was the poet, *par excellence,*
of the city of the dead.

One night Eliot went with his brother to hear a performance
of Stravinsky's *Le Sacre du Printemps.* "At the end of the performance Tom stood up and cheered." Sencourt makes the comment that "Stravinsky was providing what Joyce provided in
prose," and defines it as "the sordid." [15] Eliot was cheering for
modernity, however sordid it might be.

Life, too, is an "influence." Walking late at night and seeing two rats jump down from a pile of garbage outside a restaurant and disappear through an opening in the gutter . . . The happiness of an evening at the music halls of which he was so fond . . . Not to mention Vivien's sitting at her dressing table, combing her long black hair out tight and fiddling whisper music on those strings. . . .

Eliot told Conrad Aiken that "although every evening he went home to his flat hoping that he could start writing again, and with every confidence that the material was *there* and waiting, night after night, the hope proved illusory: the sharpened pencil lay unused by the untouched sheet of paper." Aiken mentioned this to a friend who was being analyzed by Homer Lane, and Lane said, "Tell your friend Aiken to tell *his* friend Eliot that all that's stopping him is his fear of putting anything down that is short of perfection. He thinks he's God." When Aiken relayed the message to Eliot he was "literally speechless with rage," both at Aiken and Homer Lane. "The *intrusion,* quite simply, was one that was intolerable." But Aiken was convinced that "it did the trick, it broke the log-jam." A month or two later Eliot went to Switzerland, and there wrote *The Waste Land.*[16]

But, in fact, *The Waste Land* wasn't written in Switzerland—it had been in the making for years. Aiken himself says that when he saw the finished poem he recognized passages such as the one beginning "A woman drew her long black hair out tight," which he had known before as "poems, or part poems, in themselves."[17]

In September Eliot was in poor health and Vivien arranged for him to see a specialist. The advice he received was to go away at once for three months "quite alone, and away from anyone." He was not to exert his mind at all, and "follow . . . strict rules for every hour of the day." The prospect, Eliot wrote Richard Aldington, filled him with dread.[18] But he went—Lloyds giving him sick leave with pay—and he chose Margate, the resort town south of the Thames estuary. He did not go alone, however—Vivien went with him. "I could not bear the idea of starting this treatment quite alone in a strange place," he wrote to Aldington. "I have asked my wife to come with me and stay with me as long as she is willing."[19]

From Margate he wrote to Julian Huxley saying that he was doubtful of the "specialist's" ability to understand his case. ". . . he is known as a nerve man and I want rather a specialist in psychological troubles." Ottoline Morrell had advised him to go to Vittoz in Lausanne, and had told him that Huxley had been to see Vittoz.[20] Huxley replied favorably and Eliot thanked him. English doctors, he said, seemed to specialize "either in nerves or insanity." [21] He wrote to Richard Aldington about his change of plan. "I am satisfied," he said, "since being here, that my 'nerves' are a very mild affair, due not to overwork but to an aboulie and emotional derangement which has been a lifelong affliction. Nothing wrong with my mind. . . ." [22]

On 12 November he left Margate. He stayed in London for a few days, then crossed with Vivien to Paris. He left her there and proceeded to Lausanne. "The great thing I am trying to learn," he wrote his brother, "is how to use all my energy without waste, to be *calm* when there is nothing to be gained by worry, and to concentrate without effort." He said that he was much better and not miserable—there were people in Lausanne of many nationalities, which he always liked—and he was "well enough to be working on a poem." [23]

Eliot finished his drafts of *The Waste Land* in Lausanne. When he went to Margate he had with him typed drafts of Parts I and II, and most of Part III, to the end of the "episode of the typist." He also had "a bundle of drafts and fragments of unworked-up poems." In Lausanne he wrote the final part, "What the Thunder Said." [24]

In early January 1922 on his way back to London, he stayed for some days with Pound in Paris; and they went through the drafts together. Pound wrote to Quinn: "Eliot came back from his Lausanne specialist looking O.K.; and with a damn good poem (19 pages) in his suitcase; same finished up here." [25] The poem wasn't quite finished, however. When Eliot went back to London he continued making cuts and revisions, and sending manuscript to Pound for his advice. Most of Pound's suggestions were aimed at cutting out passages where Eliot was writing parodies, using a style or rhythm "that was not for him a voice of feeling." [26] For instance, right at the start . . . the fifty-five lines describing some boyos having a night out. Eliot was trying to do for lowlife in verse what Joyce had done in the novel.

> First we had a couple of feelers down at Tom's place,
> There was old Tom, boiled to the eyes, blind,
> (Don't you remember that time after a dance,
> Top hats and all . . .[27]

They went to dinner and a show. "I tried to put my foot in the drum and didn't the girl squeal." They went to "Myrtle's place." "Get me a woman, I said; you're too drunk, she said. . . ." It finished with, "So I got out to see the sunrise, and walked home." Well, the whole passage would have to go. He couldn't keep up the Irish part. And there was no necessity for it, except to point up the theme of pleasure-seeking and failure, and there was plenty of that elsewhere. Besides, the lines were too descriptive—what Pound called work "of the second intensity."

"April is the cruellest month" was the right beginning.

> April is the cruellest month, breeding
> Lilacs out of the dead land, mixing
> Memory and desire . . .[28]

Chaucer had started his pilgrims off in April.

> Whan that Aprille with his shoures soote
> The droghte of March hath perced to the roote . . .[29]

A number of lines written in imitation of Pope would have to be omitted. You couldn't parody Pope unless you could do the same thing better. Besides, *The Waste Land* shouldn't read like a sixth-former's joke. So out came Fresca:

> The white-armed Fresca blinks, and yawns, and gapes,
> Aroused from dreams of love and pleasant rapes.[30]

Also the fishing expedition. Tennyson? That had to come out.

Eliot wanted to know what Pound thought of printing "Geron-tion," his poem about the "little old man," as "a prelude in book or pamphlet form."[31] Pound advised against it. "To be more lucid still, let me say that I advise you NOT to print 'Gerontion' as a prelude."[32]

He already had a point of view with Tiresias. The old man would be confusing. Besides, "Gerontion" was an idea complete in itself. It would mislead the reader into thinking that this was what *The Waste Land* was about. The poem would be stopped before it was fairly started.

Eliot was humble and grateful, inclined to put himself entirely in Ezra's hands. Since the fishing expedition had been omitted, should he omit Phlebas also?[33] This was overdoing the humility, and Pound wrote in alarm, "I DO advise keeping Phlebas. In fact I more'n advise. Phlebas is an integral part of the poem; the card pack introduces him, the drowned phoen. sailor. And he is needed

ABsolootly where he is. Must stay in." Then Eliot got a grip on himself and took Pound's best advice: "Do as you like about my obstetric effort." [34] He rejected some suggestions, especially those that had to do with changing the sound of words and lines. There were wavelengths on which T. S. Eliot and Ezra Pound did not hear alike. Pound thought that in the line, "Filled all the desert with inviolable voice," the word "inviolable" should be omitted.[35] Eliot decided it should stay.

In the last part, written in Lausanne, the poem gathered and spoke with a sure voice:

> After the torchlight red on sweaty faces
> After the frosty silence in the gardens

Above it Pound wrote, "OK from here on *I think*." [36]

Pieces fell into place; mistakes were crossed out once and for all—for example, lines where the "young man carbuncular," having made love to the typist, paused in the yard "to urinate, and spit." Pound wrote against this, "probably over the mark." [37]

Vivien contributed to the revision. She enthused over the part beginning, "Do you know nothing? Do you see nothing?" "Wonderful," she wrote beside it, "& wonderful." [38] The more the poem had to do with Tom and herself, the better she liked it. But she wanted a line left out: "The ivory men make company between us." [39] Something too personal . . . known to Tom and herself.

She had an ear for Cockney voices, a better ear than his. In the pub scene where the women were talking about Albert and Lil, and Lil's friend was reporting what she had said to her, Vivien wrote in the margin, "If you don't like it you can get on with it." [40]

Pound's editing of *The Waste Land* is famous. "There is, I think," says Helen Gardner, "no other example in literature of a poet submitting his work for criticism to another poet of equal stature and accepting radical criticism." [41] The world of scholars and the world of poets are far apart: what strikes Gardner as unique is a perfectly ordinary occurrence among poets.

Some think that to admit Pound's help is to diminish Eliot's achievement. But it is a lot easier to make improvements on a poem than to write it. The real work was feeling. It was anxiety and desolation. What Eliot says of Pascal seems to have been true of himself: ". . . he was at the time when he received his illumination from God in extremely poor health; but it is a commonplace that some forms of illness are extremely favorable, not only to religious illumination, but to artistic and literary composition. A piece of writing meditated, apparently without progress, for months or years, may suddenly take shape and word; and in this state long passages may be produced which require little or no retouch."

He was referring to "What the Thunder Said," the part that had come all at once. He had nothing to say for the cultivation of "automatic writing" as a model for the writer; he doubted if these moments could be cultivated; but "he to whom this happens assuredly has the sensation of being a vehicle rather than a maker." [42]

Eliot and Pound knew who had done the work, and Eliot did not feel that to admit Pound's help would cost him anything. To the contrary, he wanted the manuscript preserved as evidence of the difference Pound's editing made.[43] Eliot's admirers, however, are not so charitable. (Nor are Pound's. There is a quarrel between the camps as to who shall have the spoils.) Sencourt was one of those who had little good to say of Pound or his editing. He said, "Whether Pound's judgement was competent I would strongly question." [44] He thought it was hard to find an "ordered sequence" between the sections of the poem when Pound was through with it. And T. S. Matthews thinks that the heroic couplets in the manner of Pope might have been left in. "They are not as good as Pope, but they are better than most such imitations." [45]

The aim of Pound's editing, as with everything he did, was to remove the second-rate. As for the absence of an "ordered sequence," this was not Pound's doing but Eliot's. In any case, most readers, once they have got past the initial strangeness, are able to understand *The Waste Land.* Many have found it fascinating, and this is partly due to there not being an "ordered sequence." The thoughts in the poems arise as they do in life. We feel that we are experiencing life, not listening to a description. We live the poetry before we feel a need to understand it.

The Waste Land is composed of different voices. They merge in the mind of an observer—one consciousness, like the fog in "Prufrock," that floats into all the corners. Let this be called Tiresias. (When an idea is in the air, it takes root in different places: Apollinaire's *The Breasts of Tiresias* had recently been performed in Paris. It caused a sensation.) "Just as the one-eyed merchant, seller of currants, melts into the Phoenician Sailor, and the latter is not wholly distinct from Ferdinand Prince of Naples, so all the women are one woman, and the two sexes meet in Tiresias. What Tiresias sees, in fact, is the substance of the poem." [46]

Tiresias is remarkably like Jung's Collective Unconscious.

> If it were possible to personify the unconscious, we might call it a collective human being combining the characteristics of both sexes, transcending youth and age, birth and death, and, from having at his command a human experience of one or two million years, almost immortal. If such a being existed, he would be exalted above all temporal change; the present would mean neither more nor less to him than any year in the hundredth century before Christ; he would be a dreamer of age-old dreams and, owing to his immeasurable experience, he would be an incomparable prognosticator. He would have lived countless times over the life of the individual, of the family, tribe and people, and he would possess the living sense of the rhythm of growth, flowering and decay.[47]

The vision of Tiresias ranges from London to the Nile delta. It opens on the plains of Russia where, in 1922, in the wake of the Revolution, "hooded hordes" are "swarming/ Over endless plains, stumbling in cracked earth." [48]

It ranges through time. But *The Waste Land* does not imply, as some have thought, that the past was glorious in comparison with a sordid present. Eliot is no Miniver Cheevy longing for "the days of old/ When swords were bright and steeds were prancing." [49] The flirting of a queen, Elizabeth, for a political advantage, was as sterile as fornication in a brothel. There have always been lives that were "rattled by the rat's foot only." [50]

Another way to misread the poem is to read it as mythology. Eliot himself sent readers hurrying off—with his remarks about "mythical method" and his footnotes—on a scent which, if not false, goes all around Robin Hood's barn. He induced them to put second things first. Perhaps this was deliberate—he was covering up, and there were some revelatory lines in the poem which, on second thought, he wished to disguise. In places the writing was almost confessional.

> *Datta:* what have we given?
> My friend, blood shaking my heart
> The awful daring of a moment's surrender [51]

He hastened to cover his tracks. It wasn't hard—scholars are easily lured. They went off on the track of the Grail legend, vegetation rituals and fertility rites, and mystery cults.

Not that these aren't in the poem—obviously they are. But they are not what the poetry is about. *The Waste Land* is about sexual and spiritual incapacity in the midst of "a cauldron of unholy loves." It is about the necessity for regeneration, and directives are given as to how this may be achieved: "Give, sympathize, control." *The Waste Land* is a purgatory, not the final hell some readers have taken it to be.

Robert Langbaum states that the vegetation myths are used by Eliot to diagnose modern sexual failure—they are better than Christianity for this purpose because the myths make clear that "sex and religion spring from the same impulse." [52]

But Langbaum assigns priorities: "*The Waste Land* is about sexual failure as a sign of spiritual failure." Jungians would agree: spirit is first, sex second. Jung says, "The spiritual appears in the psyche . . . as a drive, indeed as a true passion. It is no derivative of another drive, but the indispensable formative power in the world of drives." [53] Freudians, on the other hand, put sex first, spirit second; in their view *The Waste Land* would be a poem about spiritual failure as a symptom of sexual failure. But it may not be necessary to separate sex and spirit—in fact, it may be impossible. The wish to explain leads us to separate matter and spirit, but in experience and in works of art they are inseparable.

Sexual and spiritual incapacity is dramatized in the "Game of Chess" section of the poem. The woman brushes her hair so that it spreads in fiery points. The man cannot respond to her urgent questioning. All he can say is, "I think we are in rats' alley/ Where the dead men lost their bones." [54] That is, their erections.

Sex without love is a kind of rape. In *The Waste Land* every incident of sexual intercourse is presented as rape—either actual rape or dry, sterile lust, another kind of rape. In the second section, titled "A Game of Chess," the metamorphosis of Philomel is pictured above the mantel—"by the barbarous king so rudely forced." The Thames "nymphs" who have been abandoned by the "loitering heirs of City directors" bring to mind the Rhine maidens who have been bereft of their gold. The seduction of the "typist home at teatime" by the "young man carbuncular" is loveless. Afterwards she feels nothing and, in the original version, he stops in the yard outside to urinate, so that the acts of sex and urination are equated.[55] In "The Fire Sermon," one by one the voices of women explain how they were seduced and abandoned.

These are symbolic rapes. That is, they are fantasies that spring from a real situation. All these fantasies of rape and forced sex are a means of absolving oneself of guilt—that is, if one is a woman, or if one imagines oneself to be a woman, Tiresias in his female aspect. There is guilt for having had sexual intercourse or for wanting to have it. If intercourse is seen as a rape, then she is absolved of blame. After all, it wasn't her fault.

From the man's point of view—Tiresias in his male aspect— fantasies of rape serve a different purpose. They make it unnecessary for him to have sexual intercourse, provide him with an excuse for not having it. If intercourse is rape, clearly it is better not to take part.

Tiresias knows what it is to feel as a man or as a woman. He feels the sexual inadequacy of both partners. Perhaps it is more accurate to say that he has pleasure as a woman but punishes himself for it with guilt. The legendary Tiresias was asked by Jove to settle an argument he was having with his wife. The question was, who had more pleasure in sexual intercourse, the man or the woman. Jove said the woman, Juno the man. Tiresias would know, for he had lived as both. Tiresias said that Jove was right—the woman had more pleasure. Thereupon Juno made him blind. In recompense Jove gave him power of insight and a long life.

"What Tiresias sees . . . the substance of the poem" is dry, sterile lust. At the top of the social scale there is the grotesque flirting of the Virgin Queen, Elizabeth. At the bottom are the women in the pub discussing Albert, who is coming home from the army, and Albert's wife, who has had an abortion.

What you get married for if you don't want children? [56]

There is no love in these people—their lovemaking is "unholy." It presents itself to the imagination as a rape. Therefore the protagonist, the Fisher King, is impotent, and the land is infertile. To enlarge his theme Eliot refers to rites and rituals, he brings in Dido and Mrs. Porter. He speaks of the drowned or buried god and the Hanged Man. He gives the theme of impotence and sterility a wide, universal application.

But vegetation rituals, or a buried god, are not what the poem is about—it is about a situation that gives rise to fantasies. It was intense feeling that enabled Eliot to visualize the woman in the Perilous Chapel drawing "her long black hair out tight" and fiddling "whisper music on those strings." Around her were "bats with baby faces," the children of guilt. He was able to imagine it because, like Tiresias, he had lived it. "A poet," Eliot says, "may believe that he is expressing only his private experience; his lines may be for him only a means of talking about himself without giving himself away; yet for his readers what he has written may come to be an expression both of their own secret feelings and of the exultation and despair of a generation." [57]

The Waste Land has been so taken. And this was not wrong—we cannot arrive at the universal except by way of the particular: the classically "impersonal" poem must include the "personal." There is a danger, however, in taking *The Waste Land* to be representative of the "feelings of a generation." Eliot complained about this way of reading it: "When I wrote a poem called *The Waste Land* some of the more approving critics said that I had expressed 'the disillusionment of a generation,' which is nonsense. I may have expressed for them their own illusion of being disillusioned, but that did not form part of my intention." [58]

What does this mean? Like other of Eliot's disclaimers it can be misleading. *The Waste Land* does, in fact, express despair and disillusionment, as any reader can see. But it does so only up to a point, then there is a turning toward regeneration. Perhaps this was what Eliot meant: or perhaps he was only speaking, to use his description of Harry in *The Family Reunion,* like a prig.[59] At times Eliot could be awfully superior.

There is an end to the despair and an end to the impotence. The images for this are explicitly sexual.

> Only a cock stood on the rooftree
> Co co rico co co rico
> In a flash of lightning. Then a damp gust
> Bringing rain [60]

One critic has said that the tragedy of *The Waste Land* is that the rain does not come. One wonders what text she had been reading. And there are others who still read the poem as an expression of despair. But the thunder says: "*Datta:* give. *Dayadhvam:* sympathize. *Damyata:* control." A clearer set of directives it would be hard to imagine.

The one who says "I" in the poem, the connector—"I can connect nothing with nothing"—has not himself arrived at the point of being able to give, sympathize and control, but he knows what has to be done. In the meantime he will set his life in order. And he will speak like Hieronymo in fits and starts, pretending to be mad, so that his enemies won't smell him out and destroy him before his plans are ripe. He has not yet come to the point of taking action, but he knows the way. The land is still unregenerate, but we are on the road to Emmaus.

"The poem turns out more positive than we used to think it." [61] Indeed it does. We are reminded by Margolis that as early as 1927 Eliot was taking issue with I. A. Richards' assertion that in *The Waste Land* he had achieved "a complete separation between poetry and belief." Eliot said that the doubt and uncertainty so evident in the poem were "merely a variety of belief." He acknowledged that it would not inevitably be orthodox Christian belief, but "I cannot see," said Eliot, "that poetry can ever be separated from something which I should call belief." [62]

Elizabeth Drew finds a Jungian pattern in all Eliot's work, a progression from "psychic sterility" to faith. "The central experience which informs most of the poetry of Eliot is this same age-old pattern of symbolic death and birth, lived through as an intense personal experience and accepted as the central truth of a religious faith." [63] There are symbols occurring in dreams that represent the progress of the psyche. Jung says, "If the conscious will is collaborating with the revelations contained in the dream symbols, there is an apparently purposive sequence of images creating the gradual shift from the ego as the centre of being, to a different centre." The sequence is as follows: going down into darkness, to the water; journeying under the sea or a lake, or in the belly of a beast, or in the guise of a Fisher King; meeting with the Shadow, "the inner realities of a man's own unconscious," which may be transposed into monsters, dragons, and ordeals. It means, Drew says, "a repudiation of the old practical guides of the ego, and the allowing of the ego to be object not subject; the experience of 'not doing.'" [64]

But in Eliot's case there has been no ego, or very little ego, to start with. In the Bradleyan view of things, to which he subscribed, there is no separation of subject and object—no ego. How then is there to be a shift from the ego?

It is not possible to set forth on the Quest unless one has an identity. "A gentle knight was pricking on the plain"—so starts a famous epic. We know that he is a knight and gentle. It does not start by saying that "a lack of self-awareness could be observed in the vicinity of X." One must begin with one's life. One must have a life in order, as religion recommends, to lose it.

Those, on the other hand, who try to leap directly to Heaven are more likely to land in the Paradise of Fools, or in the Hell of Hypocrites. It would be a mistake to think, from reading a Jungian interpretation, that Eliot had only to step into the "collective unconscious" as into an elevator, and be carried up. He had first to construct, or reconstruct, an ego. He had to separate himself, the subject, from the sensory world, the object. He had to break with the Bradleyan view of the universe.

When he began writing *The Waste Land* he was more worn down than usual. He had come to a dead stop. Usually he defended himself against the intrusion of other people's lives, their insistent questioning, their demands that he respond. But on this occasion, being so worn down, he put up no defense. He surrendered and let them speak. He let the voices have their way and fear express itself in any shape it willed. And he was not annihilated. He had imagined dying, and still he lived. He had a life, it seemed, apart from the voices. In the language of religion he had died and been reborn. In the language of psychoanalysis, he had gone a journey into the unconscious; he had struggled with his fears and brought them to light. As a result, he had strengthened his ego. "Where id was, there shall ego be."

Drew says that "The surrender has been made but it still seems a surrender to death, and the possibility of rebirth is still without substance or outline." [65] This is a curious remark, in view of the signs of regeneration—a damp gust bringing rain; the admission of

> The awful daring of a moment's surrender
> Which an age of prudence can never retract [66]

and the voice of the thunder: "Give, sympathize, control." The thunder would hardly speak these directives unless there were a definite hope.

There are many ways to read *The Waste Land,* almost as many ways as there are critics. Hugh Kenner has explained that before Eliot wrote the poem he had been reading Mark Van Doren's study of Dryden in order to review it. *The Waste Land* takes Dryden's *Annus Mirabilis* for a model; like Dryden's poem it is a commentary on London. In Eliot's time as in Dryden's, London had suffered from a war and a pestilence (after the Great War, the influenza epidemic). In his original version of "The Fire

Sermon" Eliot looked at London through various Augustan modes. "The rest of the poem seems to have been planned around it, guided by the norms and decorums of an Augustan view of history. When the plan faltered and changed, the historical norms changed too." Kenner then proceeds to show resemblances between *The Waste Land* and Virgil's *Aeneid*. In the *Aeneid* the Sybil of Cumae enjoins Aeneas to find the golden bough and perform the rite of burial for his drowned companion; there are resemblances between the Great War and the wars of Rome and Carthage; the woman in the "Game of Chess" resembles Dido. This is one way to read *The Waste Land:* it will cease to be convincing when readers take it to be the only way, which some are sure to do.[67]

New ways continue to be found. But one thing does not change: *The Waste Land* remains a poem of "intense personal experience," the expression of one man's view of the world, things he has seen and heard, his suffering, the rhythms of his utterance. "To me," said Eliot, "it was only the relief of a personal and wholly insignificant grouse against life; it is just a piece of rhythmical grumbling." [68] This is too modest. Eliot had two different ways of explaining himself, both of which are misleading. In one mood he would pontificate, denying that anything he wrote had any connection with his life. He spoke, as it were, with the voice of an institution. In the other mood he expressed bewilderment that anyone could take anything he said to have a deeper meaning than appeared on the surface. Nevertheless, what he expressed frivolously is true: *The Waste Land* is "the relief of a personal . . . grouse against life." It is "rhythmical grumbling" of a high order—it grumbles like thunder.

The Waste Land is a poem of feeling. This is why it has given pleasure to many people and, it seems, will continue to do so. Eliot did not sit down with a copy of Jessie L. Weston's *From Ritual to Romance* and undertake to write a poem about the Grail legend, or with *The Golden Bough* to write about vegetation ceremonies. As he says in a footnote, the symbolism is incidental.[69] He speaks of the drowned god and the Fisher King to give his experience a wider application; these are the limbs of the poem, but the body is his anguish, his struggle to disengage a self from the enclosing sensory world. The self was never strong, and it has been damaged by some sexual experience so that it gives birth to nightmare images. The task within the poem is to construct a new sense of self—to disengage an ego from the sensory world that threatens to overwhelm it. This task the poem achieves in the conclusion. The margin of victory is narrow and the protagonist retires to set his lands in order.

The Waste Land has been criticized for presenting life from too narrow a viewpoint—"Life isn't like that." But the way to the universal is through the particular, and no poetry strikes us more vividly with the force of a personal utterance.

12

Dreamcrossed Twilight

In 1922 Pound thought of raising a subscription for Eliot so that he would be able to give up his job at the bank and devote himself to writing. Pound aimed at thirty donors, each to give ten pounds a year. The scheme, to which he gave the name *Bel Esprit*, was advertised in *The New Age*, and several people were willing to subscribe, including Lady Ottoline Morrell, John Quinn, and Leonard Woolf. But it proved embarrassing to the recipient and he declined.

This year, however, saw the founding of *The Criterion*. Among Eliot's friends were Violet and Sidney Schiff; Sidney Schiff wrote under the pseudonym "Stephen Hudson"—he had translated some of Proust's writing; Violet Schiff had translated Charles-Louis Philippe's *Marie Donadieu*. The Schiffs did a good deal of entertaining at their house in Cambridge Square and at Eastbourne. At the Schiffs' Eliot met Lady Rothermere, wife of the first Viscount Rothermere, who owned *The Daily Mail, The Sunday Dispatch,* and *The Evening News.* This is one version—according to another, Eliot met Lady Rothermere through the efforts of Richard Cobden-Sanderson.[1] In any case, Eliot persuaded Lady Rothermere to put up the money for a literary review, on the understanding that she was to have no control over editorial policy. Eliot was to receive no salary as editor, this being prohibited by his working at Lloyd's—bank employees could accept no other income.

The first issue of *The Criterion* appeared on 15 October 1922.

The leading feature was *The Waste Land,* without the notes. In the following month the poem appeared in the United States, in *The Dial.* It wasn't just an appearance, it was a boom. Scofield Thayer and J. S. Watson, editors of *The Dial,* presented Eliot with the two-thousand-dollar Dial Award for "service to American literature."

Reviewers, however, were not so discerning. In the *New States-man and Nation,* 4 November 1922, there was a notice that "several separate poems entitled *The Waste Land*" had appeared in *The Criterion.* On 20 September 1923 *The Times Literary Supplement* described the poem as "parodying without taste or skill." In America Louis Untermeyer referred to the allusions in the poetry as "weak burlesque." F. L. Lucas, who wrote for the *New Statesman,* deplored the symbolism; Eliot, he said, had "sacrificed his artistic powers on the altar of some fantastic mumbo-jumbo"; he thought that "this unhappy composition should have been left to sink itself." [2] But the effect of a literary work does not depend on what reviewers say, and *The Waste Land* struck readers of poetry like a thunderbolt. They argued over it, the poem was quoted and parodied, people said that it expressed the despair of modern life. In Germany the critic Ernst Robert Curtius said that it expressed the suffering of the German soul in defeat.[3] In America the poet William Carlos Williams took *The Waste Land* almost as a personal affront—he said that Eliot had sent everyone back to the classroom.[4] *The Waste Land* continued to provoke discussion. The poet Hart Crane felt that he had to show up Eliot by writing a big poem about myths and modern life. But unlike *The Waste Land* his poetry would be romantic and optimistic. When *The Bridge* failed he killed himself.

Eliot was a celebrity. Richard Aldington, in *Stepping Heaven-ward,* a thinly disguised account of Eliot's career, says of Eliot, whom he calls Cibber, "Wherever you went in evening dress you were bound to hear people discussing Cibber." [5]

Eliot had two strings to his bow—he was a critic as well as a poet. *The Sacred Wood* had been hailed by Bonamy Dobree as "the most important book of criticism since the *Preface* to *Lyrical Ballads* and *Biographia Literaria.*" [6] Now, as editor of *The Criterion,* Eliot was able to influence, then to command literary taste.

There is something repellent about literature as a career—the gatherings to which influential people are invited, the intriguing, the planning of strategy—and the reputation of Eliot as a poet has suffered for his reputation as a careerist. Today, when literary life is less formal, Eliot's way seems forbidding, certainly nothing to be desired. But his politicking was by no means unusual. It may be the conservative style rather than the thing itself that people find offensive. At the present time the style is to be sincere. In time, however, writers who now seem totally "honest" may turn out to have been literary men after all.

When Conrad Aiken arrived in London he found Eliot "rootedly established, both socially and in the 'politics' (as it were) of literature." Aiken was present on the occasion of a "carefully picked quarrel . . . public, prolonged, and pointless" that exhibited the "evident streak of sadism in the Tsetse's otherwise urbane and kindly character." Aiken calls the incident an example of a "deliberate and Machiavellian practice of power-politics, of reputation-making and reputation-*un*making." [7] There was a feline side to Eliot that came out in his literary and social climbing.

In 1925 he gave up his job at the bank and joined the publishing house of Faber and Gwyer as, in his own words, a "talent scout." According to F. V. Morley, however, it wasn't for his literary acumen that Eliot was hired by Faber. "In 1925," says Morley, "I doubt if any of them saw any particular reason to defer to him in literary matters. What then were his assets? He was a gentleman; he was literate; he was patient; he got on well with difficult people; he had charm; and, he had been in the City. He had good qualifications for a man of business, and it was as a man of business, I suggest, that he was taken on." [8] According to Matthews, Eliot got the job through "the Old Boys' network." "At a weekend at All Souls, Charles Whibley put a word in Geoffrey Faber's ear. Whibley was a cantankerous literary journalist of the old school; Faber a scholarly businessman just starting his own publishing firm. The result of this word-in-ear transformed Eliot's life." [9] Faber offered a much better salary than the six hundred pounds he had been getting at Lloyd's. There was another advantage: he had found a new backer for *The Criterion*. Lady Rothermere had withdrawn her support; she had held up her end of the bargain, but she wanted a magazine with *chic*, not the serious articles Eliot was publishing for a few hundred subscribers.[10] Shortly after Eliot went to work at the publishing firm, Geoffrey Faber took over responsibility for publishing *The Criterion*.

The Eliots were able to rent a house on the edge of Belgravia. Tom and Vivien Eliot and Geoffrey and Enid Faber became good friends; every summer Tom went to stay with the Fabers at their place in Wales.

The work was pleasant. It consisted of reading manuscripts, conferring with authors, and preparing manuscripts for publication. He wrote a number of jacket blurbs. Vivien's nerves, however, were no better. She suffered from insomnia, and this would cause her to be depressed. This caused him to feel depressed in turn.[11]

"In one's prose reflections," says Eliot, "one may be legitimately occupied with ideals, whereas in the writing of verse one can only deal with actuality." [12] In his editing of *The Criterion* and writing for magazines Eliot is the reasoner, the man concerned with ideas of religion and civilization. In the poems, on the other hand, he has been compelled, by a struggle that convulses his being, to express himself. It is the poet we read—understanding the ideas, however, helps us to understand his poems.

He had Aldington for a co-editor on *The Criterion,* but Aldington soon dropped out. From 1922 to 1939, when *The Criterion* ceased, Eliot used its pages to air his views. The magazine was international and cosmopolitan: among the foreign authors published were Marcel Proust, Paul Valéry, Jacques Rivière, Ramon Fernandez, Jacques Maritain, Charles Maurras, Henri Massis, Wilhelm Worringer, Max Scheler, and E. R. Curtius. Contributors met every month in a Soho restaurant and exchanged ideas. From 1923 to 1930 they also met in the Grove pub in Beauchamp Place, near the Victoria and Albert Museum, because Herbert Read worked there. Read brought his Museum friends: among them F. S. Flint, K. de B. Codrington, A. W. Wheen, F. V. Morley, and T. O. Beachcroft.

The word was classicism. *The Criterion* was to be in harmony with the ideas of Babbitt, Maurras, and Hulme. Eliot, as we have seen, referred to Hulme's poetry in his lectures. He discussed Hulme's critical theory. Finally he drew on the theological implications of Hulme's thought. As Margolis suggests, "It may well be that it was in demonstrating the close relationship between classicism (which Eliot for some time now had embraced) and the religious attitude (to which he had not yet passed) that Hulme 'influenced Eliot enormously.' " According to Hulme, man is fallen and lives only on one plane of existence, the organic world. There are other regions "discrete and absolutely discontinuous" from the organic: mathematical and physical science; the world of ethical values. Humanism and Romanticism had confused the three regions—Hulme proposed the religious attitude: "There must be an *absolute* division between each of the three regions, a kind of *chasm*. There must be no continuity, no bridge leading from one to the other." [13]

No sooner, however, have we understood what "classicism" portends than Eliot disclaims it, saying that the antithesis between "classic" and "romantic" was merely "literary politics." [14] This is Eliot being evasive. In fact, the arguments of Hulme and Babbitt affected him profoundly—they justified his longing to be connected to a First Cause. "Order," said Hulme, "is freedom, and freedom is found in institutions." [15] To this Eliot would have said "Amen." It is not necessary to explain away his "classicism": the attitudes underlying his writing, in poetry and prose, are consistent with the principles stated by Hulme and Babbitt— eschewing verbiage, weeding out vanity, transforming the personal into matter of general concern.

In 1923 Eliot engaged with Middleton Murry in a public debate on the question of classicism versus Romanticism. Murry's magazine, *The Adelphi*, was definitely romantic—it was run, said Murry, by "a belief in life." *The Adelphi* was an "assertion of faith . . . that life is important, and that more life should be man's chief endeavour. . . . The endeavour to be true to experience strikes me at this moment as the most precious privilege of all." [16]

It strikes one that Middleton Murry was a sap. If this is Romanticism it is no better than *True Confessions* magazine, and it is easy to understand why Aldous Huxley, who was employed by Murry for a while, used him for a model for the flabby Burlap in *Point Counter Point*. "All our classics," said Murry, "are romantic." Englishmen had inherited no rules—"they must depend upon the inner voice." [17] In this, truly, Murry spoke for England: in spite of Ford Madox Ford's strictures on the English for having no theories about writing, so that they produced novels like puddings; in spite of Pound's insulting editors and reviewers;

in spite of Henry James and Flaubert, the English still believe that there is something ridiculous about taking art seriously enough to theorize about it, and they still trust "the inner voice." "The inner voice," said Eliot, meant "doing as one likes." It was the "eternal message of vanity, fear, and lust." The romantic could not distinguish between fact and fancy, whereas the classic, or adult mind, was thoroughly realist, "without illusions, without day-dreams, without hope, without bitterness, and with an abundant resignation." [18]

In 1924 Eliot published a second volume of essays, *Homage to John Dryden*. And in 1925 he published "The Hollow Men," a poem equal to *The Waste Land*. In the following years he published only a handful of poems. There were reasons: his work at Faber and editing *The Criterion* was exhausting. He wrote more than a hundred essays and reviews for the magazine, and some sixty editorial "Commentaries" besides. In one issue he is reviewing sixteen detective novels, in another six books of popular theology, and on a third occasion two books on the history of the dance.[19] His marriage was depressing. Perhaps for these reasons he published very little poetry until 1930, when *Ash-Wednesday* appeared: there are only the short *Ariel Poems* and "Sweeney Agonistes," the fragment of an "Aristophanic melodrama."

Alexander Pope complained,

> Why am I asked what next shall see the light?
> Heavens! was I born for nothing but to write?

The protest shouldn't be taken too seriously—writers complain loudly enough, Heaven knows, if nobody cares whether they publish or not. Still, there are poets who like to wait until they have something to say, who are not always trying to make a poem out of every idea that comes their way and hurrying it into print. If they do not stop writing altogether they may produce work that is truly innovative because it is the product of necessity, the recurring need to make sense of a world that is always becoming incoherent.

During these years when poetry lay idle he thought about philosophy, culture, and religion. The humanism of Irving Babbitt was inadequate to his needs. "I found no discipline in humanism," he said, looking back from the vantage of 1930, "only a little intellectual discipline from a little study of philosophy."

He became more concerned with society and less concerned with literature for its own sake. In 1928, in a preface to the new edition of *The Sacred Wood*, he explained that he had revised his opinion of the use of criticism. When he wrote the essays the problem had been "the integrity of poetry." "When we are considering poetry we must consider it primarily as poetry and not another thing." Since that time, however, his emphasis has shifted —it is "not so much a change or reversal of opinion, as an expansion and development of interests"—he is now concerned with "the relation of poetry to the spiritual and social life of its time and of other times." [20] The statement in parenthesis shows Eliot's habit of qualifying a position he has taken so as to avoid a charge of inconsistency. The statement that it is not a change of opinion is evasive. For if poetry is now to be considered in its relation to spiritual and social life, it is not being considered "primarily as poetry and not another thing," and Eliot has in fact reversed his opinion.

It has been said that his own situation as an artist compelled him to be engaged [21]—that like Yeats and Pound he moved to the right because he believed that in a free-enterprise system the arts would be commercialized and debased. Pound said so in *Mauberley* and the articles he wrote for Orage. He continued to say it in pamphlets, articles, and *Cantos*. The artist forced to compete in the marketplace and sell his wares to the public was not at liberty to create original work, to develop his own style, to finish his masterpiece.

> The "age demanded" chiefly a mould in plaster,
> Made with no loss of time . . .[22]

Yeats agreed with this, comparing the life of a painter or sculptor in the courts of Italy to the situation of the modern artist in a democratic state. The artist needed a patron who would support him while he worked—a protector. Pound believed that he had found a solution in Fascism and a patron in Mussolini. Yeats for a while believed that the Blue Shirts might be a solution, until their violence scared him off.

Wyndham Lewis described the plight of the artist in a series of articles he contributed to *The Criterion* between February 1924 and February 1925. He spoke of the popularization and cheapening of art. Democracy was anti-art. The "small man," who should be ruled in matters of art by the superior intelligence of the creative mind, was in fact dictating artistic standards through his financial control. For the artist who had to serve such people Lewis offered a rule: *"You cannot aim too low."* [23]

Eliot agreed. In *The Criterion,* June 1926, he said that the artist "finds himself, if he is a man of intellect, unable to realize his art to his own satisfaction, and he may be driven to examining the elements in the situation—political, social, philosophical or religious—which frustrate his labour. In this uncomfortable pursuit he is accused of 'neglecting his art.' But it is likely that some of the strongest influences on the thought of the next generation may be those of the dispossessed artists." [24]

It seems, therefore, that it was because he was a "dispossessed artist" that Eliot moved to the right. A Marxist might very well take this view of the matter. I do not believe, however, that it is true of Eliot—though it seems to be true of Pound. The economic pressure on Pound was very strong—he was prevented from publishing in England. He could not publish his anthology because it would compete with Palgrave's *Golden Treasury*—and Palgrave was a Jew. So Pound's Fascism and anti-Semitism were stimulated by his "situation as an artist." This was why he was obsessed with usury, why he thought it was a Jewish plot, why he was so extravagant, practically insane on the subject—it was something that had been done to him, he felt it as an injustice. Eliot's situation, however, was different. Though at first he had to struggle to make ends meet when he was a schoolteacher, reviewer, employee at Lloyd's bank, he was never prevented from publishing, and from the time that he was employed at Faber he was economically secure. In fact, others had reason to complain of him, for he was a publisher. His complaints about the "situation of the artist" and economic injustice, therefore, were merely lip service to a fashionable idea. Pound was his friend, so was Wyndham Lewis, therefore he agreed with their pronouncements on this subject. His anti-Semitism, too, was intellectually fashionable rather than heartfelt. This is why he could not understand, in later years, why people thought of him as an anti-Semite. What to the Jews had been a matter of life and death, to Eliot had been a point he was making about culture.

This, of course, does not excuse his reactionary political views or his anti-Semitism. For both he is still responsible—and he holds himself responsible. In "Little Gidding" he speaks of

> the rending pain of re-enactment
> Of all that you have done, and been; the shame
> Of motives late revealed, and the awareness
> Of things ill done and done to others' harm
> Which once you took for exercise of virtue.[25]

In the 1920's Eliot corresponded with Charles Maurras, the leader of *Action Française*. This was a movement of nationalists and anti-Semites that had originated at the end of the nineteenth century in the Dreyfus Affair. At that time Maurras wrote a newspaper article rallying anti-Dreyfusard opinion. A League of Patriots was formed; Maurras converted the League to monarchism and changed the name to *Action Française*. In 1908 a newspaper with this name was founded; it was read by people with anti-republican and proclerical sympathies. Maurras preached that France was faced with a choice between established, hereditary traditions, *le sang*, and insurrectionary forces of mercantilism, *l'or*. Jews, naturally, were in control of the gold.

Such was the movement with which Eliot sympathized. He agreed not only with Maurras's anti-Semitism, but with the wider-ranging racism of Henri Massis, an associate of Maurras, who saw "Asiaticism" and "Oriental anarchy" threatening Western civilization.[26]

It was a nasty shock to Eliot when, in December 1926, Maurras was condemned by the Vatican and his works placed on the Index. The reason was that he had used the Church for his own political purposes—because it provided order—without subscribing to the dogma. The effect on Eliot was to alienate him from Roman Catholicism—he agreed with Paul Elmer More that neither the Bible nor the Pope could be held an absolute guide in spiritual matters. More proposed a church in which the believer would be guided by authority yet be free to reject parts of the tradition that he could not accept.[27]

Eliot remained sympathetic to Maurras. Eliot's famous statement that he was "classicist in literature, royalist in politics, and anglo-catholic in religion," was taken from a description of Maurras in *La Nouvelle Revue Française*.[28]

It has been suggested that Eliot was a reactionary because he was an expatriate. Uprooted people, so runs the argument, feel a need to belong; therefore they ally themselves with established institutions, with the class that is most secure. But not all ex-patriates move to the right and make anti-Semitic statements.

Besides, Eliot was not an uncritical admirer of things British. He said, "No one can be so aware of the environment of stupidity as the Englishman; no other nationality perhaps provide so dense an environment as the English." [29] Eliot did not want to live in America; he had no liking for a republic; he preferred English manners and institutions, and he had married an Englishwoman. Therefore he lived in England, but as an intellectual he had his work cut out, penetrating the "denseness."

He chose to move among people of some social standing. E. M. Forster has a comment on this: "One has a feeling at moments that the Muses are connected not so much with Apollo as with the oldest country families. One feels, moreover, that there is never all this talk about tradition until it has ceased to exist, and that Mr. Eliot, like Henry James, is romanticizing the land of his adoption." [30] Donald Davie remarks that in the opinion of Englishmen of his generation and younger, "Eliot knew England and the English very imperfectly, after thirty years." And he says that Eliot's sense of Britain is "offensively metropolitan . . . his England is to all intents and purposes London, or at most the home counties." [31]

In 1927 Eliot became a British citizen. In the same year he was confirmed in the Church of England. Now that we have all Eliot's works and a fair idea of his life we can see that it is all of a piece. His mockery of a torpid Church in "The Hippopotamus" is not inconsistent with his beliefs as a Christian. The despair in *The Waste Land* is not inconsistent with the calm in the *Quartets*. It used to be thought that there was a difference in the attitudes of the pre- and the post-Anglican Eliot, but there is no real difference, only the bringing of his attitudes into line with Christian doctrine.

Eliot's religious conversion was more important than his change of citizenship. William Chace has said, "No land can be Eliot's home, no party is worth his allegiance, all the modern ideologies are poor substitutes for faith—even political power itself is useless." [32] As we have seen, he had found humanism very inadequate. "The difficult discipline," he said, "is the discipline and training of emotion . . . and this I have found only attainable through dogmatic religion." [33] He said, "Where there is no vital connection, the man may be a brilliant virtuoso but is probably nothing more." [34]

In a letter to Paul Elmer More, dated "Shrove Tuesday, 1928" (it should probably be dated 1929), he gave a more personal expression of the feelings that led to his conversion. He said that he was amazed at the existence of people for whom religion was wholly unnecessary. They might be good and happy; they seemed to be unconscious of any void, "the void that I find in the middle of all human happiness and all human relations, and which there is only one thing to fill. I am one," said Eliot, "whom this sense of void tends to drive toward asceticism or sensuality, and only Christianity helps to reconcile me to life, which is otherwise disgusting." [35]

On 29 June 1927, he established his vital connection. The baptism was performed at Finstock in Oxfordshire, the Rev. William Force Stead officiating. Eliot and Stead were friends; they had met at one of Pound's gatherings. Stead was an American, he wrote verse, and he had recently been appointed Chaplain of Worcester College, Oxford. Two other fellows of the college, H. V. F. Somerset and B. H. Streeter, stood as godparents. According to Mrs. Eliot and the Rev. J. C. S. Nias, who furnished an account of the events, Eliot was confirmed immediately after his baptism by the Bishop of Oxford in his private chapel.[36] But according to Stead the confirmation did not take place until the next morning. He tells us that during the baptism the front door of the church was locked and a guard was posted in the vestry while Eliot stood at the baptismal font.[37]

What were they afraid of—that someone might see him becoming a member of the Church? We are told that Jesus was baptized in a river—anyone passing by could have seen it. But Eliot was baptized behind a locked door, with a guard posted. These proceedings seem typical of Eliot's Christianity—it was exclusive.

The years right after his conversion were the worst. In time he mellowed and was less severe in his attitude to himself and others, but at first he had the dogmatism of a convert. He said that religion had brought him "at least the perception of something above morals, and therefore extremely terrifying; it has brought me not happiness, but the sense of something above happiness and therefore more terrifying than ordinary pain and misery; the very dark night and the desert." [38] There was much emphasis on damnation in Eliot's religion. "I am really shocked by your assertion that God did not make Hell," he wrote to More. "It seems to me that you have lapsed into Humanitarianism. . . . Is your God Santa Claus?" [39] Humanitarianism he defined as "an excessive love of created beings." [40]

We have been told, however, that God is love, that without charity man is a sounding brass and tinkling cymbal. It is hard to find charity in Eliot's *ex cathedra* pronouncements—his Christianity is for the not-so-happy few. This is the Eliot who was overheard saying on the telephone, "Will you tell her ladyship that I am unable to come to lunch with her because I don't accept invitations from ladies I have not met, nor from one who invites me without my wife, nor from one who is divorced." [41] It is certain that this Eliot would not have lunched with the Magdalene. This is the thinker who said that "Where you find clear thinking, you usually find that the thinker is either a Christian (if he is a European) or an atheist." [42] This is the author of the statement, "My general point of view may be described as classicist in literature, royalist in politics, and anglo-catholic in religion." [43] This is the Eliot who describes tradition as consisting of the habitual actions of "the same people living in the same place." It proceeds from "blood kinship." "The population should be homogeneous; where two or more cultures exist in the same place they are likely to be fiercely self-conscious or both to become adulterate. What is still more important is unity of religious background; and reasons of race and religion combine to make any large number of free-thinking Jews undesirable. There must be a proper balance between urban and rural, industrial and agricultural development. And a spirit of excessive tolerance is to be deprecated." [44]

He didn't have to worry about excessive tolerance—the National Socialists in Germany were preparing a final solution of the Jewish question. At this point, however, we must not hasten to place Eliot in the circle of Hell to which, prayer book in hand, he seems to be hastening. Eliot was not a Fascist, though he has been called one. The name-calling comes mainly from the Left; but as Leftists include a good number of Stalinists, their judgment in matters of conscience leaves something to be desired.

In 1928, commenting in *The Criterion,* Eliot said that the statement of policy by *The British Lion,* the organ of the British Fascists, was "wholly admirable." [45] In July 1929 we find him saying, "I confess to a preference for fascism in practice, which I dare say most of my readers share; and I will not admit that this preference is itself wholly irrational. I believe that the fascist form of unreason is less remote from my own than is that of the communists, but that my form is a more reasonable form of unreason." [46] Nine years later he remarks: "But Mr. Day Lewis suffers from the weaknesses of most Englishmen of his belief. There is nothing, for these people, to be said for fascism." [47]

In 1937 when Oxford University decided not to send representatives to Germany to attend the Bicentenary celebrations of the University of Göttingen, as a protest against the imprisonment of scholars, Eliot condemned the decision.

This is the case for regarding Eliot as a fascist. On the other hand, fascism then did not have the meaning that it has for us today—it did not smell of the death camps. Moreover, Eliot did not take an active part in politics; as Chace points out, he had no connection with English fascist groups. There is no record of any claim on him by Oswald Mosley, "nor does Colin Cross, the historian of *The Fascists in Britain* . . . think it worthwhile even to mention him."

In an article, "The Literature of Fascism," published in *The Criterion* in December 1928, Eliot criticized fascism as being a panacea. What he himself desired was "decentralized royalism, the humble citizen deriving his comforts from the privileged and hereditary class." [48]

He said, "The human craving to believe in *something* is pathetic, when not tragic. . . . The popular result of ignoring religion seems to be merely that the populace transfer their religious emotions to political theories. Few people are sufficiently civilized to afford atheism. . . . So far as bolshevism is a practical way of running Russia—if it is—for the material contentment of Russians, it seems to me worthy of study. So far as it is a kind of supernatural faith, it seems to be a humbug. The same is true of fascism. There is a form of faith which is solely appropriate to a religion; it should not be appropriated by politics." [49]

In *The Criterion* of July 1929 he said, "What I find in both fascism and communism is a combination of statements with unexamined enthusiasms. A revolutionary idea is one which requires a reorganization of the mind; fascism or communism is now the natural idea for the thoughtless person." [50]

In 1934 he published in *The Criterion* an essay by the Roman Catholic historian Christopher Dawson, "Religion and the Totalitarian State," in which Dawson said: "There is an obvious and apparently irreducible opposition between Communism and Christianity. . . . Communism, in fact, challenges Christianity on its own ground by offering mankind a *rival way of salvation*." [51]

Eliot was not a Fascist, but he was opposed to Communism. Therefore the Communists called him a Fascist.

13

Prayers to Broken Stone

"THE Hollow Men" is the poem of despair *The Waste Land*
was supposed to be. But it is not the poet's despair—the poet is
saved by his works. Hollow men "grope together/ And avoid
speech," but poetry speaks, even though it be

> As wind in dry grass
> Or rats' feet over broken glass
> In our dry cellar [1]

The poem makes a whispering sound and, one by one, desolate
images swim into view. They impressed themselves on the consciousness of a generation. For a time, says Edmund Wilson, young
poets "took to inhabiting exclusively barren beaches, cactus-grown
deserts, and dusty attics over-run with rats." [2] Wilson speaks of
"Gerontion" and *The Waste Land,* but the images he lists are
more strongly emphasized in "The Hollow Men."

"The Hollow Men" was the more disturbing because it was not
explicit, could not be explained away. There are three kingdoms
in the poem: death's dream kingdom, death's other kingdom, and
the twilight kingdom. And there are eyes "I dare not meet in
dreams/ In death's dream kingdom." [3] This is Symbolist writing.
"Nature," said Baudelaire, "is a temple, in which living pillars
sometimes utter a babel of words; man traverses it through forests
of symbols, that watch him with knowing eyes." [4] Mallarmé said
that poetry should suggest, never state. "To name a thing is to
suppress three quarters of the joy of the poem, which consists

in guessing, little by little; suggestion makes the dream." [5]
Whereas *The Waste Land,* once the references have been un-
raveled, is as clear as a nightmare, "The Hollow Men" is as vague
as a dream.

Modern poetry moved from Symbolism to Imagism to Surrealism—with lesser movements such as Futurism and Dada coming
in and out. Eliot did the opposite—he moved from Imagism back
to Symbolism. Hugh Kenner has said that Eliot never was an
Imagist: his images were always symbols. This may be true—
nevertheless, there is a marked increase in symbolic values from
"The Hollow Men" on.

But meanings are deliberately left vague. Therefore, to say that
the eyes are the eyes of saints, that death's other kingdom is
Heaven, that death's dream kingdom is this world, that by
"dreams" are meant visions or works of art, and that the twilight
kingdom is death, is to reduce to one clear meaning poetry that
was written to suggest many things that are not clear.

"The Hollow Men" moves to its conclusion with a phantasmagoric nursery rhyme: "Here we go round the prickly pear." [6] A
sepulchral voice says that there is a Shadow that falls between the
motion and the act. This is cut across by a fragment of the Lord's
Prayer. The sepulchral voice speaks again. A plaintive voice says
that life is very long. The poem begins to stammer, then it goes
back to the nursery with a cheerful song of annihilation: "This is
the way the world ends / Not with a bang but a whimper." [7]

The bitter saying has been remembered, especially by those
who were young at the time. It was one of the touchstones of the
Lost Generation.

"The Hollow Men" is a balancing of Eliot's earlier and later
styles. Like a nineteenth-century Symbolist he speaks of "Sunlight
on a broken column," "a fading star," a "Multifoliate rose." This
is the symbolism of his later style. On the other hand there is an
admixture of the earlier kind of imagery that riveted attention
to the present scene, the particular experience—specific, grotesque,
enclosing. F. H. Bradley, the philosopher of experience, still stands
between Eliot and the saints, with his "Rat's coat, crowskin,
crossed staves." [8] His baleful, desiccating influence has not yet
been overcome.

In *The Waste Land* Eliot had moved beyond Bradley. He had
arrived at a vision of what must be done, and was able to set his
ideas in order. Then he wrote nothing for a while, for he wrote

only under the pressure of need. Then, once more, writing "The Hollow Men," he submitted to Bradley, stepping back in order to leap—into the Church.

The fragments of "an Aristophanic Melodrama" that Eliot did not complete, "Sweeney Agonistes" and "Fragment of an Agon," have the old preconversion nightmare thoughts. Sweeney tells his rapt friends that he knew a man once "did a girl in," and that "Any man has to, needs to, wants to/ Once in a lifetime, do a girl in." [9] The words seem to have been written for jazz—"The drama was originally ritual," says Eliot, "and ritual, consisting of a set of repeated movements, is essentially a dance." The trouble with modern theater is that "we have lost the drum." [10] In these fragments the words move to a drumbeat, with syncopation.

Once Sweeney forgets who he is and talks about "Birth, and copulation, and death," [11] but otherwise the language is on the level of vaudeville and popular songs. Eliot has an ear for clichés —there is an inevitability about his clichés that is very gratifying.

> Klipstein: London's a fine place to come on a visit—
> Krumpacker: Specially when you got a real live Britisher
>   A guy like Sam to show you around.
>   Sam of course is at *home* in London
>   And he's promised to show us around.[12]

Eliot was converted to Anglo-Catholicism in 1927. Some readers think that nothing he wrote from that time on is as good as "The Hollow Men," *The Waste Land,* and "The Love Song of J. Alfred Prufrock"; that the later poetry is less intense; that it is less interesting because it is religious. Edmund Wilson, criticizing Eliot in 1929, said: "The Church is now practically impossible as a solution to our present difficulties because it is so difficult to get educated people to believe in its fundamental doctrines." [13] And recently Robert M. Adams remarked: "I am not the first to sense a kind of shrinking from hard ideas to soft ones, from an order reached or at least sought through vision to an order standing this side of vision and substituting for it." [14]

On the other hand there are those who think that Eliot's poetry increased in meaning and skill after his conversion. Helen Gardner asserts that *Four Quartets* is "Mr. Eliot's masterpiece," [15] and Elizabeth Drew concurs: *Four Quartets* has all the qualities of the earlier poetry, but "whereas in the early poems these qualities had often to be asserted through a *dislocation* of language, in *Four Quartets* they are knit into a perfect articulation of sound and movement and meaning." [16]

It is not always evident, but the reader's opinion of Eliot's later poetry usually reflects his own attitudes to the Church. Readers who sympathize with Eliot's Anglo-Catholicism find the writing good; others think that it has faded.

In the late twenties he published parts of *Ash-Wednesday* and the *Ariel Poems*—the name "Ariel" has no significance, it was a series of poems by various authors, published at Christmas. Eliot's are poems of resignation, waiting for something better; there has been a revelation, then a lapsing back into the world. In "Journey of the Magi" the traveler, having returned to his own kingdom, is no longer at ease "With an alien people clutching their gods." [17] There is nothing to do but wait with a faint hope. As Eliot says in another place, mocking his own attitude: *"When* will Time flow away?" [18] The best part of the poem is the journey, exotic scenery and happenings described in matter-of-fact language:

> Then the camel men cursing and grumbling
> And running away, and wanting their liquor and women.[19]

The *Ariel Poems* are reveries—the lands and times they speak of are far away. "A Song for Simeon" shows how the method can fail; the writing is merely an echo of Scripture:

> Who shall remember my house, where shall live my children's
> children
> When the time of sorrow is come? [20]

"Animula" tells of a child's exploring the circumambient world or curling up "in the window seat/ Behind the *Encyclopaedia Britannica*." [21] The poem ends by urging the reader to

> Pray for Guiterriez, avid of speed and power,
> For Boudin, blown to pieces . . .[22]

Eliot said that the names represented "different types of career, the successful person of the machine age and someone who was killed in the last war." [23] Grover Smith has a comment on this: "At any rate they are exasperating. Eliot, having changed the men's names, has no legitimate reason to allege that they are in the poem at all; if they are in the poem, it is unfinished until the reader can identify them." In other words, if a thing cannot be looked up it has no place in a poem. Seldom has scholarship asserted its claim so firmly.

The epigraph above "Marina" is taken from *Hercules Furens.*
Hercules has slain his family, gone mad, and returned to his
senses. He asks, "What place is this, what region, what shore of
the world?" In the poem the ways leading to death are listed—
"Those who sharpen the tooth of the dog . . ." [25] et cetera. The
fear of death is offset by a vision of grace, "Marina," the lost
daughter of Shakespeare's *Pericles,* and the feeling of grace is
suggested by the place itself: gray rocks, islands, the smell of pine,
fog, the call of a thrush. Eliot is a poet of streets and furnished
rooms, but when he writes about the sea he is also a poet of nature.
The sea quickens his senses—his happiness seems to be located
permanently around Gloucester and Cape Ann.

Elizabeth Drew, as we have seen, traces in Eliot's writing a
Jungian sequence of "transformation symbols." "If the conscious
will is collaborating with the revelations contained in the dream
symbols, Jung traces an apparently purposive sequence of images
creating the gradual shift from the ego as the centre of being, to
a different centre." [26] The images of the *Ariel Poems* and *Ash-
Wednesday,* which was written concurrently, are continuations
in the sequence. After meeting with the Shadow ("The Hollow
Men"), there is a time of refraining, of not doing. The "dangerous moment" (hovering between arrested growth and renewed
fertility) is past. This does not mean that safety has been reached,
but the "new redeeming symbols" are established, enabling the
poet to feel, at least intermittently, the capacity to experience
reality, act, creation, response, spasm, existence. There is a change
of attitude. Instead of abandonment to the Shadow there is willed
renunciation and the patience of a chosen attitude. This is "not
doing" (Jung's term) rather than "doing nothing." Then the
anima archetype appears, the woman image which, when it appears in the process of spiritual regeneration, symbolizes hidden
wisdom, "the mediating function between the conscious ego and
the inner world of the unconscious." [27]

"Marina" = *anima.* And she is the daughter—that is, a child.
"According to Jung the revelation of the beginning of a new
spiritual experience is usually heralded by the appearance in
dreams of some sort of miraculous child, symbolizing the new po-
tentiality for growth and development which has awakened in the
unconscious." For this reason the poem is joyful—"the only purely
joyous poem," says Elizabeth Drew, "Eliot has ever written." [28]

"As a human construction," says Jung, "the ship has the meaning . . . of a system, method or way." [29] "I made this," says the poem, "Between one June and another September./ Made this unknowing, half conscious, my own." [30] The speaker wishes to resign his old life for the new, symbolized in the vision of "The awakened, lips parted, the hope, the new ships." [31]

Christian resignation is the theme of *Ash-Wednesday*. As usual Eliot has other writers in mind as he begins his poem, opening with a line from Cavalcanti: "Because I do not hope to turn again," [32] borrowing from Shakespeare, "Desiring this man's gift and that man's scope," [33] borrowing from St. John of the Cross: "Why should the agèd eagle stretch its wings?" [34] This line irritated Edmund Wilson; he did not know the reference and would not have liked it any better if he had. "I am made a little tired," he said, "at hearing Eliot, only in his early forties, present himself as 'an agèd eagle' who asks why he should make the effort to stretch his wings." [35] But the passage from St. John of the Cross tells of rejuvenation. "God makes [the soul] to die to all that is not naturally God, so that, once it is stripped and denuded of its former skin, He may begin to clothe it anew. And thus its youth is renewed like the eagle's and it is clothed with the new man." [36]

In every phase of his poetry Eliot has been dying and being reborn. The struggle became desperate in *The Waste Land;* after his conversion it was continued in explicitly Christian terms. *Ash-Wednesday* has been described as a *Purgatorio,* but this should not lead us to think that *The Waste Land* was an *Inferno.* Everything Eliot wrote was a *Purgatorio.*

The lines in which he prays for resignation, "Teach us to care and not to care/ Teach us to sit still," are more Buddhist than they are Christian.[37]

The opening of the second section, which was published in 1927 as a separate poem, is one of Eliot's memorable dramatic scenes.

> Lady, three white leopards sat under a juniper-tree
> In the cool of the day, having fed to satiety
> On my legs my heart my liver and that which had been contained
> In the hollow round of my skull . . .[38]

In *The Dark Night of the Soul* St. John of the Cross locates physical strength in the legs, emotion in the heart, sensuality in the liver, and sense perception in the skull. So the living man has been thoroughly consumed by the leopards, clean as a whistle, and is ready to embark on a new life, if such be the will of God. Where have the white leopards come from? Once Eliot was asked the meaning of the leopards and the juniper tree, and he simply repeated the line: "Lady, three white leopards sat under a juniper tree." This was a Symbolist answer.

The lady here addressed is like Dante's "Ladies that have intelligence of love," bearer of the grace he is hoping for. Eliot writes of her in a paraphrase of the Litany to the Virgin. There are other lines from Scripture and lines from Catholic ritual: in the third section, the Act of Humility; in the fourth, the prayer "Salve Regina." Writing such as this helped to make Eliot unpopular with his liberal, anti-Catholic readers. As we have seen, Edmund Wilson had little patience with it. With the spread of Marxism among intellectuals in the thirties, Eliot's Catholic references seemed arcane, if not downright perverse. They seem less so today; at least, they are no more dated than the Marxism of the thirties.

In the third section the speaker retraces his past; he climbs a staircase. Looking down he sees his former self struggling "with the devil of the stairs who wears/ The deceitful face of hope and of despair." [39] To be resigned is to have passed beyond both hope and despair; the speaker has rid himself of "an excessive love of created beings," [40] himself included. Yet he cannot expect a reward for these merits: that would be self-interest, defeating the process of his "dying." Eliot's is a very scrupulous kind of Christianity; few people could measure up to it. He said so himself: "The number of people in possession of any criteria for discriminating between good and evil is very small." [41]

Climbing the stairs the speaker recalls the pleasures of sensuality. The lines are remarkable for their rhythm—only a master of verse could have written them.

Blown hair is sweet, brown hair over the mouth blown,
Lilac and brown hair;
Distraction, music of the flute, stops and steps of the mind over
    the third stair,
Fading, fading . . .[42]

The effect Eliot is striving for in *Ash-Wednesday* is what he calls "the high dream." [43] He wishes to create a poetry of vision, images that abstract us from the world and suggest states of grace. "While jewelled unicorns draw by the golden hearse" is such an image.[44] For many readers, however, it is not applicable to their own experience. There seems to be a discrepancy between the language and life—just such a discrepancy as Eliot criticized when he spoke of the poets who came after the Metaphysicals. In Milton and Dryden, he said, there had been a "dissociation of sensibility." There are readers, even Catholics, for whom unicorns, golden hearses, yew trees, blue rocks and ivory gates hold no significance. They don't object to Eliot's being religious, but they would prefer poetry that had something to say about life as they know it.

To this he might have replied, "Precisely. You have had no experience of 'the high dream,' therefore I am trying to show you what it is like."

His model was Dante. Dante, he said some years later, had been "the most persistent and deepest influence" on his verse.[45]

The poet whose name with the public stood for modernism was now its avowed opponent. Modernism was, he said, "a mental blight which can affect the whole of the intelligence of our time. . . . Where you find clear thinking, you usually find that the thinker is either a Christian (if he is a European) or an atheist; where you find muddy thinking you usually find that the thinker is something between the two, and such a person is in essentials a Modernist." [46]

He was concerned for society; he believed that only Christianity could save it. "The World," he said, "is trying the experiment of attempting to form a civilized but non-Christian mentality. The experiment will fail; but we must be very patient in awaiting its collapse; meanwhile redeeming the time: so that the Faith may be preserved alive through the dark ages before us; to renew and rebuild civilization, and save the World from suicide." [47]

Speaking on the BBC in 1932 about "The Modern Dilemma," he urged the need for religious faith. There were three challenges to Christianity: communism, psychology, and science. Communism was a rival religion and of course he did not believe in it. Science he saw as no great threat, but psychology was menacing—it ignored the "more intense, profound and satisfying emotions of religion." (His attitude to psychology, however, was ambivalent. In this talk he acknowledged that it could be an ally of religion, and *The Criterion* published several essays on psychology.) His aim, he said on the BBC, was to show that a "Christian organization of society" was possible.[48]

Eliot was proselytizing, moving toward the position he would take in 1939 when he proposed a "Community of Christians," consisting of "both clergy and laity of superior intellectual and/or spiritual gifts" that would form the mind and conscience of the nation. The other two parts of society would be the leaders—who would not have to be believers—and the workers, that is, those who were preoccupied with their jobs. For the workers there would be rituals and traditions—they could not be expected to think deeply on religious matters.[49]

As Chace points out, Eliot's plan for society includes a revenge against the lower middle class by whom he has been threatened all his life. Democratic society caters to the lower middle class, and it is their bad taste that makes culture what it is. In the new dispensation this class will be taught to accept new ideas and new art.

But it is not only Sweeney and his friends who will have to be instructed. Some artists, too, are in error. In *After Strange Gods,* a book made out of lectures he delivered in 1933 at the University of Virginia, Eliot set about showing what was wrong with other authors.

This book is a curious production. It has never been reprinted, and Eliot is reported to have said that he was sick when he wrote it—referring to the part that had to do with D. H. Lawrence.[50] Lawrence was one of the authors he said had gone wrong because they were not orthodox. So had Katherine Mansfield in her stories, Pound in *A Draft of XXX Cantos,* W. B. Yeats in general, Thomas Hardy, and even Father Hopkins. In Lawrence's story, "The Shadow in the Rose Garden," there was an absence of any moral or social sense. Mansfield's "Bliss" neglected "the moral issue of good and evil." Pound's hell had neither dignity nor tragedy and, ignoring "essential Evil," it implied a heaven "equally trivial and accidental." Hardy, in his story, "Barbara of the House of Grebe," had written "solely to provide a satisfaction for some morbid emotion." Yeats's poetry showed what happened when "a highly sophisticated lower mythology" was substituted for "a world of real Good and Evil, of holiness or sin." Hopkins was no better— he was too verbal, he offered only technical tricks. Joyce alone escaped chastisement; Joyce alone had created works "penetrated with Christian feeling." Eliot said that Joyce was "the most ethically orthodox of the more eminent writers" of his time.[51]

Orthodox, Orthodox, wha believe in John Knox . . . The trouble with all these writers, Joyce excepted, was that they were not orthodox. In them the decline of Christian values was manifest —they had no sense of original sin. Hence their works failed— without original sin, the human beings presented in poetry and fiction must become "more and more vaporous."

So Eliot unfurled the banner of orthodoxy in Virginia. Nor did he confine his remarks to authors. He said that the Civil War was "certainly the greatest disaster in the whole of American history," and that "the influx of foreign populations had almost effaced the American 'tradition' in some parts of the North." [52] Sweet music to the ears of Fugitives and Agrarians!

At the same time that he was recommending orthodox views, in his private life Eliot was suffering from unorthodox behavior. He was married to a woman who would throw the beads of her necklace onto the floor and pretend they were animals, and tell him to drive them back to their stall.[53] This was when he was preparing to go to the States—his first trip in seventeen years. He was to deliver the Charles Eliot Norton lectures at Harvard.

Vivien and her brother Maurice accompanied him to Southampton. On their way to Waterloo Station to catch the boat train they discovered that Vivien had left behind some of Tom's indispensable papers, locked in the bathroom. He stopped the taxi and asked a friend who was following in a second cab to go back to the flat and retrieve the papers. The friend returned at top speed, a boy was pushed through a window into the bathroom, the papers were found, and Eliot had them a few minutes before the boat train started.

Sencourt tells the story.[54] In the absence of an official biography the reader who wishes to know about Eliot's life must go to Sencourt, Matthews, and other self-appointed biographers who have not had access to Eliot's correspondence. It is said that they have relied on hearsay. But the policy Eliot himself began, of concealing his life (yet at the same time hinting at it in his writing), has been continued after his death, and there has been no official biography. It is likely that when one does appear it will be like a wedding too long deferred: no one will come to it. Readers will have figured out the important matters for themselves, and the official biography will not change their attitudes. No doubt, however, as with other such works we shall have information as to

Eliot's whereabouts at all times, and we shall be told that he was a model husband.

He lectured at Harvard on "Studies in the Relation of Criticism to Poetry in England"—later published as *The Use of Poetry and the Use of Criticism.* He lectured on Elizabethan criticism and literature, on the Augustans, with particular praise for Dryden, on Wordsworth's *Preface,* and Coleridge's *Biographia Literaria.* There was a lull of two months for examinations and the vacation, then he resumed with a lecture on Shelley and Keats. This was the famous attack in which he confessed that he found Shelley's ideas repellent. This set Shelley studies back thirty years; then a new generation of critics who liked Shelley "crept out again to feel the sun," and a new generation of readers discovered that Shelley was a genius, after all. Whereupon they said that Eliot was a humbug.

He spoke on Matthew Arnold, the apostle of culture whom in some ways he resembled. But there was something missing in Arnold: "auditory imagination"—Arnold didn't have much of an unconscious. And, of course, the author of "Dover Beach" lacked faith.

He concluded with some remarks on contemporary criticism: Maritain, Brémond, Rivière, Herbert Read, and Ivor Richards. His listeners drank in his words. They were conscious of being in the presence of the most influential critic of all, who could make or destroy a reputation with his words.

When he returned to England he did not return to Vivien. Instead he went to live with Frank Morley and his family in Surrey. Eliot had a separate cottage where he could think and write. In the winter he returned to London and found accommodations in a guesthouse in Cortfield Road. St. Stephen's Church, in Gloucester Road, was within walking distance. He became a friend of Father Eric Cheetham of St. Stephen's, and left the lodging-house to live with Father Cheetham and his curates.

His wife continued to occupy their flat. He had made a settlement so that she was not in want of anything material.

In *The Family Reunion,* the play Eliot wrote a few years later, Harry thinks that he pushed his wife overboard.

Vivien Eliot is said to have appeared at her husband's lectures wearing a sign: "I am the wife he abandoned." She turned up at his plays.[55]

It is no wonder that Harry in *The Family Reunion* keeps seeing the Furies.

He was no longer content to write for the few readers of verse. "Of what use is this experimenting with rhythms and words, this effort to find the precise metric and the exact image to set down feelings which, if communicable at all, can be communicated to so few that the result seems insignificant compared to the labour." [56] And in 1933, writing on *The Use of Poetry and the Use of Criticism*, he said, "The poet naturally prefers to write for as large and miscellaneous an audience as possible." The poet would like to think that what he wrote had "some direct social utility," would like to be "something of a popular entertainer, and be able to think his own thoughts behind a tragic or a comic mask." [57]

The theater was the place for this kind of poetry. Eliot's interest in playwrighting went back to undergraduate days at Harvard when he studied drama with G. P. Baker, who was concerned about the future of drama. He had studied the Elizabethan and Jacobean dramatists. He liked the music halls. His poems were dramatic: "Prufrock" was a monologue; *The Waste Land*, a poem for voices; "Sweeney Agonistes" and "Fragment of an Agon" were experimental theater, words that moved to the beat of a drum.

In October 1933 E. Martin Browne, the director of religious drama for the Anglican diocese of Chichester, commissioned Eliot to write a pageant play, to raise contributions for church-building. He fulfilled his commission, using the music halls as a model for Cockney dialogue in prose and, at the other extreme, the Scriptures of Isaiah and Ezekiel as a model for choruses in verse. Reviewers were encouraging: the *Times* remarked that *The Rock* was purposive.

The choruses were included by Eliot among his poems. They are less intense than the verse of the separate poems and better suited to the stage. Eliot has hit on a middle style between poetry and prose in which he can get his ideas across to the theater audience and still have the rhythm and forward march of verse. In this middle style he is able to range from formal to colloquial speech, and sometimes he telescopes the two levels in a way that has become his specialty. It is common enough with poets who followed Eliot—in the thirties, Auden and his friends practically made it their stock-in-trade, so that we are likely to forget that

Pound and Eliot were the first to make it popular in English. This telescoping of levels is more than a mannerism: either by bringing together two levels of language or two different kinds of image, past and present, an eternal landscape and a passing scene, the style demonstrates one of Eliot's main ideas: "The desert is squeezed in the tube-train next to you." [58]

He has said it frequently. The chorus in *The Rock* says it:

> In every moment you live where two worlds cross,
> In every moment you live at a point of intersection.
> Remember, living in time, you must live also now in Eternity.[59]

He will be saying it in "Burnt Norton": "All time is eternally present." [60] It is the mystery of incarnation, the central tenet of Christian faith, the most important idea that Eliot as a Christian has to deal with.

"You neglect your shrines and churches," the chorus tells the audience.[61] The solution for social problems is:

> A Church for all
> And a job for each
> Every man to his work.[62]

This was in the Depression, when the unemployed stood around on streetcorners. In Germany they were gathering to vote the National Socialists into power. In the face of this, there is something quixotic about a pageant that shows how churches are built, together with scenes from church history—the conversion of King Sabert by Melletus, Rahere's building of St. Bartholomew's, and so on. The chorus advances with its line of four or three stresses, its speech combining the desert and the Tube:

> And the wind shall sáy: 'Here were décent gódless péople:
> Their ónly monumént the ásphalt róad
> And a thoúsand lóst golf bálls.' [63]

It is easy, however, to push the technique too hard:

> Remembering the words of Nehemiah the Prophet: 'The trowel
> in hand, and the gun rather loose in the holster.' [64]

This unbending creaks. It is like the language Auden and his friends made in their verse plays, chatty and out of date.

He had already used the four-stress line, the language ranging "from doggerel to exaltation," in "Journey of the Magi." He would use it in plays from now on. It was, says Hugh Kenner, his "last feat of technical innovation," producing finally the self-lessly transparent verse of "Burnt Norton," where the words "appear to be writing themselves." [65]

The Rock, however, is not dramatic. A hooded, silent figure represents the Church as witness; the lines spoken by the chorus represent the Church in action. We see obstacles the Church must face in the modern world: want of money, hostile political forces —Blackshirts, Redshirts, Plutocrat. The characters are stereotypes —there is nothing in the pageant to show that Eliot can write a play.

But he was a tough-minded workman; he wanted to write plays that could be acted before an audience, and he set about learning how. But they must be in verse—he wanted to engage the audience on more than one level, and only verse drama could do this. He thought they would "stand" some poetry—not as much as an Elizabethan theater audience, nevertheless, if it were entertaining . . .[66]

With *Murder in the Cathedral* he succeeded. He wrote it for the Canterbury Festival of June 1935, and it was performed a few yards from the spot where Thomas Becket suffered death. The play has often been performed—audiences have listened to the chorus of the women of Canterbury, the arguments of the Tempters, have witnessed Thomas's struggles with his conscience, have seen the bestial Knights, and have been enthralled when the Knights, coming forward, address the audience in a familiar, friendly way, making them accomplices in the crime. In this work Eliot proved that he could write brilliantly for the theater.

He proved it again in 1949 with *The Cocktail Party.* It was a hit on Broadway—people could be heard debating what it meant. They were puzzled by the psychiatrist-priest, Harcourt-Reilly. Was he Hercules? They did not know how to take the scene in which the characters stood around sipping cocktails and discussing Celia's martyrdom.

So Eliot began a new career in middle age. The achievement was mainly technical. Some of the difficulties in his life that have been regarded as marital or spiritual may have been difficulties with art: the need to finish "Prufrock," to find a voice in which to write it, to dissociate the character from himself; the effort to make fragments of *The Waste Land* cohere; the need to find symbols for religious states of feeling, a new language for the "higher dream."

And now, for the plays, a level of poetry that audiences would stand . . . If he used poetry equal to his best the audience would stop listening. This had not happened when Shakespeare wrote, for Shakespeare's audience had no democratic prejudices. Poetic speech did not strike them as strange—it was as natural as the other kind. In the twentieth century, however, imaginative, obscure speech strikes an audience like cold water. Only words that sound as though they might be said in the street or an ordinary house win acceptance. Hence the impoverishment of thought and feeling in the theater. But he intended to resuscitate verse drama, and to some extent he succeeded. It was, like everything else he did, a triumph of technique.

He once remarked, "We cannot say where technique begins and ends." [67]

In "Little Gidding," after the "dead master" has listed "the gifts reserved for age"—a sad catalogue—he says,

> From wrong to wrong the exasperated spirit
>   Proceeds, unless restored by that refining fire
>   Where you must move in measure, like a dancer. [68]

Eliot wrote in measure. This is why his life was happy as he grew older. And why, for the sake of comparison, the prose writer Edmund Wilson became more exasperated. Wilson has been called a great critic, yet he had a thoroughly prosaic mind—there is no evidence that he was able to hear and feel verse on the highest level.

There is no sufficiency in prose. It is written with appetite and reason. There is no measure to it, only the energy of the writer. But the body fails with age; reason and appetite fail. An aging writer of prose is an exasperated, dissatisfied man.

But a line of poetry is like dancing—the words have definite positions in time and space. The poet knows that after he is gone they will continue to dance.

14

Sitting Still

IN the summer of 1934 when Eliot was on vacation in Gloucester-shire he visited a manor house built over the ruins of an earlier house burned two centuries before. He walked about in the formal garden. Later he wrote a poem in which he incorporated, as he usually did, some lines left over from an earlier piece of writing— lines discarded from *Murder in the Cathedral*. He gave the poem the title "Burnt Norton." In 1940 he wrote another poem on the same plan and titled it "East Coker." "The Dry Salvages" fol-lowed the next year, and "Little Gidding" the year after that. The four poems were published together in 1943 with the title *Four Quartets*.

Four Quartets came at the right time and had the right size. It was time for Eliot to produce what, especially among Anglican readers, might be regarded as a "major" poem. "The major poet's work must have bulk," says Helen Gardner, "he must attempt with success one or other of the greater poetic forms, which tests his gifts of invention and variation; he cannot claim the title on a handful of lyrics however exquisite." [1]

Most poets would agree that the title is not worth claiming on this condition. Not worth claiming in any case, for there are a num-ber of major poets whom nobody reads. Better to be a minor poet with Robert Burns, César Vallejo, and the anonymous author of "Western wind, when wilt thou blow," which has only four lines, than a major poet according to the rules laid down in universities.

The writing in *Four Quartets* is deliberate. The five-part divi-

179

sion of each quartet seems to have been imitated by Eliot from his own *Waste Land*.[2] With Pound's help he had discovered the organic structure of that poem. He now borrowed the idea in order to write the quartets. It is also possible that he had in mind the five-part division of Beethoven's *Quartet in A Minor, Opus 132*.

There are carefully worked out correspondences from one quartet to another. The theme of time is introduced in the first section of the first quartet, reintroduced in the first section of the second quartet, and so on. There are also correspondences in the technique of verse from one section to another: for example, in each quartet the fourth section is a lyric poem.

Each quartet is set in a place with which Eliot has either a personal or family connection. As we have seen, "Burnt Norton" is named after the house and garden he visited in the Cotswolds. "East Coker" is the village in Somerset where the Elyots lived for two centuries and from which Andrew Eliot set out for America. The first section contains some phrases taken from *The Boke named the Governour* by Sir Thomas Elyot, a grandson of Simon Elyot who lived in East Coker. "The Dry Salvages" (pronounced to rhyme with "assuages") are *les trois sauvages,* a group of rocks with a beacon off the northeast coast of Cape Ann where Eliot used to sail as a boy. "Little Gidding" was an Anglican community in Huntingdonshire founded in 1625 by Nicholas Ferrar and his family. Charles I came to Little Gidding in 1633, 1642, and in 1645 after his defeat at Naseby. The poets Herbert and Crashaw visited there.

In each quartet a season is described: spring (or early summer), summer, autumn, and winter.

Each quartet has in it one of the four elements of Heraclitus's flux: air, earth, water, fire.

Each quartet speaks of one aspect of divinity: the Unmoved Mover, the redeeming Son, the Virgin, the Holy Ghost.[3]

Each quartet treats of one way of looking at time: as memory, as cyclical pattern, as flux, as the revelation of the meaning of history.[4]

Drew describes the four poems together as a *mandala*—the Sanskrit word for "magic circle." The design of a circle divided into four parts, with a center, is found in Christian churches and Tibetan monasteries. It is called the sun wheel. It combines a circular rotary motion (frequently it is rotating light), some ele-

ment of "fourness," and "the all-important centre." In religious
mandalas the center is a figure of Christ or Buddha within a rose
or lotus pattern. In secular mandalas the figure may be a flower,
sun, star, or pool of water. The circle of the mandala stands for
wholeness of being; the center suggests "the point at which resolution of opposites occurs which makes such a sense of wholeness
possible." [5]

> Jung traces the insistence upon 'fourness' which the mandala
> dreams and drawings always possess, to some inexplicable con-
> stituent in the unconscious mind which is constantly asserting
> itself in symbol. He calls it 'the archetypal image of God as
> manifested in his creation,' citing the visions of Ezekiel and the
> Apocalypse as literary illustrations. He comments: 'The central
> Christian symbolism is a Trinity, but the formula of the uncon-
> scious mind is a quaternity. To the unconscious there seems to
> be something wholer about fourness than threeness.[6]

Throughout the quartets Eliot contemplates two worlds, "the
turning world" of perpetual change, and "the still point," the
inner life of the spirit. Another way to put it is, time and eternity.
    The problem is to understand how they are related.
    Perhaps not so much to understand as to feel the emotional
equivalent of understanding, which is faith. "The poet who 'thinks'
is merely the poet who can express the emotional equivalent of
thought." [7]
    The poem, however, does not proceed by faith—it proceeds by
reason. The argument of the five parts of "Burnt Norton" has been
summarized by C. K. Stead as follows.

1. The movement of time, in which brief moments of eternity
   are caught.
2. Worldly experience, leading only to dissatisfaction.
3. Purgation in the world, divesting the soul of the love of
   created things.
4. A lyric prayer for, or affirmation of the need of, Intercession.
5. The problems of attaining artistic wholeness which become
   analogues for and merge into, the problems of achieving
   spiritual health.[8]

As in other poems there is a struggle to arrive at, or show the
way to, "spiritual health." The scarecrow in the way is time. All
of time is always present. Time past and time future are concepts—
they exist only in our consciousness, and this is of the present time.

Therefore the past is present and cannot be changed. The past cannot be made over, and we are imprisoned, locked in experience.

We are still contending with F. H. Bradley! It seems that we can never get past him. The poetry still has to extract an ego, has to keep extracting it, from the fixating, isolating experience of present time. There have been struggles and partial victories in *The Waste Land* and *Ash-Wednesday*. The struggle seems to be continuing in *Four Quartets*.

In *Four Quartets* the stakes appear to be greater. The poetry is visibly struggling to create what Elizabeth Drew calls "another centre" and an Anglican might call an idea of God. This is one reason that some readers regard *Four Quartets* as Eliot's greatest work: the terms are explicit. But in *The Waste Land* the same struggle was taking place. The difference is that there the issue was in doubt; in *Four Quartets* it has been resolved before the poetry begins. *The Waste Land* is a poem of religious struggle; *Four Quartets* is a commentary upon it. *The Waste Land* shows the process of arriving at belief; *Four Quartets* comments upon it after it has happened.

Readers who do not wish to go through the process may prefer the commentary.

Getting back to the argument: It appears that time cannot be redeemed. There can never be a new start; man is bound on the wheel of experience and tortured by knowledge. For the Christian or Buddhist, however, there is a way out. As Eliot is living in a Christian society he discusses the problem in Christian rather than Buddhist terms: the Christian knows that divinity entered the world, lived in time, and returned to eternity. This is the Incarnation, a mystery, to be apprehended by faith. "The hint half guessed, the gift half understood, is Incarnation." [9] For those who have faith in the Incarnation, who believe in the divinity of Jesus Christ, there is a share in eternity. The Christian escapes from time through faith in the Redeemer.

> All shall be well and
> All manner of thing shall be well
> By the purification of the motive
> In the ground of our beseeching [10]

This, then, is the argument of the poem. It has been criticized by William F. Lynch, S.J., who finds fault with Eliot for trying to transcend ordinary life, living only for the intersection where the timeless enters and life may be escaped. Eliot's imagination dwells on epiphanies—another word might be "symbols"—the element of fire, the day of Pentecost, the descent of the Holy Ghost. He does not wish to move with the world as it "moves/ In appetency, on its metalled ways," [11] with "the strained time-ridden faces/ Distracted from distraction by distraction." [12] Eliot, says Fr. Lynch, "is attracted above all by the image and the goal of immobility." And this is wrong—"what we must do is go along with the time-ridden faces. . . . Jumping out of our human facts will not help at all, and will produce nothing but further strains. The only answer, as in every case, would seem to be to deepen the fact and its possible levels, to enter more deeply into it." [13]

Stead's analysis of the argument and Fr. Lynch's opinion help us to grasp Eliot's conscious intent and to see how he went about planning *Four Quartets*. But poetry is work of the emotions, it works through the body, and what Eliot said early in his career is true: "Many men will admit that their keenest ideas have come to them with the quality of a sense perception; and that their keenest sensuous perception has been 'as if the body thought.' " [14] Whatever philosophers or theologians may say, readers of poetry will be moved by passages that seem "as if the body thought," and will pass by passages that are merely arguing. They will find much of *Four Quartets* inferior to Eliot's early poetry. There is too much of this:

> But to apprehend
> The point of intersection of the timeless
> With time, is an occupation for the saint—
> No occupation either, but something given
> And taken, in a lifetime's death in love,
> Ardour and selflessness and self-surrender.[15]

"If we learn to read poetry properly," Eliot said in an address at Concord Academy in 1947, "the poet never persuades us to believe anything. . . . What we learn from Dante, or the Bhagavad-gita, or any other religious poetry is what it *feels* like to believe that religion." [16] The trouble with the passage quoted above is that it is trying to reason us into belief. "The Quartets," says Robert M. Adams, "offer an effort at affirmation, a weak two cheers for Incarnation. The one thing they do not convey is a sacramental view of the world, a rich dwelling in the holy joy of ordinary things." [17]

This is strong criticism, and other readers are not enthusiastic. Yet most would admit that there are passages of considerable beauty interspersed with passages of argument and exposition. The encounter with the "dead master" in "Little Gidding" is justly famous—Eliot said he had found it harder to write than any poetry of the same length.[18] There are other places that are equally memorable—for example, the lines about the rose garden at the very beginning, which present a moment both in and out of time.

> Dry the pool, dry concrete, brown edged,
> And the pool was filled with water out of sunlight,
> And the lotos rose, quietly, quietly,
> The surface glittered out of heart of light,
> And they were behind us, reflected in the pool.
> Then a cloud passed, and the pool was empty.
> Go, said the bird, for the leaves were full of children,
> Hidden excitedly, containing laughter.
> Go, go, go, said the bird: human kind
> Cannot bear very much reality.[19]

In January 1947 Eliot's wife Vivien died in a mental hospital in London. She had been confined since shortly before the Second World War. On a cold morning Eliot, her brother Maurice and the Fabers went to her burial. It is reported that Eliot's grief was "abnormally great," that he showed "unmistakable traces of remorse," that he said, "I've not a single second of happiness to look back on, and that makes it worse." [20]

It is hard to know what people are really feeling at weddings and funerals. Eliot had been married to the deranged woman for thirty-two years. Hugh Kenner points out that critics of *The Waste Land* speak of a drowned god and rites of the Nile—but have they thought that it might be drowning Vivien that Eliot had on his mind? In the "Game of Chess" section the woman offers to rush out with her hair down like Ophelia, and Ophelia's voice says goodnight to the "sweet ladies" in the pub. Ophelia's end was drowning. There are also, says Kenner, some revealing lines in *Ash-Wednesday*. The Lady who sits apart when the speaker has been eaten by the leopards, "withdrawn/ In a white gown," is very like a lady in a mental hospital. The "Lady of Silences," the "end of the endless/ Journey to no end," may have been Eliot's wife.[21]

In *The Family Reunion* Harry says of his wife, drowned at sea:

> One thinks to escape
> By violence, but one is still alone
> In an over-crowded desert, jostled by ghosts.[22]

Harry says that he pushed his wife overboard. Yet she is "nearer than ever," and *they*, the Furies, are always near.[23] These hints are all we are likely to know of Eliot's feelings about his separation from Vivien, her illness and death.

In 1948 he was awarded the Order of Merit. This is given by the King to twenty-four men and women he considers to have done distinguished work in their various walks of life. Eliot dined with the King and Queen. Later in the year he had an audience with Pope Pius XII. On this sixtieth birthday a T. S. Eliot *Festschrift* was published with contributions by distinguished authors.

He was offered a visiting fellowship to the Institute for Advanced Studies at Princeton, and in September sailed for New York, bringing with him the manuscript of a new play, *One-Eyed Riley* (to be retitled *The Cocktail Party*). He settled in Princeton near Trinity Church so that he could go to Mass every morning.

He went to see Pound in St. Elizabeth's. Ezra lectured him about "the Times Slithery Souplement and about Faber and Faber's obligation to launch the documents of a real paideuma, Kung for example. . . . And was there no one to translate the seven volumes of Frobenius's *Erlebte Erdteile?*" [24]

What Eliot had once said of William Blake was true of Pound: "There was . . . nothing to distract him from his interests or to corrupt these interests: neither the ambitions of parents or wife, nor the standards of society, nor the temptations of success." [25] Single-mindedness had been Blake's strength, and it was Pound's. But there was a disadvantage: "the dangers to which the naked man is exposed. His philosophy, like his visions, like his insight, like his technique, was his own. And accordingly he was inclined to attach more importance to it than an artist should." [26] This was what made Blake eccentric, and it accounted for the formlessness of his works. It accounted, also, for the formlessness of Pound's *Cantos*. "You cannot create a very large poem without introducing a more impersonal point of view, or splitting it up into various personalities." [27] The Possum had said that Blake "did not see enough, became too much occupied with ideas," whereas "What his genius required and what it sadly lacked, was a framework of accepted and traditional ideas which would have prevented him from indulging in a philosophy of his own, and concentrated his attention upon the problems of the poet." [28] From the framework of a Church the Possum looked forth on Ezra explicating Frobenius. Yet once more he heard Ezra's ideas about banking. It was not all Ezra's fault, thought the Possum in a pitying mood—it was the fault of the world, which had failed to provide what such a poet needed.[29]

Eliot had been at Princeton only a few weeks when news came that he had been awarded the Nobel Prize for literature. He went to Stockholm to receive it, dined with the King and Queen of Sweden, and did not return to New Jersey.

He returned to the flat in London he shared with John Hayward. He had moved there a few months ago. In 1926, when Eliot gave the Clark Lectures at Cambridge, Hayward was one of six undergraduates given the privilege of having breakfast with the visitor. Hayward was now an editor of English classics and the editor of *The Book Collector*. He and Eliot shared an interest in grammar, syntax and etymology. In good weather Eliot could be seen pushing Hayward in his wheelchair to Battersea Park or the grounds of Chelsea Hospital. For Hayward was an invalid—he had muscular dystrophy.

The flat was in Cheyne Walk, above rooms once inhabited by Henry James. It was comfortably furnished and steam-heated. Eliot's bedroom, however, was austere, with a single electric bulb and a crucifix over the bed. He worked standing up, at a typewriter placed on a stand. "It is a mystery to me," he said, "how anyone can write poetry except on a typewriter." [30]

He was doing very nicely. The Nobel Prize brought eight thousand pounds. *The Cocktail Party* earned him twenty-nine thousand pounds, of which all but four thousand was taken by the government as income tax. Eliot said, "I thought that I had at last provided something for my declining years, but I was disappointed." [31] Nevertheless, in 1950 the income from his salary at Faber and Faber, and from his books, amounted to four thousand pounds. And his rent and other expenses came to only one thousand pounds.[32]

He gave half his time to his duties as an editor at Faber, the rest to his writing. Occasionally he had to prepare a lecture. After the war he had made a six-week lecture tour of Germany, beginning in Hamburg and ending in Munich. He spoke to the Germans of the need for European unity, the hope for unity in the Christian tradition. It was a topic he had stressed for years in *The Criterion* until, on the eve of war, he stopped publishing the magazine. Everything then had seemed to be coming apart; there was not much hope of a European community of "a few intelligent people." But in Germany among the ruins once more he dared to hope.

In 1956 he gave a lecture at the University of Minnesota to a crowd of thirteen thousand. They had to use the football stadium. Eliot was reported to have been paid two thousand dollars, the biggest lecture fee on record. This was the occasion on which he poked fun at his own "Notes on *The Waste Land*," of which critics made so much.

But the time had passed when everything he said or wrote gave off a sparkle. These days when he labored he was likely to bring forth, with an "If and Perhaps and But," what looked like a mouse. It was hard to tell the difference between one of T. S. Eliot's definitions, arrived at after a struggle, and anybody's platitude. At times you could hardly make out what he was saying, so woolly was the prose. "We can, I think, accept without much difficulty the apparent paradox that the European poet is at the same time no less, but in a way rather more positively a man of his particular race, country, and local culture than is the poet appreciable only by his compatriots." [33] This is from the lecture on Goethe. Ronald Duncan asked him, "Isn't it a bit of a grind for you to write about Goethe?" "It is," he said. "I can't stand his stuff." [34] Nevertheless he gave the lecture, to an audience at Hamburg University, on the occasion of his receiving the Goethe Prize. He had become an institution.

His listeners took the will for the deed. When they listened to Eliot speak it was not only the present words they heard—they were remembering things he said long ago, sentences that had become part of their lives:

"Some one said: 'The dead writers are remote from us because we *know* so much more than they did.' Precisely, and they are that which we know." [35]

"The poet must become more and more comprehensive, more allusive, more indirect, in order to force, to dislocate if necessary, language into his meaning." [36]

They remembered,

> O O O O that Shakespeherian Rag—
> It's so elegant
> So intelligent [37]

Honors accumulated. Was there ever a poet so honored during his lifetime? He had an honorary degree from St. Andrews; he was an honorary fellow of Magdalene College, Cambridge, and of Merton College, Oxford. He was invited to open an exhibition, "Le Livre Anglais," in Paris—the President of France, the British Ambassador, and other dignitaries attended. In 1954 he was awarded the Hanseatic Goethe Prize; in 1959 the Dante Gold Medal, which he received at a ceremony in Florence. He was awarded the American Medal of Freedom. He was president of the Classical Association, the Virgil Society, and the London Library.

Surely there had never been a poet who belonged to so many clubs. He was a member of the Oxford and Cambridge; of the Burke Club, a Tory dining club for Members of Parliament and Journalists; of The Club, which consisted mainly of peers. He joined the Garrick and the Athenaeum. He served on committees, as had his Unitarian grandfather. He gathered with other important men at The Moot, to discuss important questions. He did not spend much time at the club for pleasure's sake, but he understood the life of a St. James's Street Cat.

> So, much in this way, passes Bustopher's day—
> At one club or another he's found.[38]

Which brings us to the cats. People in faraway places, in America and Australia, knew about T. S. Eliot and cats. He had written a funny, affectionate book of verse about them.

> Macavity, Macavity, there's no one like Macavity,
> For he's a fiend in feline shape, a monster of depravity.
> You may meet him in a by-street, you may see him in the square—
> But when a crime's discovered, then *Macavity's not there!* [39]

As with everything he wrote, there were different levels of meaning. There was a level for the nursery, a level for logicians, and a level for the Church. Macavity was a case of not seeing is believing: *Credo quia impossibile est.* The unseen Macavity is a more practical cat—we believe in him more—than cats we have actually known.

In his sixties he began to suffer from emphysema, a disease of the lungs. In order to relieve this in the winter he would travel to Cape Town, usually with the Fabers.

In 1949 a new secretary came to work at Faber and Faber. Valerie Fletcher was twenty-two. At her school in Yorkshire she had been noticed for "her cheerful character and intellectual and physical competence." [40] Her ambition was to be secretary to a famous writer. She was secretary to Charles Morgan the novelist before becoming Eliot's. (Morgan is one of the curiosities of literature—regarded on the Continent as an outstanding English novelist, he is scarcely read in England.) Valerie Fletcher was Eliot's secretary for seven years, the fairy number. Then they were married.

As with every important step Eliot took in his personal life— his first marriage, his confirmation—the second marriage was "prepared as secretly as if it had been a conspiracy." [41] In one account, Eliot did not inform John Hayward of his plans in advance, he waited until after they were married. "Why didn't you tell me before?" Hayward is reported to have asked. To which Eliot replied, "Well, John, I thought you would be so cross." [42] The official version, however, "vouched for by the present Mrs. Eliot," has Eliot telling Hayward about it two days before the wedding. Hayward takes the news of Eliot's leaving "extremely well." Eliot promises to pay three hundred pounds a year of the four hundred and seventy pounds' yearly rent for the next four years, and keeps his promise.[43]

As time went by Hayward told resentful stories about Eliot's leaving to get married. John Hayward has been called "the most malicious gossip in London." [44] There have been as many claimants to this as to the title of the wickedest woman in London, but if Hayward told the stories attributed to him he was surely a contender. In one account Eliot handed him a letter breaking the news and hovered around while he read it. Hayward said, "Sit down, my dear Tom, and let's talk about it." Eliot replied, "Oh, no, no, I can't, the taxi is waiting." [45] Hayward is also reported to have said that Eliot had been removing his clothes by stealth from the flat for weeks before his departure, and that he telephoned to say he was married and not coming back. "Think of the treacherousness of a man taking all his shirts and all his ties, little by little!" [46]

Shortly before the ceremony at St. Barnabas's, Eliot discovered that Jules Laforgue had been married in the same church.

The wedding took place, by special dispensation, at six-thirty in the morning. Then the newlyweds flew to Nice for their honeymoon.

Everyone who saw Tom and Valerie Eliot together thought that they were happy. They were given to holding hands and doting on each other in public. They set up housekeeping in a ground-floor flat in Kensington. "Tom Eliot," Aldous Huxley remarked, "is now curiously dull—as a result, perhaps, of being at last happy in his second marriage." [47]

They made three trips to the Caribbean in winter. Tom preferred to go by ship. En route they visited the United States and he showed Valerie around. When they were in New York they stayed rent-free as guests in the apartment of Margot Cohn, a friend who had a business in rare books and manuscripts. There Eliot saw old friends and new poets, and consented to be interviewed. He was friendly; he made the drinks himself, pouring jolting glassfuls of whiskey. Valerie came in now and then, a handsome, cheerful woman, and they would exchange affectionate words.

In *The Cocktail Party* Reilly says of marriage, "The best of a bad job is all any of us make of it." [48] Seeing Tom and Valerie together it was impossible not to think that his attitude to marriage and other matters would have been different had he been married to someone like Valerie in the first place. But that was like wondering what T. S. Eliot would have been like if he had been someone else.

> Two live as one
> One live as two
> Two live as three
> Under the bam
> Under the boo
> Under the bamboo tree [49]

He was sitting wrapped in a white bathrobe on a beach of white sand. A sparkling blue sea covered with whitecaps stretched to the horizon. White clouds drifted lazily and an occasional seagull was blown from right to left. The breeze was warm, and along the beach the tops of coconut trees swayed in circles.

The proper spelling was "coconuts." But in the film they had spelled it wrong. He ought to write to Groucho about it—perhaps Groucho could have it corrected. Every time they showed the film, there it was: *The Cocoanuts.*

> Tell me in what part of the wood
> Do you want to flirt with me?
> Under the breadfruit, banyan, palmleaf
> Or under the bamboo tree? [50]

Valerie was splashing about in the water. He felt too lazy to swim. But in a little while he would join her. The water, like the sky, was warm.

> Doris: That's not life, that's no life
>   Why I'd just as soon be dead.
> Sweeney: That's what life is. Just is
> Doris: What is?
>   What's that life is?
> Sweeney: Life is death.
>   I knew a man once did a girl in— [51]

A cloud passed over the sun. Then the shadow passed and the waves danced.

Valerie swam a few strokes. He ought to get in a little swimming before lunch.

He no longer "ought" to do anything. Most of his life had been spent doing what had to be done. They thought that you chose to write poetry, for example. Bad poets might, but it had not been true for him—he had had no choice. Writing had been a necessity. He had had to write poems in order to get rid of something in himself. He had said it more than once: "The progress of an artist is a continual self-sacrifice, a continual extinction of personality." [52]

He had done all that he could, and there was no longer any need to do anything. He wouldn't get up. Definitely. He'd just sit and watch her swim.

III

William Carlos Williams,
or Experience

15

Mr. and Mrs. Williams

HIS earliest memory was of the blizzard of '88. He had been put outdoors and he yelled to be taken in, out of the wind and cold. That same spring he went out with a handful of salt to try to catch some sparrows because his Uncle Godwin told him to.

His mother said, though he did not remember it himself, that when he was a child he used to beat the drum accurately. His Uncle Irving hit the big drum slowly, Bam! Bam! Then William would come in on the small drum, rapidly, Bam bam! They said that his timing was perfect. And his mother remembered the first time he'd laughed out loud. "Pop was chopping down a small tree. Each time he'd swing an axe and I heard it wham into the wood, I'd let out a wild cackle of delight." [1]

His mother came from Mayagüez in Puerto Rico. Her maiden name was Raquel Hélène Hoheb. She was half French—the other half a "mixed breed," Dutch, Spanish and Jewish.[2] "How many generations they had been in Mayagüez and how they had mixed with the Spanish, is completely lost." [3]

Her brother Carlos was sent to Paris to study medicine, and when he returned to Puerto Rico he saw to it that his sister was sent there to study painting. This was in the late eighteen-seventies, the time of Cézanne and Renoir. Raquel Hélène did not meet painters of this kind, however; she was a good Beaux Arts student, assiduously copying the masters and carrying out her exercises. She had a Grand Prix to show for it, a few gold medals which all

195

her life she kept hidden in a trunk, some charcoal sketches, and a portrait of herself by a cousin named Ludovic. The portrait, significantly, was unfinished. Then the money ran out and she had to return to Puerto Rico. Money wasn't the only reason—she was afraid of the improper advances of the father of the two girls with whom she was staying. In any case, she left Paris. She left the chestnut trees, the smell of turpentine and paint, the shuttered room overlooking a cobbled street. They had been the best years of her life. She was heartbroken, "her preparations for a career unfinished." [4]

All the races and colors of the earth mingled in the West Indies. Luchetties, Gordons, Monsantos, Kruegers . . . She married an Englishman named Williams. William George Williams. He brought her to the United States and they settled in Rutherford, New Jersey.

Raquel Hélène was a defeated romantic. "Despondency, discouragement, despair [were] periodic factors in her life. Under it [lay] the true life, undefeated if embittered, hard as nails, little loving, easily mistaken for animal selfishness." [5]

She told anecdotes of her girlhood in Puerto Rico. "The *guave* you find growing more in the country, like a plum. Yes, they eat them raw—they are very good. The *mango* they plant in yards like our apple-trees or peach-trees. . . . Then there is the *caimito*. It is round like an apple and bright green but inside it is pure white, like milk. Toledo always called me *cara de caimito,* because when I was young my face was round like that."

"We never went bathing at the sea. What! take off our clothes where men could see us! . . . When the Americans went there and went bathing in their suits with the men, the people were scandalized."

"When the little negro boys would be swimming someone would watch, then there would be a cry. Here comes a *baracuta!* and everybody would scramble to get on shore. Once your father was just going to dive in when he looked down and saw one quiet in the water looking up at him and—and waiting." [6]

William George Williams had travelled in South and Central America. He told fascinating stories of his adventures. Once on a journey by mule in Costa Rica he was short of food and ate pâtés of black ants. He remembered Bluebeard's castle, from his own childhood on the island of St. Thomas. He told of the great earthquake and tidal wave of the seventies when ships were stranded high and dry and it was thought that at any moment the island would sink.

He was a gentleman, curiously mild. His son William did not remember seeing him angry except once, when he tried to force him to eat a tomato. William detested tomatoes. "He attempted to jam the fruit down my throat, but he never did that again." [7]

Mr. Williams lived in America till the end of his life, but never became an American citizen. He remained an Englishman. "He was too English," says his son, "for me ever to be able to talk with him animal to animal." [8] The "curious mildness" of the father came to mean, for his son the poet, that English life was restrained, English traditions remote, English poetry lacking in animal vitality. He hated that tomato.

A few days after his father died, on Christmas Day 1918, William dreamed that he saw him coming downstairs; in his hand he had some business letters on which he was concentrating. "I noticed him and with joy cried out, 'Pop! So you're not dead!' But he only looked up at me over his right shoulder and commented severely, 'You know all that poetry you're writing. Well, it's no good!' I was left speechless and woke trembling. I have never dreamed of him since." [9]

All his life William Carlos Williams wrote "in the American grain" in order to prove his father the Englishman wrong. All his life he refought the American War of Independence, breaking loose like the colonies from English force and culture. He concentrated his attack on language, for language is the chief tool of empire—certainly it has been so for the English, and Macaulay revealed the secret, not meaning to, when he said that an Englishman would rather do without India than without the works of Shakespeare. In fact, the two were one: it was not just powder and shot, but English voices, that conquered the natives of India and New Zealand. The young lieutenants steadied themselves with English on the slope at Talavera. The massed battalions of the French were taken in enfilade, they received the fire of English humor and fancy all at once, and shriveled like straw in an oven.

> Or like the snow falls in the river—
> A moment white, then melts for ever . . .[10]

Actually, it was a Scotsman who wrote this. But the Scots are practically English, a conquered race, and at Waterloo they died for the King's English in rows.

Not so the Americans. They were beyond the pale, had put themselves there by revolting against the King (whether George or William). As a consequence they were punished—they had no poets. There were American humorists such as Artemus Ward, and Western characters like Joaquin Miller, but where was the American Tennyson, the American Keats? American writers were tolerable only when, like Henry Wadsworth Longfellow, they sounded like transplanted Englishmen.

This prejudice, maintained by American critics in the Genteel Tradition and endemic in American universities, exasperated William Carlos Williams. It was all the more annoying because the English had, indeed, been wonderful poets. It is a complex fate being an American, said Henry James, and Whitman bears witness to the backward pull of tradition even as he proceeds to dismiss it:

> Dead poets, philosophs, priests,
> Martyrs, artists, inventors, governments long since,
> Language-shapers, on other shores,
> Nations once powerful, now reduced, withdrawn, or desolate,
> I dare not proceed till I respectfully credit what you have left,
>   wafted hither:
> I have perused it—own it is admirable, (moving awhile among it;)
> Think nothing can ever be greater—nothing can ever deserve
>   more than it deserves;
> Regarding it all intently a long while—then dismissing it,
> I stand in my place, with my own day, here.[11]

It is not that the past was wrong, but that it is not the present; not that England is a bad place to live, but that it is not America. The war of American writers against English tradition is a civil war and therefore all the more urgent for those who are engaged in it. There were American writers at the turn of the century who were content to ape the English, but William Carlos Williams carried the war into the new century. It was as though he were compelled to by the symbolism of his life, having an English father.

William George Williams had been brought from England to the United States by his mother. There was a story that when she was a young girl in London she was "picked up by a well-to-do London family by the name of Godwin." William Godwin's wife was Mary Wollstonecraft, Shelley's mother-in-law, and "the whole lot of them supporters of the principle of free love." William

Carlos Williams lets his fancy play on this: "God knows of the intimacies of my grandmother and the set that surrounded her in those years; we have only evidence of it in her devotion to the name of Godwin which she gave her child." [12]

Her own name was Welcome. Nevertheless, the ship bringing her and her five-year-old son ran aground on Fire Island. For a quiet man, Mr. Williams had had an adventurous life. His mother was married again, to a photographer from St. Thomas in the West Indies. So it was that he was raised there, in the tropics. From St. Thomas they moved to Puerto Plata. Most of their friends were English.

Mr. Williams spoke Spanish as easily as he spoke English. His work required it—he was at one time the advertising manager of a firm that did business in South America. He loved to read more than anything else, even more than working in his garden. "He invariably spoke with a distinguished choice of his words," says William Carlos Williams. "It sometimes exasperated me." Mr. Williams was a liberal and something of a socialist. He and Mrs. Williams helped to found the Unitarian Society of Rutherford. The children were raised as Unitarians and attended Sunday school.

His greatest love was for Shakespeare and he read all the plays to the family. He also read aloud the dialect poems of Paul Laurence Dunbar. "We were not an especially literary family," says his son William, "but loved to read anything, anything that came along." [13] There was a copy of Dante's *Inferno* with engravings by Gustave Doré. This was not read aloud, but William came back time after time to look at the "magnificent nude figures of damned and beautiful ladies of antiquity." They scared him but he kept coming back, sneaking a look when he thought no one was looking.[14] He was profoundly disappointed, failing to discover "the anatomical secrets which so fascinated [him] at the time." [15]

In the same way he would eavesdrop at night when he was supposed to be asleep and his father was reading some "forbidden novel" aloud to his mother. "I remember hearing, as much as I could stay awake for, du Maurier's *Trilby*, with the particular delight of a child taking part in something that had been forbidden." [16] So he heard about Svengali the evil Jew, and Trilby, and Little Billee. He named two of his pet mice Trilby and Little Billee. But after this account of forbidden things he says, "My father was not one to keep anything from me if he thought I could understand it." [17] He seems to be of two minds when speaking of his father; his remarks give an impression of frustrated love—he was never able to explain his feelings to the "curiously mild" Englishman.

William discovered Charles Darwin's *The Descent of Man* and *The Origin of Species* on the "library" shelves in the parlor. His father promised him a dollar apiece if he would read them; he took up the challenge and read them avidly.[18] He also read Herbert Spencer, "but his habit of dictating to an amanuensis while in the act of rowing a boat impressed me more than did the text." He read the beginning of *The Canterbury Tales*. But his real love was for Palgrave's *Golden Treasury of English Verse* "leading to the *Endymion*." [19]

Mr. Williams and his half-brother Godwin, who lived with them, played the flute accompanied by Mrs. Williams on the piano.

Mrs. Williams was a medium. Her husband was accustomed to seeing her go into a trance and speak with a voice that was not her own. When it happened in front of the boys, however, they were startled. "So these are the boys," she said. "How they have grown. Come here, my dears, and let me see you." She said that she was "Lou Paine." Then the seizure passed. Lou Paine was the wife of an old friend then living in Los Angeles. Mr. Williams made enquiries; it turned out that at the time of Mrs. Williams' seizure Lou had been ill—in fact, had been given up for dead following an abdominal operation. Her spirit, however, had returned to her body, or some such explanation.[20]

Before there was a Unitarian church in Rutherford, Mr. and Mrs. Williams held spiritualistic séances at one house or another. When Mrs. Williams was in one of her trances she would be possessed by an uncontrollable shaking of the head. It could happen anywhere and at any time. "I even saw it happen once," says William, "while she was playing the piano at Sunday school. Ed and I were horribly embarrassed." But most often it occurred at home, "under strained emotional circumstances as after the death of some friend or intimate, but not necessarily involving the appearance of that particular person." [21]

By "appearance" he means the way in which his mother would indicate the presence of a spirit. The boys dreaded these occasions. There would be a fixed look in her eyes, her face would flush, she would reach for a hand. She struggled to clasp it but was unable to. Her face became contorted. Someone suggested a name—she shook her head violently, no. Finally the right name was spoken, she grasped the hand in both of hers, and the presence left.

Mr. Williams believed that the seizures were authentic—the remark, coming suddenly in Williams' *Autobiography*, suggests that they were not. "Pop believed literally, I think, in their authenticity: that the spirits of the dead did materialize through her and did try to reach us." But Mrs. Williams' son seems to have had his doubts: "Why they should want to come I never could understand." [22]

As we have seen, Mrs. Williams played the piano for the Sunday school. Mr. Williams was the superintendent, and held the position for eighteen years. Young William sang in the choir. At some time in early adolescence, he tells us, he determined to be perfect. "The fascination of it still affects me: Never to commit evil in any form, never especially to lie, to falsify, to deceive, but to tell the truth always, come what might of it. The elevation of spirit that accompanies that resolve is a blissful one." [23]

From an early age William Carlos Williams was unusually aware of his locality. "Of mixed ancestry," he says, "I felt from earliest childhood that America was the only home I could ever possibly call my own. I felt that it was expressly founded for me, personally, and that it must be my first business in life to possess it; that only by making it my own from the beginning to my own day, in detail, should I ever have a basis for knowing where I stood. I must have a basis for orienting myself formally in the beliefs which activated me from day to day." [24]

Just over the back fence was Kipp's woods, "our wilderness." The boys could sit on the fence and talk by the hour. He knew every tree in the wood, hickory, chestnut and dogwood. He went shooting robins with a BB gun. He watched Mr. Kipp kill a squirrel. He hit the tree with a wooden maul; the squirrel popped out; he hit the tree again, the squirrel fell to the ground and the dog killed it. He watched two dogs coupling. But what he really learned was "the way the moss climbed about a tree's roots, what growing dogwood and iron wood looked like." He got to know the box turtle and the salamander. It was a pleasure to remember the flowers: "The slender neck of the anemone particularly haunts me for some reason and the various sorts of violets—the tall blue ones, those with furry stems and the large, scarce, branching yellow ones, stars of Bethlehem, spring beauties, wild geranium, hepaticas with three-lobed leaves." His pleasure in flowers was unbounded and secret. He was comforted by the flowers.[25]

He needed comforting, for he was an unhappy, disappointed child. "It was due to the mood of our home," he says in a letter to his wife Florence.[26] What mood was this? It may have been imparted by his mother, who had given up her career as an artist in order to marry the Englishman Williams, "To have children and to—exhale her fragrance—or lack of it—into the surrounding air." "A woman creates a son and dies in her own mind. That is the end. She is dead, she says."[27]

So the English had killed art.

But this wasn't the whole of it. He was unhappy on his own behalf. He had "eager desires, which no world, and certainly not the Rutherford of those days, could satisfy. I do not say it was not good for me but I never could do what I really and violently wanted to—either in athletics, studies or amorous friendships— so I was gnawing my insides all day long.

"And yet," he continues, "underneath it all there was an enormous faith and solidity. Inside me I was like iron and with a love for the world and a determination to do good in the world that was like the ocean itself. I had a mountainous self pride and a conviction that could afford to adventure and decide for myself."[28]

When Mr. Williams was on a prolonged business trip in South or Central America they stayed at the Bagellon house, a run-down farm on the outskirts of town. It was a huge building with a porch all around it and with a cupola on top from which, through a telescope, he once looked at the moon.[29]

He explored Rutherford, a young Columbus extending his world of streets, houses and fields. In those days there were no sewers, no water supply, no gas, no electricity, no telephone, not even a trolley car. It was an America that some look back to with nostalgia—the Fourth-of-July-picnic, surrey-with-the-fringe-on-top America of popular song. "From the cistern the water was pumped by a hand pump in the kitchen into a tin-lined wooden tank in the attic. Ed and I got a dime apiece for an hour's pumping when it was needed."[30]

There was boyish mischief, in spite of the resolution to be perfect, such as the time the boys were trespassing in Kipp's rye field and "old man Kipp and his colored hand" crept up on them.

Kipp chased them and they ran. "But I ran right into Kipp's arms. He grabbed me by the throat and, lifting me, half-threw, half-kicked me over the fence." [31]

Straight out of *Tom Sawyer!* And there was no viciousness in it. They didn't set out to destroy anything, like those of a later generation who burned and uprooted the old man's crops and drove him out of business.

There was a Becky in the scene—a Becky with falling drawers. He went for a walk in the woods with her and Lizzie Nevins. Lizzie said, "Wait here a minute, her drawers are falling down." So he waited while they went behind a tree and refastened the garment. Then Lizzie urged them to be alone: "Go ahead, you two. Go over there in the rye field if you want to and I'll watch. Go on. She wants you to. She told me she did. Go on."

He and the girl sat in the middle of the rye field looking at each other, "too embarrassed even to open our mouths to ask a question." [32]

There were characters such as Uncle Godwin, their father's half-brother who was never quite right in the head. "A grand rouser of a child's imagination," he taught William a rhyme he never forgot:

> Oh boys keep away
> From the girls I say
> And give them plenty of room
> For when you come to wed
> They'll bang you on the head
> With the bald-headed end of a broom.

Uncle Godwin finally tried to attack William's friend Jim Hyslop, and had to be put away in the asylum.[33] Good American stuff, this!

Mr. Williams' mother lived with them. She tried to take William over as though he were her child. "But once Mother lost her temper and laid the old gal out with a smack across the puss that my mother joyfully remembered until her death." [34] More heartwarming Americana!

There were memorable occasions such as the Iveson wedding in the mansion across the street. "The worm of gaslights from the house to the street was lighted, the house ablaze with lights, the guests arriving from the railroad station—a continuous row of carriages—it was the finest sight I ever saw." [35]

One gets the picture—an American life. All that is needed is a brass band—trombones, trumpets, drum—the fire department, the police, veterans of Chancellorsville and Cold Harbor, veterans of Manila Bay, and the boy scouts. "William Carlos Williams, an American life."

Not quite. The more we examine this seemingly typical life, the more it shoots off at odd angles. In the middle of an idyllic narration, for example, there is a mention of disappointment, some veiled melancholy. A sense of despair caught from his mother's discontent . . . transmitted in words or by sighs heaved from a depth. It erupted in the terrifying séances.

Terror, he says, dominated his childhood. What kind of terror? From what cause? He does not say—instead he chooses to lapse into indirection. Though for the most part William Carlos Williams is a clear writer—he is famous for insisting on clarity and plain speech—at times he can be maddeningly opaque. He says, "I had the normal fears, naturally, but they could be condoned, not the terror that flared from hidden places and all 'heaven.' " [36] What does this mean? That he was terrified by thoughts of heaven and hell? Some Latin darkness creeps in here, by way of Raquel Hélène. There is something terrifying—certainly it is not typically American—about this overhanging mother. Passion . . . unpredictability . . . art that has been baffled and paces to and fro. Sometimes it seems possessed—its features are distorted. It seems to be struggling and it speaks an unknown name.

"A childlike innocence, unaffected by age with its maddening mutilations—remains still her virtue. To some it is childish, all the characteristics of a spoiled child—which she was—with her bad temper, fears, vindictiveness of an undisciplined infant. To others an indestructibleness, a permanence in defiance of the offensive discipline which is only a virtue to those who wish to flatten out every rebellious instinct down to a highway levelness for their own crazy facility. Be that as it may she has not given in. And is still, as a child, amused." [37]

Raquel Hélène was poetry. When he speaks of his mother's character William Carlos Williams is speaking of what poetry should be. It is as innocent as a child. It is "in defiance of the offensive discipline." It is amused.

He speaks of "a secret life he wanted to tell openly," a "secret world of perfection." [38] This is the echo of his mother who, he tells us, "retreated to her dreams." [39] It was not merely a retreat—

it was a preference. She cherished her loves and hates in secret. So does poetry. Poetry is another, secret world, created in spite of this. Poetry is a passionate spirit, not amenable to discipline. It is sympathetic to those whom the world thinks "bad."

All his life William Carlos Williams would be fascinated by those whom the world thought "bad." "It isn't because they fascinated me by their evildoings that they were 'bad' boys or girls." As with other of Williams' sentences, something has gone wrong with this one—the idea has been put the wrong way round. But the next sentence is clear: "It was because they were there full of a perfection of the longest leap, the most unmitigated daring, the longest chances." [40] His sympathy for "bad" types came from his understanding of his mother's hidden life, her rebellious, passionate, vindictive streak. He was drawn to the "bad" boys and girls in the Rutherford public schools—as later, when he was a doctor, he would be drawn to the poor and outcast. There was poetry in their lives. "The underlying meaning of all they want to tell us and have always failed to communicate is the poem, the poem which their lives are being lived to realize. No one will believe it. And it is the actual words, as we hear them spoken under all circumstances, which contain it." [41] Therefore poetry should be written with the sound of speech.

On the other hand was his English father and the Unitarian church. The need to succeed. He couldn't indulge his passions, be one of the "bad" ones—he would have to find a way to fit poetry into his life without disrupting it.

There was one girl, one "ignorant, fulsome bit of flesh" that almost caused him to flunk out of grammar school. "I almost ruined my young days over her." [42] There is a self-destructive side to Williams—he admires people who are willing to let themselves go entirely. "The woman who throws herself from the rocks into the sea has more gist, more force than the sum of every college." [43] So it is not to be a typical life after all, though it may seem so on the surface; it is to be rebellious, even desperate at times. There is a part of his mind, like his mother's life, that has been repressed. "Under that language to which we have been listening all our lives a new, a more profound language . . . It is what they call poetry." [44]

One night when Mr. Williams came home he announced that he was going to Buenos Aires to set up a factory for the manufacture of Florida Water and would not be back for a year. As he would be absent there was no reason for them to stay in Rutherford. How would they like to go to Europe for a year? They were all for it—"Mother wanted to return to Paris for one last look before saying good-bye to her romantic youth." [45]

So it was that William, aged fourteen,[46] and his brother Ed, a year younger, went to school at the Château de Lancy near Geneva. "We were mere infants, hundreds of years younger than most of the sixty-two other boys there." William climbed the mountain slopes and went bird-nesting "with Leon Pont, of Rajputana, India—a wild guy if there ever was one." Once he was caned on his bare bottom "by the British contingent, the older boys of the school, for dropping a paper water-bomb on the head of a boy named Potter." They held him down by his hands and feet in order to cane him. There was no need for that. "I would not have moved—and didn't. Do you think an American would have turned a hair for an Englishman?" [47]

He continued his researches into nature. "My greatest joy was still the *ruisseau,* the icy-clear mountain brook running beside the soccer field, and the flowers growing about it, that spring, before the fields had been mowed. There I first became acquainted with the native yellow primrose, so delightfully sweetscented. The green-flowered asphodel made a tremendous impression on me. I collected all such flowers, as many as I found, and pressed them between the leaves of a copybook. I grew tall and strong for my age." [48]

He played soccer, swam in the lake at 10° centigrade, collected stamps. And there was "General deviltry of all sorts." He was particularly impressed with the dark-complexioned student named Joncelin who got into fights—once he threatened to stab "Tum Devis, a Siamese prince." At sunset Joncelin rode his bicycle at breakneck speed through the paths. "The rest of us would be lolling around when suddenly he'd be at it, slowly at first, then faster and faster until he'd be rounding those turns in the semi-dark, reversing himself, coming out and driving in again round after round like a madman." [49] Throughout his life any demon-driven behavior fascinated Williams, any action that broke through conventions and seemed to be making its own laws, discovering its own form, like a work of art. He prized the dark people whose lives, as often as not, ended in disgrace, obscurity, disease.

Then their mother took them to Paris, where they lived with their cousins the Truflys in Montmartre. They wore knee breeches

and attended the Lycée Condorcet. William excelled at jumping—
"I could jump higher than any but one of the boys in the school."
He had a French cousin who was always urging him to give his,
the cousin's, enemies a *coup de poing Américain*—an American
punch in the snoot—but he had no real wish to. "How could I
walk up to a guy and slug him for no reason at all?" [50]

As they hadn't learned French at Geneva—everyone there spoke
English—they were at a disadvantage in the Lycée, so their mother
took them out and had them tutored by an aunt. Tante Alice
Monsanto had been one of their mother's best friends in the
seventies, the dear Beaux Arts days, now gone beyond recall.

They mixed with a Paris crowd on holiday, they saw a man
operating a puppet theater, they watched the *Petoman!* "who let
farts! at command! Very French and hilariously funny, ending as
always with the grand release of all the residual air that had been
pumped into his rectum with a bicycle pump—'Ma Belle-Mère!'
My mother-in-law." [51]

It was the time, Williams tells us, of the Dreyfus trial. There
was violent anti-Semitic feeling which showed itself even in the
middle of the Carnival, "though in a good-natured vein, it must
be said." [52] Good-natured violent anti-Semitism . . . it beat the
Petoman hands down.

They made the usual tourist pilgrimage to the Catacombs, the
Eiffel Tower, various churches. One night they made a circuit
of the clubs in Montmartre.

In the spring of 1899 they returned to Rutherford. The boys
went back to public school where the teaching wasn't distinguished
and where, says William, he "re-encountered some of the same
girls that he had known in the eighth grade." [53] He was pretty
wild, and the outlook wasn't promising. "I went through hell,"
he would tell his son William thirty-five years later, "what with
worrying about my immortal soul and my hellish itch to screw
almost any female I could get my hands on—which I never did."
He was maladjusted—having grown up in "a more or less civilized
environment." [54]

To curb this propensity it was decided to take him out of the
high school in Rutherford and enroll him at Horace Mann in
New York City, where the teaching was reputed to be better. The
school was on Morningside Heights, near Columbia University,
so that every morning William and Ed took a train, crossed to
Manhattan on the ferry, and rode the El up to 116th or 125th

Street. The brothers were closely knit by these experiences, until they quarreled over a girl.[55]

William took the course in science—chemistry rather than Greek. He studied a little Latin, French (which he spoke), English, German, mathematics, chemistry, physics and "the elements of joinery." The classes were large and serious, and he worked with enthusiasm.

In English he was taught by Uncle Billy Abbott, who, for the first time in his life, made him feel the excitement of great books.[56] For the first time he actually looked at a poem, and he found it interesting. "I read *The Ancient Mariner, Lycidas, Comus* and studied out a process that was unfamiliar to me. I read *L'Allegro* and *Il Penseroso*." [57]

He had his first literary success, writing a paper that retold a story by Robert Louis Stevenson, about a man on a canoe trip who fell into the water. But he held on to his paddle. William made a point of this—he had not lost his paddle.[58]

He enjoyed the history of Greece and Rome and England. And French. But mathematics was not his forte. The mathematics master, Mr. Bickford, gave him a pass in algebra, however. "You'll never be a mathematician, Williams," he said, "but you show an understanding of the process. And I'm going to pass you." It was the most intelligent verdict, and from a teacher, that he ever encountered. "It is hard to realize how important such a moment can be in a man's life. That single piece of intelligence had more to do in straightening my difficulties, in putting me on a correct course than any single thing that I can remember. He saw my mind and realized what it was not intended to perform. And he acted accordingly. That's what it means, at best, to be a teacher." [59]

He went out for athletics. He was too light for football, but he did well at baseball and track. But he overdid the track, strained his heart sprinting an extra lap, and had to give up athletics.

Lust "burned him to a cinder in those days." Then he went through a "stage of asceticism"—providentially, for it took up the space between his passion for athletics and the passion for art.[60]

Up to the age of eighteen he had no intention of being a writer or doing anything in the arts. He tried a little painting, using his mother's old tubes of paint.

Then he wrote his first poem. "[It] was born like a bolt out of the blue. It came unsolicited and broke a spell of disillusion and suicidal despondency."

> a black, black cloud
> flew over the sun
> driven by fierce flying
> rain

He was filled with joy when he wrote it, "mysterious, soul-satisfying joy." Then he thought, How could the clouds be driven by the rain? Stupid.

But the joy remained. "From that moment I was a poet." [61]

How had this come about? He wanted to protest against the "blackguarding" and beauty of the world. The only way he could find was poetry—and prose to a lesser extent. So he gradually began to learn, very slowly. He had to cling to what he had and not relinquish it in the face of tradition. Tradition was the enemy—there were good safe stereotypes everywhere. He had to learn to let himself go. But there was the danger that if you let go you ran into chaos. So he had to invent, or try to invent. Not speaking English—speaking American, helped a lot.[62]

"Words offered themselves and I jumped at them. To write, like Shakespeare! and besides I wanted to tell people, to tell 'em off, plenty. There would be a bitter pleasure in that, bitter because I instinctively knew no one much would listen. So what? I wanted to write and writing required no paraphernalia. That was the early skirmish, ending with the spontaneous poem—a black, black cloud, etc." [63]

His present objective, however, was to be a doctor, like his mother's brother Carlos after whom he was named. He reasoned that this would give him freedom—having an income would enable him to write just what he liked. "No one, and I meant no one (for money) was ever (never) going to tell me how or what I was going to write. That was number one." [64]

16

The Sensible Choice

WILLIAM Carlos Williams did not go to college—he went directly from high school to medical school at the University of Pennsylvania. He had to meet their entrance requirements, that was all. He was the second youngest in a class of one hundred and twenty.

No sooner had he begun studying medicine than he wanted to quit and devote himself to writing.[1] It would be a recurring complaint. Twenty-seven years later, in answer to the question, "What should you most like to do, to know, to be? (In case you are not satisfied)," he replied, "I'd like to be able to give up the practice of medicine and write all day and night." [2]

But he didn't. At times he claimed that the practice of medicine gave him the material of stories and poems—it even gave him the language of poetry.[3] But the overriding argument was that the income from his medical practice enabled him to write just as he pleased. He did not relish the Romantic idea of suffering for art— he was no Chatterton. "I would not," he says, "court disease, live in the slums for the sake of art, give lice a holiday." He saw his life as divided between medicine, "work," and his writing, and he attributed each part to the influence of one parent. "I would not 'die for art,' but live for it, grimly! and work, work, work (like Pop), beat the game and be free (like Mom, poor soul!) to write, write as I alone should write, for the sheer drunkenness of it . . . And complete defiance of the world or what might come after it, if anything." [4]

There was a disadvantage—he could not find time to read the things he liked. "I shall never forget with what fascination I read *Les Misérables,* which I had just discovered, in the original, when I should have been hard upon normal anatomy. I am a slow reader." [5]

He had to omit reading for pleasure, and he never became in any sense a scholar. He was ignorant of literature as it is taught in universities. He would not be able to range widely like Pound, nor deeply like Eliot. As a result, all his life Williams resented scholars, especially those who were employed in departments of English. Williams speaks of professors and departments of English so frequently and with such rancor that it is clear he thinks they have done him harm. What right do they have to teach literature? Writing is hard work, a task, and these parasites attach themselves. . . . He feels about scholars as some people feel about priests—they exploit religion.

Perhaps he feels that their way of life is a reproach. They have chosen to live by words and to risk financial insecurity; in a competitive society they have at least the courage of inertia. But far from being sympathetic, Williams adds his voice to the chorus of Americans who condemn the scholar's life as unmanly.

When he speaks of universities he sounds paranoid: "I am looked on by our teachers as though I were mad. They are threatened in their tenure of office. They literally want to kill me. I have seen it in their faces." [6] The grievance goes back to student days when he planned his life so that it would be divided between medicine and writing, with no time to read. He bore a lifelong grudge against those who, like Chaucer's clerk, spent all they had on books and went threadbare.

To say that an attitude is personal, however, does not show that it is wrong—no doubt Martin Luther was moved by feeling as well as by logic when he posted the ninety-five theses—and Williams' dislike of the academic mind has a good deal to be said for it. Anyone who has worked in a university knows how stultifying this can be. Some teachers are lazy, some teach without love of the subject, others are concerned only with getting ahead. When Williams was a young man the teaching of literature was dismal— only the "classics" were taught and gentility prevailed.

This was the period when Doubleday, the publisher of Dreiser's *Sister Carrie,* tried to break the contract on the ground that it was an immoral book. *Sister Carrie* was published, but without advertising so that only a few hundred copies were sold. Thanks to writers such as Dreiser, however, the Genteel Tradition had to step down, and the intellectual climate in universities has changed since William Carlos Williams attended the University of Pennsylvania. Today almost anything can be taught in a university. Indeed, the revolt against tradition has been more radical than writers may have wished. In the nineteen-sixties young people frequently expressed their indifference to writing of any kind—no one who heard the contempt with which one of the Beatles in a movie spoke the word "book" will easily forget it.

The traditional view of literature when Williams was a young man, and his decision to be a doctor rather than a scholar, have had lasting effects. Writers influenced by Williams still nourish suspicion of the Establishment, and poets who go from one university to another reading their poems are heard to say that there is no room for creativity in the System.

In his first year at the university he made friends with Charles Demuth, who developed into a painter. They met "over a dish of prunes at Mrs. Chain's boarding house on Locust Street and formed a lifelong friendship on the spot." At this time Williams himself was undecided whether to be a writer or a painter—he had puttered with his mother's old paint tubes from time to time. He decided for writing: "I coldly recalculated all the chances. Words it would be and their intervals: Bam! Bam!" [7]

Having decided to be a writer he set about reading Keats in earnest. He had first read Keats in Palgrave's *Golden Treasury,* in the parlor at home. Keats had been a medical student—that is, a surgeon's apprentice, walking the wards of Guy's and St. Thomas's Hospitals and assisting with operations—nevertheless he was a poet. Williams pored over Keats' *Endymion,* the long poem about the shepherd who falls in love with the moon-goddess Cynthia, and with an Indian maiden, then discovers that the two are one. The theme appears later in Williams' writing as an apology for sexual infidelity, though he does not seem conscious of its origin. At first, however, it was the superficies that he imitated, Keats' style and manner of narrative, if the meanderings of *Endymion* can be called a narrative. *"Endymion,"* he says, "really woke me up." [8] What woke him, perhaps, was the sexual suggestiveness of the poem. He set about writing a long narrative poem in Keats' style.

At the same time he kept a notebook in which he wrote Whitmanesque thoughts, "a sort of purgation and confessional, to clear

[his] head and [his] heart from turgid obsessions." He filled twenty-three copybooks with his thoughts. For many years they were a precious comfort; then he lost them.[9]

He met Ezra Pound. From the beginning Pound assumed the role of mentor. He was more sophisticated; he had left Keats behind "and gone madly on, even to Yeats." (Yeats came to Philadelphia in the flesh in 1903 and read to the students, but Williams did not hear him.)[10] "Ezra, even then, used to assault me," William says in his *Autobiography,* "for my lack of education and reading." Ezra thought that he was an expert on everything—he told William that he should study the differential calculus. In return William told him that he could use a course in anatomy.[11]

Ezra dressed like a poet, and spoke and behaved like a poet. Unlike William he was going to be a poet or bust. This put people off—they thought him arrogant and affected. But William considered him more deeply. There were differences in their attitudes —Ezra never explained his writing or joked about it, as he did. Ezra was "cryptic, unwavering and serious in his attitude toward it. He joked, crudely, about anything but that."

Ezra was "the livest, most intelligent and unexplainable thing [he'd] ever seen, and the most fun—except for his often painful self-consciousness and his coughing laugh." He was a delightful companion if you saw him now and then over the years, but you wouldn't want to see him often or long. "Usually," says William, "I got fed to the gills with him after a few days. He, too, with me, I have no doubt."

Ezra was "often brilliant, but an ass." "But," says William, "I never (so long as I kept away) got tired of him, or, for a fact, ceased to love him." Sometimes Ezra looked as though he would kick you in the teeth, but that was all show—he was too gentle at heart. "And he had, at bottom, an inexhaustible patience, an infinite depth of human imagination and sympathy." [12]

It is good to have this estimate of Pound's character from a man who knew him well over the years. Williams' "brilliant, but an ass" rings true; so does his remark about Pound's "human imagination and sympathy." His praise of Pound can be trusted, for he was willing to point out his faults. Years later when Pound supported the Fascists he condemned him in plain terms.

Pound was writing a sonnet a day and some of the poems that appear in his first book, *A Lume Spento.* He came to Williams' room and read them aloud.

> Exquisite loneliness:
> Bound of mine own caprice,
> I fly on the wings of an unknown chord
> That ye hear not,
> Can not discern.
> My music is weird and untamèd . . .[13]

The poems were frequently inaudible, his voice trailing off in the final lines "from his intensity." Williams didn't want to hurt his feelings, but now and then he would explode—how could he be expected to have an opinion of the poetry if he couldn't hear the lines? But all Ezra wanted was an audience.[14]

Ezra was learning to fence, Italian style, from the Penn coach. Then he quit fencing and took up lacrosse. He was always jumping from one thing to another, thinking he had attained mastery. William, who had learned to fence in Paris, went out for the university team. When he came to see Ezra in Wyncotte, Ezra invited him to pick up one of his father's walking sticks and have a friendly bout. William obliged and placed himself *en garde,* whereupon Ezra rushed at him, lunging wildly, and struck him above the right eye and laid him out. William threw down his stick and told Ezra what he thought of him. But Ezra was triumphant—with that one blow he had vanquished, in the person of their representative, the entire fencing team of the University of Pennsylvania.[15]

It was the same with Ezra's music—he could never learn to play the piano, though his mother tried to teach him, but he "played" for all that. When he came on a visit to the Williams' house he sat down at the piano and let fly. "Everything, you might say, resulted except music. He took mastership at one leap; played Liszt, Chopin —or anyone else you could name—up and down the scales, coherently to his own mind, any old sequence. It was part of his confidence in himself. My sister-in-law," William says, "was a concert pianist. Ez never liked her." [16]

Ez saw himself as a Ronsard. Once he asked William to accompany him on a romantic mission, to pick up a "particularly lovely thing in her early teens" whom he'd seen coming home from school. So they accosted her, one on each side. William was not interested—at least, so he says—and he found the whole thing ridiculous, but Ez addressed her in his best romantic manner. "The poor child was all but paralyzed with fear, panting to the point of speechlessness as she just managed to say in a husky voice,

'Go away! Please go away! Please! Please!' " William dropped back
but Ezra continued a few more paces before he quit; then he
bawled William out for giving up too easily. William told him
again what he thought of him.[17]

In these anecdotes William is always being taken to task by
Ezra for one thing or another. Then he tells him off. The relationship is that of a follower who reminds himself from time to time
that he should appear more like an equal. There is something too
compliant in Williams' attitude to Pound.

They met two girls by moonlight near a school at Chestnut Hill.
"Equally futile." Williams speculates that one of the girls may have
been the Mary Moore to whom Pound dedicated a book—"Mary
Moore of Trenton, N.J." He has heard that Pound used to visit
at the Moores' and, having once entered through one of the French
windows, ever after insisted on entering the house in that way.
"That's all I know of Mary Moore," he says, "a queen of the man's
youth." [18]

Pound was no lady-killer, not then at any rate. Williams says in
a letter that Pound was "a most gingerly and temperate young man
in everything that I had occasion to observe. If he ever got under
a gal's skirts it must have been mainly with his imagination." And
he didn't drink. It was hard to figure why in 1905 he "was ban-
ished by his father to the sticks"—that is, Hamilton College. It
might have been for refusing to do anything but what he pleased
in his classes, or for spending more cash than the old man could
give him.[19]

What William could not stand was Ezra's posturing as a poet.
This was "old hat"—the artist aping the gentry whom he pretended
to despise. Williams saw a different role for himself as artist. "My
upbringing assumed rather the humility and caution of the scien-
tist. One was or one was not *there*. And if one was there, it be-
hooved one to be at one's superlative best, and, apart from the
achievement, a thing in itself, to live inconspicuously, as best as it
might be possible, and to work single mindedly for the task. Not so
sweet Ezra." [20]

So Williams unlike Pound would live inconspicuously. But
though Williams speaks of humility he is not humble—rather, he
is proud. "My furious wish," he says, "was to be normal, undrunk,
balanced in everything. I would marry (but not yet!), have children
and still write, in fact, therefore to write." [21] He would live a
"normal" life in order to write about it. Pound, on the other hand,

would live like a poet—he was a romantic, a born impersonator. With a fencing foil he impersonated D'Artagnan, at the piano he impersonated a concert pianist. He took part in a university production of Euripides' *Iphigenia in Aulis* as one of the women in the chorus, wearing a toga and a blond wig, tearing at the wig and waving his arms and heaving his massive breasts "in ecstasies of extreme emotion." [22] Ez would be anything, but his favorite role was that of romantic poet, a Ronsard. "At Hamilton he was the laughing-stock of the place with a continuous impersonation of Ronsard." William thought the posturing ridiculous, but he thought he understood why Ezra did it: "He put that on no doubt to shield himself from too close approach by the yokels." [23]

William Carlos Williams, on the other hand, would spend his life among the yokels, listening to the story of their lives and treating their diseases. At the same time he would be perfecting his art. His way was no less adventurous than Pound's, and he was just as proud. Only by leading an ordinary life, working every day, marrying and raising children, could a man have the knowledge that would enable him to create works of art that spoke for and to other men. "Every man," he says, "is like me. . . . I'm not neurotic. That's just what I'm not. I'm just like everybody else. That's my pride. I'm proud. Hellishly proud that I'm just the core of the onion—nothing at all. That's just what makes me so right. And I *know* I'm right." [24]

He worked at his long poem in the manner of Keats' *Endymion*. His brother Ed, who was studying architecture at M.I.T., had a professor of English named Arlo Bates. Ed spoke to Bates about his literary brother William and arranged for William to meet the professor.[25]

William brought his *"Endymion* manuscript" with him. (The Whitmanesque notebooks, however, he did not bring—they were not "literature.") When he entered, Mr. Bates was sitting at a small desk near the window—a tall, middle-aged man with white hair. William asked him if he thought that he should quit medicine and write or go on with medicine. He offered the poem in evidence. Bates looked through it carefully while the author sat and sweated.

The poem was set in medieval times, with castles and kings and princes. It opened with a Keatsian sonnet followed by an "Induction" in blank verse. A prince was married to a beautiful lady. But at the feast after the wedding someone, for some undisclosed reason, put poison in a cup. This killed everybody except the

prince. He was saved by his old nurse; she gave him an antidote
and dragged him out of the pile.

Then the poem itself began to unroll. The prince woke to find
that he had been transported to a foreign country. He was
lying in a forest and there had just been a storm. He was lying in
the debris of fallen leaves and branches. Some people came by and
he accosted them, but they did not speak his language. Then he
had a dream, out of a print by Boecklin—he dreamed that he was
transported to Boecklin's *Insel des Todes* in a boat. There the
narrative bogged down. The author planned to write this part in
heroic couplets, like the scene with the players in *Hamlet,* but this
proving difficult, he left it unfinished and hurried on to the exciting parts.

The prince went wandering about, trying to get home and discover what had happened to him. He could not recall the details
but he "sensed" that there had been a beautiful bride, a father and
a mother. That a disaster of some sort had occurred . . .

So he wandered through scenes of nature—trees for the most
part, and forests—"wandering at random, without guide, alone." [26]

The narrative lacked, shall we say, incident. The professor put
it down, thought a while, and delivered an opinion: "I can see that
you have a sensitive appreciation of the work of John Keats' line
and form. You have done some creditable imitations of his work.
Not bad. Perhaps in twenty years, yes, in perhaps twenty years you
may succeed in attracting some attention to yourself. Perhaps!
Meanwhile, go on with your medical studies."

Then, as professors are likely to do, he opened a desk drawer
and showed the young man some pages of his own. "I, too, write
poems. And when I have written them I place them here—and—
then I close the drawer."

William thanked him and left.[27]

Twenty years! That would be 1925. It was a long time to wait
for "some attention."

But the air outside was sweet. He stood on the sidewalk overlooking the Charles Basin. It would be working as a doctor, then,
not just writing. He felt relieved—he couldn't stand the idea of
being just a writer.

Professor Doolittle was astronomer at the university, and being
invited to dinner at the Doolittles' was like going to Laputa.
At table the professor scarcely focused on anything nearer than

the moon. When he showed signs of being about to engage in human discourse Mrs. Doolittle, who was considerably younger than he, silenced everyone with a look. The professor would deliver himself of some observation. They waited respectfully to be sure that he had finished, then resumed their chattering.[28]

The Doolittles had a daughter named Hilda. She was tall and blond, with a long jaw but gay blue eyes. William wrote his brother Ed about her: "She is tall, about as tall as I am, young, about eighteen and, well, not round and willowy but rather bony, no that doesn't express it, just a little clumsy but all to the mustard. She is a girl that's full of fun, bright, but never tells you all she knows, doesn't care if her hair is a little mussed, and wears good solid shoes. She is frank and loves music and flowers and I got along with her pretty well." [29]

She was, in his opinion, much like her father, though the professor seemed to pay her no particular attention. "There was about her that which is found in wild animals at times, a breathless impatience, almost a silly unwillingness to come to the point. She had a young girl's giggle and shrug which somehow in one so tall and angular seemed a little absurd." [30] She fascinated him, though he was not in love with her. He left the loving to Pound—"Ezra was wonderfully in love with her and I thought exaggerated her beauty ridiculously." [31] He, for his part, thought she was just a good guy and enjoyed, uncomfortably, being with her. She wasn't inviting but irritating, "with a smile."

He took her to a Mask and Wig tryout, and got some dirty looks from Ez. "For God's sake," he told him, "I'm not in love with Hilda nor she with me. She's your girl and I know it. Don't be an ass." [32] As a matter of fact he had met someone else at the Mask and Wig in whom he was really interested: "She is of French descent," he wrote Ed, "and a college graduate, which is a combination hard to beat. . . . She is the first girl into whose eyes I have looked and forgotten everything around me. My, but she has fine eyes. I came home feeling sort of funny, so I sat down and wrote a sonnet to her brown eyes. Isn't that fierce?" The poem followed:

> Last night I sat within a blazing hall
> And drank of bliss from out a maiden's eyes.
> The jeweled guests passed by as forms that rise
> The charm in dreams the sleepy night for all
> Sped nameless on, no face can I recall.

> Those eyes, those eyes, my love entombed lies
> In their deep depths beyond recalling cries
> As lost as rings adown a well that fall . . .[33]

Und so weiter. It didn't make sense, but he had captured, more or less, the style of Keats' early poems, the cloying begemmed style Keats took from Leigh Hunt, and his theme of swooning, "Sinking away to his young spirit's night,—/ Sinking bewilder'd 'mid the dreary sea . . ." He wondered if his sonnet were any good: "I like it well, but of course that may be the false pride of a father in a sickly baby." [34] "Sickly" was good criticism.

He took Hilda walking in the "really lyrical Upper Darby country of those days." There were deep blue hyacinths in a gully beside the road. Hilda told him she was studying Greek and had heard that he too was writing poetry. The "too" hurt—Ezra, of course, was the hero. William didn't want to talk about his poems in any case; he didn't think he had produced anything yet that was worthy of notice.

Oh well, Hilda told him, she had been writing too. "Some translations," she added modestly, for nothing anyone did could bear comparison with the works of Ezra.

They wandered along, Hilda letting her skirt trail carelessly, "no hips, no nothing, just Hilda." They climbed over fences. She had a careless way of stepping over. Edmonson, who had been on a group walk with Hilda, confided in William that a fellow couldn't help looking sometimes, she was that careless.

A storm was brewing and William suggested that they turn back. But she wanted to know if when he sat down to write he liked everything neat and in its place. He said that he liked things neat. For her part, she said, she found it a great help to spill some ink on her clothes, so that she would approach the act of composition with an indifferent attitude toward the mere means of writing.

There were thunderclaps, then the rain came toward them. They were at the edge of a pasture. But instead of running for cover Hilda sat down in the grass and waited. "Come, beautiful rain," she said, holding out her arms. "Beautiful rain, welcome." The rain came pelting down. William had to stay with her—it was her party—but he didn't share her mood. "It didn't improve her beauty or my opinion of her—but I had to admire her if that's what she wanted." [35]

She and Ezra were two of a kind.

Together William and Hilda discovered *Aucassin and Nicolette* and Villon, puzzling over the old French, and Rabelais in Urquhart's translation.

About a year after the incident of the rain there was a party at Point Pleasant on the Jersey coast. When William arrived he found that Hilda had almost drowned. There had been a storm and the sea was still heavy, but "Hilda was entranced. I suppose she wasn't used to the ocean anyhow and didn't realize what she was about. For without thought or caution she went to meet the waves." She was knocked down and dragged in the undertow, and if one of the party hadn't been a strong swimmer this might have been the end of Hilda. She was unconscious when they pulled her out.[36]

H. D.'s poem "Oread" may have originated in this episode. A few years later Hilda Doolittle began to publish her poems under the initials H. D. Pound says that he started the Imagist movement, gave it the name, in order to bring H. D.'s poetry to the public.

> Whirl up, sea—
> Whirl your pointed pines,
> Splash your great pines
> On our rocks,
> Hurl your green over us,
> Cover us with your pools of fir.[37]

"Without thought or caution . . ." Professor Doolittle's daughter was, in William's words, "all to the mustard." (Huckleberry Finn might have said that she had "sand.") Richard Aldington, who was married to her, said that H. D. was "more distinguished . . . than Ezra, both as a person and as a mind." This is typical of Aldington, who seldom praised anyone unless it were to put down someone else. Aldington says that he has never known anyone, not even Lawrence, who was H. D.'s equal in aesthetic appreciation. "Lawrence was more keenly aware of the living world, but he was almost blind to the world of art." To look at beautiful things with H. D. was a remarkable experience. She had a genius for appreciation, a "severe but wholly positive taste." She lived on the heights and never wasted time on what was inferior.[38]

With this prettily turned compliment to himself—seeing that he was married to H. D. he must have shared the heights—Aldington sketches H. D.'s remarkable personality. To correct the picture, however, it should be said that Pound's mind does not seem inferior to H. D.'s, and that Lawrence had keen and original appreciation for art. His descriptions, in *Twilight in Italy,* of the Christs in roadside shrines, are an astonishing *tour de force.*

William had few friends—Ezra Pound, Charlie Demuth, and a man in his early fifties named John Wilson who was a failure as an artist. Wilson painted, out of his head, landscapes with cows that sold at from ten to twenty dollars. He loved painting—it was all that he could do and all he wanted to do. Wilson had a wife who was able and good-natured, and a daughter Dorothy, and maybe they were thinking of William's marrying her. But when he agreed to take her to a dance and showed up in a tux the night *following* the event, they gave up the idea. On Sunday afternoons William would sit in Wilson's north-light studio watching him paint, over and over again, trees and cows and sky. One day Wilson gave him a canvas and some brushes and told him to paint. He did—"That was fun." [39]

His other Sunday occupation was churchgoing. He had to count his pennies to see if he could ride the trolley down Chestnut Street to the First Unitarian Church where Reverend Ecob held forth. "He was a small, gray-haired fellow, an ex-Presbyterian who, more than a little to his family's discomfiture, had taken to Unitarianism, that most unpopular, almost non-Christian faith. Certainly un-Christian to popular belief." Ecob had three daughters who seemed ill at ease over their father's falling-off from orthodoxy. "The Ecob girls," says Williams, "especially the youngest, were a possible solution to my secret misery but . . . I was poor, poor." [40] The misery was sexual frustration. He speaks of this and of his poverty in other writings besides the *Autobiography.* Most of Williams' fiction is taken from his experiences and he doesn't care who knows it—"The artist," he remarks, "is always and forever painting only one thing: a self portrait." [41] In his play *A Dream of Love* the character "Doc" speaks of his experiences in medical school in terms that clearly apply to the author: "I must have had a guardian angel watching over me among the back streets of Philadelphia! Maybe I frightened them—or looked too poor. Frightened them because I looked too poor. That must have been it." [42] With other writers we must be on guard against thinking that they are writing about themselves—with Williams the reverse is true: almost everything he wrote is autobiography.

In grade school and at the university he suffered from sexual frustration. He blames the system of education, "our masters, who suppress us." [43] He would have agreed with Blake, and with Freud, that there is a conspiracy of the old to suppress the young:

> And priests in black gowns were walking their rounds,
> And binding with briars my joys and desires.[44]

It was sexual activity they aimed to bind. And the cord was money or the lack of it. He would not have been rejected if he had not been poor.

He took the Ecobs' youngest daughter out walking, though he felt she didn't like, and possibly hated, the sight of him. When he put out his hand to help her climb a slope she pulled her arm away and said, "Don't touch me!" They parted company on the spot.[45]

One Sunday after church he was invited home to have lunch with the family. He went ahead with the girls on the trolley, then discovered that he didn't have a cent in his pocket, and they had to pay his fare. It was the kind of incident that finished him in their eyes.[46]

Sexual desire, poverty, humiliation . . . this is the picture Williams draws of his life as a young man. It would have been the same for other young men. There were some who had money, but in fact money didn't buy everything—in middle-class families at the start of the century it didn't buy relief from sexual desire and a tormented conscience. It would be a mistake to think, as Williams apparently does, that his torments were extraordinary.

When the Ben Greet Players did a performance of *As You Like It* he didn't have the dollar's admittance fee. The play was to be given outdoors on the Botanical Garden lawn. Going along the path by the frog pond, backstage, he saw two of the actresses "in costume lying at ease on the brilliant grass, talking together. Goddesses! If that is not agony, to see, to desire and not to know how to begin, then I have never known it." He managed to circumvent the guards and sneak through the gate without paying. Someone shouted, but he kept on going. All the seats were taken, so he lay on the grass, close to the actors. "You might say that from that time on I never took a complete breath all afternoon until it was over." [47]

In the *Autobiography* and the letters he wrote to his mother and brother, Williams seems to have been an ordinary young man, as much like others as he could have wished to be. He hopes to get into the Mask and Wig, and achieves his ambition—he plays Polonius in *Mr. Hamlet of Denmark* and goes on a tour with the company, ending in Washington. There he brings down the house with an impromptu line kidding Teddy Roosevelt, who is on a bear hunt in the Ozarks. He has a heady sense of what it means to hold an audience in the palm of one's hand. He is the hero of the hour.[48]

He goes dancing. "I had the first dance with Miss Ecob. It was a two-step, and I got along all right but next came a waltz. Oh, boy." [49]

When he writes to his mother he makes resolutions. "One thing I am convinced more and more is true and that is this: the only way to be truly happy is to make others happy. When you realize that and take advantage of the fact, everything is made perfect." [50]

He is still thinking of perfection. In response to a letter from his mother in which she has found fault with him and cast aspersions on his judgment, he expresses some very strong resolutions indeed. "I want you to believe these few statements once for all. . . . First, that I never did and never will do a premeditated bad deed in my life. Also that I have had and never will have anything but the purest and highest and best thoughts about you and Papa, and that if anybody ever says a word contrary to your wishes or high ideals I never fail to fight them to a standstill. . . . I have always tried to do all that you and Papa wished me to do and many times I have done things against my own feelings and convictions because you wanted me to. . . . Still, Mama dear, I know you are right and I am wrong. Don't think I blame you, for a second; I don't, but feelings will come.

"This may sound harsh but I do not mean it to be so. I try to do right and then I am blamed for doing wrong and really it is hard to be happy then." [51]

Some of the idealism is due to Williams' character and the character of Mr. and Mrs. Williams, but it should not be taken to mean that there was anything extraordinary about his relationship to his parents. At the turn of the century children placed a great deal of importance on trying to please their parents. They aimed to be dutiful and obedient, and they worried about sin—that is, the evils of sexual indulgence. We do not know what faults William's mother was taxing him with . . . she probably feared that he was going "wild"—he had a history of girl-chasing in grade school—and warned him against evil company and dissipation. The usual parental advice of the time . . . So he responded as young American males did by assuring his mother that he was high-minded.

He was also writing to his brother Ed, to whom he felt very close—he speaks of it as a "passionate identification" that lasted until they fell in love with the same girl. She was one of two sisters—Ed became engaged to the one William wanted, whereupon he married the other. It was the end of their identification and, William says, of his youth. "Something profound did happen, something moving and final." [52] He writes to Ed about meeting girls, but there is nothing that could be blamed, even by Unitarian standards: "We talked of the finest things: of Shakespeare, of flowers, trees, books & pictures and meanwhile climbed fences and walked through woods and climbed little hills till it began to grow dusky when we arrived at our destination. We had by this time, as you imagine, gotten pretty well acquainted. She said I was Rosalind in *As You Like It* and she was Celia, so I called her that, although her name is Hilda." [53]

"She said I was Rosalind . . . and she was Celia." He did not see the significance of this. Hilda Doolittle preferred women to men, but such things were not understood in Philadelphia at the beginning of the century.

He continued writing to Ed after he left the university. He was still idealistic—he said so himself: "I am not even remotely cynical." He had ambitions, "dreams that merely to mention is too daring, yet I'll tell you that any man can do anything he will if he persists in daring to follow his dreams." [54]

But sex stood in the way. "To do what I mean to do and to be what I must be in order to satisfy my own self I must discipline my affections, and until a fit opportunity affords, like no one in particular except you, Ed, and my nearest family. From nature, Ed, I have a weakness wherever passion is concerned. No matter how well I may reason and no matter how clearly I can see the terrible results of yielding up to desire, if certain conditions are present I might as well never have arrived at a consecutive conclusion for good in all my life, for I cannot control myself. As a result, in order to preserve myself as I must, girls cannot be my friends."

He has contempt for those who fail for lack of determination. "If a man fails in attempts too great for him he is a better man than the whimpering weakling who is frightened away by obstacles." [55]

There was nothing unusual about these attitudes, though they may seem so now. Like other middle-class men in the early years of the century Williams was going to have a devil of a time fighting his instincts in order to succeed and be respectable. Sexual freedom and making a place for oneself in society were clearly opposed. This was hard enough for the average man to face, but for one who wanted to be a poet it was almost impossible. Poetry implies a certain degree of freedom—it has even been said, by no less an authority than Plato, that a man has to be out of his mind in order to write poetry.

But, as Williams saw it, according to the plan he had made for himself, he would have to be "balanced in everything." [56] Writing required inspiration—"drunkenness" was the word he used [57]—but he could only afford to be drunk at certain times. He wouldn't be able to live carelessly like Ezra and Hilda, "yielding up to desire." He couldn't go running into the waves.

"It was money that finally decided me. I would continue medicine, for I was determined to be a poet." [58]

It was the sensible choice. After all he was living in America.

17

A Proposal of Marriage

H E was interning at the old French Hospital opposite the Lincoln Tunnel on West Thirty-fourth Street. He worked at his long poem on weekends, "coming home stinking of ether and going back Sunday evening to resume the hospital grind." [1] His friend J. Julio Henna on the staff urged him to marry a South American widow with a million dollars. The young doctor didn't bite, but he did follow through on another of Henna's suggestions: he accompanied an old Mexican on the train back to Mexico, keeping him alive so that he could die in his bed. For this he was paid in twenty-dollar gold pieces. [2]

He decided not to be a surgeon—he didn't fancy a life spent "dabbling in people's guts." He would take another internship in obstetrics and diseases of children, then go in for general practice. He planned to live in the suburbs. [3]

He was one of a crew of happy, nurse-chasing young internes. There were four, if you counted Krumwiede the pathologist whom they called "The Wrath of God" from the way he looked at breakfast. There was Smith who fell on his back beside a recently operated-on and beautiful girl patient—he had been trying to do a handstand on the bar at the foot of her bed—his feet hit her pillow! Maloney, who was dismissed because he complained about the food . . . and Gaskins, hilariously comical and the best pal in the world. "Eberhard came after Maloney had been fired. He was a fat guy from Brooklyn." [4]

There was a nursing school at the hospital. They'd sneak the girls out on to the roof at night and hide behind the water tank and look at the stars. "But my life was too hard," he says, "for much gaiety of that sort." Old Eberhard, who was always trying to incite him to bitchery, told him that he had two girls for them in a room over in Brooklyn. Williams didn't go. "He was disgusted with me for not stepping out and later told me he'd had a time taking care of both of them." [5]

Interning brought out a side of Williams that had been suppressed up to then. It was the most carefree time of his life. He didn't have to worry about the future—he was in it, sink or swim. And he had the company of young men to whom nothing was sacred. It came as a relief after living up to the standards set by his parents. In the French Hospital young Doctor Williams was able to lift the veil and see that behind it was just life, that was all. He chose obstetrics so that he could look through the mystery of childbirth and know everything that had been hidden. He was fascinated with women. Yet, though his curiosity should have been sated, to the end of his life he seems not to have lost it. The curiosity was derived as much from fear as love. "Determined women," he says, "have governed my fate." [6] And he says of his mother: "When she herself was unable to fulfill her desires for personal accomplishment, she transferred her ambitions to her children." [7]

Though he was inhibited he took a vicarious joy in the exploits of his companions—just as at the university while he ridiculed Pound's manner of approaching women he envied his assurance. At the hospital there was an Irish maid who "inhabited a skin as tightly packed with goodies as a young intern could desire to pinch." Eberhard grabbed her, she swung at him and ran, and his arm went through the glass door. Everyone vanished except young Doctor Williams, who was on duty as Senior in charge. Sister Superior arrived on the scene and enquired what had happened. He had to tell her. "Well," she said, "as long as it's you . . ." [8] He was not wicked. But he rejoiced in the wickedness of his companions.

He came to know all kinds of people. For example, a poor whore who had been mutilated . . . He hardly knew women and felt tender to them all, "especially, like any man, if they retained some vestige of beauty." This woman was young and full-breasted. She had been cruelly beaten—her eyes were closed, her mouth cut, her arms bruised and bleeding. "But the thing that knocked me over was that her breasts were especially lacerated and on one could be seen the deeply embedded marks of teeth, as if some animal had attempted to tear the tissues away." [9]

There was the injured workman who, when they took off his dirty overalls, turned out to be wearing a woman's chemise and panties and silk stockings, and to have shaved his legs. He was married—his wife came to the hospital, in distress over his condition. Then a big limousine drew up, from which emerged an unforgettable figure of a man, over six feet tall and so well dressed that he made everyone about him look like a lackey. He gave instructions for his friend the workman to be given a private room and the best of everything.[10]

Williams had begun the immersion in experience that would provide him with the material of his poems and stories. Most of his writing was derived from experience. He liked to think that he worked according to a theory, that he was discovering the laws inherent in art. Being "objective" . . . It was the temper of the time—Joyce, Pound and Eliot recommended "impersonality." He liked to think of himself as a "pure" artist—to tell the story of the woman in the Daniel Gallery who looked at a painting and said, "But Mr. Hartpence, what is all that down in this left hand lower corner?" Hartpence came close and inspected the painting. "That, Madam," he said, "is paint." [11] Nevertheless, Williams believed that experience signifies something. His writing is full of life observed in the belief that it holds a secret.

His work as a doctor furnished him with characters and incidents. He recalled things he saw on his rounds, what people said, the accounts they gave of their lives. In this he resembles Whitman, who tended the sick during the Civil War. Randall Jarrell, in his introduction to Williams' *Selected Poems*, underlines the resemblance. "Williams," he says, "has the knowledge of people one expects, and often does not get, from doctors; a knowledge one does not expect, and almost never gets, from contemporary poets." With Williams the reader has "the amused, admiring and affectionate certainty that one has about Whitman: *Why, he'd say anything!* creditable or discreditable, sayable or unsayable, so long as he believes it." Williams' poems are like Whitman's in that they are full of what is ugly as well as what is clear, delicate, and beautiful. Both writers have their faults, but these are canceled out by a quality they have in common: "a wonderful largeness, a quantitative and qualitative generosity." [12]

Williams, however, seems not to have been conscious of the

resemblance. As Hyatt H. Waggoner points out, he did not read Whitman with sympathy.[13] His remarks show that he did not perceive Whitman's skill as a writer of verse: "Whitman," he says, "was a romantic in a bad sense . . . He composed 'freely,' he followed his untrammeled necessity." [14] Not until the 1940's when Williams delivered a lecture on Whitman to the English Institute does he seem to have read Whitman's poems carefully, and his remarks on this occasion, reducing the meaning of *Leaves of Grass* to "democracy," show no real understanding of Whitman's ideas. A few years later he returned to his old way of talking about Whitman: " 'free verse' since Whitman's time has led us astray . . . Whitman was right in breaking our bounds but, having no valid restraints to hold him, went wild." [15]

He may have seen the resemblance but been unwilling to admit it. Whitman was "romantic." Williams admired the romantic elements of his mother's character, but would not admit them in himself. Wallace Stevens, in the preface he wrote for Williams' *Collected Poems,* said that he was romantic. "There are so many things to say about him. The first is that he is a romantic poet. This will horrify him. Yet the proof is everywhere." [16] It did horrify him, and the preface was never reprinted. Romanticism was formlessness. He rejected it—he was creating a new form, an American measure to replace the meter of England.

But though Williams did not wish to be identified wth Whitman, they were alike in their belief in the intrinsic value of experience. "As the youthful Whitman accepted what he called 'materialism,' but then 'imbued' it with spirit, so Williams, determined to be a 'realist,' looked long and hard at *things*—and found in them the source and sufficient basis for dream." [17]

Say it, no ideas but in things.[18]

He was a doctor and his practice lay among the poor. This would keep his attention fixed on things. Moreover, he would reside in one place all his life. Imbuement with a vengeance! The son of the Englishman who grew up in St. Thomas and the half-Basque, half-Jewish mother who grew up in Puerto Rico would put down roots in Rutherford, New Jersey. Pound had left the States and gone roaming like a vagabond, picking up ideas. Pound could afford to wander—his family went back to Colonial days. But the Williamses were islanders—their hold on the mainland was precarious. Mrs. Williams had no friends in Rutherford—she "kept a secret and soul-consuming longing for Paris! Paris!" She wasn't antagonistic to Rutherford but felt ill at ease, and was virtually unknown in the town.[19]

Who could feel like an American, having such parents? When William and Ed were children, "There above them, as they played, leaned nothing of America, but Puerto Rico, a foreign island in a tropical sea of earlier years—and Paris of the later Seventies." [20]

Though he had been raised in Rutherford, wth Kipp's woods just over the back fence, and had gone to public schools, he felt like an outsider. If he didn't hang on and strike deep he would be easily uprooted. Especially by desire. So it was to be Doctor Williams of Rutherford, going his appointed rounds and paying close attention to things.

Ideas are like the wind, but things you can see and touch, and the things people tell you, are real. It doesn't matter if what they say happened really happened, or if they really feel what they say—the act of saying is real. Your listening to it is real. Language is reality. And as we are Americans it is the American language.

Whitman said, "I am the man—I suffer'd—I was there." [21] Williams put it to himself in the same way: "One was or one was not *there.*" [22]

His profession called him away from himself. "They call me," he said, "and I go." [23] He was paid little or nothing for his visits. "It was not money. It came of his sensitivity, his civility; it was that that made him do it." [24] He admired the toughness of the poor, their ability to survive—"indestructibleness," such as his mother had. He admired their willingness to risk everything. They were like artists who risk everything when they compose or paint. "It's the anarchy of poverty," he said, "delights me." [25] But there were times when he felt anything but generous—like Doc Rivers in his story he had a side that was "aloof, a little disdainful, impatient with fumbling humanity." [26] The poor need our compassion but this does not make them lovable. Maybe you feel an attachment, but to call it love doesn't render the feeling. "Give it an enema," says the doctor in "Life Along the Passaic River." "Maybe it will get well and grow up into a cheap prostitute or something. The country needs you, brat. I once proposed that we have a mock wedding between a born garbage hustler we'd saved and a little female with a fresh mug on her that would make anybody smile." [27]

People were like poems—especially among the poor you saw that life was there for its own sake, like the life in a poem. Moral-

ity had nothing to do with it, nor beauty in the old sense. Ugliness
is truth, as much as beauty ever was. "A thing of beauty," Keats
says at the beginning of *Endymion,* "is a joy for ever:/ Its loveliness increases . . ." Williams says in *Paterson:*

> And the guys from Paterson
>   beat up
> the guys from Newark and told
> them to stay the hell out
> of their territory and then
> socked you one
>   across the nose
>   Beautiful Thing
> for good luck and emphasis
>   cracking it
> till I must believe that all
> desired women have had each
>   in the end
>   a busted nose
> and live afterward marked up
>   Beautiful Thing
>   for memory's sake
> to be credible in their deeds [28]

Medical practice enlarged his experience, taught him something about people, gave him incidents for his writing. It enabled him, also, to think of himself as a theorist, to believe that
he was writing in an objective manner, and writers need some
sustaining belief. But it is possible to exaggerate the "largeness"
and "generosity" of Williams' disposition, and Jarrell's introduction is too cheerful. There were days when Williams would gladly
have thrown in his hand, especially when he thought of the time
lost tending the sick or delivering babies that might have been
given to his writing.

He would write on a typewriter in his office. When a patient
entered he put it aside. When the patient left, he went back to
his writing. This is well known, and it is something to be wondered at—it may even make the writer who asks for a certain
amount of quiet, uninterrupted time feel that there must be
something wrong with him. But in fact Williams frequently complained about the arrangement, so that it took the rough side of
his wife's tongue to make him stop. From *A Dream of Love* we
get an idea of what these conversations were like.

Myra: Really, Dan. I'm getting awfully fed up with this routine.
       The same thing, the same thing, over and over and over
       and over.
Doc: Me too.
Myra: Why don't you quit then?
Doc: On what? I haven't got enough money to quit on—at my
       age.
Myra: Just quit. . . .
Doc: I think you took a swig of something out there in the
       kitchen.
Myra: You coward. You haven't got the nerve . . . Why don't
       you give up being a half-time writer if you like to write
       that much? Why don't you make a decision one way or
       the other? I'll do it for you.[29]

Williams was no simple lover of humanity, nor was he happy
about his medical practice. On the other hand he wouldn't give
it up.

From the French Hospital he went to the Nursery and Child's
on Sixty-first Street and Tenth Avenue. There he received his
training from Charles Gilmore Kerley—a lucky break, as Kerley
was one of the leading pediatricians of the day.

This was in Hell's Kitchen, and the hospital faced the most
notorious block in the district. People didn't go out unaccom-
panied after dark. There were shootings and near riots practically
every weekend. And the management of the hospital was riddled
with corruption. But there was plenty of work. He delivered three
hundred babies and faced every conceivable complication. He
liked the women he worked alongside. "They led a tough life
and still kept a sort of gentleness and kindness about them that
could, I think, beat anything a man might offer under the same
circumstances." [30]

He had a halfway affair with the night superintendent of
nurses. They would meet at night in the pharmacy. She was
pretty but hardly an intellectual—a futile, dispirited, lonely sort
of woman. She was older than he and had a sad story—"The
place was full of sad stories." She invited him up to the room
where she lived. There was little more than a bed, a dresser, and
a chair. "The poor child"—the *Autobiography* speaking—"The
poor child seemed really poor and humiliated in such surroundings." He wanted to lie on the bed with her but she shook her
head, no. "Just say one word," she told him, "and you can have

everything I've got." The word was marriage and he didn't say it.[31]

Every month the hospital had to send in a report to Albany of the number of admissions and discharges; in return they received funds commensurate with these figures. One day Doctor Williams, as Resident Surgeon, was asked by Miss Malzacher, Secretary of the Board of Governors, to sign his name to one of these reports. He said that he could not without first seeing the records. He was told that he could not see them; they were confidential. He was adamant, and the report went to Albany without his signature. Then hell broke loose—the operating funds were being withheld. Pressure was brought to bear by the hospital chief of staff and the other physicians—he still refused to sign. So it was arranged for the treasurer of the hospital to sign the report instead, and Doctor Williams was suspended for two weeks for insubordination.

But Albany was still not satisfied—they still wanted his signature. Miss Cuthbertson, who was in charge of the nursing program, urged him to stick to his guns. One day Miss Cuthbertson discovered Miss Malzacher and the President of the Board doing something obscene in the Board Room. "There it was, plain as daylight, the whole reason why the woman was being allowed to get away with her petty graft." He thought of calling in the newspapers but "Pop advised me against it." Finally he resigned. "My days of internship were over. Not a single doctor of the attending staff had stood by me. To hell with them all, I thought." [32]

Ezra had published his first book. William found fault with it —there was "poetic anarchy" in the work, and personal bitterness; he feared it might offend the public. Pound wrote from London ticking him off—W. B. Yeats had pronounced the poems charming, though he had some reservations about the morals and future of the author. "I doubt," Pound said in his letter, "if you are sufficiently au courant to know just what the poets and musicians *and* painters are doing."

William had spoken of the "ultimate attainments of poetry." What were they? Ezra said that for his part he aimed to "paint the thing" as he saw it. He didn't write for the public—he wrote "To such as love this same beauty that I love somewhat after mine own fashion." Also he didn't want to bore people.[33]

The word "bore" sounded a knell. William thought about his long poem, "Philip and Oradie," that was patterned on Keats' *Endymion*. Before Ezra left for Europe he had seen the poem and judged it great. He could imagine what the new, sophisticated Ezra would say if he looked at it now. One day he disposed of the manuscript. In later years he couldn't recall what he had done with it. Maybe he burned it.

But if Ezra Pound could publish a book, why shouldn't William Carlos Williams? He collected some of his short poems. His father had a friend named Reid Howell who had been a printer in New York and had now opened a shop in Rutherford. He agreed to do the job for fifty dollars—the deal to include a small book by Jim Hyslop on his observations of insects in the neighborhood. So *Poems* by W. C. Williams was printed—twenty-two pages. The title page was designed by the author's brother: borders of flowers and two epigraphs—one from Keats: "Happy melodist forever piping songs forever new"—the other from Shakespeare: "So all my best is dressing old words new/ Spending again what is already spent." The edition of one hundred copies was full of errors and it was not distributed. The author's father made corrections and suggestions, most of which he adopted, and a revised edition, again of a hundred copies, was published in May 1909. It retailed at twenty-five cents and was reviewed in the *Rutherford American:* "It may well be hoped that, in his busy professional life, Dr. Williams will find more odd moments in which to record his open-eyed interest in the things of beauty, the mind and the spirit. We are reminded that the father wields a graceful poetic pen, and are pleased to notice how gracefully the mantle of good literary expression falls upon the son." [34]

One sonnet may stand for the whole. It is titled "The Uses of Poetry" and dedicated to H. D.

> I've fond anticipation of a day
> O'erfilled with pure diversion presently,
> For I must read a lady poesy
> The while we glide by many a leafy bay,
>
> Hid deep in rushes, where at random play
> The glossy black winged May-flies, or whence flee
> Hush-throated nestlings in alarm,
> Whom we have idly frightened with our boat's long sway.

> For, lest o'ersaddened by such woes as spring
> To rural peace from our meek onward trend,
> What else more fit? We'll draw the light latch-string
>
> And close the door of sense; then satiate wend,
> On Poesy's transforming giant wing,
> To worlds afar whose fruits all anguish mend.[35]

This is strikingly similar to the early poetry of Keats—wandering in woods, paddling in streams, munching apples and sucking strawberries. There is a lady in the case, but where Keats sees women as nymphs and would like "To woo sweet kisses from averted faces,—/ Play with their fingers, touch their shoulders white/ Into a pretty shrinking with a bite/ As hard as lips can make it . . . ," the chaste medical practitioner wishes "to close the door of sense"—leave sensuality behind and fly with poetry to worlds "whose fruits all anguish mend." The language is that of "poesy," with inversions, archaisms, and traditional epithets. It is the antithesis of Williams' later style.

Williams' father played an important part in the transaction. Pound always insisted, Williams says, that he didn't stress sufficiently the influence of his father as well as mother on his development. "Oh, the woman of it is important," Pound would say, "but the form of it, if not the drive, came . . . from the old man, the Englishman." Williams' father was a stickler for fundamentals and once he started something would see it through to the bitter end to see what it amounted to. "If he couldn't understand a thing at last, he'd reject it, which was not Mother's saving way of facing the world." [36]

What does this mean? Williams' prose is frequently a little "off." At times he does not write, as he claims, American—he writes Mumble. Perhaps the sentence means that Mrs. Williams accepted everything as it came.

Williams is proud of the clarity of his father's mind, his ability to go straight to the point. Once when Pound came to Rutherford he read his poems aloud. They didn't go down well, Mr. Williams finding fault with one poem especially. "What are all the jewels you speak of?" he wanted to know. Ezra explained: they were the backs of books in a bookcase. Oh, said Mr. Williams. He could see why, as a student and poet, Pound treasured books and thought of them as jewels. But if he wished to make an intelligent impression on the reader, if it was books he was talking about why didn't he say so?

Williams says that Pound seems never to have forgotten the lesson. This is a revealing statement—it reveals Williams' need to keep abreast of Pound. If Pound never forgot the lesson, then his development as a theorist was due to the teaching of Mr. Williams. A neat way of bringing the credit back home! And of making himself appear more knowledgeable than Pound, for William Carlos Williams knew more about poetry than his father.[37]

If Williams had hoped that his first book would impress Pound he was quickly disabused. Pound wrote to him as though he were a child that hadn't known better: "As proof that W. C. W. has poetic instincts the book is valuable. Au contraire, if you were in London and saw the stream of current poetry, I wonder how much of it you would have printed? . . . Individual, original it is not. Great art it is not. Poetic it is, but there are innumerable poetic volumes poured out here in Gomorrah . . . Your book would not attract even passing attention here. There are fine lines in it, but nowhere I think do you add anything to the poets you have used as models. . . .

"If you'll read Yeats and Browning and Francis Thompson and Swinburne and Rossetti . . . And if you'll read Margaret Sackville, Rosamund Watson, Ernest Rhys, Jim G. Fairfax . . .

"Read Aristotle's *Poetics,* Longinus' *On the Sublime,* De-Quincey, Yeats' essays."

He had sent Pound his book hoping for praise. In return he received a reading list.

Pound's concluding words, however, were the kind of encouragement that he alone was able to give, recalling the poet to a high sense of his task. "Remember a man's real work is what *he is going to do,* not what is behind him. Avanti e coraggio!" [38] Pound was not infallible—Yeats and Longinus we know, but who was Jim G. Fairfax? Pound's advice was not always right, but it sounded great.

"In the Spring of 1909"—*Autobiography* speaking—"I observed Flossie, the kid, on Park Avenue in Rutherford, and my whole life came to a head." [39] But from what he says elsewhere their encounters weren't so decisive—it wasn't love at first or second sight. He was in love with Flossie's sister, and it was only when she chose his brother Ed instead that he proposed to Flossie.

Williams' engagement, says Mike Weaver, was "his first act of daring and resolution"—up to that his life had been extremely conventional.[40] But Williams' experiences in Hell's Kitchen had been anything but conventional, and what is most evident about his engagement is that there was no passion in it. As he had "coldly recalculated all the chances" when he decided to be a writer rather than a painter, so he made some recalculations and proposed to Florence. *The Build-Up*—the last volume in the trilogy he wrote about Florence Herman and her family—shows that he went about getting married with a sense of urgency, even desperation, but nothing that could be called love. Marrying Florence Herman was a way to control his life and to survive. His mother had a will to survive—she had given up passion and survived.[41] He saw the same quality in Florence—they would manage to survive together.

In *The Build-Up* Williams is "Charlie Bishop," Florence Herman is "Florence Stecher," Williams' brother Ed is "Fred," and Florence's sister Charlotte is "Charlotte" or "Lottie." Lottie is a concert pianist. "At the piano she was queen. Perhaps the very feeling of frustration she induced in her suitors came from that. She was really, at that time, such an accomplished pianist and there was such a mystery about her as she played her Schumann, her Debussy, her Chopin, that they were overawed. They simply did not dare." [42]

The Build-Up is autobiographical—more revealing than the *Autobiography*—and what Williams says about "Charlie" is true of himself: he did not dare. He observed Lottie "closely for a year . . . her lanky thighs as she sat at the piano; her skinny legs; her large, mysterious eyes. Surely she was no beauty, but he had to acknowledge that she was disturbing, to say the least." Lottie wanted to be a great artist, to be admired and successful. She read his first book of poems and said, "I don't think a poem, to be a poem, should use ugly words, dirty words, vulgar . . . A poem should be beautiful. And you can write beautifully. But you seem to want to spoil everything. Why is that? I don't understand you," she would say.[43]

Brother Ed also wants Lottie. He is competing for a prize in architecture, the *Prix de Rome,* and is determined that if he wins he will ask Lottie to marry him. He wins the prize and the family is overjoyed—he will go to Rome and William will go to Europe too. Ed tells William to ask Lottie to choose between them. William says that he won't. So Ed goes, proposes, and is accepted. On hearing the news William flings his arms about his brother and "goes mad." Ed is embarrassed—he loosens his brother's hold and flees.

William wonders if Ed has acted decently, and decides that he has—to perfection. But "Something had come to an end. It was a deeper wound than he should ever thereafter in his life be able to sound. It was bottomless."

Then he makes a decision. "He ground his teeth, he fought back his unreasoning tears. And then it left him. Like a flash. He made up his mind and was determined to act upon it." [44]

The decision is to marry Lottie's sister. These, then, are the facts—omitted from the *Autobiography*, where Williams merely says, "I observed Flossie, the kid, on Park Avenue in Rutherford, and my whole life came to a head." It is enough to make you throw the *Autobiography* out the window. But he wasn't setting out to conceal anything—he had been writing autobiography all his life, in poems, stories and novels. He was writing about Flossie and himself in a novel, so when he wrote the *Autobiography* he thought that he could leave it out.

The Build-Up goes on to describe Flossie's feelings. She is in love with Charlie Bishop (William). "Not that the Bishop boy had ever addressed more than a passing word to her, but she had not given up hope. She loved him. It was unreasonable. Nothing would ever come of it. But she liked his nose. What a silly thing! But there it was, she loved him, secretly."

William was grieving. He stayed at home looking out the window or lying on his bed. He wouldn't eat. His mother urged him to. "He felt sorry for her, helpless as she was, and smiled." He took some of the soup she made, and on the third day went out of doors.

At this point William's life begins to take on overtones of Scripture.

After all, he said to himself, the world goes on as usual no matter how we feel about it. No, I'll be damned if it will this time. It's going my way.

So he phoned Flossie and went over to see her. They sat on the porch awhile, then, "Florence," he said, "will you marry me?"

She said, "You don't love me. You love my sister."

"I do not love your sister."

"But you don't love me."

"I don't love anyone," he said, "but I want to marry you. I think we can be happy." [45]

> Was ever woman in this humour woo'd?
> Was ever woman in this humour won?

There follows an explanation of his feelings. He was not in love for the time being, but if she loved him and would have him, "here he was at her feet." He now realized that Flossie was "love itself." He had been conscious of her presence in his environment but had rejected the feeling. Now he himself had been rejected. This brought them together: "He had a fellow feeling for her." "Together they, having found out what love is, having been rejected, and what it could do, with their eyes open, could and would face it together.

"One thing was certain, he was not going to start over again what he had in this tragic experience already been through." [46]

This is revealing. What had he been through? Love and rejection. He wasn't going to risk that again. Just as at the university he had decided to be a doctor because a life of art was too risky, now he decided to marry a woman he did not love, because love was too risky.

Lottie represented the life of art as well as passion—so that in being rejected by Lottie he had been rejected by the life of art as he had feared all along that he would be. In fact, he had arranged to be rejected, by not proposing and sending his brother instead.

He was very much the son of Mrs. Williams, who had given up her life as an artist in order to marry and have children. The reason for her choice had never been disclosed—there were too many reasons. Was it lack of money? The advances of the father of the girls? The behavior of Alice Monsanto? "If Alice had not been so mean perhaps I would have stayed there longer." [47] But in fact she had lacked confidence in her ability and chosen security instead. Similarly, Williams doubted his ability to make a go of it, and settled for marriage to a woman he did not love.

"She loving him and therefore willing to take his lead, they could—for he would teach her what comes after love—they two could make a life of it. They might even conceivably make a superb life of it.

"There is a sort of love, not romantic love, but a love that with daring can be made difficultly to blossom. It is founded on passion, a dark sort of passion, but it is founded on passion, a passion of despair, as all life is despair." [48]

But there was no passion in his proposal of marriage. Williams feels guilty about this—therefore he uses the word passion, trying to give it a different meaning, one that will be acceptable to himself and to others. Through a simple defense mechanism he seeks to divert attention from his painful failing. "Passion" usually means sexual passion—he uses it in some metaphysical sense, meaning "despair," and starts talking about life in general. What appears to be his failure as a man was really, it seems, a philosophical problem that he had solved. To perfection.

"And it would never come to an end. It would be a marriage that would be founded on human understanding that would be difficult but passionate, passionate as one says of a saint—those saints that were womanly, or, like St. Francis, full of compassion. It would be like no other love that had been conceived between a man and a woman." [49]

So they would live like saints. In the meantime, however, it was just Flossie and Bill, with not much yearning on his part. Mr. Williams had said that if Ed won the *Prix de Rome,* Bill could go to Europe too. So to Germany he went, to study pediatrics. He chose Leipzig because that was where Flossie's sister had studied. He went, he says, "with half a kiss from my bride to be." [50]

Half a kiss being better than none.

Mike Weaver shares Williams' philosophical view of the proceedings. He says that Williams' "swift appraisal of the practical, economical Florence, which replaced his long devotion to the mooning, musical Charlotte, was not so much a spontaneous gesture as a deliberate act of will." Williams, it seems, had been influenced by reading a book, Otto Weininger's *Sex and Character.* Weininger argued that "woman was essentially substance, subject to man's genial capacity for forming her . . . Woman was passive, man active; woman wholly sexual in her nature, man only partly so. But if man was genial, the quality of genius was not hereditary like talent but strictly individual; any man with sufficient nerve and strength could develop it." So when Williams says, "It's going my way," he is exerting his will in accordance with Weininger's thesis. Seen in this light, his proposing to Flossie was a stroke of genius.[51]

It seems more likely, however, that he married her because he thought she could save him. Especially from the "passion" for which, he told his brother Ed in a letter, he had a weakness . . . "I can see the terrible results of yielding up to desire." [52]

18

Modernity

How shall I be a mirror to this modernity?

"The Wanderer"

H E did not like what he saw of the Germans—they were not gifted with inspiration. He condemned their militarism: they feared France and England and hoped to overcome their fear not by faith in the brotherhood of man but by an army to crush and kill.[1]

That year he went over to London and saw Ezra in his habitat —Church Walk, Kensington. Ezra introduced him to Mrs. Shakespear and her daughter. One evening they went to hear Yeats reading poems by candlelight. When they entered he was reading, of all things, Dowson's "Cynara." In a beautiful voice . . . but it wasn't Williams' dish. After a while he and Pound started to leave, but Yeats called out, "Was that Ezra Pound who was here?" He had something to say to Pound, so Ezra returned "and remained a few additional moments with the great man while we waited." This may have been, says Williams, the first time Pound met Yeats.[2]

The word "great" as he uses it is ironic. He is not taken in by the posturing of men such as Pound and Yeats.

He went with Pound to a lecture Yeats gave with Sir Edmund Gosse presiding. Yeats spoke of the young men of the nineties, Lionel Johnson among them, who had been denied an audience in England. What else was left for them but "drunkenness,

242

lechery or immorality of whatever other sort?" At this point Sir
Edmund banged his palm down on the bell beside him. Yeats
tried to continue—the bell rang again. Pound and Williams
failed to speak up in support of Yeats. "What a chance it had
been for me," Williams says, "but I wasn't up to it . . . and so
I sank back once more into anonymity." [3]

He didn't shine in public, couldn't think on his feet. He wasn't
cut out for the occasions that were Ezra's meat and drink. Ezra
didn't shine either, but he wasn't embarrassed—he behaved in a
manner he had got out of books, unconscious of the effect this
might be having on others.

There was the time that Ezra stared at the woman in the
National Gallery. She was a tall, wan creature, a "curious, detached figure." Ezra postured, leaning back on his cane (did he
have a cane? perhaps not), his legs apart, his pointed beard atilt,
and stared at her. She was conscious of it and "began to move
her thighs and pelvis in such a way that it became very apparent
that she was greatly moved and excited." Then there came a
snigger from the ceiling—some workmen had been watching the
scene. Ezra stopped staring at the woman and stepped back and
stared at them until they stopped sniggering. By this time the
woman had vanished. She may well, Williams speculates, have
served as the model for the one in *Mauberley* whom Pound com-
pares to a skein of silk blown against the railing.[4]

> She would like some one to speak to her,
> And is almost afraid that I
> will commit that indiscretion.

The poem he is thinking of is Pound's "The Garden," in *Lustra*.[5]

During his year abroad Williams traveled to Paris and Italy,
where his brother Ed showed him around. He gazed at buildings,
statues, and pictures. Then he went to Spain. One evening in
Toledo he drank wine with some shepherds and listened to a
man play the guitar. "That's another place," he thinks, "in which
I might have stayed forever without loss." But the thought is
followed by another: "They might have robbed me, stuck me
with a knife and thrown the body over the cliff and no one the
wiser for it." [6]

So back to Rutherford . . . "Home and the practice of medicine had begun." [7]

In 1911 he bought his first Ford. It was a beauty with brass rods in front holding up the windshield, and acetylene lamps, but no starter. Sometimes on a winter day he would crank the car for twenty minutes until he got it going, then, in a dripping sweat, go in and take a quick bath and change his clothes, before setting out on his calls.[8]

He saw Floss every day. "Happy days and nights—if lovers are ever happy!"

They waited three years to be married. Three years was too long—he "wore the streets out between the two houses"—yet when he looked back he thought that the long period of breaking in was all that had made their later marriage bearable. He had to do a lot of readjusting to come out softened down for marriage. "My mind was always rebellious and uneasy. This was to be my wife-to-be, excluding all the rest. How could one stand or understand it? And yet, there was Flossie, no Venus de Milo, surely—Flossie, in some ways hard as nails, thank heaven. She had to be." [9]

They were married in December 1912 and went to Bermuda for their honeymoon. They bought a house at Number 9 Ridge Road. Then Floss was pregnant.

One day he was digging a trench for rhododendrons in front of the house when a young woman he knew came walking down the street.

"Happy?" she said.

"Sure," he said, "why not?"

She laughed and kept on walking. What was biting her, he wondered. Then he thought about the question. Was he happy? Who could tell? [10]

He had begun by imitating Keats. Now he imitated Pound, who himself was writing imitations of Renaissance poetry, pre-Raphaelite poetry, and Robert Browning.

In these prewar years Pound was in the ascendant. He published book after book. He knew Yeats and other famous authors. He was beginning to have a reputation in London. In comparison with Pound, Williams was a nonentity.

Therefore he took Pound as his mentor and heeded his advice. He observed the laws Pound handed down. These were the years in which Pound led the Imagist movement—Williams became an Imagist, more deeply committed to the principles than Pound himself. Williams was a slow reader—he lingered behind, still considering, while Pound went leaping ahead, changing from one thing to another. Williams believed . . . he believed in Ezra Pound. He took to heart the Imagist principles that writing must be based in sensory experience, and that poetry does not declaim or explain, it presents.[11] He held to these principles all his life.

Pound was his master. This is evident in Williams' fascination with Pound's theatrical behavior and his way of approaching women. There was a good deal of the woman in Williams, he liked to explain. He accepted Weininger's division of male and female psychology. Writing to Viola Baxter Jordan he said, "Men disgust me and if I must say it fill me with awe and admiration. I am too much a woman." [12] He liked theatricals himself, but had subdued that part of his character in order to be a doctor and family man. He remained fascinated, however, with people who dared to act their dreams.

He submitted to Pound's authority. And Pound was two years younger! He swallowed his pride and submitted. It was hard, for he had a pride of his own—prided himself on being ordinary. Like Whitman he contained multitudes.

For the time being he set himself to imitating Pound. He wrote Renaissance poems in Ezra's English:

> Lady of dusk-wood fastnesses,
>> Thou art my Lady.
> I have known the crisp, splintering leaf-
>> tread with thee on before,
> White, slender through green saplings . . .[13]

He wrote a rhyming imitation of Pound's imitations of Browning's dramatic monologues. He began with a Poundian exclamation:

> It is useless, good woman, useless: the spark fails me.
> God! yet when the might of it all assails me . . .[14]

He wrote an imitation of the spirit, if not the technique, of H. D.'s pseudo-Greek poems:

> So art thou broken in upon me, Apollo,
> Through a splendor of purple garments
> Held by the yellow-haired Clymene . . .
>
> . . . .
> This is strange to me, here in the modern twilight.[15]

It was not just strange, it was alien to Williams, for unlike H. D. he wanted to be modern. In the year following the publication of these poems he wrote, "How shall I be a mirror to this modernity?" [16]

Pound undertook to help Williams as, within a short time, he would be helping Eliot. He saw to it that seven of Williams' poems were published as a group in *The Poetry Review,* London, "With Introductory Note by Ezra Pound." This was Williams' first appearance in a magazine. Pound arranged for Williams' second book, *The Tempers,* to be published by Elkin Mathews, his own publisher. The book appeared in September 1913. Pound reviewed it himself in *The New Freewoman.* He praised the vigor of the poems. The emotions expressed were original and this gave hope for Williams' future work.[17]

Pound recommended the publication of four of Williams' poems in *Poetry,* Chicago, Harriet Monroe's magazine.[18] But William and Harriet did not see eye to eye. She found fault with some of his lines and he assumed the role of an iconoclast: "The poet comes forward assailing the trite and established while the editor is to shear off all roughness and extravagance." [19] Williams means: "while the editor thinks that he must shear off. . . ." He did not have time to spare—when he wrote prose he was content to approximate a meaning.

His tone in their subsequent correspondence became downright insulting: "I wish you well in your work but I heartily object to your old-fashioned and therefore vicious methods." [20]

Williams now thought of himself as a modern poet "assailing outworn conventions." In March 1913 his wife gave him a copy of Whitman's poems. Though he seems to have gotten very little from Whitman—only the idea of writing free verse—Whitman's emphasis on contemporaneity appealed to him. The air was full of new ideas, *l'esprit nouveau* as they called it in France. Modern art began in the prewar years—it seems to have been stimulated by the approaching cataclysm. In 1913 the Armory Show in New York introduced works by Cézanne, Gauguin, Renoir, Matisse, Picasso, Braque, Picabia, Gleizes and Duchamp, the most sensational being Duchamp's "Nude Descending a Staircase." There were innovations in the dance, led by Isadora Duncan and Ruth St. Denis. Among poets there was talk of Futurists and Imagists.

Williams frequented artistic circles in New York. He found

that he could have his cake and eat it too—being Doctor Williams in Rutherford and William Carlos Williams, poet, in Manhattan. He took Floss to parties, then he started leaving her home.[21] She didn't seem to enjoy the company of artists and writers as much as he did, and besides it was inconvenient—there was the trouble of getting someone to stay with the child. They agreed, however, that for the sake of his writing he should keep in touch with what was going on. He would try not to stay out late—he couldn't afford to anyway, seeing that he had to be up early in the morning. He cranked the Ford and headed for New York.

The party might be at the "sumptuous studio" of Walter Arensberg.[22] Arensberg edited *The Glebe*. Ten numbers appeared, one being Pound's Imagist anthology, *Des Imagistes*. "Arensberg could afford to spread a really ample feed with drinks to match. You always saw Marcel Duchamp there. His paintings on glass, half-finished, stood at one side. . . ."[23] Man Ray might be there or Charles Sheeler. Or Charlie Demuth, Williams' old friend from student days. Isadora Duncan was there.

In 1914 Williams began meeting poets associated with *Others*, Alfred Kreymborg's magazine. "There was . . . wild enthusiasm among free verse writers. . . . Good verse was coming in from San Francisco, from Louisville, Kentucky, from Chicago, from 63rd street. . . ."[24] On Sunday afternoons the *Others* crowd would congregate at the Kreymborgs' house in Grantwood, New Jersey. "On every possible occasion," says Williams, "I went madly in my flivver to help with the magazine which had saved my life as a writer. Twenty-five dollars a month kept it going. . . ."[25]

He came to know Wallace Stevens and Marianne Moore, poets like himself, and Kenneth Burke, the poet and critic who became a lifelong friend. He knew Maxwell Bodenheim and Malcolm Cowley. He went to literary gatherings in the Village. Amy Lowell was there, smoking a cigar.

Amy was involved in Imagism. In fact, she had taken it over and Pound had dropped it. Just as well . . . she had heard that he was being dropped himself by everyone in London. Pound was impossible, an egotist. On the other hand, truly great poets had sympathy. As Keats said, "If a sparrow come before my window, I take part in its existence and pick about the gravel."

Williams had had enough of Keats. He went over and talked to Charlie Demuth. He loved Charlie's attitude to life—sophisticated, sharp-witted, irreverent. It corresponded to his own appetite for "something new . . . Something to enliven our lives by its invention, some breadth of understanding, some lightness of touch." [26] Charlie didn't like the taste of liquor but found that the effect on his mind was delightful. Li Po had written his best poetry while being supported in the arms of the Emperor's attendants and with a dancing girl to hold the tablet.[27]

Were there any dancing girls present? One or two, said Charlie, one or two.

In March 1914 Williams' "The Wanderer" appeared in *The Egoist,* London. The poem of three hundred lines announced his intention to be modern. It was in free verse and the theme was new: the Wanderer immersed himself in the stream of life, symbolized by the Passaic River. The river was filthy, but he bathed in it. In this manner he was reborn—he became the river and knew everything it knew.

Keats says that beauty is truth. Williams was taking a different view: "We have discarded beauty; at its best it seems truth incompletely realized." [28] The new poetry would include:

> Faces all knotted up like burls on oaks,
> Grasping, fox-snouted, thick-lipped,
> Sagging breasts and protruding stomachs . . .[29]

The Wanderer is taken by his muse to the city. For this purpose she has transformed herself:

> Ominous, old, painted—
> With bright lips, and lewd Jew's eyes . . .[30]

She shows him Broadway, a breadline, and a strike. Then she leads him through the meadows of New Jersey to the Passaic. She dabbles her hands in the filthy water and bathes both their foreheads. She tells him to enter the river: "Enter, youth, into this bulk," and tells the river, "Enter . . . into this young man." He enters the river and, he says, "I knew all—it became me." [31]

This is Whitmanesque—the sense of absorbing everything, becoming it.

The Wanderer is transformed and sees the last of his old self being borne off by the water. "I could have shouted out in my agony/ At the sight of myself departing." But there is some happiness left: "deep foliage, the thickest beeches . . ./ Tallest oaks and yellow birches." There are birds. The place, "For miles around, hallowed by a stench," shall be the temple of poetry.[32]

As with much that Williams wrote, "The Wanderer" echoes Keats. Here the echoes are of Keats' "Ode to Psyche":

> Yes, I will be thy priest, and build a fane
> In some untrodden region of my mind . . .

At this time the Imagist movement was flourishing. The typical Imagist poem was brief and restricted to presentation of sensory details. Then the concept of Imagism degenerated—anything written in free verse was thought to be Imagist. The unsure taste of Amy Lowell and Harriet Monroe was responsible for this, Pound having left the movement.

For a while Williams considered himself an Imagist. "The immediate image, which was impressionistic, sure enough, fascinated us all. We had followed Pound's instructions, his famous 'Don'ts,' eschewing inversions of the phrase, the putting down of what to our senses was tautological and so, uncalled for, merely to fill out a standard form. Literary allusions, save in very attenuated form, were unknown to us. Few had the necessary reading."

The public thought that the Imagists had definite ideas, but the Imagists themselves were not so sure. "No one knew consistently enough to formulate a 'movement.' We were restless and constrained, closely allied with the painters. Impressionism, dadaism, surrealism applied to both painting and the poem. What a battle we made of it merely getting rid of capitals at the beginning of every line!" [33] It was the line that really concerned them, "the poetic line and our hopes for its recovery from stodginess." [34] That, and the structure of the poem . . . "Imagism was not structural: that was the reason for its disappearance." [35] The mere presentation of an image was not enough.

Williams worked at his writing like a painter or sculptor, struggling with the material. He was having trouble with his lines— "The Wanderer" moved in jerks and gasps. He was not happy with the freedom of free verse. As for structure, the poem had none; it was episodic, like the discarded poem modeled on *Endymion.*

The air was full of theories. Poetry must cleave to the senses— but it was also true that poetry was nothing without imagination. "The thing that stands eternally in the way of really good writing is always one: the virtual impossibility of lifting to the imagination those things which lie under the direct scrutiny of the senses." [36] Were these ideas contradictory? It didn't matter. Ideas were like tubes of paint—they were not what you looked at. The poem was an object—a shape and a sound.

He did not hold theories—he had them, which is a different thing entirely. He echoed Weininger's views of psychology. Then he discovered Kandinsky's ideas about art. There are, said Kandinsky, three modes of expression, and he listed them in an ascending order of importance:

1. A direct impression of nature, expressed in purely pictorial form. This I call an 'Impression'.
2. A largely unconscious, spontaneous expression of inner character, non-material in nature. This I call an 'Improvisation'.
3. An expression of slowly formed inner feeling, tested and worked over repeatedly and almost pedantically. This I call 'Composition'. Reason, consciousness, purpose, play an overwhelming part. But of calculation nothing appears: only feeling.[37]

Kandinsky's treatise *On the Spiritual in Art* was well known among writers and artists. Marsden Hartley met Kandinsky in Germany in 1912 and 1913, and extracts from the treatise were printed in Alfred Stieglitz's *Camera Work*. The third idea stated above sounds like a description of Williams' poetry: "An expression of slowly formed inner feeling, tested and worked over repeatedly and almost pedantically . . . But of calculation nothing appears: only feeling."

There were other ideas in Kandinsky that agreed with ideas Williams had been developing out of the circumstances of his life. An artist must express his personality. He must express what is characteristic of his epoch—this is the element of style, "composed of the speech of the epoch, and the speech of the nation." And he must express what is particular to all art everywhere—elements that are not bound by time or space. If the first two principles are observed, the third will follow of its own accord. But— and this is important—if the third element, the "eternal qualities," are emphasized, the work of art will not reach a contemporary audience. This last idea, says Mike Weaver, helped Williams to develop the idea of "locality" with which he belabored Pound and Eliot.[38]

Between 1913 and 1916 Williams wrote poems that fitted Kandinsky's description of an "impression." "If one were to turn for an analogy in painting for the poems in the collection *Al Que Quiere,* it would be to the Ashcan school of realism, in which the dignity of human life was rendered by impressionistic means." [39]

> the old man who goes about
> gathering dog-lime
> walks in the gutter
> without looking up
> and his tread
> is more majestic than
> that of the Episcopal minister
> approaching the pulpit
> of a Sunday.[40]

Apart from the realism of the subject, the most noticeable change is in the use of words and the shaping of lines as units. The lines are tight and short, and they seem to break with a purpose. There is a clear reason, for instance, why one line, "And his tread," has only three syllables which must be uttered slowly. The syllables in their ponderousness and sound represent the walk of the lime-gatherer.

This is like a poem written a hundred years before—Wordsworth's poem about an old man gathering leeches. Whether or not Williams is conscious of the resemblance, in his attempt to dignify the ordinary he resembles Wordsworth. Moreover, his insistence on the use of the American idiom is like Wordsworth's argument, in *Lyrical Ballads,* for "a selection of language really used by men." "I have wished," says Wordsworth, "to keep the Reader in the company of flesh and blood." [41] It is equally true of Williams.

Most of the poems in *Al Que Quiere* are written in short lines because, Williams says, his writing reproduces the pace of his speech. "I didn't go in for long lines because of my nervous nature. I couldn't. The rhythmic pace was the pace of speech, an excited pace because I was excited when I wrote." [42] The idea that poetry should reproduce the rhythms of speech or feeling has now become so common that it passes unnoticed. But when Williams started writing this was a new idea. Traditionally poems had been written in meter—the rhythm of the line was determined not by the feelings of the poet but by literary conventions.

The poems in *Al Que Quiere* look carved—a block of lines counterpoised by another block. Not the traditional division of the poem in stanzas mechanically repeated. Williams works in blocks of rhythm as a sculptor works in marble or a painter in colors. A Williams poem is irregular—but not free verse, "the senseless / unarrangement of wild things." [43] There is an organic relationship between one part and another. Therefore it is as difficult to represent Williams' poetry with quotations as it would be to represent a statue by a finger or a painting by a few inches of the canvas. "My liking," he says, "is for an unimpeded thrust right through a poem from the beginning to the end, without regard to formal arrangements." [44]

The poetry is concentrated. This he has learned from the Imagist movement. A poem may be only a few lines.

> It's a strange courage
> you give me ancient star:
>
> Shine alone in the sunrise
> toward which you lend no part! [45]

The writing is vivacious; it conveys a sense of enjoyment. This is not common—in Chinese or Japanese poems perhaps, but not in our traditions. The English or American poem traditionally has set out to do something, to make a statement or move the reader. But in many of Williams' poems the aim is enjoyment, nothing more.

> if I in my north room
> dance naked, grotesquely
> before my mirror
> waving my shirt round my head
> and singing softly to myself:
> "I am lonely, lonely.
> I was born to be lonely,
> I am best so!" . . .[46]

This is original, and when poetry speaks of "Old men who have studied / every leg show / in the city . . ." we are hearing a language that has not been in American poetry since Whitman. It has what Williams calls "the inclusive sweep of the great tradition." [47]

Al Que Quiere has been said to mark the start of Williams' metric experiments. [48] But it was more than a beginning—after *Al Que Quiere* though he varied he did not radically change his style.

At this point, when he had achieved a kind of mastery, began the trouble of his life.

There is nothing in literary history quite like the feelings William Carlos Williams had when he thought about T. S. Eliot. Byron said of Keats, who had apparently been killed by bad reviews of his poems, " 'Tis strange the mind, that very fiery particle, / Should let itself be snuff'd out by an article." Stranger still for one writer to dislike another to the point that, like King Charles' head, he sees him everywhere. In the middle of an essay on Marianne Moore, Williams interjects, "It is a talent which diminishes the tom-toming on the hollow men of a wasteland to an irrelevant pitter-patter." [49] In an essay on Karl Shapiro, "Well, you don't get far with women by quoting Eliot to them." [50]

He wishes that Eliot were dead. "Let us once and for all understand," Williams writes to Kay Boyle in 1932, "that Eliot is finally and definitely dead." [51]

There are reasonable explanations for his dislike of Eliot. It was natural for him to oppose Eliot's Anglophilia, believing as he did in the value of locality. Then Eliot was converted to Anglo-Catholicism, and Williams thought it was eyewash: "Every little cleric who happens to bleat and consider himself an artist because of his association with the Church has no title whatever to consider himself so for that reason." [52] And Eliot was no lover of democracy —nor was Williams in certain moods, but he did have an affection for ordinary people.

But the difference in their ideas does not account for Williams' virulent hatred of Eliot. Nor did it begin, as is commonly thought, in 1922 with the publication of Eliot's *Waste Land*. It began years before, when Pound discovered the American poet he had been hoping for and it was not Williams. "Here is the Eliot poem," Pound wrote to Harriet Monroe in 1914. "The most interesting contribution I've had from an American." [53] From then on it was clear that with Pound it was Eliot who came first. He continued to be interested in Williams, but did not expect great things of him, nothing to what might be expected of Eliot.

Williams had followed Pound, even unto the Renaissance. He had been loyal to Ezra. "There are people," he wrote Harriet Monroe in 1915, "who find E. P. chiefly notable as a target—and yet they cannot perceive his greatness." [54]

Now he felt betrayed. And with Eliot's success he felt even worse. The publication in 1917 of Eliot's *Prufrock and Other Observations* cast him into the shade. There was, for example, an English critic who said that American poets were no good, with the exception of Eliot. The critic's name was Jepson and it seems that he lived in Kensington—like Pound, though Williams did not say so. Williams said, "There is always some everlasting Polonius of Kensington forever to rate highly his eternal Eliot. It is because Eliot is a subtle conformist. It tickles the palate of this archbishop of procurers to a lecherous antiquity to hold up Prufrock as a New World type. Prufrock, the nibbler at sophistication, endemic in every capital, the not quite (because he refuses to turn his back), is 'the soul of that modern land,' the United States!"

Jepson had praised Eliot's "La Figlia Que [sic] Piange," the delicate rhythm, et cetera. "IT CONFORMS," Williams shouts, that's why Jepson likes it. He admits that there is "a highly refined distillation" in the poem, a "conscious simplicity." The line "Simple and faithless as a smile and shake of the hand" is perfect. But the last stanza is made almost unintelligible by straining after a rhyme, "the very cleverness with which this straining is covered being a sinister token in itself." He sees Eliot's rhyming as sinister —it conceals some deeper, evil purpose.[55]

He was so hurt by Pound's preference for Eliot over himself that he never forgave Eliot and for a while he had harsh things to say about Pound. "E. P.," he said, "is the best enemy United States verse has."[56] He visualized an international congress of poets—Remy de Gourmont had called for one. "I do believe," Williams wrote, "that when they meet Paris will be more than slightly abashed to find parodies of the middle ages, Dante and *langue d'oc* foisted upon it as the best in United States poetry."[57]

He was no longer willing to accept Pound's tutelage from the other side of the Atlantic. "Criticism must originate in the environment that it is intended for."[58]

But he did not long direct his fire against the one who had actually hurt him. He did not hate Pound. It was the favorite he hated, Eliot with his coat of many colors. And to this day Williams' admirers have carried on the vendetta against Eliot. They would like his works to be erased from the memory of men. As this cannot be arranged, the next best thing is to misread them. " 'The Waste Land,' " says James Breslin, "is a kind of anti-epic, a poem in which the quest for meaning is entirely thwarted and we are left, at the end, waiting for the collapse of western civilization."[59]

Paterson, on the other hand, is a "pre-epic, showing that the process of disintegration releases forces that can build a new world." [60] It seems that for Williams to be a great poet, it must be proved at any cost that Eliot is not.

But Williams was not so different from Eliot as he has been made to seem, and at this time he was feeling a bit like Prufrock himself, anticipating middle age: "In middle age the mind passes to a variegated October. This is the time youth in its faulty aspirations has set for the achievement of great summits. But having attained the mountain top one is not snatched into a cloud but the descent proffers its blandishments quite as a matter of course. At this the fellow is cast into a great confusion and rather plaintively looks about to see if any has fared better than he." [61]

He wondered if he had made the right choice. Pound was in London doing what he liked, writing, while he had to practice medicine. There was something ludicrous about his position, for an artist. "I have defeated myself purposely," he said, "in almost everything I do because I don't want to be thought an artist. I much prefer to be an ordinary fellow. I never wanted to be separated from my fellow mortals by acting like an artist." [62] But the price of being an ordinary fellow came high. "He would want to be quiet, want to relax, and had to go on without respite. To hell with home, his kids, herself, everything . . . if he could only get out and away—anywhere." [63]

The suburbs were getting him down. He was becoming dull. So he turned to women for excitement—"the quiver of the flesh under the smooth fabric." [64]

"I have discovered," Williams says in the Prologue to *Kora in Hell*, "that the thrill of first love passes!" This was written when he had been married six years. He goes on to say, "I have been reasonably frank about my erotics with my wife. I have never or seldom said, my dear I love you, when I would rather say: My dear, I wish you were in Tierra del Fuego."

Once more, Williams' prose is a little "off." His saying that he has been frank about his erotics with his wife is not followed, as we expect, by his saying that his wife knows about his affairs. It is followed by something quite different. The confusion comes of his setting out to say something, then thinking better of it and saying something else that shows him in a better light. But he does not rewrite the first part of his thought.

He goes on to say, "I have discovered by scrupulous attention to this detail and by certain allied experiments that we can con-

tinue from time to time to elaborate relationships quite equal
in quality, if not greatly superior to that surrounding our wedding."

As Williams' wedding was delayed three years, this is nothing
to brag of.

He concludes the glimpse into his marriage with the statement
that the best times have followed the worst. "Periods of barrenness
have intervened . . . our formal relations have teetered on the
edge of a debacle to be followed, as our imaginations have per-
mitted, by a new growth of passionate attachment. . . ." [65]

He was the straying husband who knows that he will be forgiven. This is shown in the following dialogue from his play, *A
Dream of Love*. The play is autobiographical, so much so that the
poem Doc reads to Myra, "Love Song," which he wrote when
they were first married, is included in Williams' collected poems.[66]

Myra: . . . what would you do without all your women, dar-
       ling?
  Doc: I'd find one up a tree somewhere.
Myra: You sure would. And drag her down by the hair—if she
       didn't drop on you first from a low branch. I don't care—
       so long as I have my garden.

       . . . .

Myra: . . . you went to a hotel with that woman.
  Doc: Sure. Anything you can do you must do. I'm not proud.
       If it comes my way I do it.[67]

It was a common enough way of looking at sex. Williams seems
to have suspected that it was too common, for he tried to describe
it as romantic: the other women were visionary, or his wife was
all women, subsuming the rest. In "The Basis of Faith in Art"
he has this conversation with his brother:

Did it ever occur to you that a marriage might be invigorated by
deliberately breaking the vows?

That is impossible.

Nothing is impossible to the imagination.[68]

Nevertheless, he was feeling disillusioned. There was no letup
in his work as a doctor. His affairs provided only temporary relief.
He was past thirty and he was not famous—it seemed unlikely

that he would ever be, living in Rutherford. It was one of the low points of his life. It compelled him to think—to think things through and see where he stood and why. It was not the kind of thinking philosophers do—it came of a way of life, not out of books. Kandinsky was not as convincing as "The odor of the poor farmer's fried supper . . . mixing with the smell of the hemlocks, mist . . . in the valley." [69]

"The local is the universal." [70] And "There is no universal except in the local." [71]

Believing this enabled him to make a new start. And developing the belief he found others who held it too. John Dewey said, "The local is the only universal, upon that all art builds." [72] Keyserling said the same thing in different words. Williams had discovered it for himself, by living in Rutherford. He had to believe it. But it wasn't just a matter of necessity—he had chosen to live where he did. He might have lived in Toledo—"That's another place in which I might have lived forever." Or in London, like Pound and Eliot. But he had chosen to live here—so it was a matter of conviction, not mere necessity. Other men dreamed, but he had vision—he saw life as it was.

Keyserling said, "Every autochthonous culture in the world began as a local culture. Culture is always a daughter of spirit, married to earth. A man who is not yet the native son of a soil can conquer matter spiritually only on a small scale." [73] Williams believed this. From this time forward he strove to emphasize the "universality of the local. From me where I stand to them where they stand in their lives here and now. . . ." [74]

The word "local" may be misleading. It doesn't mean Rutherford, nor even America—it means experience, of which sensory experience is primary—"a local definition of effort." [75] This is how locality comes in, but the emphasis isn't on the locality; it is on the experience. As the point is so important we had better have it in his own words: "We have said simply and as frequently as possible and with as many apt illustrations as we could muster that contact with experience is essential to good writing or, let us say, literature. We have said this in the conviction that contact always implies a local definition of effort with a consequent taking on of certain colors from the locality by the experience, and these colors or sensual values of whatever sort are the only realities in writing or, as may be said, the essential quality in literature. We have even given what seem to be definite exceptions to the rule: unattached intelligence (the Jewish sphere), virtuosity (Russian violinists)." [76]

The corollary is opposition to those who do not show "local definition of effort." In his opinion, Pound and Eliot do not show it. "Being inclined to run off to London and Paris, it is in-explicable that in every case they have forgotten or not known that the experience of native local contacts which they take with them, is the only thing that can give that differentiated quality of presentation to their work which at first enriches their new sphere and later alone might carry them far as creative artists in the continental hurly-burly. Pound ran to Europe in a hurry. It is understandable. But he had not sufficient ground to stand on for more than perhaps two years. He stayed fifteen. Rereading his first book of poems it is easy to see why he was so successful. It was the naive warmth of the wilderness—no matter how presented. But in the end they played Wilson with him.

"Unfortunately for the arts here, intelligence and training have nearly always forced a man out of the country. Cut off from the dominant of their early established sensory backgrounds these expatriates go a typical and but slightly variable course there-after."

It is not surprising that Williams has been called provincial.[77] He seems to think that American writers should stay in America and write about local subjects. In the 1920's expatriatism was an issue, with writers such as Pound, Eliot, Hemingway and Fitz-gerald preferring to live in Europe and others arguing for America. "I remember," says Fitzgerald, "a fellow expatriate opening a letter from a mutual friend of ours, urging him to come home and be revitalized by the hardy, bracing qualities of the native soil. It was a strong letter and it affected us both deeply, until we noticed that it was headed from a nerve sanitarium in Pennsyl-vania." [78]

Williams tried to remove the impression that by "locality" he meant simply place. In a letter to Pound—"For the luv of God snap out of it! I'm no more sentimental about 'murika' than Li Po was about China or Shakespeare about Yingland or any damned Frog about Paris. I know as well as you do that there's nothing sacred about any land. But I also know (as you do also) that there's no taboo effective against any land, and where I live is no more a 'province' than I make it." [79]

The argument against expatriatism is not chauvinistic—it is a matter of aesthetics: "He who does not know his own world, in whatever confused form it may be, must either stupidly fail to learn from foreign work or stupidly swallow it without knowing how to judge of its essential value." [80]

Therefore it appears that when Williams argues for the local he means the artist's sensory experience rooted in place—not merely staying in one place. Locality is "the sense of being attached with integrity to actual experience." [81] Yet Williams was so attached to one place that the meaning has been taken to be this. The place for him was Number 9 Ridge Road. He persuaded himself that it was, making a virtue of necessity. Believing this enabled him to believe in the importance of what he was writing, even if it were only a few lines dashed off about something he had seen that day. Living in Rutherford was as significant as living in London or Paris. No one, not even Eliot, could know what he knew—no one else could be William Carlos Williams.

19

Words and Their Intervals

THOSE were the days. "I can see old Marsden now. . . ." [1]
After the war intellectuals started moving into the territory
opened up by the "lunatic fringe" of the prewar years.[2] New
faces appeared: Wallace Gould and Charles Henri Ford, Matthew Josephson, Djuna Barnes, Hart Crane. *The Dial* started
publishing. Margaret Anderson and Jane Heap edited *The Little
Review,* which published Joyce's *Ulysses.*

Charlie Demuth was around, and in the midtwenties Williams
came to know Charles Sheeler. These painters had been born in
the same year as Williams. They came from similar backgrounds
—they had been at the Philadelphia Academy of Fine Arts when
he was in medical school. They had broken with their early work
as he had—Sheeler stopped painting Fauvist landscapes, Demuth
his "vaudeville watercolors"—in order to paint their subjects in
a more naturalistic way. They adapted the techniques of international movements, Futurism, Cubism, and Imagism, in order
to develop their own Precisionist school of painting. The painters
and the poet were close friends; they frequented the art gallery
in New York run by the photographer Alfred Stieglitz at 291
Fifth Avenue, later An American Place.[3]

Demuth, Sheeler and Williams shared the same attitudes; it
was not influence in the common meaning of the term—they
painted and wrote alike because they thought alike. Williams
thought of poetry as though it were painting. The poem was not
a vehicle for thought but a physical object, an organization of

sounds and rhythms.[4] Painting, in the modern period so far removed from representation, enabled poetry to see its aims more clearly. "Such a painting as that of Juan Gris," Williams wrote in *Spring and All*, " . . . is important as marking more clearly than any I have seen what the modern trend is: the attempt is being made to separate things of the imagination from life, and obviously, by using the forms common to experience so as not to frighten the onlooker away but to invite him." [5] In the *Autobiography* he says that it was the step of using words for their tactile qualities, "the words themselves beyond the mere thought expressed," that distinguished modern writing.[6]

James Guimond points to similarities between Williams' poems and the paintings of Demuth and Sheeler. Demuth was the enemy of stupidity and drabness; he gave witty titles to his paintings. There is a Demuth painting of a grim water tower and chimney titled "Aucassin and Nicolette." Sheeler is "the man of integrity, full of respect for the commonplace, which he clarifies and organizes so that each object's identity is based upon a fresh perception of its unique qualities, its denotations, rather than its utilitarian or sentimental connotations." Both painters used local materials: "Demuth decorated barns near Lancaster with Pennsylvania Dutch hex signs; one of Sheeler's best works is his tempera and crayon 'Bucks County Barns,' an exquisitely precise rendition of contrasting native materials, weathered grey wood and sandy yellow stone." [7] As Williams says in *Spring and All*, " 'Beauty' is related not to 'loveliness' but to a state in which reality plays a part." [8]

The arts were flourishing. Extraordinary talents would appear and cause a sensation. "Once, Mayakofsky read aloud for us his 'Willie the Havana Street Cleaner.' A big man, he rested one foot on top of the studio table as he read. It was the perfect gesture." No one could understand a word of the reading, but they were impressed with the sounds and the intense seriousness of the Russian poet.[9]

At that time artists and writers lived as in the opinion of Monsieur Homais artists and writers always do. "These great artists are all night-birds. They need to lead rackety lives, to stimulate their imagination. They die in the workhouse, though, not having the sense to put a bit by when young." [10]

The Baroness Elsa von Freytag Loringhoven, for example . . . She was a sculptor and an artists' model, now fifty years old. She sent Williams a photograph of herself, "8 × 10, nude, a fine portrait." She pursued him, and several others—Wallace Stevens was afraid to come below Fourteenth Street because of her. She had an intimate talk with Williams and advised him that what he needed to make him great was to contract syphilis from her and so free his mind for serious art. She pursued him to Rutherford. One night he was called out to attend a sick baby. When he stepped outside it was the Baroness—she grabbed his wrist and said, "You must come with me." He refused, so she hauled off and hit him with all her strength. A few months later she waylaid him again, but this time he flattened her with a punch. Then he had her arrested. "What are you in this town?" she yelled, as the police took her away. "Napoleon?"

He was really crazy about her. He gave her money to get out of the country—which someone stole. He gave her some more and she went. Then he heard she had been killed. As a practical joke some Frenchman turned on the gas jet while she slept.

Between 1920 and 1923 Williams was associated with Robert McAlmon on the magazine *Contact*. McAlmon had served in the Canadian army during the war. Then he was a flyer out on the Coast. Then he lived on a scow in New York harbor. He was a "coldly intense young man with hard blue eyes" who, when Williams met him, was making a living posing nude for mixed classes at Cooper Union.[12] McAlmon had a fierce belief in the need for contact with the soil, due perhaps to his experiences in the air and on the scow. "Contact meant coming in to land or stepping ashore."[13] He wrote a fable for *The Ace,* a magazine of aviation, describing how glad he had been to return to earth, "something that had been and would continue to be," after his flights in the sky.[14] A subsequent issue of *The Ace* presented a manifesto on the influence of aviation on art: the "air-centaur" would scorn earthbound thinkers who built reputations upon "the little ripples of character accentuation, native to all men, but with them displayed in the spotlight of self-adoration." Through his experience in the air the flyer would develop his individuality.[15] This was the kind of thing Futurists had been saying in Europe for some time. McAlmon agreed with the manifesto in its contempt for New York artists and writers who herded together. He disagreed, however, with the idea that art must be disconnected from nature and that "we must forget the specific in our contemplation of the general." [16] McAlmon's creed was contact with the soil.

This suited Williams, who had his own theory of locality, and there was another aspect of McAlmon's thinking he found congenial. McAlmon drew his attention to an article by Mary Austin attacking certain New York Jews—Stieglitz, Stein, Orenstein, Rosenfeld and Oppenheim, friends of Waldo Frank, whose book, *Our America,* she was reviewing. These Jews believed that literature must be Americanized. The mystique came of their familiarity with the country around Broadway and Fifty-ninth Street. McAlmon reacted against Frank; in his contributions to *Contact* he attacked what he called "Semiticism," and later from France he wrote of "Jew-York." [17]

This did not displease Williams. He was anti-Semitic himself —in this, too, he was "ordinary." In Rutherford, as in the suburbs of Philadelphia where Pound grew up, Jews were regarded with suspicion. One of the teachings of Christianity was that Christ was killed by the Jews. Jews were said to be moneylenders, and there was talk of the Protocols of Zion, an international Jewish conspiracy. Williams was no Christian, but he shared the prejudice of his neighbors.

Williams' *The Great American Novel,* published in 1923, concludes with anti-Semitism, almost as though this were the whole point of the novel—it is teetering on the edge. In the final paragraphs he talks about the manufacture of "shoddy." Linda Welshimer Wagner, in her discussion of the passage, praises the "Spanish irony" of the writing.[18] She fails to mention, however, that the person who is described as making shoddy out of filthy rags and marketing it to an unsuspecting public is a Jew.[19] Other of Williams' admirers have failed to notice his anti-Semitism.

His most offensive writing on the subject occurs in the novel *A Voyage to Pagany,* published five years later when anti-Semitism had become common, even chic, among intellectuals. The hero—like most of Williams' heroes he is unavoidably recognizable as Williams himself—is put off by the Jewishness of Michelangelo's statue of David, "The too big hand, the over-anxious Jewish eyes. The neurasthenic size of the thing. . . ." [20] On a train he is unfortunate enough to meet with "a fat old Jew and his blubber wife." Later, ". . . the old Jew woman, having eaten too much, struggled over legs, flung open the door, and vomited full into the corridor—then came back, as she must have done, and slept again—perfectly unconcerned." [21] There are other references of the kind: "the stinking Jews," "A Jew of the usual objectionable type." [22]

Contact meant contact with experience. McAlmon was looking for writers who would "favor direct experience of life before intellectualism of any kind." [23] This was right up Williams' alley.

With its anti-intellectualism and anti-Semitism *Contact* held seeds of the Fascism then spreading among European writers, but in the United States what writers say has little importance, either good or bad. Only four issues of *Contact* saw the light— "some fine poems by Marianne Moore, Hartley and a few others," "direct, uncompromised writing," but "Nobody bought—and there was much else in the wind." [24]

Then McAlmon sailed for Europe. He had been planning to sail on a freighter to China, but something happened that changed his plans: H. D. arrived in New York on her way to California, "Same old Hilda, all over the place, looking as tall and as skinny as usual." She was traveling with a friend named Bryher, "a small, dark English girl with piercing eyes." Williams and McAlmon had tea with them at the Belmont Hotel. Then McAlmon had a card from Bryher in California—she was on her way back to England with H. D. and wanted to marry him.

Bryher turned out to be the daughter of Sir John Ellerman, "the heaviest taxpayer in England." "Bob," says Williams, "fell for it." Bob and Bryher were married and had a suite on the White Star liner *Celtic,* reserved by the father of the bride. The night before sailing there was an "intimate supper" in a small dining room at the Hotel Brevoort. Williams was divided between joy for his friend's good fortune and sadness at their parting. "Bryher was there, H. D. was there, not joining too excitedly in the ceremonies." Flossie was there, and Marianne Moore, "and good old Marsden, the most wonderful of party men."

Two days later Floss and Bill received a postcard representing a scene from a current play, men and women with their hands in a pot full of money. The card was signed D. H. Williams accused H. D. of being the sender—she denied it violently. He did not believe her.

So "Bob left and took his disastrous story with him." [25] Presumably Williams means the story of Bryher's relations with

H. D. The next time he saw the McAlmons, in Paris, H. D. was with them, looking silently on. It was like the Hemingway story, "The Sea Change."

As a result of his marrying Sir John's daughter McAlmon was able to start a publishing venture, Contact Editions, and bring out important writing in Paris: Gertrude Stein's *The Making of Americans,* the early Hemingway, Williams' *Spring and All.*

At that time, Williams says, writers and artists were full of energy—they had rediscovered a "primary impetus, the elementary principle of all art, in the local conditions." [26] And he was hitting his stride. In September 1920 he published *Kora in Hell: Improvisations.* It was published by the Four Seas Company, Boston, the author contributing two hundred and fifty dollars to the cost of publication. He had tried writing something every day without planning—prose reflections—putting down anything that came into his head, writing at any hour of the day or night. He didn't revise, though he did tear up some of what he wrote. Some of the pieces could not be understood, so he wrote interpretations beneath the improvisations. He got the idea from a book, the poems of Pietro Metastasio, Pound left when he came on a visit.[27]

Parts of *Kora* are Kandinsky's "direct impression of nature, expressed in purely pictorial form." [28] There are the thoughts of the writer: "After thirty years staring at one true phrase he discovered that its opposite was true also." [29] And the work of the doctor: "Stupidity couched in a dingy room beside the kitchen. One room stove-hot, the next the dead cold of a butcher's ice box. The man leaned and cut the baby from its stem. Slop in disinfectant, roar with derision at the insipid blood stench: hallucination comes to the rescue on the brink of seriousness: the gas-stove flame is starblue, violets back of L'Orloge at Lancy." [30]

Kora has instances of the "poetic prose" that was fashionable at the time. The manner was carried over from the cult of beauty in the 1890's—in the hands of writers such as James Branch Cabell it would have a revival in the 1920's. The style was marked by archaic words, literary turns of phrase, and irony. It struck readers as very sophisticated. In *Kora* Williams tried to show that though he lived in New Jersey he could be as sophisticated as writers who lived in Greenwich Village. "There was a baroness lived in Hungary bathed twice monthly in virgins' blood." [31] The sentence might have come from Cabell's *Jurgen*.

In 1921 Williams published, with the same publisher and on the same terms, a book of poems titled *Sour Grapes*. People jumped at the title—it showed that he was frustrated and disappointed. Instead of living like a poet he lived in the suburbs. "The young Frenchmen, yes, they really let go. But you, you are an American. You are afraid (this from the women and the men also) you are afraid. You live in the suburbs, you even *like* it. What are you anyway? And you pretend to be a poet, a POET! Ha, ha, ha, ha! A poet! You!"

"But," says Williams, "all I meant was that sour grapes are just the same shape as sweet ones:

Ha, ha, ha, ha!" [32]

If this was what he intended he failed to take into account the plain meaning of the words. *Sour Grapes* means just what he says people took it to mean: frustration. In spite of his insistence on using the "American language," Williams can be surprisingly unaware of the effect words actually have. This is most evident when he writes expository prose and tries to reason —not so evident in the short stories, which approach poetry and are among the best of the kind. Prose allowed him to think loosely. On the other hand when he wrote poetry he wished to shape it "to perfection." He was driven by a need to be perfect, almost despair. It *had* to be right. "Most of my life," he said, "has been lived in hell—a hell of repression lit by flashes of inspiration, when a poem such as this or that would appear." [33] His need to write a poem went back to the times he sought to please his father and mother by being perfect. The feeling of repression forced the poem into its necessary form as it escaped.

"To me at that time," Williams said, "a poem was an image, the picture was the important thing. As far as I could, with the materials I had, I was lyrical, but I was determined to use the material I knew and much of it did not lend itself to lyricism." [34]

Besides their visual qualities the poems have a natural phrasing and movement of the line that give an impression of sincerity. In the poem, "To a Friend Concerning Several Ladies," Williams described his immediate surroundings:

> You know there is not much
> that I desire, a few chrysanthemums
> half lying on the grass . . .

But, he says:

> But there comes
> between me and these things
> a letter
> or even a look—well placed,
> you understand,
> so that I am confused, twisted
> four ways and—left flat,
> unable to lift the food to
> my own mouth:
> Here is what they say: Come!
> and come! and come! And if
> I do not go I remain stale to
> myself and if I go—

If he goes to the city which he can see at night blazing in the
distance, perhaps he will get some good out of it. Out of the
woman, that is. For there is "no good in the world except out
of/ a woman and certain women alone/ for certain things."
But "what if/ I arrive like a turtle,/ with my house on my
back . . . ?" [35]

Here is the famous sincerity that distinguishes the style of
Williams. The effect is got through natural-seeming sentences
and right visual images: "like a turtle,/ with my house on my
back." It is not easy to find poems in English that give the appearance of sincerity. The English tradition is to embellish a
thought, create a work that will be splendid, a poetry machine
that will carry the writer out of himself and beyond the reach
of criticism—the "great poem," suitable for anthologies. For
poetry that seems to speak as men do we may go to Burns,
Wordsworth and Whitman. There are specimens of sincerity
here and there, and then there is William Carlos Williams.
Sincerity was his style. For this he gave up nearly everything
else and was obscure. When Williams was young he was over-
shadowed by Eliot. Then Auden's style caught on; young poets
imitated his catchy stanzas full of references to spies, nervous
disorders, Kierkegaard, whatever was intellectually fashionable.
Later, when fame still eluded him, Williams saw audiences
flocking to readings by a young Welsh poet; [36] they liked the
stentorian voice on the platform though they could not have
said what all the fuss was about.

He sacrificed fame for sincerity. He was like a monk who has
taken a vow. A Buddhist monk—some of the poems are close

in spirit to Buddhism. The intent to live here and now, to be conscious of everything he can see, hear, touch and taste, is reminiscent of Buddhist teaching. "Your ordinary life, that is the way," says the Buddhist Nansen. Williams' way was as ordinary as he could make it; at the same time he strove to lift things into perfection, the Nirvana of art.

> So much depends
> upon
>
> a red wheel
> barrow . . .[37]

From where does vision proceed? From the life of the poet. Nancy Willard says, "For Neruda, Rilke, Williams and Ponge, the question of how to write is a question of how to live." [38] To understand Williams' poems we must understand his life. This is not true of Pound and Eliot whose experiences passed through a process of dramatization before they issued as art.

Did Williams know anything about Buddhism? He had read *haiku,* the Japanese poems of seventeen syllables which suggest a scene and trigger a perception. All the Imagist poets read *haiku.* They did not know that *haiku* embody Buddhist teachings, but they learned something of the technique. Like a Buddhist monk giving a *koan* to his disciple, the Imagist poem presented, it did not explain. It was up to the recipient to make what he could of it. The truth must be experienced, not merely apprehended with the abstracting, reasoning mind.

Williams seems to have had a particular fondness for "The Great Figure," the poem he placed at the end of the book. Demuth did a painting based upon it. On a hot day in July Williams was walking to Marsden Hartley's studio on Fifteenth Street. There was a clatter of bells and a fire engine passed the end of the street. He turned just in time to see a golden figure 5 on a red background flash by. "The impression," he says, "was so sudden and forceful that I took a piece of paper out of my pocket and wrote a short poem about it." [39]

> Among the rain
> and lights
> I saw the figure 5
> in gold
> on a red
> firetruck

> moving
> tense
> unheeded
> to gong clangs
> siren howls
> and wheels rumbling
> through the dark city.[40]

He seems to feel this is the way poems should always be written
—straight from experience.

Once he and Marsden were standing on the Erie platform in
Rutherford, waiting for the train that was to take Marsden back
to New York. An express train roared by, "right before our faces
—crashing through making up time in a cloud of dust and sand
so that we had to put up our hands to protect our faces.

"As it passed Marsden turned and said to me, 'That's what
we all want to be, isn't it, Bill?'

"I said, 'Yes, I suppose so.' " [41]

The drive and heat of the period were what made it great.
Yes, and locality—that it was happening here and now, on the
Erie platform in Rutherford, in the Village on Fifteenth Street.

Then, he says, their world caved in. *"The Dial* brought out
The Waste Land and all our hilarity ended. It wiped out our
world as if an atom bomb had been dropped upon it and our brave
sallies into the unknown were turned to dust."

A sentence that follows is famous: "Critically Eliot returned
us to the classroom."

This occurred just when Williams and his friends were "on
the point of an escape to matters much closer to the essence of
a new art form itself—rooted in the locality which should give
it fruit. I knew at once that in certain ways I was most defeated." [42]

Meaning, it seems, that of all the artists of the local who were
defeated, he suffered the most. Presumably because he was the
most committed to the theory.

It seems that it was Eliot's erudition, the allusiveness of *The
Waste Land,* that had done so much harm. The poem was anything
but local; it ranged in time from the Crucifixion to the Great
War, in space from the Ganges to the Thames. It did not appear
to have come out of experience—one or two of the early reviews
had even suggested that it was a parody of literature of the past.

Syntax and grammar desert Williams when he thinks about Eliot: "Eliot had turned his back on the possibility of reviving my world. And being an accomplished craftsman, better skilled in some ways than I could ever hope to be, I had to watch him carry my world off with him, the fool, to the enemy." [43] So it was merely Eliot's skill that made him successful—this from Williams, who in other places declares that technique is everything: "It is in the minutiae—in the minute organization of the words and their relationships in a composition that the seriousness and value of a work of writing exist—*not* in the sentiments, ideas, schemes portrayed." [44]

Truly, when he tried to reason he was inconsistent, and when he talked about Eliot he hardly made sense. If only Eliot had stayed in America! "We needed him in the scheme I was half-consciously forming." [45]

One is reminded of the cry of the Baroness Elsa von Freytag Loringhoven: "What are you in this town? Napoleon?"

It is possible that Williams did not enjoy Eliot's work, could not put aside his ideas of what poetry should be and experience the poetry of *The Waste Land.* But if he was unable to read Eliot it was because, in the first place, he did not want to. There is no getting around it—he was envious. He envied Eliot's success and growing reputation, he envied his friendship with Pound and the high opinion Pound had of Eliot's writing. Williams had already been wounded by this—the fame of *The Waste Land* rubbed salt into the wound.

> . . . inwardly he chawéd his own maw
> At neighbor's wealth, that made him ever sad.[46]

There was apprehension mixed with his envy. Writing to John Riordan in 1925 he said, "I must say Eliot inspires me with dread—since I see him finished and I do not find myself stepping beyond him. Since I cannot compete with him in knowledge of philosophy, nor even in technical knowledge of the conned examples of English poetry which he seems to know well—what is left for me but to fall back upon words? There they are just as they always were and the art of using them is no more dependent upon philosophic catastrophes or past examples of writing than are the words themselves . . .

"The words are there quite apart from any theory of arranging them. . . ." [47]

What the soothsayer says to Mark Antony concerning Octavius might have been said to Williams concerning Eliot:

> Thy lustre thickens
> When he shines by. I say again, thy spirit
> Is all afraid to govern thee near him:
> But he away, 'tis noble.[48]

But people did not fail to read Williams because they were reading Eliot—to paraphrase Bentley, no writer is ever put down by another writer, only by himself. Eliot succeeded because he had great talent and his poetry expressed what people were feeling at the time. Williams' poetry didn't. He would have to wait —he had always been a slow starter.

In the meantime it wasn't *The Waste Land* that did him harm; it was the feeling that he was in competition with Eliot. " 'History is England,' yodels Mr. Eliot. To us this is not so, not so *if* we prove it by writing a poem built to refute it—otherwise he wins!!" [49] Williams said this after Eliot had published *Four Quartets*. Even by his own theory it doesn't make sense, for England was where Eliot lived, his "locality." Therefore, for Eliot history had to be English.

As long as Williams kept thinking that Eliot might "win" he kept losing, for if we fear a thing enough we come to believe that it is true. He felt that Eliot had won and he was out of the running. Williams didn't withdraw to the extent of giving up poetry, but in the thirties he concentrated on prose fiction. And when he did write a poem he set limits to it, leaving "philosophy" to Eliot and restricting himself to using just words —"The words are there quite apart from any theory of arranging them." He tried to use words as though they didn't have meanings and made dry work of it. He might have enjoyed himself more if he hadn't thought Eliot was watching.

Spring and All, published in 1923 by McAlmon's press in Paris, is a kind of watershed—after this Williams begins concentrating on prose. In *Spring and All* he achieves what he has set out to do; he is always a poet, even when he makes mistakes —what he says of Marianne Moore's writing is true of his own: "She writes sometimes good and sometimes bad poetry but always—with a single purpose out of a single fountain which is of the sort." [50]

The book consists of a handful of poems and some short chapters of prose, thoughts about art and writing. He is especially concerned with the use of imagination. The artist uses what he has observed but out of this he makes a nature of his own.

"Crude symbolism" is empty—comparing anger with lightning, flowers with love. It is marked by the use of the word "like." Typing by association kills imagination. Evocation of images for their own sake also kill it.[51] His object in the present book is to write about "the 'nature' which Shakespeare mentions and which Hartley speaks of so completely in his 'Adventures': it is the common thing which is anonymously about us." [52]

This sounds as though he has suddenly reverted to naturalism. Not so. His writing will be "in the realm of the imagination as plain as the sky is to a fisherman . . . The word must be put down for itself, not as a symbol of nature but a part, cognisant of the whole—aware—civilized." [53]

He is also concerned with form and the difference between poetry and prose. The difference is not that poetry is written in a pronounced rhythm. It is that poetry and prose have different origins and a different purpose. "Poetry feeds the imagination and prose the emotions, poetry liberates the words from their emotional implications, prose confirms them in it." [54]

In poetry the words have a direction that is separate from meaning. "To understand the words as so liberated is to understand poetry." [55] Writing is not music and has nothing to gain by trying to be like music—"the conditions of music are objects for the action of the writer's imagination just as a table or—" [56]

Having said this, Williams immediately contradicts himself—it seems that writing should be like music after all. " . . . the writer of imagination would attain closest to the conditions of music not when his words are disassociated from natural objects and specified meanings but when they are liberated from the usual quality of that meaning by transposition into another medium, the imagination." [57]

This is Surrealism, the doctrine being followed by André Breton, Louis Aragon and other writers in Paris. Surrealism presented objects in all their concrete reality—there was nothing symbolic about Surrealist painting or poetry—but the objects were divorced from their functions, the chair placed upside down. When Williams speaks of "liberation from the usual quality of that meaning by transposition into another medium, the imagination," he is recommending Surrealism.

But there is nothing particularly Surrealist about his poems. For all his talk of imagination and the need to transform the world, he was fond of it as it was. "I can't write fiction," he told Pound. "All I do is try to understand something in its natural colors and shapes." [58] His poems are a selection and rearrangement of things so that we can look at them hard, but the things have not been divorced from their usual qualities. Williams disliked the thought of divorce, either in life or art.

Spring and All contains the poems with the famous beginnings, "By the road to the contagious hospital," and "The pure products of America/ go crazy." [59] The language of these poems is not particularly American, but the content is: American landscape, American lives. There is something about this content that would not have sounded right in iambic pentameter. It goes better in irregular feet.

Sincerity becomes confession in the poem that begins "What about all this writing?" The poem is about love in the city—not any city, but Manhattan of the Wrigley's sign and warm summer nights.

> You lay relaxed on my knees—
> the starry night
> spread out warm and blind
> above the hospital

Their lovemaking is watched by the chairs, the floor, the walls, "they which alone know everything/ and snitched on us in the morning." The poem ends:

> but I merely
> caressed you curiously
>
> fifteen years ago and you still
> go about the city, they say
> patching up sick school children [60]

How are we to describe the form of poetry such as this? Williams thought a great deal about the structure of his poems. "IT IS THE FORM . . . I have tried so hard to make this clear: it is the form which is the meaning." [61] Yet, confronted with the broken shape of his writing on the page, we are tempted to say it is the shape of thought, and let it go at that.

James Breslin has done more. He speaks of the recurrence and "jagged, circling movement" of Williams' thinking, and undertakes to show how this "extends down into the most minute workings of the poem—the line itself." The lines end with "prepositions, adjectives, conjunctions, subjects, transitive verbs —all words we know will be followed by objects, modifiers, and so on." The effect is to prevent "quick movement through a conventional form." There is a "halting, disjunctive sequence of sharply defined images." The aim is to "break through the reader's protective shell, jar his relaxed euphoria," to force the reader's attention "down into an independent world of objects, solid and distinct in themselves yet fluid in their combinations." [62]

Williams says, "By the brokenness of his composition the poet makes himself master of a certain weapon which he could possess himself of in no other way. The speed of the emotions is sometimes such that thrashing about in a thin exaltation of despair many matters are touched but not held. . . ." [63] No wonder some readers have found his method unpalatable. There is an element of bullying about it. Readers, especially those whose idea of verse is the regular beat of iambic pentameter, dislike being hauled about so. They don't want poetry that, as Keats said of Wordsworth's poetry, "has a palpable design upon us." "Let us have the old Poets, and Robin Hood." [64]

"The rhythmic unit," says Williams, "usually came to me in a lyrical outburst." [65] The poem began to move in units of two lines, say, or three:

> Now the grass, tomorrow
> the stiff curl of wildcarrot leaf

> One by one objects are defined—
> It quickens: clarity, outline of leaf [66]

The unit would expand, then again it would contract. He had a "rationale of organic form, the art object as a machine made of words, searching for its own autonomous shape." [67]

The origins of the forms his poetry took were as mysterious to him as they are to us.

Those were the days. "*Everyone* was in Paris . . . Sat at Dôme, saw Kiki, Mary Reynolds, etc. Sat at Dôme with Antheil. . . ." [68]

"The next day it was raining but cleared, and the sun came out brightly. Rode a bus to the Louvre and walked thence, buying a few stamps at the outdoor market on the Champs Elysées for Bill. At the hotel neither trunk nor baggage had arrived; ate at Trianon, then to Dôme. Met Hemingway on the street, a young man with a boil on his seat, just back from a bicycle ride in Spain. . . ."

Bob McAlmon told Bill and Floss about an incident the year before when he was coming back from Spain with Hemingway. The train stopped and the passengers got off for a breath of air. There was a dead dog beside the track, belly swollen, "skin . . . iridescent with decay." McAlmon wanted to get away from the stink, but Hemingway got out his notebook and, to McAlmon's disgust, started taking notes in minute detail, "describing the carcass in all its beauty."

Bob showed them around. Williams had been nervous about seeing him again—the last time they had met had been at the Brevoort in New York. Bob was stouter, far less youthful and less discerning.[69] But Bill got over his uneasiness—Bob and he still had a common need, the "desire to get down to some sort of sense about writing." He still loved Bob.[70]

Bill and Floss had decided to risk everything. They left the kids at home—Bill aged nine and Paul aged six—and set out to see the world. McAlmon took them under his wing. He was at home in Paris. He was always doing something for someone—spending money like a prince. At one point he was giving the young American composer George Antheil a hundred dollars a month. He fed the Joyces. He gave big parties. "It was Sir John's money, but if Bob hadn't earned it, nobody ever earned a nickel." Bryher and H. D. were off somewhere together in Switzerland. McAlmon told them about "long train trips about the continent with the two women quarreling in the compartment driving him nearly insane, hard to go on like that." [71]

McAlmon had a way of insulting people with his "blinkless and cold-eyed remarks," calling them liars to their faces. Then the bartender had to pull him over the counter—McAlmon weighed only 150 pounds—and keep him out of sight till he sobered up.

McAlmon took them to see Brancusi in his studio. Bill offended Brancusi by saying that Pound, whose opera *Villon* had just been performed at the Théâtre des Champs Elysées, didn't know one note from another.

They met Sylvia Beach, who had a bookshop on the rue de l'Odeon, a sanctuary for writers. And Man Ray did some photographs of Bill Williams. But when he got the finished pictures he was furious—they made him look like a fool. And they were expensive—the six prints cost more than the hotel bill! There had been a beautiful girl present in the studio while Bill was having his picture taken. Man Ray's assistant. She gave him a penetrating look . . . he regretted not having got to know her better. He was infuriated when he saw the photographs. Man Ray had asked him to close his eyes a little—this gave him a sentimental, inexperienced appearance. He felt humiliated, especially when he thought of the "beautiful, courageous girl a thousand years off, experienced, unobtainable—in the background," laughing at him.[72]

They had dinner at the Joyces', James and Nora (née Barnacle —he'd married her, Joyce said, because she'd stick). "Here's to sin!" said McAlmon, raising his glass. "I won't drink to that," said Joyce. McAlmon laughed and took it back, and they all sipped their wine in silence. The exchange seemed significant. Everything people say in Paris seems significant.

One night McAlmon gave a party for Floss and Bill at the Trianon. Tables were pushed together. "I was in the middle facing the wall, Floss next to me on the right with Joyce and Ford Madox Ford opposite, their wives and the others close about us; Harold Loeb with Kitty Cannell, Antheil, Marcel Duchamp. Bill Bird, Man Ray, Mina Loy and her daughter, Sylvia Beach, Louis Aragon; some were invited and some merely showed up (at Bob's expense)." [73]

The reporter of dead dogs, however, was not in evidence. He was writing short stories. Some day he would put these people in a novel that would make him rich and famous.

Bill Williams had to make a speech. All eyes were upon him —what could an American say that would be significant? "I had nothing in common with them." Nevertheless he made his speech. He told them that in Paris he had observed that "when a corpse, in its hearse, plain or ornate, was passing in the streets, the women stopped, bowed their heads and that men generally stood at attention with their hats in their hands. What I meant was my own business, I did not explain, but sat down feeling like a fool." [74]

It was a bad moment, he tells us. Indeed it must have been— the party had been subjected to some of his expository prose. What he meant exactly was known to him alone.

He did not shine in Paris. He felt himself "with ardours not released but beaten back in this centre of old-world culture where everyone was tearing his own meat, warily conscious of a newcomer but wholly without inquisitiveness." [75] They weren't interested in his thoughts.

He had been thinking more and more about what it meant to be an American, and had brought with him drafts of chapters of a book he was writing on the subject. He was thinking of a chapter on Daniel Boone. To Boone the Indian was the best teacher. Boone didn't want to be like an Indian, though they wanted to adopt him into their tribe—he wanted to be himself in the new world. To possess the land as the Indian had possessed it. The Indian was not to be feared and exterminated—he was the natural expression of the place. It was up to the white man to discover the natural expression of his place.[76]

On the other hand were those who brought their Old World habits and obsessions with them—men like Cotton Mather, who thought in abstractions. "Trustless of humane experience, not knowing what to think, they went mad, lost all direction. Mather defends the witchcraft persecutions." [77]

The day after the party at which not only had Williams failed to shine, but with a foolish speech had brought upon himself incomprehension then gathering contempt in all their eyes, he went for a walk by himself, alone. He bought a pear and ate it. He discovered the Place François Ier by himself and admired the "French austerity of design, gray stone cleanly cut and put together in complementary masses. . . ."

> I am lonely, lonely.
> I was born to be lonely,
> I am best so! [78]

Like Columbus, De Soto, and Daniel Boone. Explorers are always lonely.

"Paris," he wrote to Kenneth Burke, "would be wonderful if I could be French and *Vieux;* it would be still more wonderful if I could only want to forget everything on earth. Since I can't do that, only America remains where at least I was born." [79]

Gertrude Stein felt as he did about locality. "After all," she wrote, "anybody is as their land and air is . . . It is that which makes them and the arts they make and the work they do and the way they eat and the way they drink and the way they learn and everything." [80] But Gertrude Stein lived in Paris. So did Hemingway—an American author if ever there was one—and he would write about Americans who lived in Paris and went to bull-fights in Spain. After this he would write a novel about the retreat from Caporetto.

Truly, as Henry James said, it is a complex fate being an American.

Bill and Floss traveled south to Carcassonne and the Riviera, to Rome and Vienna. On their return to Paris they found the pace quicker than before. They saw a good deal of Ezra and Dorothy Pound. The Pounds were living in a big studio with a courtyard. Ezra and Bill talked about Renaissance music, theory of notation, melody and time. A sense of time, Bill felt, was Ezra's chief asset as an appreciator of music. He could be listened to on the subject of melody, the musical phrase, and the early composers. But he knew nothing about tones, and his opinions of music in general were suspect.

Dorothy Pound disliked Paris, "as much because of its people as its winter weather, neither fish nor flesh." On the other hand she adored Italy. She showed them her paintings, linear and gray like herself, and gave them a painting of rocks on the Dartmouth moors, "cubistic in feeling, flat and cold." Pound made tea over the spirit lamp that seemed to be his specialty. Then they went to supper—Williamses, Pounds and Hemingways. Afterwards they went to a prize fight where Floss—to his horror and astonishment, Bill says—pounded on the back of the man in front of her, screaming "Kill him! Kill him!" The man the back belonged to was Ogden Nash.

They saw more of the Pounds and came to know Hemingway better. Bill played tennis with Hemingway and Harold Loeb, and he performed a small operation on the Hemingway baby, retracting the foreskin. "He naturally cried, to his parents' chagrin."

Then the Williamses sailed back to America where Bill understood things in their natural (native?) colors and shapes.

But Floss and Bill looked back on their time in Europe as a high point of their lives. "*Everyone* was in Paris—if you wanted to see them." Nancy Cunard and Iris Tree, for example . . . Bill thought Nancy was wonderful. "They were riding above the storm in Paris that we were witnessing. Nancy Cunard straight as any stick, emaciated, holding her head erect, not particularly animated, her blue eyes completely untroubled, inviolable in her virginity of pure act."

Épatante, as the French say.

Nancy and her mother, Lady Cunard, used to visit the Williamses in their pension at Villefranche. And there were the Birds, Bill and Sally. Bill could be wild—one night he wanted them all to go to Marseilles for bouillabaisse. "But I couldn't see it though Floss would have gone."

There was the time the innkeeper called Bill aside and asked him if either he or McAlmon would be willing to sleep with his, the innkeeper's wife, so that she could bear a child. He was impotent, having suffered a wound . . .

> "You mean . . ." I began.
> "Yes, precisely that."
> "But you would shoot a man who would so presume."

Nothing came of it—neither Bill nor Bob being willing to oblige. Still, the incident was so typically French!

They heard that Eliot had appeared in Paris while they were there. He came to the Dôme and other bars in top hat, cutaway, and striped trousers. "It was intended as a gesture of contempt and received just that." [81]

Not even T. S. Eliot could spoil "Their Trip Abroad."

20

River of Experience

The world appears as something more epic than dramatic.
William James

HE had often thought he would give up his medical practice and devote himself to writing. Until he was forty he practiced medicine "in a continuously surly mood at the overbearing necessity for it—wanting always to do something else: to write! Why? Because then only, when he was stealing time for his machine and paper, did he live." [1] So he traveled to Europe with Floss to see what the other way of life would be like. France was the place for a life devoted to art. When his mother was asked where she would like to go to study painting, "To France! to FRANCE! to *FRANCE!*" she cried.[2] Now McAlmon and Pound were in Paris. Everyone was in Paris.

But he found he didn't fit in. He couldn't live like the expatriates—he needed his locality, and this meant his medical practice as well. From this time on he was reconciled to his life in Rutherford. He would still rebel against the demands made upon him, but *au fond* he felt he had made the right choice. There would be no changes—he would build on what had gone before, not seek to escape.

When he came back he joined the staff of the Passaic General Hospital. To be eligible he had to have an office in Passaic as well as his office in Rutherford. Now he had hospital rounds as well as office consultations and house calls. It was a routine, and sometimes he kicked over the traces. These were the Prohibition years—people felt obliged to drink. He did too, though he had no liking for it. "I always grow amorous, then remorseful, waking (as I never hope to do again) with a head split in half with pain." [3]

In 1927 he traveled to Europe again, this time with a different purpose. The boys were going to school in Switzerland and Floss would stay with them. He would return to Rutherford by himself. There was a family tradition of children being schooled in Europe—Ed and he had spent a year abroad—the change would break up the "staleness of schooling and experience" young Bill and Paul had got into. [4]

But husbands and wives do not live apart just so that their children can study abroad. There was a rift between them, suggested by the words, "whatever I have done to lessen myself in your eyes." [5]

Writing to Floss in mid ocean, on the ship carrying him back to America, he reviewed his early life and the reason for their marriage. "I was a disappointed and unhappy—lit by wild flashes—boy, though this is true I am a most happy man. And the greatest thing which has caused that has been yourself." She had seen and understood him, uncannily, and he in a flash of intuition had known that she was the "queen of the world" for him at that moment. "I tell you now that feeling went through my whole body like sweetest nectar and that I knew it would last forever."

He had been "wild then, hurt and crazy," but she had seen the tremendous reserve of strength in him. No one else had seen it. This was a stroke of genius on her part. [6]

He was always trying to make up to Floss for having married her on the rebound from Charlotte. Now he reinterpreted the facts so that their marrying each other had been pure intuition. He was continually trying to see it that way. Then he would tire of the effort—you can't lick Original Sin, anyway!—and find another woman. In the *Autobiography* he speaks of "Flossie, my wife, who is the rock on which I have built. But," he adds, "as far as my wish is concerned, I could not be satisfied by five hundred women." [7]

Floss said that a period in their lives had ended and now they were entering a new phase. They were going on. [8] But for a year they would not be living together.

In his letter he told her that he had met a man on the ship who wondered at the arrangement, saying, "It's a question whether a man can continue continent that long." He answered that these days "there was as much question about a woman as a man in such cases." The man said that women didn't have any difficulty keeping out of trouble unless they went looking for it, but a man was always billygoating around.[9]

During their separation, he assured her, he would work and persist.[10]

And he did, writing poems, stories and essays. Among his projects was a novel about Floss, starting from the moment of birth. This was something he knew—very few novelists can have been privileged to know a heroine so well.

> In prehistoric ooze it lay while Mrs D wound the white twine about its pale blue stem with kindly clumsy knuckles and blunt fingers with black nails and with the wiped-off scissors from the cord at her waist, cut it—while it was twisting and flinging up its toes and fingers into the way—free.[11]

It was a "pure book" without sentimentality, telling not what might have happened, or the reader might like to have had happen, but what really did happen.[12] It was sincere—the reader would have to look in other places for an exciting story, unusual characters, or "view of life."

This year his mother kept house at Number 9 Ridge Road. One Sunday E. E. Cummings came out to Rutherford. Williams had given him directions for finding the house, but one o'clock came and still no Cummings. Knowing his reputation for "indifference to conventional order," Williams went out to look for him. He found him wandering on Park Avenue, looking in the store windows at shoes, an Easter card, a brace and bit in Dow's hardware store. He conveyed him home where Mrs. Williams had fixed a chicken for lunch. Afterwards they played with a batch of Persian kittens on the dining room table. Mrs. Williams thought Cummings gentle but strange.[13]

Williams met Louis Zukofsky in New York. Then Williams, Zukofsky, Charles Reznikoff and George Oppen would meet in Zukofsky's basement apartment in Brooklyn Heights. There they formulated the Objectivist theory of the poem and inaugurated the Objectivist Press which published three or four books, Williams' *Collected Poems* among them, before it folded.

Objectivism meant "not an objective viewpoint, but to objectify the poem, to make the poem an object. Meant form." [14]

This was what Oppen said. On the other hand, Reznikoff said it meant "writers publishing their own work." [15] The Objectivists were fearfully self-conscious and at the same time fled from definition as from the plague.

Objectivism existed before the movement, and its name was Williams. The theory evolved out of his practice. As he tells it, there were a number of poets who were dissatisfied with Imagism. Imagism had got rid of verbiage but deteriorated into shapeless free verse. But the poem was an object—it made its meaning by its form.[16] Williams had been writing for years in "organic forms." This was picked up by the Objectivists—not the other way round. He continued to write the poems he would have written in any case.

Labels such as Objectivism have a scientific ring. Therefore they are attractive to writers, who have only vague ideas about what they are doing and would like some of the feeling of security that attaches to the sciences in our time. The labels are useful for publicity—in the art world they seem indispensable in order to sell pictures—and later they are useful to critics so that they can make sense out of masses of writing. This goes with this, and that goes with that, and before you know it a thousand books have been reduced to the dozen that count. At least, they can be arranged in piles.

But the catchier the label, the more likely it is to be misleading. Objectivism sounds as though it means impersonal writing, and critics have taken it to mean just this: "As an Objectivist, Williams carried the earlier impersonality of his Imagist poetry to its logical extreme." [17] And some of Williams' own remarks are misleading; writing in 1937 he says, "In my own work it has always sufficed that the object of my attention be presented without further comment. This in general might be termed the objective method." [18] It sounds as though subjectivity has no part in the writing of the poem. But in fact the subjective response is an essential part of the Objectivist poem.

This is understood if instead of using scientific terms such as "rays of the object brought to a focus" we think of Objectivism as an organic process. This was the way Williams preferred to think. The best description of Objectivist writing is found in some observations he made about writing short stories. It is the method of empathy, "feeling into" the thing you describe.

Crawl into the man's head and how get inside a woman's head, being a man? That is the *work* of the imagination . . . This is where the *imitation* of nature takes place. There is no copying here.

You *are* now nature: given a set of circumstances—a woman: a man—names:

What is there to do?

Now go ahead and do it. Name the actions and perform them —yourself.

This is something that you yourself (as "Jim Higgins") have very little to say about (you become a nonentity, like Shakespeare). You are in the creative process—a function in nature— relegated to the deity.

You have now entered what is referred to as the divine function of the artist.

Let's keep away from frightening words and say you are nature —in action.

It is an action, a moving process—the verb dominates; you are to *make*.[19]

This is the process described by Keats: "A Poet is the most unpoetical of anything in existence; because he has no Identity— he is continually informing and filling some other Body."[20]

Objectivism meant concentrating on objects with the aim of finding a specific form for the emotion induced by this contemplation. The aim was imitation in Aristotle's sense, not copying. The poet's thought was an essential part of the poem—in fact, the thoughts he had as a result of contemplating the object would be the form and substance of the poem. "A personal structure of relations might be a definite object, or vice versa."[21]

Williams says there is "a shape for each piece of writing consonant with its subject, tone, and intended impact," and this grows logically from the writer's real concern with the piece of work before him.[22] Zukofsky says, "You live with the things as they exist and as you sense them and think them. That's the first thing, and that I call *sincerity* in an essay that was printed at the back of that *Poetry* number. Otherwise how sincere your intentions doesn't matter. The rest is, once you do that, you do put them into a shape that, apart from your having lived it, is now on its own, and that's what goes into the world and becomes part of it."[23]

The poet learns from nature how to create. "An objective— nature as creator—desire for what is objectively perfect. . . ."[24] Then he sets about making his poem, which is not a copy or representation of physical objects in nature but a "thing of words" invented "in a manner determined by the nature of his perception." [25]

Boone does not try to act like an Indian. He learns from the Indian how to be himself.

If this is understood we won't be misled by Objectivist language: "An objective—rays of the object brought to a focus. . . ." [26] We may even enjoy the use of photography as a metaphor. The lens of the camera forms an image of the object being photographed by bringing its rays into focus. The depth of field—the area within which objects in a picture are visible—is narrowed but made more intense. Therefore, "To objectify an image means both to intensify its qualities and to blur or eliminate the features of its surroundings. In the same way, a person who is 'objective' eliminates all irrelevant or accidental responses in order to 'focus' his mind more entirely on the subject of his experience." [27]

Images taken from science—Eliot's "finely filiated platinum" for the mind of the poet, Zukofsky's "rays . . . brought into a focus" for the process of contemplation—are . . . images. They are not explanations. But it sometimes happens that the writer who invents them begins to believe them literally. Eliot in his criticism spoke for "impersonality" to an extent not warranted by his poems. And Williams took Objectivism to mean a kind of word-painting. "It all went with the newer appreciation, the matter of paint upon canvas as being of more importance than the literal appearance of the image depicted." [28] With painting in mind he wrote "Nantucket."

> Flowers through the window
> lavender and yellow
>
> changed by white curtains—
> Smell of cleanliness—
>
> Sunshine of late afternoon—
> On the glass tray
>
> a glass pitcher, the tumbler
> turned down, by which
>
> a key is lying—And the
> immaculate white bed [29]

"Nantucket" was in the *Collected Poems 1921–1931* put out by the Objectivist Press. It might have appeared in any of Williams' books from 1917 on. Reading "Nantucket" is like being there with the flowers and white curtains. But in other poems where Williams takes Objectivism to mean words-as-paint there is a less pleasing result:

> The stem's pink flanges,
> strongly marked,
> stand to the frail edge,
> dividing, thinning
> through the pink and downy
> mesh—as the round stem
> is pink also—cranking
> to penciled lines
> angularly deft . . .[30]

This is dull stuff. Poetry, whatever its name, requires the active cooperation of the "subjective" poet.

Objectivism did not make a splash—nothing to compare with the Imagist movement. The reason is that Imagism, rightly understood, had implied all that Objectivism set out to do. If Imagism were regarded as mere photography, then indeed Objectivism, with its theory of free creation, was a step forward. But in good Imagist poetry nature was merely a start—poetry had its origin in sense perception, but only its origin—the poem itself was a new creation. This is also a definition of Objectivist writing. Therefore the new movement had nothing to add, unless it were a clearer understanding of Imagism. But the Objectivists were not clear men. They were so dedicated to precision, niggling over words and phrases, that they found it almost impossible to reveal their thoughts. They were not understood, so they avoided the public. Then they avoided one another. "Nothing much," says Williams, "happened in the end." [31]

We are entering the Depression. Words such as Objectivism fade upon the blowing of a horn, not to be heard for thirty years. The password is social realism. In the glare of necessity the avant-garde movements will seem to have been irresponsible.

Williams' savings were wiped out in the stock market crash. He had been hoping to retire at fifty, but he entered the Depression struggling with hands and feet. In this, too, he was like everybody else. We have the books to prove that he was writing, but the period leaves a dim impression. Williams had always felt that he represented America. Now there was a slump in his career corresponding to the fortunes of the country.

He was approaching fifty. This is a bad time for writers, especially in the United States, where the emphasis is on youth. Much is forgiven the youthful writer who has his fame before him, but at fifty the case is different. If he is not famous by this time, chances are he will never be. There are days when he feels that it doesn't matter how well he writes, no one is paying attention. They were more interested when he was younger and wrote worse.

Literary careers that had begun brilliantly in the twenties did not flourish in the Depression. Writers endured the slump in different ways: Eliot by proselytizing for his church, Pound by advocating Social Credit. Doctor Williams did his rounds.

He was sympathetic to the poor. He knew from his own experience what it was like to be outside—when Eliot was taken up and *The Waste Land* set the tone; when, in Paris, his speech fell flat and the others at the table looked at him in a certain quizzical way. He knew what it was to be "ignored, maligned, left unnoticed." [32] So were the American people during the Depression.

He wrote stories about them. Short stories—the *genre* seemed suited to the times. As for form, a doctor's appointments have a beginning and an end.

His own grievances gave him insight to their lives: he knew why they lied and cheated and snatched so eagerly at pleasure. They wished to escape from the dreary day. They were rebellious like his mother and himself. "There is something there, underneath the dynamo of intelligence—of life itself that is crude, rebellious—the lack of which, or denial of which . . . makes an ass." [33]

> Why do I write today?
>
> The beauty of
> the terrible faces
> of our nonentities
> stirs me to it . . .[34]

He was stirred by "The Girl With a Pimply Face." [35] One day he called on a poor family to attend to a sick infant and found a young girl in charge to whom he took an instant liking. "She was just a child but nobody was putting anything over on her if she knew it, yet the real thing about her was the complete lack of the rotten smell of a liar. She wasn't in the least presumptive. Just straight."

She had dropped out of school. And she had "a terrible complexion, pimply and coarse." He told her how to treat it by using hot water and ice. On a subsequent call he met the mother, who implored him to save her baby. She pleaded poverty and delayed paying his fee. The father, when he met him, was indifferent.

One day he heard some of his colleagues discussing the family: it seemed that they had money but were always trying to evade payment. The mother was always drunk on whiskey—as for maternal feeling, she would let the baby cry until the neighbors complained to the police.

> But what about the young girl, I asked weakly. She seems like a pretty straight kid.
>
> My confrere let out a wild howl. That thing! You mean that pimply faced little bitch. Say, if I had my way I'd run her out of the town tomorrow morning. There's about a dozen wise guys on her trail every night in the week. Ask the cops. Just ask them. They know. Only nobody wants to bring in a complaint. They say you'll stumble over her on the roof, behind the stairs anytime at all. Boy, they sure took you in.
>
> Yes, I suppose they did, I said.[36]

The point is, however, that it's not he who has been fooled but the others with their cynical view. They don't take into account what he actually experienced. And his feelings prove to have been right after all. When he goes back to the house for the last time the girl tells him that the baby is much better. She has followed his advice and her complexion is clearing up. Moreover she is back in school: "I had tuh." The point is one Chekhov would have approved—he trusted in science and compassion.

Williams' prose is matter-of-fact and the dialogue seems accurate. He doesn't exaggerate, resisting the temptation to be satiric—he is of the people, not above them. At the beginning of a story he may be aloof, even contemptuous of the characters, but as he gets to know them he shares their point of view. This is a theme in all Williams' writing—starting from a point outside or above the material, then being dragged down into it. He immerses himself in the "filthy" river and is reborn.

This is like the myth of Kora. Jerome Mazzaro has shown that Williams would assume a "dual Kora-Demeter role as voyager and rescuer." The repeated use of the myth in his earlier poems "suggested that these descents and returns were related to a psychological need to 'gather the assets of the whole personality' into the form of a personified thought of moments of despair and spatial closure, 'and with this united strength to fling open the door of the future.'"[37]

But the river appears more often than Kora and is more representative of Williams' thinking: he was not one for the depths of Jungian symbolism. He was extremely distrustful of psychoanalysis—he called the unconscious a "low level of invention."[38] It is all right to give the subconscious play in order to see what it turns up, but poetry is written by the conscious brain.[39] In reading Williams one impression we definitely do not receive is of a mind that expressed itself through the symbolism of the Jungian or any other kind of unconscious. He preferred the surface, the river to the cave.

In *A Voyage to Pagany* the river is the Arno, "the prototype of art. Useless river—as far as itself is concerned. It was the Arno, before Florence, gathering tribute from the fields—a workaday river—countryman, maker, poet—poetic river."[40] In *Last Nights of Paris,* a novel by Soupault that Williams and his mother translated, there is a description of the Seine.

> On the river floated a scum of objects, pieces of wood, nameless debris gliding to their destiny . . . Now my mind would stem the current, and now abandon itself to the flow. Now I wished to look for causes, motives, and now I willingly accepted my ignorance, my simplicity.[41]

Williams' second collection of stories was *Life Along the Passaic River.*

> The boy is drifting with the current but paddling a little also toward a couple of kids in bathing suits and a young man in his shirt sleeves, lying on what looks to be grass but is probably weeds across the river at the edge of an empty lot where they dumped ashes some years ago, watching him.[42]

The river as a symbol of life . . . how often have we seen it! Shelley has such a river in *Alastor.* So do many other poets, and every year the high school valedictorian writes one into his speech.

The river was used by William James to describe a philosophy: "The pragmatic method, in its dealings with certain concepts, instead of ending with admiring contemplation, plunges forward

into the river of experience with them and prolongs the perspective by their means." [43] The river is as necessary to the pragmatist as moon and stars to the romantic.

The pragmatist believes in learning as he goes. In this he differs
from the rationalist. The rationalist holds that there are absolute
truths, founded for eternity. But, says the pragmatist, he forgets
that his truths were taken from experience. The rationalist has a
set of fixed ideas in the light of which he tries to order existence.
But he is out of touch with concrete particulars.

At the other extreme from rationalism lies empiricism, the
belief that there is nothing beyond the material universe. This
is a gloomy prospect: old age, a cooling planet, extinction of life
in the universe. And it would be a mistake to think that men
need not concern themselves about such matters: "The absolute
things, the last things, are the truly philosophic concerns: all
superior minds feel seriously about them, and the mind with
the shortest views is simply the mind of the more shallow man." [44]

Pragmatism undertakes to supply what is deficient in these
philosophies. "The pragmatic method is primarily a method
of settling metaphysical disputes that otherwise might be in-
terminable. Is the world one or many?—fated or free?—material or
spiritual? . . . The pragmatic method in such cases is to try
to interpret each notion by tracing its respective practical consequences. What difference would it practically make to any one
if this notion rather than that notion were true?" [45]

The pragmatist asks, Does it work? He is willing to entertain
any belief that will make men happy. He is not opposed to faith
—on the contrary, he sees the river of experience issuing in a sea,
"a more of the same quality as oneself." [46]

To the rationalist everything already exists in the mind of
God—our part is to know our place. Pragmatism on the other
hand believes that the universe is being created and man has a
share in the creation. There is a meaning in things, and no
meaning apart from things. "Say it, no ideas but in things." [47]

> Lotze has in several places made a deep suggestion. We naively
> assume, he says, a relation between reality and our minds which
> may be just the opposite of the true one. Reality, we naturally
> think, stands ready-made and complete, and our intellects super-
> vene with the one simple duty of describing it as it is already.
> But may not our descriptions, Lotze asks, be themselves impor-
> tant additions to reality? And may not previous reality itself be

there, far less for the purpose of reappearing unaltered in our knowledge, than for the very purpose of stimulating our minds to such additions as shall enhance the universe's total value.[48]

This passage in James describes Williams' creed as an artist. Whitman would have subscribed to it. He said, "I consider *Leaves of Grass* and its theory experimental—as, in the deepest sense, I consider our American republic itself to be, with its theory." [49]

Williams began working with the river as a symbol in "The Wanderer." He used it again in "Paterson," the poem that won the Dial Award in 1926.[50]

The award no doubt affected him powerfully. Writers who take a stand against tradition are likely to be nervous about the value of their own productions. They are grateful for praise, and if anyone gives them an award they think he must have extraordinary judgment and it is a sign this is the direction they must follow. The Dial Award—given to Eliot a few years before—confirmed Williams in the way he was going. It was a mandate to write an epic poem. "There would be four books following the course of the river whose life seemed more and more to resemble my own life as I more and more thought of it: the river above the Falls, the catastrophe of the Falls itself, the river below the Falls, and the entrance at the end into the great sea." [51]

This was his theme. The plot would be to present the totality of experience in that place, Paterson and environs. He visualized the city as a giant lying opposite a mountain (Garret Mountain). The mountain was Paterson's wife and the other women in the poem. The Passaic coming over the Falls was the voice of the people, multitudinous. From this sound it was the poet's task to pick out the thread of true language, poetry.

He began planning *Paterson* in 1928.[52] Eight years later he was writing to Pound about "that magnum opus I've always wanted to do: the poem PATERSON. Jeez how I'd like to get at that. I've been sounding myself out in these years working toward a form of some sort." [53]

The poetry was the sound of many voices, and he put in prose as well: letters, journalism, statistics. Recently the American painter Stuart Davis had been juxtaposing colors, fragmenting the subject and reorganizing it to make "a new reality of paint surface." This, Williams said, was exactly what he was trying to do in words.[54]

Life seemed to cooperate in the writing of *Paterson*. In 1938

Williams received some curious letters from a man named David
Lyle, a radio expert and instrument engineer who lived nearby.
Lyle was trying to establish a connection between abstract codes
of communication like Morse and patterns of human behavior.
He wanted to find a language which would "illustrate the common basis of all organisation and so open the way to a sense of
common purpose in the world." He thought he had found a
method in his "multiple letters," a stream of news items, facts,
ideas. "The arbitrariness of Lyle's sampling, the correlation of
trivia with permanence, was emphasized by his habit of giving
the elapsed writing time; he matched whatever happened to be
passing over the Falls as he wrote." [55]

Williams had the text typed without the indentations so that it
ran in a stream. He changed the addresses, "Dear Dr. Williams,"
to "Dear Noah," and the signature "David Joseph Lyle" to
"Faitoute," He Who Does Everything. So the giant Noah Faitoute
Paterson was conceived, listening to the roar of the Falls. Paterson is the city; he is also the poet. As Noah he survives—and survives the flood of texts in *Book Three*. As Faitoute he is the man
of many responsibilities, many wives.[56]

> Paterson lies in the valley under the Passaic Falls
> its spent waters forming the outline of his back. He
> lies on his right side, head near the thunder
> of the waters filling his dreams! Eternally asleep,
> his dreams walk about the city. . . .

The dreams of Paterson are the people of Paterson. They are
"automatons"

> Who because they
> neither know their sources nor the sills of their
> disappointments walk outside their bodies aimlessly
>   for the most part,
> locked and forgot in their desires—unroused.[57]

It is not necessary to point out correspondences between the
poem and Williams' life—we would have to recite the whole—
but here is one at the start. The citizens who have not been
roused, who walk outside their bodies, are like the young medical
student who wandered in the streets of Philadelphia.

He himself was Paterson. Once, referring to a young poet,
Williams said, "I like the lack of choice and the complacency
with which he takes it for granted that merely by being where he

happens to be he transforms the place to his desire." [58] Yet he
believed that a poem had its own independent reality. "An artist
should always speak in symbols even when he speaks most pas-
sionately; otherwise his vision becomes blurred. He has to hold
his objects away from him to be able to see them clearly." [59] How
are these different ideas to be reconciled? By the man, the
style, the poem itself. "It is in complexities that appear finally
as one person that the good of a life shows itself—ringing all together to return the world to simplicity again." [60]

Poems, even epic poems, usually have an ending. But true ideas,
says William James, "lead us into useful verbal and conceptual
quarters as well as directly up to useful sensible termini. They lead
to consistency, stability and flowing human intercourse." [61] The
poem of experience has no ending.

As he worked he was beset by doubts. "It's very hard to treat
of American things and name them specifically without a sense
of bathos, of bad sentimental overlap resulting." [62] *Passaic,* the
nineteenth-century poem by Thomas Ward, was on his mind. It
was picturesque writing, in iambic pentameter and couplets.
Ward had taken for his hero Sam Patch, who jumped from the
Falls. Williams was using Patch too, to show the hunger of the
crowd for wonders, freaks, a new form of expression. Patch faltered in midair and fell to his death. He failed to find the right
language. Was *Paterson,* too, a mistake?

He took notes when he was on a W.P.A. writers' project, making
a guidebook to Bergen County. He borrowed Herbert A. Fisher's
manuscript, "Legends of the Passaic." He consulted with Kathleen
Hoagland, who was writing a novel based on local history. [63] But
all this, as Louis Zukofsky says, "is not to be pointed up for the
sake of dullness." [64]

He put Floss in the poem. She was the first of the wives of the
African chief, nine on a log, one behind the other.

> the first wife
> present! supporting all the rest growing
> up from her—whose careworn eyes
> serious, menacing—but unabashed; breasts
> sagging from hard use .   .
>
> Whereas the uppointed breasts
> of that other, tense, charged with
> pressures unrelieved   .

> and the rekindling they bespoke
> was evident.[65]

It has been said of Williams that "The reaffirmation of his wife was contained in the seriousness of his dalliance with other women." [66] This is like the solution of Keats' *Endymion:* the Indian girl turns out to be Cynthia the moon-maiden.

Book Four describes Paterson's meetings with Phyllis, a girl from the back country. She is also being courted by a Lesbian who talks like the Old World:

> Let's change names. You be Corydon! And I'll play Phyllis. Young! Innocent! One can fairly hear the pelting of apples and the stomp and clatter of Pan's hoofbeats.[67]

Phyllis tells Paterson, "I don't know why I can't give myself to you. A man like you should have everything he wants . . . I guess I care too much, that's the trouble." [68]

Maybe he should have taken her, that was what she wanted. But the language he was seeking had to give itself; it could not be taken by force.

One idea came from Pound:

> That sovereignty inheres in the **POWER** to
> issue money, whether you have the right to
> do it or not.
>
> >   don't let me crowd you.
>
> If there is anything here that is OBskewer   ,   say so.[69]

The lesson of the Master, in his very words . . .

In 1934, reviewing Pound's new *Cantos,* Williams echoed his ideas about monetary reform as though they were his own. "Usury—the work of double-crossing intellectual bastards in and out of government and the church—rules the world and hides the simple facts from those it torments for a profit. . . ." [70] Two years later he was still approving of Pound's ideas: "The American political upheaval having for the moment practically eliminated the Communist party from our midst, it would seem to me THE moment for redirecting sane minds toward the need for an acute radicalism—which would concern precisely the things your nine or ten categories included." [71]

But when Pound came out for Mussolini, Williams started

calling him an ass. He saw Pound in May 1939 when he was visiting the States. Williams described Pound's demeanor in a letter to McAlmon: Pound was being very mysterious about his comings and goings while in the country, keeping his whereabouts more or less secret. Williams thought he was somewhat uncertain about the reception he would get if he came out openly with his Fascist opinions. Now Pound was protesting that he was not a Fascist. They had met affectionately and said nothing.[72]

On a subsequent meeting he again studied Ezra and found him evasive—he would not answer directly. But, said Williams, "He does have some worthwhile thoughts and projects in hand. I like him immensely as always, he is inspiring and has much information to impart but he gets nowhere with it. . . . The man is sunk, in my opinion, unless he can shake the fog of fascism out of his brain during the next few years, which I seriously doubt that he can do." [73]

Pound didn't. Still, a year later Williams could say, "Ezra is an important poet, we must forgive him his stupidities: I do, no matter how much he riles me." [74]

One night in July 1941 the voice of Ezra was heard on short-wave radio prophesying woe to the Americans if they opposed Hitler and Mussolini. In the course of the broadcast Pound made one of his jocular, unfunny asides: "As my friend Doc Williams of New Jersey would say . . ."

Williams had two sons in the Navy. As a result of the war his work load had increased. He felt that he was a patriot and did not want to be associated with the Fascist Pound. He rushed to the typewriter and fired off an article that appeared with the ominous heading, "Ezra Pound: Lord Ga-Ga!" (Lord Haw-Haw, the English traitor, was hanged). The trouble with Ez, he said, was that he was not content to be a great poet, he was always setting himself up as an expert on matters about which he knew nothing. He had done so with painting and music. Pound had always been "a spoiled brat, with a spoiled brat's self assurance and overweening desire to occupy the center of the stage."

Pound was for civilization as long as it meant rule by the few who, "in his maimed opinion," were civilized. But he lacked a knowledge of man, plain and simple. He knew nothing about the people, "the great leaven of the world without whose tonal tides to support them, all men become tyrants and beasts in the end." He quoted from Pound's Canto XX:

>Compleynt, compleynt I hearde upon a day
>Artemis singing, Artemis, Artemis
>Against pity lifted her wail . . .

Williams paraphrased this to mean, "Keep what is 'good,' keep what is lovely. Let all that is ugly be clean slain." He found it a doctrine "stale as Egypt, completely blasted by every competent mind of the present era." Certainly there must be "totalitarianism of economic effort," the Church had taught that from the beginning, but not at the cost of human slavery. That was putting the cart before the horse with a vengeance.[75]

Pound's mention of his name had immediate repercussions. Doc Williams of New Jersey received a visit from an FBI man who wanted to know how well he knew Pound and if he, Williams, were a loyal American.[76]

In spite of this, Williams retained his affection for Pound as a man and admiration for his poetry. In February 1944 he said, "I have made up my mind to defend him if I am ever called as a witness in his trial. . . ." [77]

There was no trial. Instead, Williams visited Pound in St. Elizabeth's Hospital.

The government spy's question caused Williams to have a curious reaction. After he has told about the incident in his *Autobiography* he begins listing names—not because these men and women were loyal, or American, or close friends. But they did exist . . . he seems to be trying to assure himself of their reality. Perhaps this is all we know in the end. Hemingway said about war, it comes down to the naming of places. And life comes down to a list of people—there seems to be no reason for life but life itself. "So here is Pound confined to a hospital for the insane in Washington . . . McAlmon working for his brothers in El Paso; Hemingway a popular novelist; Joyce dead; Gertrude Stein dead . . . Nancy Cunard still alive, thin as paper as she is . . . Charles Demuth dead; Marsden Hartley dead . . . T. S. Eliot a successful playwright . . . " [78]

The names went on, a river flowing to the sea.

21

Symbolic Lives

[Eli] Siegel: . . . as I said, you're right now the most talked of person writing poetry in America.

Williams: You think so.

Siegel: Yes. I don't go in for schmoozing.

The Williams-Siegel Documentary [1]

WHEN William Carlos Williams looked back on his career as a writer it hadn't been a success, not by any visible standard. In 1938 he told Alva Turner he had received in royalties for his last two books the sum of two hundred and thirty dollars— "covering the work of a ten or fifteen year period, about twelve dollars a year." [2] Nor could he console himself with the thought that he had had a *succès d'estime.* "I haven't been recognized," he wrote his son William, "and I doubt that my technical influence is good or even adequate." [3]

There were some bitter conversations at 9 Ridge Road:

Myra: . . . we've been plenty kicked around by all kinds of people—your literary friends and the shits of this town— I don't know which is worse. They were all out for themselves, every one of them—and to use you, if they could. But you can't say that of me.

Doc: That I'll agree to.[4]

He gave some poetry readings at colleges, in the enemy camp. But he was no crowd-pleaser. In any case, he told Srinivas

Rayaprol, there is something wrong about reading poetry in public. Either the room is wrong or the people who come are the wrong sort. Perhaps they only seem so because both they and the reader are embarrassed—at shouting poems in public when poetry is intimately personal. Poems need to be warmed and loved; they require close attention. Reading in public leads the poet into selecting the obvious and passing over what is delicate or questionable.[5]

There is the man in the audience who wants to know why modern poetry is obscure. There is the man who thinks he should be in your place and who asks a question that is not a question, implying that you have "sold out"—you are making a lot of money by these readings. There is the man who, while you are still breathing hard, hands you his own poems to be read on the spot. And how does one go about getting a book published?

After the reading there is a reception at which the poet may meet the faculty, looking down their noses. When they were young they too wrote poems; then they became serious and took the Ph.D. Now they write articles about English literature. This is demonstrably serious—they are promoted for it. One of them is writing an article on Barnabe Googe.

Why all the fuss about new poetry? There is still a great deal of work to be done in the thirteenth century.

I hope you are not still a friend of Pound's, Doctor Williams?

Williams continued to inveigh against academics. In the 1940's the New Criticism was prevalent and critics put on airs. They would approach the poem—with "armed vision," one said, "an armed assembly," said Williams [6]—and proceed to inspect it. A touch of sentimentality here, a mixed metaphor there, and *pouf!* another poet disposed of.

He came to know some of these people, however, and found they were not monsters. They seemed so only when, emboldened with ink, they savaged white paper. In person they were eager to be liked and seemed as nervous as writers about what they were writing. He had the impression that if he had been nicer to them over the years they would have been nicer to him. He might have enjoyed a success like Eliot's!

He actually took part in a writer's conference in Utah. For two weeks he talked to the students about "modern verse." There were a half dozen visiting writers with their wives living in one house. Allen Tate was there with his wife Carolyn Gordon. Ray West was there, also Mark Schorer, Walter Van Tilburg Clark, Brewster Ghiselin, and Eric Bentley. There was a lot of work, with workshop meetings, lectures, and conferences with individual students.[7]

There is no letup; they get you coming and going. They think you want to talk about poetry all the time.

He got along well with his fellow advisers. "Too bad that such meetings do not occur oftener among writers." [8] This was before universities caught onto the idea that Creative Writing pays. Thirty years later poets and novelists would be able to meet one another at writers' conferences all over the United States. Aspiring writers would travel from one conference to another, revising their stories or poems in accordance with suggestions, hoping to find one visiting professional writer who would say, "At last I've found what I'm looking for," and, removing his pipe and staring at the group with a solemn expression, "I shall undertake to see that this manuscript gets published, myself."

The body was beginning to turn against its poet. In 1946 Williams was operated on for a hernia; the operation had to be repeated. In 1948 he had a heart attack and was confined to his bed for three weeks. In March 1951 he had a slight stroke.

This was the year he published the fourth, and seemingly final, part of *Paterson*. It met with a cool reception. There were critics who had been cool to his writing from the start. R. P. Blackmur said, "Dr. Williams has no perceptions of the normal; no perspective, no finality—for these involve, for imaginative expression, both the intellect which he distrusts and the imposed form which he cannot understand." [9]

Randall Jarrell had praised *Book One,* saying that *Paterson* might turn out to be "the best very long poem that any American has written." His review of *Book Four* took it all back. *Paterson* was so disappointing that he did not wish to discuss it at any length. Williams had adopted a Pound-like "Organization of Irrelevance." All three later books were "worse organized, more eccentric and idiosyncratic, more self-indulgent, than the first." As a result of his being the last poet of his generation to be appreciated, Williams had now been overvalued. The fact was that he was a *"very* limited poet" by nature and commitment, "volunteering for and organizing a long dreary imaginary war in which

America and the Present are fighting against Europe and the Past." Jarrell finished with the unkindest cut of all: he said that a comparison of *Paterson* and *Four Quartets* clearly demonstrated Williams' defeat in his "long one-sided war with Eliot." [10]

Williams never got over this review. Ten years later he was still bringing it up in conversation. Jarrell, he said, was clever but shifty—making his way up in the world and willing to change his opinions. Marianne Moore hadn't liked *Book Four* either.[11]

What else could he have done? How else ended the poem? After all, a poet isn't a moralist. The fact is that the Passaic is polluted. And it empties into Newark Bay. So he had to deal with perversion in *Book Four*. "If you are going to write realistically of the conception of filth in the world, it can't be pretty. What goes on with people isn't pretty. With the approach to the city, international character begins to enter the innocent river and pervert it; sexual perversions, such things that every metropolis when you get to know it houses. Certain human elements can't take the gaff, have to become perverts to satisfy certain longings." [12]

So he defends *Paterson* with the argument that it is true to fact. "No ideas but in things" apparently means "No ideas, just things." This is the kind of statement that makes people say that Williams had no ideas. Yvor Winters called him an ignorant man, and Winters was only saying what others thought.

But Williams was trying to defend his poem as a mother defends her child, with the nearest words. He knew very well that adherence to fact is no way to write poetry or anything else— he had often said so. As for the poet's not being a moralist, "Every minutest thing that is part of a work of art is good only when it is useful." [13]

He was aware that *Paterson* hadn't come off. In 1950 he spoke of a "failing experiment." "The poem to me (until I go broke) is an attempt, an experiment, a failing experiment, toward assertion with broken means but an assertion, always, of a new and total culture, the lifting of an environment to expression. Thus it is social, the poem is a social instrument—accepted or not accepted seems to be of no material importance. It embraces everything we are." [14]

This is desperate. And reading *Paterson, Book Four* is not a happy experience. The Wanderer's immersion in the river has

made him filthy, but where is the rejuvenation? An account of
a man's killing his infant daughter—rant about money—Lesbian
conversations—an account of the murder of an old couple—the
execution of the murderer—

> This is the blast
> the eternal close
> the spiral
> the final somersault
> the end [15]

—is this an argument for living in New Jersey?

The trouble was in the conception. By identifying his hero
Paterson with the city, and language with the river, he ensured
that the poem would be despondent—a poem about "blockage"
one reader calls it[16]—issuing in despair. "I took the river as it
followed its course down to the sea; all I had to do was follow
it and I had a poem." [17] Did he really think it was going to be
that easy? How could he, after his own "Objectivist" statements
about not merely copying nature but learning from nature how
to create?

Paterson was not "objective." It had no shape of its own, just
incidents. What was *Paterson*? A man? A city? An idea? Readers
cannot agree what the poem is about. One says that it is "an
attempt to gain some understanding of contemporary life by
means of a thorough examination of a specific place." [18] Another
describes the "central theme of *Paterson*" as "the poet's attempt
to find a language by which to express the beauty that is 'locked'
in the mind." [19] Another says, "*Paterson* is not primarily concerned with language . . . it is rather a study of man's search
for relationships with other people." [20]

Long ago Williams had written: "The thing that stands
eternally in the way of really good writing is always one: the
virtual impossibility of lifting to the imagination those things
which lie under the direct scrutiny of the senses." This time
he failed to lift them, and "The senses witnessing what was
immediately before them in detail [saw] a finality which they
[clung] to in despair, not knowing which way to turn." [21] The
poem ran out in Newark Bay.

Williams' admirers are defensive of *Paterson*. One says, "Many
readers will not want to make the extensive commitment the

poem requires. That, of course, is their choice; but it is a choice that precludes them from making value statements about the poem." [22] By this argument every work is good; there is no bad writing, only a failure of readers to sympathize.

But Williams was not his admirers—he knew that something had gone wrong. Writing to Sister Bernetta Quinn he said, "I feel extremely grateful for your discernment. Even if the poem were now lost I should be satisfied; it CAN be understood." [23] It needs no great insight to see that to his mind the poem was lost, like the poem modeled on Keats' *Endymion* lost long ago. Or had it been burned?

This was a pattern of behavior: to attempt the great work that could be accomplished by effort and perseverance. He was trying to please . . . especially his mother. Like D. H. Lawrence, Williams had an ambitious mother. " . . . her life had a definite form and purpose—not by any means sentimental: it was based on somewhat rigid loyalties to the ideal. When she herself was unable to fulfill her desires for personal accomplishment, she transferred her ambitions to her children." [24]

But then he would let it go. After *Paterson* Williams gave up the ambition of creating a poem that would astonish the world and put Eliot in his place. Many writers have the idea of creating some great work that will justify them, bring everything to a climax and make it unnecessary for them to endure the "whips and scorns of time,"

> The insolence of office, and the spurns
> That patient merit of th' unworthy takes . . .

Keats was always thinking of Fame. "I have asked myself so often why I should be a Poet more than other Men,—seeing how great a thing it is,—how great things are to be gained by it— What a thing to be in the Mouth of Fame. . . ." [25]

Failure was therapeutic for Williams. Long ago in "The Wanderer" he had spoken of entering the river and being reborn. Just so, submergence in *Paterson* freed his imagination. He was through with facts and a sense of obligation. Now he could write as he liked, poems that spoke about his feelings. In this, too, he was like his mother, whose life at the end, "tired of pretense to gain attention," came out into "a sort of clearing, what a man or woman might have been had he or she walked out simply into the street and existed." [26] And this was the coming style. William

Carlos Williams would have a following in a generation that "walked out simply into the street and existed."

Pound taught that "a new cadence means a new idea." This was part of the Imagist teaching. "As regarding rhythm: to compose in sequence of the musical phrase, not in sequence of a metronome." [27] Williams learned from the Imagists to write free verse—the rhythm determined not by feet but cadence, the way the stresses fell in speech. The line ended where he felt it should end, and he usually wrote short lines.

But free verse "amounted to no more . . . than no discipline at all." [28] He wanted a "measure" in the American idiom, to replace the English foot. In his introduction to the poems of Byron Vazakas, published in 1946, Williams said that what was needed was "a line loose as Whitman's but measured as his was not." In Vazakas' grouping of four lines he had found the solution, the "cadence of the musical phrase." Vazakas wrote:

> In the railroad station, the
>   crowd is assembled, lugubrious
>   as umbrellas expecting rain.
>   The terminus tall windows arch
>
> With requiem glow above the mausoleum
>   marble floors; and groups that
>   at the gates will be the mass
>   that weeps and prays, are [29]

"He has completely done away with the poetic line as we know it," said Williams. Vazakas had invented a "workable expedient" to replace it, a measure based not upon convention but upon music, an "auditory measure." At the same time he had "made a transit from English, for us an hieratic language, to our own spoken tongue, freeing that to its own melodies." [30]

The unit of rhythm was measured by time, not stress. "The passage of time (not stress) is the proper (democratic) key to the foot (approaching Athens)—and music." [31]

Words and their intervals. Bam! bam!

Williams first used the "auditory measure" in *Paterson, Book Two,* beginning with the line, "The descent beckons. . . ." In 1955 he said that this passage had prompted his "solution of the problem of modern verse." [32] Apparently he had forgotten about Vazakas.

He called the unit of rhythm the "variable foot": "The foot not being fixed is only to be described as variable." [33] And divided the line in three steps down—each step to be counted as "a single beat." [34]

<blockquote>
The descent beckons
    as the ascent beckoned
        Memory is a kind
of accomplishment
    a sort of renewal
        even
an initiation, since the spaces it opens are new
places
    inhabited by hordes
        heretofore unrealized
of new kinds—
    since their movements
        are towards new objectives
(even though formerly they were abandoned) [35]
</blockquote>

This is usually referred to as the triadic line. Williams used it for most of the poems in *The Desert Music and Other Poems* (1954) and *Journey to Love* (1955). Only twice, however, does it appear in his last book, *Pictures from Breughel and Other Poems* (1962).

Poems Williams wrote at other times in his life can be arranged in triadic lines. He was now making plain to the eye what had always been plain for the ear. The following lines are from "The Cod Head" (1934):

<blockquote>
Miscellaneous weed
strands, stems, debris—
firmament

to fishes—
where the yellow feet
of gulls dabble [36]
</blockquote>

They could be triadic lines:

<blockquote>
Miscellaneous weed
    strands, stems, debris—
        firmament
to fishes—
    where the yellow feet
        of gulls dabble
</blockquote>

In a letter to Mike Weaver, Hugh Kenner has suggested that Williams' use of the three-part line came from his inability to read after the brain damage of his strokes. "His eyes could follow a line but not jump back and locate accurately the beginning of the next line . . . I'm convinced that the 3-ply typography of his late verse was originally a set of helps (with the tab stops) for just such line-finding in rereading." [37] Weaver himself has a different explanation: "The origin of the three-part line was probably Pound's original printing of 'In a Station of the Metro':

> The apparition   of these faces   in the crowd . . ."

To rearrange these groups of three in a "step-down line," says Weaver, was a "natural, if unconscious," development of the idea of the musical phrase.[38]

Is there an "American measure"? Americans use the English language; even colloquial American phrases contain the feet used in English verse. How then can there be a distinctively American measure? And can there be such a thing as a "variable foot"?

Alan Stephens considers the matter from a different angle. He says that though there is no measurement, "no definite and re-current combination of stressed and unstressed syllables," Williams' line does have a definable identity. ". . . a line is a line because, relative to neighboring lines, it contains that which makes it in its own right a unit of the attention. . . ." Moreover, the line "has a norm against which it almost constantly varies . . . the formal architecture of the sentence." He goes on to say that this principle also underlies verse in meter; audible rhythm is not the "supreme fact" of the line of verse, and so "Dr. Williams will have been working in the tradition all along." [39]

Doctor Williams would not have been happy to hear it, for he insisted on the variable foot's being a measurement in time. It was a unit of rhythm, not a form of sentence structure.

To the question whether there is an "American measure" the answer is yes, with an explanation. If we compare the verse made by Williams and younger American poets with verse being written in England, it is clear that the Americans have abandoned traditional English meters and are following patterns of American speech. This makes a great difference. Whatever the "variable foot" may be—it seems to vary with the individual—it is certainly not the iambic foot still favored by English poets. So in effect there is an "American measure," if only because it is plainly not English.

Williams was the poet—after Whitman—who gave American poets the confidence to use their own patterns of speech in poetry.

In 1948 Williams was offered the Chair of Poetry at the Library of Congress. He put off taking it so that he could help his son William get started in medical practice and wind up his own. Then he had a heart attack and, in March 1951, a cerebral stroke.

This was the period in which Alger Hiss was found guilty of treason and Senator Joseph McCarthy began investigating the loyalty of Americans in government. A woman named Virginia Kent Cummins, who controlled a little magazine in Roanoke, Virginia, called *The Lyric,* undertook the investigation of poets. The campaign began with an essay in *The Lyric* on "The Treason of 'Modern' Poetry." Then Robert Hillyer, who had led the attack on Pound's Bollingen award, appeared on the masthead. Three months later Mrs. Cummins announced that she had established a Foundation for Traditional Poetry and in its name Hillyer had been awarded a thousand dollars.

Mrs. Cummins presided over *The Lyric* for three years. During this period she mounted attacks on Pound, Eliot, Auden, Spender, Marianne Moore, Cummings and Williams. The issue of *The Lyric* that announced Hillyer as vice-president of traditional poetry denounced Williams' poem, "History of Love," as obscene and his "Russia" as treason. The editor noticed that Williams was now "one of the Fellows in American Letters (of the Library of Congress) which honored Ezra Pound." "A scandalous thing," cried Mrs. Cummins, "has been done to the name of my Library of Congress."

So Williams' friendship with Pound was to be charged against him and at the same time he was accused of being Red. In Autumn 1952 *The Lyric* brought an open letter accusing Williams of having signed the Golden Book of American Friendship with the Soviet Union; having urged greater cooperation with Stalin; having demanded an end to the House Committee on Un-American Activities; and having defended "the policies and practices of the Communist Party." [40]

It was true that Williams had lent his name to pro-Soviet appeals. He was a typical fellow traveler, as ignorant as other Americans who supported Stalin. It need hardly be pointed out, however, that during the Second World War Russia and the United States were allies. And the fact is that Williams was opposed to the Communist Party. "My own feeling," he said, "is that the worst element we have to face is the Communistic one." [41] His only affiliation, outside the Democratic Party, was with the American Social Credit Movement.[42]

But this was witch-hunting time and distinctions went by the board. Mrs. Cummins' accusations were reported in the newspapers, and in Congress "Javits (Rep.) pointed out that the Ezra Pound clique among the library fellows had been strengthened by the appointment of William Carlos Williams as a member." [43] The upshot was that Williams withdrew. Speaking of it five years later, his wife said, "What the whole mess did was drive Bill into a serious mental depression. I am convinced if Bill had gone down as he was able to, he would have been as he is now. Coming after the stroke, it was too much; it set him back tragically, kept him from poetry and communication with the world for years." [44]

In mid-August of 1952 Williams had another stroke. This was more severe: his right arm was paralyzed—the writing arm—and he lost the power of speech. He was confined to the house. In the spring of 1953 he spent two months at Hillside Hospital in Glen Oaks, New York, and he continued to receive psychiatric treatment until 1957.[45] During this time he suffered a severe depression and partial loss of memory. It did not, however, stop his writing as the statement by his wife suggests. Like his mother, who for the last years of her life had been an invalid and practically blind, Williams had a determination to survive, "an indestructibleness, a permanence in defiance of the offensive discipline." [46] He continued to write—in fact, during these years he did what many consider to be his best work. Parts of the long poem, "Asphodel, That Greeny Flower," were published in magazines between 1952 and 1955 under the heading, "Work in Progress."

Sickness and age drove him to create. "When you're through with sex, with ambition, what can an old man create? Art, of course, a piece of art that will go beyond him into the lives of young people, the people who haven't had time to create. The old man meets the young people and lives on." [47]

"The Sparrow" was also published during this period. He dedicated it to his father, maybe because Mr. Williams had been a chirpy, strenuous bird. He had written another poem about a sparrow years ago:

> Shabby little bird
> I suppose it's
> the story every-
> where, if you're
>
> domestic you're drab
> Peep peep!
> the nightingale
> 's your cousin but
>
> these flagrant
> amours get you no-
> where . . .[48]

Now he considered the subject more carefully. The poem might be about his father—it was certainly about himself. It was also, like Keats' "Ode to a Nightingale," an enquiry into the nature of poetry. The phrase in the earlier poem, "the nightingale's your cousin," is more than a hint; Williams must have had in mind, over a long period of time, the contrast between the American sparrow and the English nightingale.

In Keats' poem the nightingale, having completed his song, vanishes into a dim forest. The poet would like to follow, to swoon away with pleasure. But as he is a man he cannot; he has to remain in the world "where men sit and hear each other groan."

Williams' "The Sparrow" makes a very different impression. The sparrow is an indefatigable fornicator—extremely busy—nothing melancholy about him or dim about his habitat. *En plein jour*. This life, persisted in, becomes a kind of success—in any case, it gives the sparrow a character. Life becomes art . . . the life is symbolic finally . . . the sparrow itself flattened on the sidewalk.

Not only Keats' nightingale comes to mind but also the urn that says:

> "Beauty is truth, truth beauty,"—that is all
> Ye know on earth, and all ye need to know.[49]

The sparrow says:

> This was I,
> a sparrow.
> I did my best;
> farewell.[50]

"It is the poem of his existence that triumphed finally." The urn

speaks of beauty, and the nightingale tempts us away from the
world, but the sparrow reconciles us to the world; his body is
pressed into it:

> flattened to the pavement,
>   wings spread symmetrically
>   as if in flight,
>   the head gone,
>   the black escutcheon of the breast
>   undecipherable
>   an effigy of a sparrow,
>   a dried wafer only . . .[51]

In Keats there is a separation that leaves him forlorn: poetry is
in another world:

> Was it a vision, or a waking dream?
>   Fled is that music:—Do I wake or sleep? [52]

The sparrow says, "This was I." Poetry is the shape I myself make
in the world.

Poets since Williams have taken this way of thinking to mean
that if they write about themselves the result will be poetry.
Williams knew better: his sparrow is "a poetic truth/more than
a natural one." [53] The lusty crying of the sparrow is "more related
to music than otherwise." [54] Life is the substance, but it has to be
worked over.

He believed in work—this was what sustained him. He was not
a religious or political man. The nearest he came to any faith
was a belief in experience. He agreed with William James: "When
a moment in our experience, of any kind whatever, inspires us
with a thought that is true, that means that sooner or later we
dip by that thought's guidance into the particulars of experience
again and make advantageous connection with them." [55] And he
agreed with Wordsworth:

> There are in our existence spots of time,
> That with distinct pre-eminence retain
> A renovating virtue.[56]

He believed: "If your interest is in theory . . . and your mind
is alive and you're trying to improve your poems technically you
will produce the work, and will never cease to produce it." [57]

Paterson, Book Four included a letter from "A. G.," who introduced himself as a young poet living in Paterson. This was Allen Ginsberg. The letter gave an account of his life to date and stated his intention to be a poet. He looked to Williams as a master: "I know you will be pleased to realize that at least one actual citizen of your community has inherited your experience in his struggle to love and know his own world-city." [58]

This was the harbinger of Fame. Ginsberg went forth and with his *Howl* became famous. Other poets followed in his steps and the audience for poetry—at least, poetry readings—increased greatly. Thousands who had never read a poem by Williams now knew of his existence as the spiritual father of the Beats.

Fame, that had fled his embrace, came knocking at the door of 9 Ridge Road. She wished to inform him that he was also to have an academy of his own.

In his *Autobiography,* published in 1951, Williams had included a passage by Charles Olson describing "Projective Verse." Olson said that "the poem itself must, at all points, be a high energy-construct and, at all points, an energy-discharge." He spoke of "FIELD COMPOSITION" and said that "FORM IS NEVER MORE THAN AN EXTENSION OF CONTENT." [59] Such were the formulas of a new school of poets who borrowed their ideas from Williams and Pound, but mainly Williams.

Williams' sayings were the rules of Projective Verse. "No ideas but in things" was explained by Olson to mean that every element of the poem must be treated as a solid: "the syllable, the line, as well as the image, the sound, the sense." Williams' "poem as a field of action" became Olson's "composition by field," "kinetics" by which the poem shaped itself. Williams said, "The only reality we can know is *MEASURE*." [60] In Olson this became "LAW OF THE LINE." "I am dogmatic that the head shows in the syllable." "The line comes (I swear it) from the breath, from the breathing of the man who writes, at the moment that he writes." Williams said, "Our poems are not subtly enough made, the structure, the staid manner of the poem cannot let our feelings through." [61] Olson said, "A poem is energy transferred from where the poet got it . . . by way of the poem itself to, all the way over to, the reader."

Olson became rector of Black Mountain College in North Carolina and in 1953 he invited Robert Creeley to edit *Black Mountain Review.* Then Creeley and Robert Duncan came to teach at the school where Joel Oppenheimer, Ed Dorn and Paul

Williams were continuing students. Four poets, Paul Blackburn, Paul Carroll, Larry Eigner and Denise Levertov, who had been publishing in Cid Corman's *Origin*, now published in *Black Mountain Review*. The magazine was not exclusively "projective"; the final issue, in 1957 when the college was forced to close, listed Ginsberg as contributing editor. Among the writers were William Burroughs, Gary Snyder, Jack Kerouac and Michael McClure.

In 1960 the Black Mountain poets, together with independent poets such as Ginsberg and Snyder, were published in an anthology. *The New American Poets* wrote in colloquial American and the rhythms of speech. They were against tradition and authority. Their attitude to sex, drugs, any kind of behavior, was: Do as you like.

This could be traced to Williams, and Henry Miller, and back to Whitman, and further back to Rousseau. It was Romanticism, belief in the innate goodness of the individual, the creed Hulme and Babbitt opposed. The "modernist" movement of 1910 had been an attempt to set up standards outside the individual. "Man," said Hulme, "is an extraordinarily fixed and limited animal whose nature is absolutely constant. It is only by tradition and organisation that anything decent can be got out of him." But now the Romantics were back in force, and one of their gods was Williams.[62]

But there was much of his mind that resisted categorizing. "A man somehow disturbed at the core," said Wallace Stevens, "and making all sorts of gestures and using all sorts of figures to conceal it from himself." [63] McAlmon, who knew him well, said, "There is so much wild imagination, audacity, and timidity, mixed up in him indiscriminately that nobody can ever know where he is, least of all himself." [64]

But though his ideas were not consistent there was a consistency that ran through them: his own individual character. He was a man of feeling—not deep, religious feeling to be sure, but rather the warm, generous feelings Europeans recognize as American. Naive, too.

He had added another, fifth book to *Paterson*, in order to retrieve it. The message was that man is to find his salvation through art. It was an old Romantic idea . . . So what! He was writing about Floss and himself, their life together. He had nothing to go on but feelings. But if a man is true to his feelings, and if he works and keeps at it long enough, he becomes his own authority.

Eliot was different. He had looked for a truth outside himself. Perhaps he had found it . . . No, that would be going too far. He had hated Eliot too long to forgive him now.

Pound said, "Bill Williams would converse with a goat if he were amiable." [65]

To Ridge Road came a number of poets and people of all kinds. "Hundred of neighbors, former patients, poets, and students ring the bell and walk in," says Edith Heal, who did just that herself. One wonders what Floss thought about it. Probably much the same as Tolstoy's wife when the "holy people" came to see Leo and sat for hours conversing. America had finally arrived at having a class of the "dispossessed" who wandered from place to place looking for someone to tell them what to do with their lives. They had long hair and were dressed in a manner offensive to the bourgeoisie. They wore amulets and beads and chanted Hindu prayers.

Floss didn't say much. "My wife," Williams remarked, "is a silent woman." This was after a reading at the Museum of Modern Art when the audience had been cool. Floss didn't express an opinion—she hadn't wanted to hurt his feelings.[66]

Other readings went better. "At Wellesley, once, they practically carried me off on their shoulders. I was speechless. You could hear a pin drop. A million girls were there . . . at least it looked that way. A bell kept ringing, it finally stopped. Floss had asked me to read the Coda to 'Asphodel' . . . I thought I didn't have time . . . but they stood on their heels and yelled . . . the girls . . . my god I was breathless, but I said do you really want more and they said yes so I read what Floss knew they would like. They were so adorable. I could have raped them all!" [67]

Floss, he told Edith Heal, was like a shot of whiskey to him, "her disposition cantankerous, like all wives, riding her man for his own good whether he liked it or not." [68]

He was writing poetry about their life together. It was a mystery. What was it that happened long ago, the time he proposed and she accepted? There were so many threads involved in the moment that he had been a lifetime trying to ravel them out. He had written three novels about Floss and her family. In the last he had lived through those days again, when Ed went off and proposed to Charlotte and was accepted. Then he asked Floss to marry him. "But you don't love me," she said, "you love my sister."

He had written about their wedding in "Asphodel," the part Floss told him to read.

> At the altar
> so intent was I
> before my vows,
> so moved by your presence
> a girl so pale
> and ready to faint
> that I pitied
> and wanted to protect you.

And:

> It is late
> but an odor
> as from our wedding
> has revived for me
> and begun again to penetrate
> into all crevices
> of my world.[69]

If that wasn't love, what was it?

When the visitor had gone he still sat at his desk. It was a warm murmuring night, sounds carrying a distance. Some people went by down the street, and a girl laughed.

> you know how
> the young girls run giggling [70]

He wrote that for the old woman. Rebellious to the last . . . she wouldn't have broken her leg if she had listened to his advice! She had to walk on an icy street! A cripple the last twenty years of her life. . . . But she outlived the Englishman, and lived to see her sons make a place for themselves.

> All this—
> Was for you, old woman.
> I wanted to write a poem
> that you would understand.

For what good is it to me
if you can't understand it?
            But you got to try hard—
But—
      Well, you know how
the young girls run giggling
on Park Avenue after dark
when they ought to be home in bed?
Well,
that's the way it is with me somehow.[71]

Afterword

All art . . . appeals primarily to the senses.

Joseph Conrad [1]

Our spirit, shut within this courtyard of sense-experience, is always saying to the intellect upon the tower: "Watchman, tell us of the night, if it aught of promise bear."

William James [2]

In the years leading up to the First World War there were experiments by Futurist poets, Imagists, and Vorticists. After the war there was a resurgence with Dada and Surrealism. These movements produced a storm of images. Whether it were Marinetti shouting about an automobile, or H. D. writing about a hot day:

> O wind, rend open the heat,
> cut apart the heat,
> rend it to tatters.[3]

the appeal was to the senses. They would have said, "to life itself."

The aim of writing, said Ford Madox Ford, is to create an illusion of life. "You attempt to involve the reader among the personages of the story or in the atmosphere of the poem. You do this by presentation and by presentation and again by presentation." [4]

T. E. Hulme, Ezra Pound and T. S. Eliot explained the nature of the new poetry. It attempted to present actuality by imitating actual processes of thought, sense perception and intuition. Its most useful tool was the image—writing that, by creating an illusion of

315

sensory life, evoked the reality of a perception. T. E. Hulme explained the process: "[Poetry] is a compromise for a language of intuition which would hand over sensations bodily. It always endeavours to arrest you, and to make you continuously see a physical thing, to prevent you gliding through an abstract process. . . . Images in verse are not mere decoration, but the very essence of an intuitive language." [5]

The "modernist" poets did not believe that poetry was a mere representation of sensory life. "In the first place," Pound said, "it is necessary to be a poet." [6] The difference between the new poetry and the old would be a shift of emphasis. There would be a minimum of interference by the personality of the writer. There would be no inflation. In short, the new poetry would not be romantic. The effect aimed at was of life, even disorder, rather than a moral judgment.

But still, "it is necessary to be a poet." The question of what poetry is always seems to return to the character of the poet. The poet, said Wordsworth in 1800, "has a greater knowledge of human nature, and a more comprehensive soul, than are supposed to be common among mankind." [7] Nearly a hundred years later, Henry James said, ". . . if I should certainly say to a novice, 'Write from experience and from experience only,' I should feel that this was rather a tantalizing monition if I were not careful immediately to add, 'Try to be one of the people on whom nothing is lost.' "

The consciousness of how much depends on his own individual mind places a great burden on the poet. The more he perceives and the more he imagines, the greater the discrepancy between his imagination and life. Hence the *poète maudit,* like the Decadent poets of the nineties, who destroys himself with antisocial behavior. Others look to a religion or a political system that will give them a sense of purpose.

Pound and Eliot were concerned with social stability—they thought this offered the best conditions for the artist. (As John R. Harrison points out, this is an error. The contrary is true: art flourishes in conditions of change—Periclean Athens, Renaissance Italy, England during the Napoleonic wars. Art fares worst in the most stable society of all, the totalitarian state.)[9] Pound preached Social Credit; then he supported Mussolini because he believed that Mussolini would support the arts. Eliot envisioned a society based on closely knit agricultural units, guided by a Christian elite. Both Pound and Eliot were hostile to the masses;

consequently, their political ideas have been ignored. Like it or not, this is the century of the common man.

William Carlos Williams was more attuned to the age. Pragmatic writing flows with experience, absorbing every idea it meets, until it reaches the sea of "a more of the same quality as oneself." In 1840 Alexis de Tocqueville, examining the young American republic, said that men were as much afloat in matters of faith as they were in their laws. Skepticism then drew the imagination of poets back to earth and confined them to the "real and visible world."

There is nothing, said Tocqueville, "so petty, so insipid, so crowded with paltry interests—in one word, so anti-poetic—as the life of a man in the United States." The poet, therefore, would not choose a particular man for his subject. Instead, he would write about "the people itself." He would write about the people "draining swamps, turning the course of rivers, peopling solitudes, and subduing nature." He would write of Providence and the destinies of mankind. Also, as the daily lives of men in a democracy were too trivial to be idealized, the poet would search below the surface to read the inner soul. "I need not," said Tocqueville, "traverse earth and sky to discover a wondrous object woven of contrasts, of infinite greatness and littleness, of intense gloom and amazing brightness, capable at once of exciting pity, admiration, terror, contempt. I have only to look at myself." [10]

Whitman seems to have been born to fill this prescription. So does William Carlos Williams. He writes about the life around him, insipid as it is, and he is called antipoetic. In *Paterson* he attempts to write of the destinies of mankind. But most of all he writes about himself, and in his last poems he writes with feeling. Williams' style, with its emphasis on "sincerity" and direct, plain speech, has been taken up by American poets; in recent years among young people it has become a standard way of writing. There have been experiments in rhythm stemming from Williams' search for "an American measure." However, his idea of the poem as an "object" with a necessary shape seems to have been lost.

There is a dimension of belief that lies beyond any particular belief. It is love, and in poets it is the love of rhythm, the sound, the falling into place of words. This is what poets still believe, after they have believed in everything else. When it comes to dealing with the world, writers are not smarter than bricklayers.—this has been shown in the lives of Pound and Eliot and Williams. If they were to be judged for their opinions, we would not be thinking about them at all.

But they loved poetry all their lives. This is what gives their characters a consistency and their writings a style. They had significant, I would say symbolic, lives. As writers they sometimes failed, and their reasoning was no better than other people's. Yet they are poets. Many feel that they are great poets—their writings give off a vibration of authority. They knew something, and this is very rare in the world. They knew themselves, what they had created out of their flesh and blood and with every fiber of their intellect. This is what is meant by having authority, or being an author.

References

Preface

[1] Mark Sullivan, *Our Times: 1900–1925*, Vol. III (1936), p. 560.

[2] Wyndham Lewis, "The Vorticist Manifesto," *Blast* No. 1 (1914).

[3] T. S. Eliot, *The Waste Land*, in *Collected Poems 1909–1962* (1963), p. 57.

[4] William James, *Pragmatism* (1949 reprint of 1907 edition), p. 121.

1   1908

[1] "Ezra Pound to William Carlos Williams, 21 October 1908," *The Selected Letters of Ezra Pound: 1907–1941*, ed. by D. D. Paige (1950), pp. 3–4.

[2] William Carlos Williams, *Autobiography* (1951), p. 57.

[3] Ezra Pound, "Scriptor Ignotus . . . To K. R. H. . . . Ferrara 1715," *A Lume Spento and Other Early Poems* (1965 reprint), p. 39.

[4] Charles Norman, *Ezra Pound* (1960), p. 28.

[5] Pound, *A Lume Spento.*

[6] "Ezra Pound to William Carlos Williams, 21 October 1908," *Letters,* pp. 4–6.

[7] "William Carlos Williams to His Mother," *The Selected Letters of William Carlos Williams,* ed. by John C. Thirlwall (1957), p. 6.

[8] Patricia Hutchins, *Ezra Pound's Kensington* (1965), p. 55.

[9] Ford Madox Ford, *The Soul of London* (1905), cited by Hutchins, p. 49.

[10] Hutchins, pp. 48–68.

[11] Ezra Pound, "In Durance," *Personae* (1926), p. 20.

[12] ———, "Hell," *Literary Essays of Ezra Pound* (1954), p. 205.

[13] Walter Pater, *The Renaissance.*

[14] Algernon Charles Swinburne, "Dolores."

[15] "Ezra Pound to William Carlos Williams, February 1909," *Letters,* p. 7.

2   Portrait of a Man with a Blue Earring

[1] Ford Madox Ford, *Return to Yesterday* (1932), pp. 356–57.

[2] William Carlos Williams, *I Wanted to Write a Poem* (1958), p. 6.

[3] William C. Wees, *Vorticism and the English Avant-Garde* (1972), p. 125.

[4] ———, p. 123.

[5] ———, p. 124.

[6] *Evening Standard and St. James Gazette,* 21 April 1909 (unsigned review), in *Ezra Pound: The Critical Heritage,* ed. by Eric Homberger (1972), p. 43.

[7] Edward Thomas, "Two Poets," *The English Review,* June 1909, cited in *Ezra Pound: The Critical Heritage,* pp. 50–53.

[8] *Ezra Pound: The Critical Heritage,* pp. 5–6.

[9] Noel Stock, *The Life of Ezra Pound* (1970), p. 4.

[10] "Ezra Pound: An Interview," *The Paris Review,* Vol. 28 (Summer–Fall, 1962), p. 40.

[11] "Ezra Pound to William Carlos Williams, 21 May 1909," *Letters,* pp. 7–8.

[12] Pound, "In Durance," *Personae,* p. 20.

[13] William Butler Yeats, *Memoirs,* ed. by Denis Donoghue (1972), p. 103.

[14] ———, p. 63.

[15] T. E. Hulme, poems printed in *Personae,* p. 252.

[16] ———, p. 253.

[17] ———, *Speculations* (1924), p. 118.

[18] Ezra Pound, "How I Began," *T. P.'s Weekly* (June, 1913).

[19] Hutchins, p. 68.

[20] "Ezra Pound to Patricia Hutchins, 20 July 1957," cited by Hutchins, p. 68.

[21] Hutchins, p. 70.

[22] *Ezra Pound: The Critical Heritage,* p. 6.

[23] ———, pp. 36–37.

[24] *Ibid.*

[25] Homberger, "Introduction," *Ezra Pound: The Critical Heritage,* p. 9.

[26] Pound, "Phasellus Ille," *Personae,* p. 63.

[27] Wyndham Lewis, *Blasting and Bombardiering* (1967 reprint of 1937 edition), pp. 272–74.

[28] Ezra Pound, in *The Nineteenth Century and After* (August, 1939), cited by Stock, p. 103.

[29] Ford Madox Ford, "Preface" to his *Collected Poems*, cited by Hugh Kenner, *The Pound Era* (1972), p. 80.

[30] "Ezra Pound to Malcolm Cowley," cited by Malcolm Cowley, *Exile's Return* (1961), p. 122.

[31] *Ezra Pound: The Critical Heritage*, p. 9.

3 Gathering the Limbs of Osiris

[1] Ezra Pound, "Arnold Dolmetsch," *The Literary Essays of Ezra Pound* (1954), p. 431.

[2] ——, *The Spirit of Romance* (1910, rev. 1952), p. 5.

[3] ——, "Cino," *Personae*, p. 6.

[4] ——, "Sestina: Altaforte," *Personae*, p. 28.

[5] ——, "Cino," *Personae*, p. 6.

[6] ——, "La Fraisne," *Personae*, pp. 4–5.

[7] Richard Ellmann, "Ez and Old Billyum," *Eminent Domain* (1967), p. 59.

[8] Pound, "La Fraisne," *Personae*, p. 5.

[9] ——, *Hugh Selwyn Mauberley*, in *Personae*, p. 197.

[10] ——, "Canto LXXXI," *Cantos* (1970), p. 521.

[11] ——, "Canto LXXXI," *Cantos*, p. 522.

[12] ——, "The Tradition," *Literary Essays*, p. 92.

[13] ——, "Cino," *Personae*, p. 6.

[14] ——, *Selected Prose: 1909–1965*, ed. by William Cookson (1973), pp. 26–27.

[15] ——, "In Durance," *Personae*, p. 20.

[16] ——, *Selected Prose*, p. 38.

[17] Donald Davie, *Ezra Pound: Poet as Sculptor* (1964), p. 24.

[18] Pound, *Selected Prose*, p. 33.

[19] ——, "Canto LXXXI," *Cantos*, p. 518.

[20] ——, *Selected Prose*, p. 38.

[21] Hugh Witemeyer, *The Poetry of Ezra Pound* (1969), p. 24.

[22] Pound, *Literary Essays*, p. 431.

[23] ——, "Ballad of the Goodly Fere," *Personae*, p. 33.

[24] "Ezra Pound to Malcolm Cowley," cited by K. K. Ruthven, *A Guide to Ezra Pound's Personae* (1969), p. 42.

[25] Yeats, in *Little Review* (April, 1914), cited by Ruthven, p. 204.

[26] Pound, "The Return," *Personae*, p. 74.

[27] Ruthven, p. 204.

[28] Pound, "The Seafarer," *Personae*, pp. 64–66.

[29] Ruthven, pp. 212–13.

[30] Pound, "Portrait d'une Femme," *Personae*, p. 61.

[31] Jules Laforgue, "Légende."

[32] Pound, "Portrait d'une Femme," *Personae,* p. 61.

[33] T. S. Eliot, *The Waste Land,* in *Collected Poems* (1934), pp. 67–68.

[34] Pater, *The Renaissance.*

[35] Pound, "Portrait d'une Femme," *Personae,* p. 61.

[36] ————, "Salvationists," *Personae,* p. 99.

[37] ————, *Selected Prose,* pp. 33–34.

4 *Il Miglior Fabbro*

[1] "Ezra Pound to Harriet Monroe," and "Ezra Pound to Amy Lowell," November 1913, *Letters,* pp. 24–26.

[2] "Ezra Pound to Harriet Monroe, September 1912," *Letters,* pp. 10–11.

[3] "Ezra Pound to Harriet Monroe, January 1915," *Letters,* p. 48.

[4] "Ezra Pound to Harriet Monroe, September 1914," *Letters,* p. 40.

[5] Stock, p. 164.

[6] Hugh Kenner, *The Pound Era* (1972), pp. 292–95.

[7] "Ezra Pound to James Joyce, 15 December 1913," *Pound/Joyce: The Letters of Ezra Pound to James Joyce,* ed. by Forrest Read (1967), pp. 17–18.

[8] Cited in *Pound/Joyce,* pp. 27–30.

[9] Ruthven, p. 158.

[10] Ellmann, "Ez and Old Billyum," *Eminent Domain,* p. 64.

[11] ————, p. 68.

[12] Pound, "Canto LXXXIII," *Cantos,* p. 534.

[13] *Ibid.*

[14] Hulme, *Speculations,* pp. 134–35.

[15] "Ezra Pound to Margaret Anderson, 17 November 1917," cited by Kenner, *The Pound Era,* p. 178.

[16] Earl Miner, "Pound, Haiku, and the Image," in *Ezra Pound: A Collection of Critical Essays,* ed. by Walter Sutton (1963), p. 128.

[17] Pound, "In a Station of the Metro," *Personae,* p. 109; "Vorticism," in *Gaudier-Brzeska, A Memoir* (1960 reprint of 1916 edition), pp. 87–89.

[18] ————, *Literary Essays,* p. 295.

[19] Kenner, *The Pound Era,* pp. 15–18.

[20] Joseph Conrad, "Preface" to *The Nigger of the Narcissus* (1897).

[21] Stock, pp. 106–07.

[22] Remy de Gourmont, *Le Problème du Style* (1902), p. 81.

[23] Pound, "A Few Don'ts," *Literary Essays,* pp. 3–4.

[24] ————, *Gaudier-Brzeska,* p. 86.

[25] F. S. Flint and Ezra Pound, "Imagism," in *The Modern Tradition,* ed. by Richard Ellmann and Charles Feidelson, Jr. (1965), p. 142.

[26] Pound, "L'Art, 1910," *Personae,* p. 113.

[27] ————, *Gaudier-Brzeska,* p. 89.

28 ———, *Literary Essays,* p. 7.

29 ———, "Fan-Piece, for Her Imperial Lord," *Personae,* p. 108.

30 Miner, p. 124.

31 Pound, "Religio," *Selected Prose,* p. 47.

32 "Ezra Pound to Homer L. Pound, 11 April 1927," *Letters,* p. 210.

33 Pound, "Canto II," *Cantos,* p. 6.

34 ———, *Gaudier-Brzeska,* p. 88.

35 ———, *Literary Essays,* p. 5.

36 ———, *Gaudier-Brzeska,* p. 85.

37 ———, *Literary Essays,* p. 5.

38 ———, p. 6.

39 ———, p. 9.

40 ———, p. 7.

41 ———, p. 4.

42 Hutchins, p. 135. See also: Christopher Middleton, "Documents on Imagism from the Papers of F. S. Flint," *The Review* (April, 1965).

43 William Pratt, *The Imagist Poem* (1963), p. 23.

44 Wees, p. 69.

45 ———, p. 88.

46 ———, p. 89.

47 ———, p. 91.

48 ———, p. 89.

49 Paolo Buzzi, from "Versi Libri," cited by Wees, p. 97.

50 F. T. Marinetti, *Marinetti: Selected Writings,* ed. by R. W. Flint (1971), pp. 3–42.

51 Richard Aldington, *Life for Life's Sake* (1941), p. 108.

52 Wees, p. 79.

53 ———, p. 82.

54 ———, p. 83.

55 ———, p. 84.

56 ———, p. 115.

57 Wyndham Lewis in *The New Weekly,* May 1914, cited by Wees, p. 101.

58 R. W. Flint, "Introduction," *Marinetti: Selected Writings,* p. 18.

59 Wees, p. 110.

60 Pound, "I Gather the Limbs of Osiris," *Selected Prose,* p. 34.

61 Wees, p. 177.

62 Pound, "Salutation the Third," *Personae,* p. 145.

63 "Ezra Pound to James Joyce, September 1915," *Pound/Joyce,* p. 46.

64 Wyndham Lewis, *Enemy of the Stars,* cited by Wees, p. 186.

65 Wees, p. 170.

66 Violet Hunt, quoted by Wees, p. 197.

67 Wees, p. 194.

68 Edgar Jepson, *Memories of an Edwardian,* cited by Wees, p. 196.

[69] Wees, p. 208.

[70] Guillaume Apollinaire, "Lundi Rue Christine."

[71] Wees, p. 70.

[72] Ezra Pound, *Gaudier-Brzeska*, p. 126.

[73] ———, pp. 120–21.

[74] Wees, p. 209.

[75] Pound, *Gaudier-Brzeska*, p. 92.

[76] ———, p. 90.

[77] ———, p. 89.

[78] ———, "Affirmations," *Selected Prose*, pp. 344–45.

[79] Clark Emery, *Ideas Into Action* (1958), p. 72.

[80] Kenner, *The Pound Era*, p. 228.

[81] William Wordsworth, "Lines Composed a Few Miles Above Tintern Abbey."

[82] Davie, *Ezra Pound: Poet as Sculptor*.

[83] Pound, "South-Folk in Cold Country," *Personae*, p. 139.

[84] ———, *Literary Essays*, p. 3.

[85] Davie, p. 45.

[86] Pound, "Song of the Bowmen of Shu," *Personae*, p. 127.

[87] ———, "The River-Merchant's Wife: A Letter," *Personae*, pp. 130–31.

[88] ———, p. 137.

[89] ———, "Vorticism," in *Gaudier-Brzeska*, p. 89.

[90] ———, *Literary Essays*, p. 5.

[91] ———, "Lament of the Frontier Guard," *Personae*, p. 133.

[92] ———, "Hugh Selwyn Mauberley IV," *Personae*, p. 190.

5 Into the Vortex

[1] Pound, "Commission," *Personae*, p. 88.

[2] ———, *Selected Prose*, p. 386.

[3] ———, "Albatre," *Personae*, p. 87.

[4] ———, "Les Millwin," *Personae*, p. 93.

[5] ———, "The Seeing Eye," *Personae*, p. 104.

[6] Homberger, *Ezra Pound: The Critical Heritage*, p. 155.

[7] Ruthven, p. 86.

[8] W. G. Hale, "Pegasus Impounded," *Poetry* (April 1919), in *Ezra Pound: The Critical Heritage*, pp. 155–57.

[9] Pound, *Homage to Sextus Propertius*, in *Personae*, p. 225.

[10] ———, p. 212.

[11] ———, p. 216.

[12] ———, p. 210.

[13] ———, p. 207.

[14] ———, p. 207.

[15] ———, p. 227.

[16] ———, p. 228.

[17] ———, p. 220.

[18] ———, p. 228.

[19] ———, *Literary Essays*, pp. 339–42.

[20] ———, *Homage to Sextus Propertius*, in *Personae*, p. 228.

[21] "Ezra Pound to John Quinn, 25 October 1919," *Letters*, pp. 151–52.

[22] This paraphrase of the theory is Mr. Donald Intonato's, who has kindly let me use it.

[23] Pound, "Cino," *Personae*, p. 7.

[24] Robert Nichols, "Poetry and Mr. Pound," *Observer* (11 January 1920), in *Ezra Pound: The Critical Heritage*, pp. 165–67.

[25] F. R. Leavis, *New Bearings in English Poetry* (1932), pp. 150–57.

[26] Kenner, *The Pound Era*, p. 408.

[27] Pound, quoted by Thomas E. Connolly, in *Accent* (Winter, 1956).

[28] Pound, *Hugh Selwyn Mauberley*, in *Personae*, p. 198.

[29] John J. Espey, *Ezra Pound's "Mauberley"* (1955), p. 16.

[30] William Cookson, "Introduction," *Ezra Pound: Selected Prose*, p. 18.

[31] Davie, pp. 91–96.

[32] Pound, "Our Contemporaries," *Personae*, p. 118.

[33] "Ezra Pound to Harriet Monroe, 12 October 1915," *Letters*, pp. 64–65.

[34] ———, p. 66.

[35] Rupert Brooke, "The Soldier."

[36] Pound, *Hugh Selwyn Mauberley*, in *Personae*, p. 203.

[37] ———, p. 197.

[38] Witemeyer, pp. 168–69.

[39] Pound, *Hugh Selwyn Mauberley*, in *Personae*, p. 199.

[40] ———, p. 189.

[41] ———, p. 197.

[42] ———, p. 202.

6 His True Penelope

[1] Stock, p. 235.

[2] T. S. Eliot, "Letter to John Quinn, 25 January 1920," *The Waste Land: A Facsimile and Transcript of the Original Drafts*, ed. by Valerie Eliot (1971), p. xix.

[3] Ezra Pound, *How to Read* (1931), pp. 10–11.

[4] "Ezra Pound to William Carlos Williams, 21 October 1908," *Letters*, p. 4.

[5] Pound, *New English Weekly* (12 October 1933), in *Ezra Pound: The Critical Heritage*, p. 268.

[6] Eliot, *The Waste Land: Facsimile*, p. xxii.

[7] "Ezra Pound to T. S. Eliot, 24 December 1921," *Letters,* p. 169.

[8] Pound, "Canto XX," *Cantos,* p. 89.

[9] ———, "Canto III," *Cantos,* p. 11.

[10] *Ibid.*

[11] "Ezra Pound: An Interview," *Paris Review,* p. 24.

[12] ———, p. 25.

[13] Pound, "I Gather the Limbs of Osiris," *Selected Prose,* p. 43.

[14] Ezra Pound, *Guide to Kulchur* (1938), p. 51.

[15] Pound, cited by Stock, p. 256.

[16] William Carlos Williams, *Autobiography* (1951), pp. 225–26.

[17] T. S. Matthews, *Great Tom: Notes Towards the Definition of T. S. Eliot* (1974), p. 85.

[18] Remy de Gourmont, *The Natural Philosophy of Love,* trans. by Ezra Pound (1931), p. 125.

[19] Mary de Rachewiltz, *Discretions* (1971), p. 127.

[20] ———, p. 110.

[21] ———, p. 156.

[22] ———, p. 197.

[23] ———, p. 144.

[24] Stock, pp. 41–42.

[25] "Ezra Pound to the Alumni Secretary of the University of Pennsylvania, 20 April 1929," *Letters,* p. 225.

[26] "Ezra Pound to William Carlos Williams, 22 November 1931," *Letters,* p. 229.

[27] Zukofsky in conversation with the author.

[28] Stock, p. 260.

[29] ———, p. 237.

[30] Kenner, *The Pound Era,* p. 146.

[31] Pound, "Canto IV," *Cantos,* p. 13.

[32] George Dekker, *Sailing After Knowledge* (1963), p. 82.

[33] Pound, "Catechism," *Selected Prose,* p. 47.

[34] ———, "A Retrospect," *Literary Essays,* p. 5.

[35] ———, "Canto II," *Cantos,* p. 6.

[36] *Ibid.*

[37] ———, "Canto XX," *Cantos,* p. 92.

[38] D. S. Carne-Ross, "The Cantos as Epic," in *Ezra Pound,* ed. by Russell (1950), p. 139.

[39] Pound, *Selected Prose,* p. 32.

[40] ———, "Cino," *Personae,* p. 7.

[41] ———, "Addendum for Canto C," *Cantos,* p. 798.

[42] ———, *Selected Prose,* p. 6.

[43] Kenner, *The Pound Era,* p. 430.

[44] Pound, "Canto LXXIV," *Cantos,* p. 449.

[45] Kenner, *The Pound Era,* p. 483.

[46] Pound, "Canto LVI," *Cantos,* p. 307.

[47] Cookson, "Introduction," *Selected Prose,* p. 9.

[48] Kenner, *The Poetry of Ezra Pound,* p. 296.

[49] Emery, *Ideas Into Action,* p. 124.

[50] Kenner, *The Pound Era,* p. 447.

[51] Pound, "Canto XIII," *Cantos,* p. 59.

[52] ———, translation of *Ta Hsio,* in *Selected Prose,* p. 16.

[53] ———, "Canto LI," *Cantos,* p. 251.

[54] ———, "Canto VIII," *Cantos,* p. 29.

[55] ———, "Paris Letter," *The Dial* (September 1922), cited by Espey, *Ezra Pound's "Mauberley"* (1955), p. 38.

[56] ———, "Canto XLI," *Cantos,* p. 202.

[57] ———, "Open Letter to Tretyakow," in *Front* (February 1930), cited by Stock, p. 296. *Front* was a Leftist magazine published in Albuquerque, New Mexico.

[58] *Ibid.*

[59] Pound, in 1935. The statement is found in his *Polite Essays* (1937). It is reprinted by J. P. Sullivan in *Ezra Pound* (1970), p. 183.

[60] Pound, "Canto LXXXIV," *Cantos,* p. 537.

[61] Stock, p. 367.

[62] Rachewiltz, *Discretions,* pp. 152–53.

[63] "Ezra Pound: An Interview," *Paris Review,* p. 46.

[64] ———, p. 44.

[65] Rachewiltz, pp. 143–44.

[66] Pound, "Canto L," *Cantos,* p. 248.

[67] ———, "Canto XCI," *Cantos,* p. 614.

[68] ———, "Canto LXXIV," *Cantos,* p. 439.

[69] "Excerpts from Pound's Broadcasts," *A Casebook on Ezra Pound,* ed. by William Van O'Connor and Edward Stone (1959), pp. 163–64.

[70] Rachewiltz, p. 241.

[71] ———, p. 243.

[72] Kenner, *The Pound Era,* p. 504.

[73] Pound, *Hugh Selwyn Mauberley,* in *Personae,* p. 193.

[74] ———, p. 194.

[75] ———, "Canto XXX," *Cantos,* p. 147.

[76] ———, "Canto LXXIV," *Cantos,* p. 441.

[77] John Keats, letter to Benjamin Bailey (November 22, 1817).

[78] Pound, "Canto XCVIII," *Cantos,* p. 685.

[79] ———, *Money Pamphlets,* No. 1 (London, 1959).

[80] Kenner, *The Pound Era,* p. 377.

[81] Pound, "Canto LXXXIV," *Cantos,* p. 539.

[82] ———, "Canto CVII," *Cantos,* p. 761.

[83] ———, "Canto CXVII," *Cantos,* p. 801.

[84] ———, *Hugh Selwyn Mauberley,* in *Personae,* p. 187.

[85] ———, an early poem, quoted by C. H. Sisson, *English Poetry 1900–1950* (1971), p. 112.

[86] Stock, p. 295.

[87] Pound, "Canto LXXIV," *Cantos,* p. 425.

[88] ———, "Canto XVI," *Cantos,* p. 69.

[89] ———, "Canto LXXX," *Cantos,* p. 506.

[90] ———, "Canto IV," *Cantos,* p. 15.

7   Cloud's Processional

[1] Stock, p. 419.

[2] ———, p. 446.

[3] Pound, "Canto LXXXI," *Cantos,* p. 521.

[4] ———, "Canto LXXXVII," *Cantos,* p. 570.

[5] William Shakespeare, *Timon of Athens.*

[6] Pound, "Canto LXXXIII," *Cantos,* p. 531.

[7] ———, p. 533.

[8] *Ibid.*

[9] Pound, "Canto I," *Cantos,* p. 3.

[10] ———, "Canto LXXIV," *Cantos,* p. 425.

[11] ———, "Canto LXXVII," *Cantos,* p. 471.

[12] ———, "Canto XLVII," *Cantos,* p. 238.

[13] ———, "Canto LXXX," *Cantos,* p. 515.

[14] ———, "Canto LXXX," *Cantos,* p. 505.

[15] Michael Reck, *Ezra Pound: A Close-Up* (1967), p. 158.

[16] Frank MacShane to the author.

[17] "Ezra Pound: An Interview," *The Paris Review,* p. 25.

[18] Pound, "Vorticism," *Gaudier-Brzeska,* p. 85.

[19] ———, "Portrait d'une Femme," *Personae,* p. 61.

[20] ———, *Gaudier-Brzeska,* p. 85.

[21] ———, "Portrait d'une Femme," *Personae,* p. 61.

8   The Author of Prufrock

[1] T. S. Eliot, *To Criticize the Critic* (1965), p. 44.

[2] Robert Sencourt, *T. S. Eliot: A Memoir* (1971), pp. 3–4.

[3] ———, pp. 5, 9.

[4] Matthews, *Great Tom,* p. 15.

[5] ———, pp. 8, 12.

[6] ———, p. 9.

[7] ———, p. 13.

[8] Sencourt, p. 6.

[9] "The Dry Salvages," T. S. Eliot, *Collected Poems 1909–1962* (1963), p. 191. Hereafter this title will be abbreviated as *C. P.*

[10] T. S. Eliot, *The Use of Poetry and the Use of Criticism* (1955), pp. 78–79.

[11] ———, p. 33.

[12] ———, p. 148.

[13] T. S. Eliot, *To Criticize the Critic*, p. 45.

[14] T. S. Eliot, "A Lyric," *Poems Written in Early Youth* (1967), p. 9.

[15] Bernard Bergonzi, *T. S. Eliot* (1972), p. 4.

[16] Sencourt, p. 18.

[17] Conrad Aiken, "King Bolo and Others, in *T. S. Eliot: A Symposium*, ed. by Richard March and M. J. Tambimutter (1965), p. 20.

[18] T. S. Eliot, quoted by Herbert Read in "T. S. E.—A Memoir," *Sewanee Review*, Vol. 74 (1966), p. 35.

[19] Sencourt, pp. 12–14.

[20] T. S. Eliot, *The Cocktail Party*, in *The Complete Poems and Plays* (1952), p. 384.

[21] ———, "Circe's Palace," *Poems Written in Early Youth*, p. 20.

[22] T. S. Eliot, cited by Bergonzi, p. 7.

[23] Sencourt, p. 29.

[24] T. S. Eliot, "Nocturne," *Poems Written in Early Youth*, p. 23.

[25] ———, p. 26.

[26] ———, in *Poetry* (September 1946).

[27] Elizabeth Drew, *T. S. Eliot: The Design of His Poetry* (1949), p. 22.

[28] *Ibid.*

[29] "Ezra Pound to Harriet Monroe, 30 September 1914," *The Letters of Ezra Pound 1907–1941*, ed. by D. D. Paige (1950), p. 40.

[30] John D. Margolis, *T. S. Eliot's Intellectual Development: 1922–1939* (1973), pp. 5–9.

[31] Conrad Aiken, *Ushant* (1971), p. 186.

[32] Grover Smith, *T. S. Eliot's Poetry and Plays* (1956), pp. 23–25.

[33] ———, pp. 20–21.

[34] T. S. Eliot, *Prufrock and Other Observations*, in *C. P.*, p. 1.

[35] John Peter, "A New Interpretation of *The Waste Land* (1952); With Postscript" (1969), in *Essays in Criticism*, Vol. XIX, No. 2 (April 1969), *passim*.

[36] ———, p. 175.

[37] T. S. Eliot, "The Three Voices of Poetry," *On Poetry and Poets* (1957), pp. 97–98.

[38] ———, "Tradition and the Individual Talent," *Selected Essays* (1950), p. 8.

[39] ———, "The Function of Criticism," *Selected Essays*, p. 18.

[40] ———, "Tradition and the Individual Talent," *Selected Essays*, pp. 7–8.

[41] ———, "Introduction" to *Le Serpent* by Paul Valéry.

[42] ———, "The Music of Poetry," *On Poetry and Poets*, p. 38.

[43] ———, *The Use of Poetry and the Use of Criticism*, pp. 118–19.

[44] ———, "The Love Song of J. Alfred Prufrock," *C. P.*, p. 7.

[45] ———, *The Use of Poetry and the Use of Criticism*, pp. 17–18.

[46] ———, "Little Gidding," *C. P.*, p. 207.

[47] ———, "The Love Song of J. Alfred Prufrock," *C. P.*, p. 3.

[48] ———, p. 6.

[49] Hugh Kenner, *The Invisible Poet: T. S. Eliot* (1959), p. 31.

[50] T. S. Eliot, "The Love Song of J. Alfred Prufrock," *C. P.*, p. 5.

[51] Ezra Pound, *ABC of Reading* (1960), p. 63.

[52] T. S. Eliot, "The Love Song of J. Alfred Prufrock," *C. P.*, p. 5.

[53] ———, *Ash-Wednesday*, in *C. P.*, p. 86.

9 "The horror! the horror!"

[1] Conrad Aiken, "King Bolo and Others," *T. S. Eliot: A Symposium* (1965), p. 21.

[2] Cited by Bergonzi, p. 23.

[3] Aiken, "King Bolo and Others," *T. S. Eliot: A Symposium*, p. 21.

[4] Kenner, *The Invisible Poet*, p. 45.

[5] Hugh Kenner and Robert Langbaum agree that Eliot understood Bradley's ideas before he had read Bradley. See Kenner, *The Invisible Poet*, p. 63, and Langbaum, "New Modes of Characterization in *The Waste Land*," in *Eliot in His Time*, ed. by A. Walton Litz (1972), pp. 122–23.

[6] T. S. Eliot, "Notes on 'The Waste Land,'" *C. P.*, p. 75.

[7] ———, *The Waste Land*, in *C. P.*, p. 57.

[8] ———, "Fragment of an Agon," *C. P.*, p. 123.

[9] ———, "East Coker," *C. P.*, p. 188.

[10] ———, "Thoughts after Lambeth," *Selected Essays*, p. 324.

[11] ———, *The Family Reunion, The Complete Poems and Plays*, p. 235.

[12] ———, "Preludes," *C. P.*, p. 14.

[13] ———, "Mr. Apollinax," *C. P.*, p. 23.

[14] ———, in *Purpose* (April/June 1931), pp. 91–92, cited by Roger Kojecky, *T. S. Eliot's Social Criticism* (1971), p. 227.

[15] Wyndham Lewis, *Blasting and Bombardiering* (1967), pp. 285–86.

[16] Smith, p. 31.

[17] ———, pp. 31–32.

[18] T. S. Eliot, "The Death of St. Narcissus," *Poems Written in Early Youth*, p. 28.

[19] ———, p. 29.

[20] Lewis, pp. 282–83.

[21] Matthews, p. 4.

[22] ———, p. 48.

[23] ———, p. 45.

[24] Lewis, p. 287.

[25] Kojecky, p. 43.

[26] Bertrand Russell, *Autobiography*, cited by Richard Ellmann, "The First Waste Land," in *Eliot in His Time*, ed. by Litz, p. 57.

[27] Kojecky, p. 43.

[28] Matthews, p. 47.

[29] *Ibid.*

[30] Ellmann, in *Eliot in His Time*, pp. 59–60.

[31] Brigit Patmore (Mrs. Richard Aldington), cited by Matthews, p. 54.

[32] Ellmann, in *Eliot in His Time*, p. 57.

[33] Kenner, *The Invisible Poet*, pp. 34–35.

[34] Marion Montgomery, *T. S. Eliot: An Essay on the American Magus* (1969), p. 5.

[35] Smith, p. 38.

[36] Paraphrase of Eliot's "Short Sketch of Rousseau's Life," in his first lecture, cited by John D. Margolis, *T. S. Eliot's Intellectual Development* (1972), p. 10.

[37] ——, pp. 10–11.

[38] *The Complete Poetical Works of T. E. Hulme*, in *Personae*, by Ezra Pound (1926), p. 253.

[39] Jane Lidderdale and Mary Nicholson, *Dear Miss Weaver* (1970), p. 64.

[40] T. S. Eliot, *New English Weekly* (Nov. 7, 1938), p. 39.

[41] Kenner, *The Invisible Poet*, p. 96.

[42] ——, p. 118. The quotation is from T. S. Eliot, "Tradition and the Individual Talent," *Selected Essays*, p. 5.

[43] T. S. Eliot, "Gerontion," *C. P.*, p. 30.

[44] ——, review of *The Education of Henry Adams*, in *Athenaeum* (May 23, 1919).

[45] *Ibid.*

[46] Ellmann, in *Eliot in His Time*, p. 61.

[47] T. S. Eliot, *The Complete Poems and Plays*, p. 356.

[48] "T. S. Eliot to Richard Aldington, 6 November 1921," cited in *The Waste Land: A Facsimile and Transcript of the Original Drafts*, ed. by Valerie Eliot (1971), p. xxii.

[49] Smith, p. 298.

[50] T. S. Eliot, "Gerontion," *C. P.*, p. 30.

[51] Wilfred Scawen Blunt, quoted by Wees, p. 23.

[52] Robert Ross, quoted by Wees, p. 23.

[53] R. D. Laing, *The Divided Self* (1970), p. 90.

[54] Michael Goldman, "Fear in the Way: the Design of Eliot's Drama," in *Eliot in His Time*, p. 165.

[55] Laing, p. 112.

[56] T. S. Eliot, "Thoughts After Lambeth," *Selected Essays*, p. 324.

[57] F. Scott Fitzgerald, "Pasting It Together," *The Crack-Up* (1931), p. 81.

[58] T. S. Eliot, "Dante," *Selected Essays,* p. 223.

[59] Sencourt, p. 85.

[60] T. S. Eliot, *The Waste Land,* in *C. P.,* p. 57.

[61] ———, p. 60.

[62] Lewis, pp. 235–36.

[63] Sencourt, illustrations following p. 78.

[64] Matthews, illustrations following p. 108.

10   Mug's Game

[1] T. S. Eliot, "The Music of Poetry," *On Poetry and Poets,* p. 26. Originally delivered as a lecture in 1942.

[2] ———, "The Frontiers of Criticism," *On Poetry and Poets,* p. 106.

[3] *Ibid.*

[4] Richard Aldington, *Life for Life's Sake* (1968), pp. 244–45.

[5] T. S. Eliot, *Selected Essays,* p. 127.

[6] ———, "Introduction," *The Sacred Wood* (1928), p. xiii.

[7] ———, "Preface," *The Sacred Wood,* p. viii.

[8] ———, p. x.

[9] "The Idealism of Julien Benda," *New Republic* (12 December 1928), cited by Margolis, p. 100.

[10] T. S. Eliot, "Preface," *The Sacred Wood,* p. viii.

[11] ———, "Introduction," *The Sacred Wood,* p. xiv.

[12] ———, "Tradition and the Individual Talent," *The Sacred Wood,* p. 52.

[13] ———, p. 58.

[14] ———, "Imperfect Critics," *The Sacred Wood,* p. 43.

[15] Mario Praz, "T. S. Eliot," in *L'Italia che scrive* (October 1956).

[16] Ezra Pound, "Arnold Dolmetsch," *Literary Essays of Ezra Pound* (1960), p. 431.

[17] T. S. Eliot, *The Sacred Wood,* p. 100.

[18] Cited by Matthews, p. 59.

[19] T. S. Eliot, "The Frontiers of Criticism," *On Poetry and Poets,* p. 106.

[20] Robert M. Adams, "Precipitating Eliot," in Litz, p. 135.

[21] Matthews, p. 81.

[22] T. S. Eliot, "Tradition and the Individual Talent," *The Sacred Wood,* p. 49.

[23] ———, p. 54.

[24] *Ibid.*

[25] ———, "The Function of Criticism," *Selected Essays,* p. 19.

[26] ———, p. 21.

[27] ———, p. 11.

[28] E.g., Leonard Unger, cited by Matthews, p. 82. Matthews seems to agree. So does Grover Smith, p. 28.

[29] Smith, p. 29.

[30] Drew, p. 37.

[31] See Hugh Kenner, "The Urban Apocalypse," in Litz, p. 35.

[32] T. S. Eliot, "Philip Massinger," *The Sacred Wood,* p. 125.

[33] "Ezra Pound to William Carlos Williams, 21 October 1908," *Letters of Ezra Pound,* p. 6.

[34] Smith, p. 40.

[35] T. S. Eliot, "Whispers of Immortality," *C. P.,* p. 45.

[36] *Ibid.*

[37] Rossell Hope Robbins, *The T. S. Eliot Myth* (1951), p. 76.

[38] T. S. Eliot, "Ode," *Ara Vos Prec* (1920).

[39] ———, "Whispers of Immortality," *C. P.,* p. 45.

[40] ———, "The Metaphysical Poets," *Selected Essays,* p. 247.

[41] ———, "Whispers of Immortality," *C. P.,* p. 45.

[42] ———, *Selected Essays,* p. 247.

[43] Richard March and M. J. Tambimuttu, eds., *T. S. Eliot: A Symposium for His Sixtieth Birthday* (1949), p. 86.

[44] T. S. Eliot, "Sweeney Among the Nightingales," pp. 49–50; and "Sweeney Erect," pp. 34–35, both in *C. P.*

[45] ———, "Burbank with a Baedeker: Bleistein with a Cigar," *C. P.,* p. 33.

[46] Smith, p. 54.

[47] Matthews, p. 163.

[48] Bergonzi, pp. 123–24.

11 Margate Sands

[1] "T. S. Eliot to John Quinn, 5 November 1919"; "T. S. Eliot to his mother, 18 December 1919," cited in *T. S. Eliot: The Waste Land: Facsimile,* p. xviii.

[2] "Eliot to his mother, 6 October 1920," cited in *The Waste Land: Facsimile,* p. xx.

[3] "Eliot to John Quinn, 9 May 1921," cited in *The Waste Land: Facsimile,* p. xx.

[4] T. S. Eliot, "Dirge," *The Waste Land: Facsimile,* p. 121.

[5] "Eliot to his brother, 15 February 1920," cited in *The Waste Land: Facsimile,* p. xviii.

[6] T. S. Eliot, *The Waste Land,* in *C. P.,* p. 54.

[7] Shakespeare, *The Tempest.*

[8] T. S. Eliot, *The Waste Land,* in *C. P.,* p. 58.

[9] ———, p. 53.

[10] Wyndham Lewis, *Blasting and Bombardiering* (1967 reprint of 1937 edition), pp. 265–70; 290–98.

[11] T. S. Eliot, *"Ulysses,* Order and Myth," *The Dial* (November 1923).

[12] Conrad Aiken, "An Anatomy of Melancholy," in *T. S. Eliot: The Man and His Work,* ed. by Tate, p. 194.

[13] T. S. Eliot, *The Waste Land,* in *C. P.,* p. 55.

[14] *Ibid.*

[15] Sencourt, p. 98.

[16] Aiken, "An Anatomy of Melancholy," in *T. S. Eliot: The Man and His Work,* p. 194.

[17] ———, p. 196.

[18] "Eliot to Richard Aldington, 'possibly 3 October' 1921," cited in *The Waste Land: Facsimile,* p. xxi.

[19] "Eliot to Richard Aldington, 'possibly 11 October' 1921," cited in *The Waste Land: Facsimile,* p. xxi.

[20] "Eliot to Julian Huxley, 26 October 1921," cited in *The Waste Land: Facsimile,* p. xxii.

[21] "Eliot to Julian Huxley, 31 October 1921," cited in *The Waste Land: Facsimile,* p. xxii.

[22] "Eliot to Richard Aldington, 6 November 1921," cited in *The Waste Land: Facsimile,* p. xxii.

[23] "Eliot to Henry Eliot, 13 December 1921," cited in *The Waste Land: Facsimile,* p. xxii.

[24] Helen Gardner, *"The Waste Land:* Paris 1922," in Litz, pp. 72–73.

[25] "Ezra Pound to John Quinn, 21 February 1922," cited by Gardner in Litz, p. 70.

[26] Gardner, in Litz, p. 92.

[27] T. S. Eliot, *The Waste Land: Facsimile,* p. 5.

[28] ———, *The Waste Land,* in *C. P.,* p. 53.

[29] Chaucer, *The Canterbury Tales.*

[30] T. S. Eliot, *The Waste Land: Facsimile,* p. 39.

[31] "Eliot to Ezra Pound, January 1922," in *Letters of Ezra Pound,* p. 171.

[32] "Ezra Pound to Eliot, January 1922," in *Letters of Ezra Pound,* p. 171.

[33] "T. S. Eliot to Ezra Pound, January 1922," *Letters of Ezra Pound,* p. 171.

[34] "Ezra Pound to T. S. Eliot, January 1922," *Letters of Ezra Pound,* p. 171.

[35] T. S. Eliot, *The Waste Land: Facsimile,* p. 11.

[36] ———, p. 71.

[37] ———, p. 47.

[38] ———, p. 13.

[39] *Ibid.*

[40] *Ibid.*

41 Gardner, in Litz, p. 87.

42 T. S. Eliot, "The Pensées of Pascal," *Selected Essays*, p. 358.

43 "T. S. Eliot to John Quinn, 21 September 1922," cited in *The Waste Land: Facsimile*, p. xxiv.

44 Sencourt, p. 105.

45 Matthews, p. 78.

46 T. S. Eliot, "Notes on 'The Waste Land,'" *The Waste Land,* in *C. P.,* p. 72.

47 C. G. Jung, "The Basic Postulates of Analytical Psychology," in *Modern Man in Search of a Soul,* trans. by W. S. Dell and C. F. Baynes (1933), pp. 215–16.

48 T. S. Eliot, *The Waste Land,* in *C. P.,* p. 67.

49 Edwin Arlington Robinson, "Miniver Cheevy."

50 T. S. Eliot, *The Waste Land,* in *C. P.,* p. 60.

51 ———, p. 68.

52 Robert Langbaum, "New Modes of Characterization in *The Waste Land*," in Litz, p. 113.

53 Jung, "On the Relation of Analytical Psychology to Poetic Art," *Contributions to Analytical Psychology,* cited by Drew, p. 10.

54 T. S. Eliot, *The Waste Land,* in *C. P.,* p. 57.

55 ———, *The Waste Land: Facsimile,* p. 47.

56 ———, *The Waste Land,* in *C. P.,* p. 59.

57 ———, "Virgil and the Christian World," *On Poetry and Poets,* pp. 123–24.

58 ———, "Thoughts After Lambeth," *Selected Essays,* p. 324.

59 ———, "Poetry and Drama," *On Poetry and Poets,* p. 91.

60 ———, *The Waste Land,* in *C. P.,* p. 68.

61 Langbaum, p. 118.

62 T. S. Eliot, "A Note on Poetry and Belief," *Enemy* I (1927), p. 16, cited by Margolis, p. 168.

63 Drew, p. 14.

64 ———, pp. 140–41.

65 ———, p. 90.

66 T. S. Eliot, *The Waste Land,* in *C. P.,* p. 68.

67 Hugh Kenner, "The Urban Apocalypse," in Litz, pp. 23–49 *passim*.

68 T. S. Eliot, quoted by Theodore Spencer, in *The Waste Land: Facsimile*.

69 T. S. Eliot, *The Waste Land,* in *C. P.,* p. 70.

12 Dreamcrossed Twilight

1 Sencourt, pp. 108–09.

2 D. E. S. Maxwell, "How the Poem was Received and its Critical Issues Defined," in Robert E. Knoll, *Storm Over The Waste Land* (1964), pp. 9–11.

[3] Sencourt, p. 108.

[4] William Carlos Williams, *Autobiography,* p. 174.

[5] Richard Aldington, *Stepping Heavenward.*

[6] Sencourt, p. 98.

[7] Conrad Aiken, *Ushant,* pp. 215–33.

[8] Cited by Kenner, *The Invisible Poet,* pp. 240–41.

[9] Matthews, pp. 85–86.

[10] T. S. Eliot, "Letter to Herbert Read," in *T. S. Eliot: The Man and His Work,* ed. Allen Tate (1967), p. 12.

[11] Sencourt, p. 122.

[12] T. S. Eliot, *After Strange Gods* (1934), p. 30.

[13] Margolis, pp. 49–50.

[14] T. S. Eliot, "What is a Classic?" *On Poetry and Poets,* p. 53.

[15] Sencourt, pp. 69–70.

[16] Margolis, pp. 273–75.

[17] *Ibid.*

[18] T. S. Eliot, "The Function of Criticism," in *The Criterion* 2 (1923), pp. 39–40.

[19] Kenner, *The Invisible Poet,* p. 242.

[20] T. S. Eliot, *The Sacred Wood,* p. viii.

[21] William M. Chace, *The Political Identities of Ezra Pound and T. S. Eliot* (1973), p. 132.

[22] Pound, *Personae,* p. 188.

[23] Margolis, pp. 76–78.

[24] *The Criterion* (June 1926), cited by Chace, p. 132.

[25] T. S. Eliot, "Little Gidding," in *C. P.,* p. 204.

[26] ———, *The Criterion* 4 (1926), cited by Margolis, p. 83.

[27] Margolis, pp. 133–34.

[28] Matthews, p. 108.

[29] T. S. Eliot, "Tarr," in *Egoist* 5 (5 September 1918), cited by Chace, p. 133.

[30] E. M. Forster, *Abinger Harvest* (1936), p. 111.

[31] Donald Davie, "Anglican Eliot," in Litz, p. 182.

[32] Chace, p. 157.

[33] Margolis, p. 127.

[34] ———, p. 101.

[35] ———, p. 142.

[36] Letters from Mrs. Eliot, January 20, 1969, and from the Rev. J. C. S. Nias, November 16, 1968, cited by Kojecky, p. 229.

[37] William Force Stead, "Mr. Stead Presents an Old Friend," in *Alumnae Journal of Trinity College* 38 (1965), pp. 59–66, cited by Margolis, p. 105.

[38] "T. S. Eliot to Paul Elmer More, 2 June 1930," cited by Margolis, p. 143.

[39] *Ibid.*

[40] T. S. Eliot, "Catholicism and International Order," in *Essays Ancient and Modern.*

[41] Sencourt, p. 147.

[42] "Commentary," in *The Criterion* 8 (1928), p. 188.

[43] T. S. Eliot, "Preface," *For Lancelot Andrewes: Essays on Style and Order* (1928), p. ix.

[44] ———, *After Strange Gods* (1934), p. 20.

[45] *The Criterion* 7 (February 1928), p. 98.

[46] *The Criterion* 8 (July 1929), pp. 690–91.

[47] *The Criterion* 16 (March 1937), p. 473.

[48] *The Criterion* 8 (December 1928), pp. 288–90, 284, cited by Chace, pp. 141–42.

[49] *The Criterion* 8 (December 1928), pp. 281–82, cited by Margolis, p. 152.

[50] *The Criterion* 8 (1929), p. 687, cited by Margolis, p. 153.

[51] *The Criterion* 14 (1934), p. 7, cited by Margolis, p. 154.

13 Prayers to Broken Stone

[1] T. S. Eliot, "The Hollow Men," *C. P.,* p. 79.

[2] Edmund Wilson, *Axel's Castle* (1931), p. 114.

[3] T. S. Eliot, "The Hollow Men," *C. P.,* p. 79.

[4] Charles Baudelaire, "Correspondances" (1857).

[5] Stéphane Mallarmé, *Divagations* (1897).

[6] T. S. Eliot, "The Hollow Men," *C. P.,* p. 81.

[7] ———, p. 82.

[8] ———, p. 80.

[9] ———, *Sweeney Agonistes, C. P.,* p. 122.

[10] ———, "The Beating of a Drum," *The Nation and the Athenaeum* (6 October 1923), pp. 11–12.

[11] ———, *Sweeney Agonistes, C. P.,* p. 119.

[12] ———, p. 117.

[13] Edmund Wilson, "T. S. Eliot and the Church of England," *The New Republic* (24 April 1929), p. 283.

[14] Robert M. Adams, "Precipitating Eliot," in Litz, p. 148.

[15] Helen Gardner, *The Art of T. S. Eliot* (1959), p. 2.

[16] Drew, p. 205.

[17] T. S. Eliot, "Journey of the Magi," *C. P.,* p. 99.

[18] ———, "Lines to a Persian Cat," *C. P.,* p. 135.

[19] ———, "Journey of the Magi," *C. P.,* p. 99.

[20] ———, "A Song for Simeon," *C. P.,* p. 101.

[21] ———, "Animula," *C. P.,* p. 103.

[22] ———, p. 104.

[23] Smith, p. 130.

[24] T. S. Eliot, "Marina," *C. P.,* p. 105.

[25] *Ibid.*

[26] Drew, pp. 140–41.

[27] ———, pp. 98–100.

[28] ———, p. 127.

[29] Jung, *Integration of the Personality,* p. 189, cited by Drew, p. 131.

[30] T. S. Eliot, "Marina," *C. P.,* p. 106.

[31] *Ibid.*

[32] ———, *Ash-Wednesday, C. P.,* p. 85.

[33] *Ibid.*

[34] *Ibid.*

[35] Wilson, *Axel's Castle,* p. 19.

[36] St. John of the Cross, *The Complete Works,* Vol. I, Bk. II, p. 418.

[37] T. S. Eliot, *Ash-Wednesday, C. P.,* p. 86.

[38] ———, p. 87.

[39] ———, p. 89.

[40] ———, "Catholicism and International Order," *Essays Ancient and Modern.*

[41] ———, *After Strange Gods,* p. 61.

[42] ———, *Ash-Wednesday,* C. P., p. 89.

[43] ———, "Dante," *Selected Essays,* p. 223.

[44] ———, *Ash-Wednesday,* C. P., p. 90.

[45] ———, "What Dante Means to Me," *To Criticize the Critic* (1965), pp. 125, 132.

[46] ———, "Commentary," *Criterion* 8 (1928), p. 188.

[47] ———, "Thoughts After Lambeth," *Selected Essays,* p. 342.

[48] Margolis, pp. 164–66.

[49] Chace, p. 179.

[50] T. S. Eliot in a conversation with Helen Gardner, November 1968, cited in Kojecky, p. 94.

[51] T. S. Eliot, *After Strange Gods, passim.*

[52] ———, p. 16.

[53] Sencourt, p. 150.

[54] *Ibid.*

[55] ———, p. 173.

[56] T. S. Eliot, "Christianity and Communism," *The Listener* (March 16, 1932), p. 382.

[57] ———, *The Use of Poetry and the Use of Criticism,* p. 154.

[58] ———, "Choruses from 'The Rock,' " *C. P.,* p. 149.

[59] ———, *The Rock* (1934), p. 52.

[60] ———, "Burnt Norton," *C. P.,* p. 175.

[61] ———, "Choruses from 'The Rock,' " *C. P.,* p. 149.

[62] ———, p. 150.

[63] ———, p. 156.

[64] ———, p. 159.

[65] Kenner, *The Invisible Poet*, pp. 292–93.

[66] T. S. Eliot, *The Sacred Wood*, p. 70.

[67] ———, *The Use of Poetry and the Use of Criticism*, p. 146.

[68] ———, "Little Gidding," *C. P.*, p. 205.

14 Sitting Still

[1] Gardner, *The Art of T. S. Eliot*, p. 3.

[2] Bergonzi, pp. 164–65.

[3] Kenner, *The Invisible Poet*, p. 307.

[4] Drew, p. 145.

[5] ———, p. 142.

[6] ———, p. 143.

[7] T. S. Eliot, "Shakespeare," *Selected Essays*, p. 115.

[8] C. K. Stead, *The New Poetic*, quoted by Bergonzi, pp. 164–65.

[9] T. S. Eliot, "The Dry Salvages," in *C. P.*, p. 199.

[10] ———, "Little Gidding," in *C. P.*, p. 206.

[11] ———, "Burnt Norton," in *C. P.*, p. 179.

[12] ———, p. 178.

[13] William F. Lynch, S. J., *Christ and Apollo*, pp. 170–71, quoted by Bergonzi, pp. 168–69.

[14] T. S. Eliot, *Athenaeum* (May 23, 1919), quoted by Bergonzi, p. 191.

[15] ———, "The Dry Salvages," *C. P.*, p. 198.

[16] ———, quoted by Drew, p. 140.

[17] Robert M. Adams, "Precipitating Eliot," in Litz, p. 150.

[18] Bergonzi, p. 171.

[19] T. S. Eliot, "Burnt Norton," *C. P.*, p. 176.

[20] Matthews, p. 138.

[21] Kenner, *The Pound Era*, p. 277.

[22] T. S. Eliot, *The Complete Poems and Plays*, p. 235.

[23] ———, p. 236.

[24] Kenner, *The Pound Era*, p. 507.

[25] T. S. Eliot, *The Sacred Wood*, p. 152.

[26] ———, p. 155.

[27] ———, p. 156.

[28] ———, pp. 157–58.

[29] ———, p. 158.

[30] Matthews, p. 162.

[31] Sencourt, p. 195.

[32] Matthews, p. 169.

[33] T. S. Eliot, *On Poetry and Poets*, p. 217.

[34] Ronald Duncan, *How to Make Enemies*, p. 384, quoted by Bergonzi, p. 179.

35 T. S. Eliot, "Tradition and the Individual Talent," *The Sacred Wood*, p. 53.

36 ———, "The Metaphysical Poets," *Selected Essays*, p. 248.

37 ———, *The Waste Land,* in *C. P.*, p. 57.

38 ———, "Bustopher Jones: The Cat about Town," *The Complete Poems and Plays*, p. 167.

39 ———, "Macavity: the Mystery Cat," *The Complete Poems and Plays*, p. 167.

40 Sencourt, p. 212.

41 ———, p. 214.

42 *Ibid.*

43 Matthews, p. 159.

44 ———, p. 156.

45 ———, p. 160.

46 *Ibid.*

47 ———, p. 172.

48 T. S. Eliot, *The Complete Poems and Plays*, p. 356.

49 ———, "Fragment of an Agon," *C. P.*, pp. 119–20.

50 ———, p. 120.

51 ———, p. 121.

52 ———, "Tradition and the Individual Talent," *The Sacred Wood*, p. 53.

15   Mr. and Mrs. Williams

1 William Carlos Williams, *The Autobiography of William Carlos Williams* (1951) p. 3. Hereafter cited as *Autobiography.*

2 ———, *Yes, Mrs. Williams* (1959), p. 3.

3 ———, p. 131.

4 ———, p. 33.

5 *Ibid.*

6 ———, "A Memory of Tropical Fruit," *A Novelette and Other Prose: 1921–1931* (1932), pp. 77–78.

7 ———, *Yes, Mrs. Williams*, p. 7.

8 "William Carlos Williams to Ezra Pound, June 1932," *The Selected Letters of William Carlos Williams* (1957), p. 127. Hereafter cited as *Letters.*

9 Williams, *Autobiography*, p. 14.

10 Robert Burns, "Tam O'Shanter."

11 Walt Whitman, "Starting from Paumanok."

12 Williams, *Yes, Mrs. Williams*, p. 6.

13 ———, p. 8.

14 *Ibid.*

15 ———, *Autobiography*, p. 15.

16 ———, *Yes, Mrs. Williams*, p. 9.

17 *Ibid.*

18 ———, *Autobiography*, p. 15; and *Yes, Mrs. Williams*, p. 8.

19 ———, *Yes, Mrs. Williams*, p. 8.

20 ———, *Autobiography*, pp. 15–16.

21 ———, p. 17.

22 *Ibid.*

23 ———, p. 27.

24 "William Carlos Williams to James Laughlin, 22 July 1939," *Letters*, p. 185.

25 Williams, *Autobiography*, pp. 19–20.

26 "William Carlos Williams to Florence Herman Williams, 28 September 1927, 7:45 a.m.," *Letters*, p. 80.

27 Williams, *Yes, Mrs. Williams*, p. 33.

28 ———, *Letters*, p. 80.

29 ———, *Yes, Mrs. Williams*, p. 6.

30 ———, *Autobiography*, p. 279.

31 ———, pp. 20–21.

32 ———, p. 21.

33 ———, p. 4.

34 ———, p. 5.

35 ———, p. 280.

36 ———, p. 3.

37 ———, *Yes, Mrs. Williams*, p. 130.

38 ———, *Autobiography*, p. 288.

39 ———, *Yes, Mrs. Williams*, p. 20.

40 ———, *Autobiography*, p. 288.

41 ———, p. 362.

42 ———, p. 287.

43 ———, "Rome," ms. cited by Mike Weaver, in *William Carlos Williams: The American Background* (1971), p. 133.

44 ———, *Autobiography*, p. 361.

45 ———, p. 28.

46 Fourteen in the *Autobiography*, p. 28; thirteen in *Yes, Mrs. Williams*, p. 11.

47 Williams, *Autobiography*, p. 29.

48 *Ibid.*

49 ———, p. 30.

50 ———, p. 35.

51 ———, p. 40.

52 *Ibid.*

53 ———, p. 43.

54 "William Carlos Williams to William Eric Williams, 13 March 1935," *Letters*, p. 153.

55 "William Carlos Williams to Harvey Breit, 18 March 1942," *Letters*, p. 193.

56 Williams, *Autobiography*, p. 44.

57 ——, p. 45.

58 *Ibid.*

59 ——, pp. 45–46.

60 ——, p. 47.

61 *Ibid.*

62 William Carlos Williams, "The Basis of Faith in Art," *Selected Essays of William Carlos Williams* (1954), p. 177.

63 ——, *Autobiography*, p. 49.

64 *Ibid.*

16 The Sensible Choice

1 Williams, *Autobiography*, p. 50.

2 ——, "Questionnaire," *Little Review* XII (May 1929), p. 87.

3 ——, "Of Medicine and Poetry," *Autobiography*, pp. 286–89.

4 ——, p. 51.

5 ——, p. 50.

6 "William Carlos Williams to Jean Starr Untermeyer, Saturday [October 1948]," *Letters*, p. 268.

7 Williams, *Autobiography*, p. 52.

8 ——, p. 53.

9 *Ibid.*

10 ——, p. 52.

11 ——, p. 53.

12 ——, pp. 57–58.

13 Ezra Pound, "Anima Sola," *A Lume Spento and Other Early Poems* (1965 reprint), p. 31.

14 Williams, *Autobiography*, p. 56.

15 ——, p. 65.

16 ——, pp. 56–57.

17 ——, p. 57.

18 ——, p. 18.

19 "William Carlos Williams to Babette Deutsch, 18 January 1943," *Letters*, p. 210.

20 Williams, *Autobiography*, p. 58.

21 ——, p. 51.

22 ——, p. 57.

23 "William Carlos Williams to Babette Deutsch, 18 January 1943," *Letters*, p. 210.

24 Williams, *A Dream of Love*, in *Many Loves* (1961), p. 209.

25 ——, *Autobiography*, p. 54.

26 ——, pp. 58–60.

27 ——, pp. 54–55.

[28] ———, p. 67.

[29] "William Carlos Williams to Edgar I. Williams, 12 April 1905," *Letters*, p. 8.

[30] Williams, *Autobiography*, pp. 67–68.

[31] ———, p. 68.

[32] *Ibid.*

[33] "William Carlos Williams to Edgar Williams, 14 January 1906," *Letters*, pp. 11–12.

[34] *Ibid.*

[35] Williams, *Autobiography*, pp. 67–69.

[36] ———, pp. 69–70.

[37] H. D., "Oread."

[38] Richard Aldington, *Life for Life's Sake* (1941), p. 111.

[39] Williams, *Autobiography*, pp. 61–62.

[40] ———, p. 62.

[41] ———, "Emmanuel Romano," *Form 2* (1 September 1966), pp. 22–25, cited by Weaver, *William Carlos Williams: The American Background*, p. 164.

[42] ———, *Many Loves*, pp. 204–05.

[43] ———, p. 202.

[44] William Blake, "The Garden of Love."

[45] Williams, *Autobiography*, pp. 62–63.

[46] ———, p. 63.

[47] ———, pp. 63–64.

[48] ———, p. 52.

[49] "William Carlos Williams to his mother, 9 December 1902," *Letters*, p. 4.

[50] "William Carlos Williams to his mother, 12 February 1904," *Letters*, p. 5.

[51] "William Carlos Williams to his mother, 8 November 1904," *Letters*, p. 7.

[52] Williams, *Autobiography*, p. 55.

[53] "William Carlos Williams to Edgar Williams, 12 April 1905," *Letters*, p. 9.

[54] "William Carlos Williams to Edgar Williams, 12 November 1906," *Letters*, pp. 13–14.

[55] ———, p. 14.

[56] Williams, *Autobiography*, p. 51.

[57] *Ibid.*

[58] *Ibid.*

17 A Proposal of Marriage

[1] Williams, *Autobiography*, p. 71.

[2] ———, pp. 71–75.

[3] ———, p. 77.

[4] ———, p. 79.

[5] ———, p. 85.

[6] ———, *Yes, Mrs. Williams,* p. 3.

[7] ———, pp. 140–41.

[8] ———, *Autobiography,* pp. 79–80.

[9] ———, p. 81.

[10] ———, pp. 82–83.

[11] ———, p. 240.

[12] Randall Jarrell, "Introduction," *William Carlos Williams: Selected Poems* (1949), pp. xiii, x, xv.

[13] Hyatt H. Waggoner, *American Poets from the Puritans to the Present* (1968), pp. 377–78.

[14] Williams, "Federico Garcia Lorca," *Selected Essays,* p. 230.

[15] ———, "On Measure–Statement for Cid Corman," *Selected Essays,* p. 339.

[16] Wallace Stevens, "Preface," *William Carlos Williams: Collected Poems 1921–1931* (1934).

[17] Waggoner, p. 380.

[18] Williams, "Paterson," *Collected Earlier Poems* (1951), p. 233. Hereafter cited as *C. E. P.*

[19] ———, *The Build-Up* (1952), p. 229.

[20] ———, *Yes, Mrs. Williams,* p. 116.

[21] Walt Whitman, "Song of Myself."

[22] Williams, *Autobiography,* p. 58.

[23] ———, "Complaint," *C. E. P.,* p. 199.

[24] ———, "Old Doc Rivers," *The Farmers' Daughters* (1961), p. 82.

[25] ———, "The Poor," *C. E. P.,* p. 415.

[26] James Breslin, *William Carlos Williams: An American Artist* (1970), p. 154.

[27] Williams, "Life Along the Passaic River," *The Farmers' Daughters,* p. 160.

[28] ———, *Paterson III* (1963), p. 153.

[29] ———, *A Dream of Love,* in *Many Loves,* pp. 117–18.

[30] ———, *Autobiography,* p. 94.

[31] ———, p. 101.

[32] ———, *Autobiography,* pp. 104–05; and *Yes, Mrs. Williams,* pp. 15–16.

[33] "Ezra Pound to William Carlos Williams, 21 October 1908," *The Letters of Ezra Pound 1907–1941* (1950), pp. 3–7.

[34] Emily Mitchell Wallace, *A Bibliography of William Carlos Williams* (1968), pp. 7–9.

[35] William Carlos Williams, *Poems* (Rutherford, N.J., 1909).

[36] ———, *Autobiography,* p. 91.

[37] ———, pp. 91–92.

[38] "Ezra Pound to William Carlos Williams, 21 May 1909," *The Letters of Ezra Pound*, pp. 7–8.

[39] Williams, *Autobiography*, p. 106.

[40] Weaver, *William Carlos Williams: The American Background*, p. 16.

[41] Williams, *Yes, Mrs. Williams*, p. 130.

[42] ———, *The Build-Up*, p. 232.

[43] ———, pp. 235–38.

[44] ———, pp. 258–59.

[45] ———, p. 261.

[46] ———, pp. 260–62.

[47] ———, *Yes, Mrs. Williams*, p. 134.

[48] ———, *The Build-Up*, p. 262.

[49] ———, pp. 262–63.

[50] ———, *Autobiography*, p. 108.

[51] Otto Weininger, *Sex and Character* (1906), p. 183, cited by Weaver, p. 18.

[52] Williams, *Letters*, p. 14.

18 Modernity

[1] "William Carlos Williams to Edgar I. Williams, 11 August 1909," *Letters*, p. 18.

[2] Williams, *Autobiography*, p. 114.

[3] ———, pp. 115–16.

[4] ———, p. 117.

[5] Ezra Pound, *Personae*, p. 83.

[6] Williams, *Autobiography*, p. 123.

[7] ———, p. 127.

[8] *Ibid.*

[9] ———, pp. 127–30.

[10] ———, pp. 132–33.

[11] ———, "A Note on Poetry," *Oxford Anthology of American Literature,* ed. by William Rose Benét and Norman Holmes Pearson (1938), p. 1313.

[12] "William Carlos Williams to Viola Baxter Jordan, 6 January 1911," cited by Weaver, p. 22.

[13] Williams, "First Praise," *C. E. P.*, p. 17.

[14] ———, "The Death of Franco of Cologne: His Prophecy of Beethoven," *C. E. P.*, p. 25.

[15] ———, "An After Song," *C. E. P.*, p. 22.

[16] ———, "The Wanderer," *C. E. P.*, p. 22.

[17] Wallace, *A Bibliography of William Carlos Williams*, p. 10.

[18] "Ezra Pound to Harriet Monroe, March 1913," *The Letters of Ezra Pound*, p. 14.

[19] "William Carlos Williams to Harriet Monroe, 5 March 1913," *Letters,* p. 23.

[20] "William Carlos Williams to Harriet Monroe, 26 October 1916," *Letters,* p. 39.

[21] Williams, *Autobiography,* p. 157.

[22] ———, "Prologue to Kora in Hell" [1918], *Essays,* p. 5.

[23] ———, *Autobiography,* p. 136.

[24] "William Carlos Williams to the Editor of *The Egoist,* 1915," *Letters,* p. 31.

[25] Williams, *Autobiography,* p. 135.

[26] James Guimond, *The Art of William Carlos Williams* (1968), p. 43.

[27] Williams, "Prologue to Kora in Hell," *Essays,* pp. 25–26.

[28] ———, "The Wanderer," *C. E. P.,* pp. 3–12.

[29] ———, p. 7.

[30] ———, p. 5.

[31] ———, pp. 11–12.

[32] ———, p. 12.

[33] ———, *Autobiography,* p. 148.

[34] *Ibid.*

[35] ———, "The Poem as a Field of Action" [1948], *Essays,* p. 283.

[36] ———, "Prologue to Kora in Hell," *Essays,* pp. 11–12.

[37] W. Kandinsky, *Concerning the Spiritual in Art,* ed. Robert Motherwell (1947), p. 77, cited by Weaver, p. 39.

[38] Weaver, pp. 37–39.

[39] ———, p. 39.

[40] Williams, "Pastoral," *C. E. P.,* p. 124.

[41] William Wordsworth, "Preface," *Lyrical Ballads* (1800).

[42] Williams, *I Wanted to Write a Poem* (1958), p. 15.

[43] ———, "This Florida: 1924," *C. E. P.,* p. 330.

[44] "William Carlos Williams to Alva N. Turner, 27 February 1921," *Letters,* p. 50.

[45] Williams, "El Hombre," *C. E. P.,* p. 140.

[46] ———, "Danse Russe," *C. E. P.,* p. 148.

[47] ———, "Against the Weather" [1939], *Essays,* p. 215.

[48] J. Hillis Miller, ed., *William Carlos Williams: A Collection of Critical Essays* (1966), p. 175.

[49] Williams, *Essays,* p. 292.

[50] ———, p. 259.

[51] "William Carlos Williams to Kay Boyle, 1932," *Letters,* p. 129.

[52] Williams, "Against the Weather," *Essays,* p. 215.

[53] "Ezra Pound to Harriet Monroe, October 1914," *The Letters of Ezra Pound,* p. 41.

[54] "William Carlos Williams to Harriet Monroe, 8 May 1915," *Letters,* p. 29.

[55] Williams, "Prologue to Kora in Hell," *Essays*, pp. 21–23.

[56] ———, p. 24.

[57] ———, pp. 23–24.

[58] "William Carlos Williams to Kenneth Burke, 26 January 1921," *Letters*, p. 48.

[59] Breslin, p. 202.

[60] *Ibid.*

[61] William Carlos Williams, *Kora in Hell: Improvisations* (1967), p. 25.

[62] "William Carlos Williams in conversation with John C. Thirlwall," "Introduction," *Letters*, p. xvii.

[63] Williams, "Hands Across the Sea," *The Farmers' Daughters*, p. 17.

[64] ———, *Kora in Hell*, p. 42.

[65] ———, *Essays*, p. 19.

[66] ———, *Many Loves*, pp. 125–26; "Love Song," *C. E. P.*, p. 174.

[67] ———, *Many Loves*, pp. 117, 206.

[68] ———, "The Basis of Faith in Art" [1937], *Essays*, p. 188.

[69] ———, *Kora in Hell*, p. 30.

[70] ———, "Introduction," *Essays*, p. 233.

[71] "William Carlos Williams to Horace Gregory, 5 May 1944," *Letters*, p. 224.

[72] Williams, *Autobiography*, p. 391. Williams is referring to Dewey's article, "Americanism and Localism," *The Dial* LXVIII [1920], pp. 687–88. "We are discovering that the locality is the only universal."

[73] Herman Keyserling, *America Set Free* (1929), p. 48, cited by Weaver, pp. 34–36.

[74] Williams, "Against the Weather," *Essays*, p. 198.

[75] ———, "Yours, O Youth" [1922], *Essays*, p. 32.

[76] ———, p. 35.

[77] By Eliot among others. "For me, without one word of civil greeting (a sign of his really bad breeding, which all so-called scholars show—protectively), he reserves the slogan 'of local interest perhaps.' " "Williams to T. C. Wilson, 12 July 1933," *Letters*, p. 141.

[78] F. Scott Fitzgerald, "Echoes of the Jazz Age."

[79] "William Carlos Williams to Ezra Pound, 23 March 1933," *Letters*, pp. 139–40.

[80] Williams, "Comment I" [1921], *Essays*, p. 28.

[81] ———, "The Work of Gertrude Stein," *A Novelette and Other Prose* [1932], pp. 108–09.

19 Words and Their Intervals

[1] Williams, *Autobiography*, p. 170.

[2] ———, p. 171.

[3] Guimond, pp. 41–42.

[4] Breslin, p. 79.

[5] William Carlos Williams, *Spring and All* (1970 reprint of 1923 edition), p. 31.

[6] ———, *Autobiography*, p. 380.

[7] Guimond, pp. 43–44.

[8] Williams, *Spring and All*, p. 46.

[9] ———, *Autobiography*, p. 163.

[10] Gustave Flaubert, *Madame Bovary*.

[11] Williams, *Autobiography*, pp. 164–66, 168–69.

[12] ———, p. 175.

[13] Weaver, p. 30.

[14] "No-Colored Encounters: Hallucinations of an Aerial Wanderer," *The Ace I*, 1 (August 1919), pp. 27–28, 36; 28, cited by Weaver, p. 31.

[15] S. MacDonald Wright, "The Influence of Aviation on Art," *The Ace I*, 2 (September 1919), pp. 11–12.

[16] ———, p. 11.

[17] Weaver, p. 33.

[18] Linda Welshimer Wagner, *The Prose of William Carlos Williams* (1970), p. 57.

[19] William Carlos Williams, *The Great American Novel* (1923), pp. 77–79.

[20] ———, *A Voyage to Pagany* (1928), p. 137.

[21] ———, pp. 174, 178.

[22] ———, pp. 178, 285.

[23] *The Ace* II (6 January 1921), pp. 14–15, cited by Weaver, p. 30.

[24] Williams, *Autobiography*, p. 175.

[25] ———, pp. 176–78.

[26] ———, p. 146.

[27] ———, *I Wanted to Write a Poem*, p. 27.

[28] Weaver, p. 39.

[29] Williams, *Kora in Hell*, p. 57.

[30] ———, p. 58.

[31] *Ibid.*

[32] ———, *Autobiography*, pp. 157–58.

[33] ———, *Spring and All*, pp. 43–45.

[34] ———, *I Wanted to Write a Poem*, pp. 34–35.

[35] ———, "To a Friend Concerning Several Ladies," *C. E. P.*, pp. 216–17.

[36] "William Carlos Williams to Srinivas Rayaprol, 24 May 1950," *Letters*, pp. 287–88.

[37] Williams, "The Red Wheelbarrow," *C. E. P.*, p. 277.

[38] Nancy Willard, *Testimony of the Invisible Man* (1970), p. 110.

[39] Williams, *Autobiography*, p. 172.

[40] ———, "The Great Figure," *C. E. P.*, p. 230.

[41] ———, *Autobiography*, p. 172.

[42] ———, p. 174.

[43] *Ibid.*

[44] ———, "Excerpts from a Critical Sketch" [1931], *Essays*, p. 109.

[45] ———, *Autobiography*, p. 174.

[46] Edmund Spenser, *The Faerie Queene.*

[47] "William Carlos Williams to John Riordan, 23 December 1925," cited by Weaver, p. 45.

[48] Shakespeare, *Antony and Cleopatra.*

[49] Williams, "The Poem as a Field of Action," *Essays*, p. 291.

[50] ———, *Spring and All*, pp. 90–91.

[51] ———, pp. 20–21.

[52] ———, p. 22.

[53] ———, p. 23.

[54] ———, pp. 89–90.

[55] ———, pp. 91, 96.

[56] ———, p. 97.

[57] *Ibid.*

[58] "William Carlos Williams to Ezra Pound, 11 August 1928," *Letters*, p. 104.

[59] Williams, *Spring and All*, pp. 12, 67.

[60] ———, pp. 40–43.

[61] ———, "Our Formal Heritage," Lockwood Memorial Library Poetry Collection, S.U.N.Y., Buffalo.

[62] Breslin, pp. 80–85.

[63] Williams, "Prologue to Kora in Hell," *Essays*, p. 14.

[64] John Keats to John Hamilton Reynolds, 3 February 1818.

[65] Williams, *I Wanted to Write a Poem*, pp. 22–23.

[66] ———, *Spring and All*, p. 13.

[67] Wagner, p. 8.

[68] Williams, *Autobiography*, pp. 190, 219; 185–234 *passim.*

[69] ———, p. 187.

[70] ———, *A Voyage to Pagany*, pp. 37–38.

[71] ———, *Autobiography*, p. 219.

[72] ———, p. 199.

[73] ———, p. 194.

[74] ———, p. 195.

[75] Cited by Van Wyck Brooks, "Introduction," *The Farmers' Daughters*, p. xiv.

[76] Williams, "The Discovery of Kentucky," *In the American Grain* (1925), pp. 136–37.

[77] ———, "The May-Pole at Merry Mount," *American Grain*, p. 80.

[78] ———, "Danse Russe," *C. E. P.*, p. 148.

[79] "William Carlos Williams to Kenneth Burke, 14 April 1924," *Letters*, p. 64.

[80] Gertrude Stein, cited by D. K. Adams, *America in the Twentieth Century* (1967), p. 215.

[81] Williams, *Autobiography*, p. 217.

20 **River of Experience**

[1] Williams, *A Voyage to Pagany*, p. 12.

[2] ———, *Yes, Mrs. Williams*, p. 33.

[3] ———, *Autobiography*, p. 239.

[4] "William Carlos Williams to Florence Herman Williams, 25 September 1927," *Letters*, p. 75.

[5] "William Carlos Williams to Florence Herman Williams, 7:45 a.m. Wednesday, 28 September 1927," *Letters*, p. 81.

[6] ———, pp. 80–81.

[7] ———, *Autobiography*, p. 5.

[8] ———, *Letters*, p. 75.

[9] ———, p. 87.

[10] ———, p. 90.

[11] ———, *White Mule* (1937), p. 1.

[12] James Laughlin, "Postscript," in *White Mule*, p. 292.

[13] Williams, *Autobiography*, p. 259.

[14] "George Oppen to Mary Ellen Solt, 18 February 1961," cited by Weaver, p. 55.

[15] Louis Zukofsky, *Prepositions* (1967), p. 41.

[16] Williams, *Autobiography*, pp. 264–65.

[17] Guimond, p. 96.

[18] Williams, cited by Horace Gregory in "Introduction," *The Oxford Anthology of American Literature*.

[19] Williams, "A Beginning on the Short Story (Notes)" [1950], *Essays*, pp. 305–06.

[20] John Keats to Richard Woodhouse, 1818.

[21] Zukofsky, *Prepositions*, p. 21.

[22] Williams, "Notes for a 1941 Harvard Talk," Buffalo Collection, cited by Wagner, in *The Prose of William Carlos Williams*, p. 13.

[23] Conversation, cited in Louis Zukofsky, *"A" 1–12* (1967), p. xii.

[24] ———, p. 30.

[25] Walter Sutton, *American Free Verse: The Modern Revolution in Poetry* (1973), p. 120.

[26] Zukofsky, *"A" 1–12*, p. 30.

[27] Guimond, pp. 95–96.

[28] Williams, *Autobiography*, p. 265.

[29] ———, "Nantucket," *C. E. P.*, p. 348.

30 ———, "The Crimson Cyclamen," *C. E. P.*, p. 397.

31 ———, *Autobiography*, p. 265.

32 "William Carlos Williams to Louis Zukofsky, 'Easter 1928,' " *Letters*, p. 96.

33 "William Carlos Williams to Louis Zukofsky, 'Oct. 22/25,' " *Prepositions*, p. 42.

34 Williams, "Apology," *C. E. P.*, p. 131.

35 ———, *The Farmers' Daughters*, pp. 117–30.

36 ———, p. 130.

37 Jerome Mazzaro, *William Carlos Williams: The Later Poems* (1973), p. 64.

38 Williams, "On Measure—Statement for Cid Corman" [1954], *Essays*, p. 340.

39 "William Carlos Williams to Harvey Breit, 18 March 1942," *Letters*, p. 194.

40 Williams, *A Voyage to Pagany*, pp. 132, 129.

41 Philippe Soupault, *Last Nights of Paris* (1929), pp. 168–69.

42 Williams, *The Farmers' Daughters*, p. 109.

43 William James, *Pragmatism* (1949 reprint of 1907 edition), p. 127.

44 ———, p. 108.

45 ———, p. 45.

46 *Encyclopaedia Britannica*, Vol. 12 (Chicago, 1947), p. 884.

47 Williams, "Paterson," in *C.E.P.*, p. 233.

48 James, *Pragmatism*, p. 256.

49 Walt Whitman, "A Backward Glance O'er Travel'd Roads" (1888).

50 Williams, "The Wanderer" and "Paterson," *C. E. P.*, pp. 10–12, 233.

51 ———, cited by John C. Thirlwall, in "William Carlos Williams' *Paterson*," *New Directions*, Vol. 17 (1961), p. 254.

52 John C. Thirlwall, "The Genesis of the Epic Paterson," *Today's Japan* IV (March, 1959), p. 65, cited by Joel Conarroe, *William Carlos Williams' "Paterson": Language and Landscape* (1970), p. 2

53 "William Carlos Williams to Ezra Pound, 6 November 1936," *Letters*, p. 163.

54 Williams, *I Wanted to Write a Poem*, p. 29.

55 Weaver, p. 126.

56 Benjamin Sankey, *A Companion to William Carlos Williams' "Paterson"* (1971), p. 45.

57 Williams, *Paterson I*, p. 14.

58 Byron Vazakas, "Introduction," *Transfigured Night* (1946), p. xi.

59 "William Carlos Williams to Oswald LeWinter, '10/10/53,' " *Letters*, p. 319.

60 William Carlos Williams, cited by Zukofsky, *Prepositions*, p. 43.

61 James, *Pragmatism*, p. 205.

[62] "William Carlos Williams to Robert Lowell, 26 September 1947," *Letters,* p. 262.

[63] Weaver, pp. 118–21.

[64] Zukofsky, *Prepositions,* p. 44.

[65] Williams, *Paterson I,* p. 23.

[66] Weaver, p. 162.

[67] Williams, *Paterson IV,* p. 187.

[68] ———, p. 181.

[69] ———, *Paterson V,* p. 254.

[70] ———, "Pound's Eleven New 'Cantos' " [1934], *Essays,* p. 167.

[71] "William Carlos Williams to Ezra Pound, 6 November 1936," *Letters,* p. 163.

[72] "William Carlos Williams to Robert McAlmon, 25 May 1939," *Letters,* pp. 177–78.

[73] "William Carlos Williams to James Laughlin, 7 June 1939," *Letters,* p. 184.

[74] "William Carlos Williams to James Laughlin, 14 December 1940," *Letters,* p. 192.

[75] William Carlos Williams, "Ezra Pound: Lord Ga-Ga!," *Decision* (September 1941), pp. 16–24.

[76] ———, *Autobiography,* p. 317.

[77] "William Carlos Williams to Robert McAlmon, 23 February 1944," *Letters,* p. 220.

[78] Williams, *Autobiography,* p. 319.

21   Symbolic Lives

[1] Martha Baird and Ellen Reiss, *The Williams-Siegel Documentary* (1970), p. 97.

[2] "William Carlos Williams to Alva Turner, 27 June 1938," *Letters,* p. 171.

[3] "William Carlos Williams to William Eric Williams, 25 September 1942," *Letters,* p. 202.

[4] Williams, *Many Loves,* p. 195.

[5] "William Carlos Williams to Srinivas Rayaprol, 29 March 1950," *Letters,* p. 281.

[6] "William Carlos Williams to Harvey Breit, 18 March 1942," *Letters,* p. 194.

[7] "William Carlos Williams to Babette Deutsch, 28 July 1947," *Letters,* p. 258.

[8] *Ibid.*

[9] R. P. Blackmur, "John Wheelwright and Dr. Williams" [1939], cited by Mazzaro, p. 14.

[10] Randall Jarrell, "Views of Three Poets," *Partisan Review* XVIII

(November 1951), pp. 698–700, reprinted in *Poetry and the Age* (1953), pp. 250–65.

[11] Williams, *I Wanted to Write a Poem*, pp. 79–80.

[12] ———, p. 79.

[13] ———, "The Basis of Faith in Art," *Essays*, p. 180.

[14] "William Carlos Williams to Henry Wells, 12 April 1950," *Letters*, p. 286.

[15] Williams, *Paterson IV*, p. 238.

[16] Mazzaro, p. 72.

[17] Williams, *I Wanted to Write a Poem*, p. 73.

[18] Conarroe, *William Carlos Williams' "Paterson": Language and Landscape*, p. 10.

[19] Sankey, *A Companion to William Carlos Williams' Paterson*, p. 27.

[20] Linda Welshimer Wagner, *The Poems of William Carlos Williams* (1964), p. 115.

[21] Williams, "Prologue to Kora in Hell," *Essays*, pp. 11–12.

[22] Breslin, p. 169.

[23] "William Carlos Williams to Sister M. Bernetta Quinn, 23 August 1951," *Letters*, p. 310.

[24] Williams, *Yes, Mrs. Williams*, pp. 140–41.

[25] John Keats to Leigh Hunt, 10 May 1817.

[26] Williams, *Yes, Mrs. Williams*, p. 54.

[27] Ezra Pound and F. S. Flint, "Imagisme," *Poetry I* (1913).

[28] "William Carlos Williams to Richard Eberhart, 23 May 1954," *Letters*, p. 326.

[29] Vazakas, "All the Farewells," *Transfigured Night*, p. 76.

[30] ———, "Introduction," p. xiv.

[31] William Carlos Williams, "Two Letters," *The Golden Goose IV* (October 1952), p. 5.

[32] "William Carlos Williams to John C. Thirlwall, 13 June 1955," *Letters*, p. 334.

[33] Williams, *I Wanted to Write a Poem*, p. 82.

[34] "William Carlos Williams to Richard Eberhart, 23 May 1954," *Letters*, p. 327.

[35] Williams, *Paterson II*, p. 96.

[36] ———, "The Cod Head," *C. E. P.*, p. 333.

[37] "Hugh Kenner to Mike Weaver, 11 February 1966," cited by Weaver, pp. 85–86.

[38] Weaver, p. 86.

[39] Alan Stephens, review of *Pictures from Breughel and Other Poems*, in *Poetry CI* (February 1963), pp. 360–62, cited by Sankey, pp. 22–23.

[40] Weaver, pp. 97–102.

[41] "William Carlos Williams to Roland Lane Latimer, 26 January 1936," cited by Weaver, p. 103.

[42] Weaver, p. 103.

[43] *The New York Post* (4 August 1949), cited by Hyatt H. Waggoner, *American Poets from the Puritans to the Present* (1968), p. 376.

[44] Williams, *I Wanted to Write a Poem,* pp. 77–78.

[45] Weaver, p. 158.

[46] Williams, *Yes, Mrs. Williams,* p. 130.

[47] ———, *I Wanted to Write a Poem,* p. 22.

[48] ———, "Passer Domesticus," *C. E. P.,* p. 456.

[49] John Keats, "Ode on a Grecian Urn."

[50] Williams, "The Sparrow," *Pictures from Breughel and Other Poems* (1962), p. 132.

[51] *Ibid.*

[52] John Keats, "Ode to a Nightingale."

[53] Williams, "The Sparrow," *Pictures from Breughel and Other Poems,* p. 129.

[54] *Ibid.*

[55] James, *Pragmatism,* p. 205.

[56] William Wordsworth, *The Prelude.*

[57] William Carlos Williams, "Symposium on Writing," *The Golden Goose* Series 3, No. 2 (Autumn, 1951), pp. 89–96.

[58] ———, *Paterson IV,* p. 205.

[59] ———, *Autobiography,* pp. 329–32.

[60] ———, "The Poem as a Field of Action," *Essays,* p. 283.

[61] ———, p. 284.

[62] T. E. Hulme, *Speculations* (1924), p. 116.

[63] *Letters of Wallace Stevens,* ed. by Holly Stevens (1967), p. 592.

[64] Robert McAlmon, *Post-Adolescence,* p. 14, cited by Weaver, pp. 162–63. The character "Brander Ogden" (Marsden Hartley) gives this opinion of Williams.

[65] Michael Reck, *Ezra Pound: A Close-Up* (1973), p. 93.

[66] "William Carlos Williams to Srinivas Rayaprol, 29 March 1950," *Letters,* p. 281.

[67] Williams, *I Wanted to Write a Poem,* pp. 94–95.

[68] ———, pp. 60–61.

[69] Williams, "Asphodel," *Pictures from Breughel and Other Poems,* pp. 181–82.

[70] ———, "January Morning," *C. E. P.,* pp. 165–66.

[71] *Ibid.*

Afterword

[1] Joseph Conrad, "Preface," *The Nigger of the Narcissus.*

[2] William James, *Pragmatism,* p. 121.

[3] H. D., "Heat."

[4] Ford Madox Ford, "On Impressionism" (1913).

[5] T. E. Hulme, *Speculations,* pp. 134–35.

[6] Pound, *Literary Essays,* p. 7.

[7] William Wordsworth, "Preface to *Lyrical Ballads*" (1800).

[8] Henry James, "The Art of Fiction" (1884).

[9] John R. Harrison, *The Reactionaries* (1967), pp. 201–04.

[10] Alexis de Tocqueville, *Democracy in America II* (1840).

Bibliography

Works by Ezra Pound:

A B C of Economics. London: Faber and Faber, 1934.

A B C of Reading. New York: J. Laughlin, 1960.

A Lume Spento and Other Early Poems. New York: New Directions, 1965 reprint.

The Cantos of Ezra Pound. New York: New Directions, 1970.

The Confucian Odes. New York: New Directions, 1954.

Ezra Pound: Translations. New York: New Directions, 1963.

Gaudier-Brzeska, a Memoir. New York: New Directions, 1960 reprint.

Guide to Kulchur. New York: New Directions, 1970.

Literary Essays of Ezra Pound, T. S. Eliot, ed. New York: New Directions, 1954.

Personae. New York: New Directions, 1926.

Pound/Joyce: The Letters of Ezra Pound to James Joyce, Forrest Read, ed. New York: New Directions, 1967.

Selected Letters of Ezra Pound: 1907–1941, D. D. Paige, ed. New York: New Directions, 1950.

Selected Prose of Ezra Pound: 1909–1965, William Cookson, ed. London: Faber and Faber, 1973.

The Spirit of Romance. New York: New Directions, 1952.

About Ezra Pound:

Chace, William M. *The Political Identities of Ezra Pound and T. S. Eliot*. Palo Alto: Stanford University Press, 1973.

Cornell, Julien. *The Trial of Ezra Pound*. New York: John Day, 1966.

Davie, Donald. *Ezra Pound: Poet as Sculptor*. New York: Oxford University Press, 1964.

Dekker, George. *Sailing After Knowledge: The Cantos of Ezra Pound.* New York: Barnes & Noble, 1963.

Emery, Clark. *Ideas into Action.* Coral Gables, Florida: University of Miami Press, 1958.

Espey, John J. *Ezra Pound's "Mauberley."* Berkeley: University of California Press, 1955.

Fraser, G. S. *Ezra Pound.* New York: Grove Press, 1961.

Gallup, Donald C. *A Bibliography of Ezra Pound.* London: Hart-Davis, 1963.

Hall, Donald, interviewer. "Ezra Pound: An Interview." *The Paris Review,* Vol. 28 (Summer–Fall 1962), pp. 22–51.

Hesse, Eva, ed. *New Approaches to Ezra Pound.* Berkeley: University of California Press, 1969.

Homberger, Eric, ed. *Ezra Pound: The Critical Heritage.* London and Boston: Routledge and Kegan Paul, 1972.

Hutchins, Patricia. *Ezra Pound's Kensington.* Chicago: Henry Regnery, 1965.

Kenner, Hugh. *The Poetry of Ezra Pound.* Norfolk, Conn.: New Directions, 1951.

————. *The Pound Era.* Berkeley and Los Angeles: University of California Press, 1971.

Leary, Lewis, ed. *Motive and Method in the Cantos of Ezra Pound.* New York: Columbia University Press, 1954.

Middleton, Christopher, "Documents on Imagism from the Papers of F. S. Flint." *The Review,* Number 15 (April 1965), pp. 35–51.

Norman, Charles. *Ezra Pound.* London: Macdonald, 1969.

O'Connor, William Van and Edward Stone, eds. *A Casebook on Ezra Pound.* New York: Crowell, 1959.

de Rachewiltz, Mary. *Discretions.* Boston: Little, Brown, 1971.

Reck, Michael. *Ezra Pound: A Close-Up.* New York: McGraw-Hill, 1967.

Russell, Peter, ed. *Ezra Pound: A Collection of Essays.* London and New York: P. Nevill, 1950.

Ruthven, K. K. *A Guide to Ezra Pound's Personae.* Berkeley: University of California Press, 1969.

Stock, Noel. *The Life of Ezra Pound.* New York: Pantheon Books, a division of Random House, 1970.

————, ed. *Ezra Pound: Perspectives.* Chicago: Henry Regnery, 1965.

Sullivan, J. P., ed. *Ezra Pound.* Middlesex, England: Penguin Books, 1960.

Sutton, Walter, ed. *Ezra Pound: A Collection of Critical Essays.* Englewood Cliffs, New Jersey: Prentice-Hall, 1963.

Witemeyer, Hugh. *The Poetry of Ezra Pound*. Berkeley: University of California Press, 1969.

Works by T. S. Eliot:

After Strange Gods. New York: Harcourt Brace, 1934.

Collected Poems: 1909–1962. New York: Harcourt Brace & World, 1963.

The Complete Poems and Plays. New York: Harcourt Brace & World, 1952.

The Criterion. London. 1922–1939.

Essays Ancient and Modern. London: Faber and Faber, 1936.

For Lancelot Andrewes: Essays on Style and Order. New York: Doubleday, Doran, 1929.

The Idea of a Christian Society. New York: Harcourt Brace & World, 1940.

Knowledge and Experience in the Philosophy of F. H. Bradley. New York: Farrar, Straus, 1964.

"Last Words." *Criterion*, XVIII (January 1939), 269–75.

Notes towards the Definition of Culture. New York: Harcourt, Brace, 1949.

On Poetry and Poets. New York: Farrar, Straus and Giroux, 1957.

Poems Written in Early Youth. New York: Farrar, Straus and Giroux, 1967.

The Rock. London: Faber and Faber, 1934.

The Sacred Wood. New York: Barnes & Noble, 1960 reprint.

Selected Essays. New York: Harcourt Brace, 1950.

To Criticize the Critic. New York: Farrar, Straus and Giroux, 1965.

"*Ulysses*, Myth and Order." *Dial*, LXXV (November 1923), 480–3.

The Use of Poetry and the Use of Criticism. London: Faber and Faber, 1933.

The Waste Land: A Facsimile and Transcript of the Original Drafts, Valerie Eliot, ed. New York: Harcourt Brace Jovanovich, 1971.

About T. S. Eliot:

Bergonzi, Bernard. *T. S. Eliot*. New York: Macmillan, 1972.

Bradbrook, M. C. *T. S. Eliot*. London: Longmans, Green, 1965.

Braybrooke, Neville, ed. *T. S. Eliot: A Symposium*. New York: Farrar, Straus, 1958.

Cattaui, Georges. *T. S. Eliot*. New York: Funk & Wagnalls, 1966.

Chace, William M. *The Political Identities of Ezra Pound and T. S. Eliot*. Palo Alto: Stanford University Press, 1973.

Drew, Elizabeth. *T. S. Eliot: The Design of His Poetry*. New York: C. Scribner's Sons, 1961.

Frye, Northrop. *T. S. Eliot*. New York: Barnes & Noble, 1963.

Gallup, Donald C. *T. S. Eliot: A Bibliography*. London: Hart-Davis, 1969.

Gardner, Helen. *The Art of T. S. Eliot*. New York: Dutton, 1950.

Kenner, Hugh. *The Invisible Poet: T. S. Eliot*. New York: McDowell, Obolensky, 1959.

————, ed. *T. S. Eliot: a Collection of Critical Essays*. Englewood Cliffs, New Jersey: Prentice-Hall, 1962.

Knoll, Robert, ed. *Storm Over the Waste Land*. Chicago: Scott, Foresman & Co., 1964.

Kojecky, Roger. *T. S. Eliot's Social Criticism*. London: Faber and Faber, 1971.

Litz, A. Walton, ed. *Eliot in His Time*. Princeton, New Jersey: Princeton University Press, 1973.

March, Richard and M. J. Tambimuttu, eds. *T. S. Eliot: A Symposium from Conrad Aiken and Others*. New York: Tambimuttu and Mass, 1965.

Margolis, John D. *T. S. Eliot's Intellectual Development 1922–1939*. Chicago: University of Chicago Press, 1972.

Matthews, T. S. *Great Tom: Notes Towards the Definition of T. S. Eliot*. New York: Harper and Row, 1974.

Matthiessen, F. O. *The Achievement of T. S. Eliot*. New York: Oxford University Press, 1958.

Montgomery, Marion. *T. S. Eliot: An Essay on the American Magus*. Athens, Ga.: University of Georgia Press, 1969.

Peter, John. "A New Interpretation of *The Waste Land* (1952), With Postscript (1969)." *Essays in Criticism*, XIX (April 1969), 140–75.

Robbins, Rossell Hope. *The T. S. Eliot Myth*. New York: H. Schuman, 1951.

Sencourt, Robert. *T. S. Eliot: A Memoir*, Donald Adamson, ed. New York: Dodd, Mead, 1971.

Smith, Carol H. *T. S. Eliot's Dramatic Theory and Practice*. Princeton, New Jersey: Princeton University Press, 1967.

Smith, Grover. *T. S. Eliot's Poetry and Plays*. Chicago: University of Chicago Press, 1956.

Southam, B. C. *A Guide to the Selected Poems of T. S. Eliot*. New York: Harcourt Brace & World, 1968.

Tate, Allen, ed. *T. S. Eliot: The Man and His Work*. New York: Delacorte Press, 1966.

Williamson, George. *A Reader's Guide to T. S. Eliot*. New York: Farrar, Straus & Cudahy, 1953.

Wilson, Edmund, "T. S. Eliot and the Church of England." *New Republic*, LVIII (April 1929), 283–84.

Works by William Carlos Williams:

Autobiography. New York: New Directions, 1951.

The Build-Up. New York: Random House, 1972.

Collected Earlier Poems. New York: New Directions, 1951.

Collected Later Poems. New York: New Directions, 1963.

"Ezra Pound: Lord Ga-Ga!" *Decision* (September 1941), 16–24.

The Farmers' Daughters. Norfolk, Conn.: New Directions, 1961.

The Great American Novel. Paris: Three Mountains Press, 1923.

In the American Grain. Norfolk, Conn.: New Directions, 1925.

I Wanted to Write a Poem. Boston: Beacon Press, 1958.

Kora in Hell: Improvisations. Boston: Four Seas Co., 1920.

Many Loves. Norfolk, Conn.: New Directions, 1961.

A Novelette and Other Prose. Toulon: Imprimerie F. Cabasson, 1932.

Paterson. New York: New Directions, 1963.

Pictures from Brueghel and Other Poems. New York: New Directions, 1962.

Selected Essays of William Carlos Williams. New York: New Directions, 1954.

The Selected Letters of William Carlos Williams, John C. Thirlwall, ed. New York: McDowell, Obolensky, 1957.

Selected Poems. New York: New Directions, 1949.

Spring and All. Buffalo, New York: Frontier Press, 1970 reprint.

"Symposium on Writing." *The Golden Goose*, Series 3, no. 2 (Autumn 1951), 86–96.

A Voyage to Pagany. New York: The Macaulay Co., 1928.

White Mule. In the Money. Norfolk, Conn., New Directions, 1937.

"William Carlos Williams: Two Letters." *The Golden Goose IV* (October 1952), 29–32.

Yes, Mrs. Williams. New York: McDowell, Obolensky, 1959.

About William Carlos Williams:

Baird, Martha and Ellen Reiss. *The Williams-Siegel Documentary*. New York: Definitions Press, 1970.

Breslin, James E. *William Carlos Williams: an American Artist*. New York: Oxford University Press, 1970.

Brinnin, John Malcolm. *William Carlos Williams*. Minneapolis: University of Minnesota Press, 1963.

Conarroe, Joel. *William Carlos Williams' "Paterson": Language and Landscape*. Philadelphia: University of Pennsylvania Press, 1970.

Guimond, James. *The Art of William Carlos Williams*. Urbana: University of Minnesota Press, 1963.

Mazzaro, Jerome. *William Carlos Williams: The Later Poems*. Ithaca and London: Cornell University Press, 1973.

Miller, Joseph Hillis, ed. *William Carlos Williams: A Collection of Critical Essays*. Englewood Cliffs, New Jersey: Prentice-Hall, 1966.
Peterson, Walter Scott. *An Approach to Paterson*. New Haven: Yale University Press, 1967.
Sankey, Benjamin. *A Companion to William Carlos Williams' "Paterson."* Berkeley: University of California Press, 1971.
Sherman, Paul. *The Music of Survival: a Biography of a Poem by William Carlos Williams*. Urbana: University of Illinois Press, 1968.
Thirlwall, John C. "William Carlos Williams' 'Paterson.'" *New Directions,* Vol. 17 (1961), 252–310.
Wagner, Linda Welshimer. *The Poems of William Carlos Williams*. Middletown, Conn.: Wesleyan University Press, 1963.
———. *The Prose of William Carlos Williams*. Middletown, Conn.: Wesleyan University Press, 1970.
Wallace, Emily Mitchell. *A Bibliography of William Carlos Williams*. Middletown, Conn.: Wesleyan University Press, 1968.
Weaver, Mike. *William Carlos Williams: The American Background*. Cambridge (England): Cambridge University Press, 1971.

General:

Adams, David Keith. *America in the Twentieth Century*. London: Cambridge University Press, 1967.
Aiken, Conrad. *Ushant, an Essay*. New York: Duell, Sloan and Pearce, 1952.
Aldington, Richard. *Life for Life's Sake*. New York: Viking Press, 1941.
Cowley, Malcolm. *Exile's Return*. New York: Viking Press, 1956.
Ellmann, Richard. *Eminent Domain*. New York: Oxford University Press, 1967.
———, and Charles Feidelson, Jr., eds. *The Modern Tradition*. New York: Oxford University Press, 1965.
Ford, Ford Madox. *Return to Yesterday*. New York: H. Liveright Inc., 1932.
Forster, E. M. *Abinger Harvest*. London: E. Arnold and Co., 1936.
de Gourmont, Remy. *The Natural Philosophy of Love,* trans. by Ezra Pound. New York: Rarity Press, 1931.
Harrison, John R. *The Reactionaries*. New York: Schocken Books, 1967.
Hulme, T. E. *Speculations*. London: Routledge and Kegan Paul, 1924.
James, William. *Pragmatism*. New York: Longmans, Green, and Co., 1949.
Jarrell, Randall. *Poetry and the Age*. New York: Vintage Books, 1955.
Jung, C. G. *Modern Man in Search of a Soul,* trans. by W. S. Dell and C. F. Baynes. London: K. Paul, Trench, Trubner and Co., Ltd., 1933.

Kandinsky, W. *Concerning the Spiritual in Art,* Robert Motherwell, ed. New York: George Wittenborn, 1973.

Laing, R. D. *The Divided Self: an Existential Study in Sanity and Madness.* Middlesex, England: Penguin Books, 1965.

Leavis, F. R. *New Bearings in English Poetry.* Michigan: University of Michigan Press, 1960.

Lewis, Wyndham. *Blasting and Bombardiering.* Berkeley: University of California Press, 1967 reprint.

Lidderdale, Jane, and Mary Nicholson. *Dear Miss Weaver.* New York: Viking Press, 1970.

Marinetti, F. T. *Marinetti: Selected Writings,* R. W. Flint, ed. New York: Farrar, Straus and Giroux, 1972.

Pratt, William. *The Imagist Poem.* New York: Dutton, 1963.

Sisson, C. H. *English Poetry 1900–1950.* London: Hart-Davis, 1971.

Stevens, Holly, ed. *The Letters of Wallace Stevens.* New York: A. A. Knopf, 1966.

Sutton, Walter, ed. *American Free Verse: The Modern Revolution in Poetry.* New York: New Directions, 1973.

Vazakas, Byron. *Transfigured Night.* New York: Macmillan Co., 1946.

Waggoner, Hyatt H. *American Poets: From the Puritans to the Present.* Boston: Houghton Mifflin, 1968.

Weatherhead, A. Kingsley. *The Edge of the Image: Marianne Moore, William Carlos Williams, and Some Other Poets.* Seattle: University of Washington Press, 1967.

Wees, William C. *Vorticism and the English Avant-Garde.* Toronto: University of Toronto Press, 1972.

Weininger, Otto. *Sex and Character.* New York: G. P. Putnam's Sons, 1906.

Willard, Nancy. *Testimony of the Invisible Man.* Columbia, Missouri: University of Missouri Press, 1970.

Yeats, William Butler. *Memoirs,* Denis Donoghue, ed. London: Macmillan, 1972.

Zukofsky, Louis. *"A" 1–12.* New York: Doubleday and Co., Inc., 1967.

———. *Prepositions.* London: Rapp and Carroll, 1967.

Index